LEADERSHIP IN
Dangerous
SITUATIONS

LEADERSHIP IN
Dangerous
SITUATIONS

A Handbook for the Armed Forces,
Emergency Services, and First Responders

EDITED BY
**Patrick J. Sweeney, Michael D. Matthews,
and Paul B. Lester**

Naval Institute Press
Annapolis, Maryland

This book has been brought to publication with the
generous assistance of Marguerite and Gerry Lenfest.

Naval Institute Press
291 Wood Road
Annapolis, MD 21402

Library of Congress Cataloging-in-Publication Data
Leadership in dangerous situations : a handbook for the Armed Forces,
emergency services, and first responders / edited by Patrick J. Sweeney,
Michael D. Matthews, and Paul B. Lester.
   p. cm.
 Includes bibliographical references and index.
  ISBN 978-1-59114-832-6 (hardcover : alk. paper) 1. Leadership—
Psychological aspects. 2. Leadership—Social aspects. 3. Crisis manage-
ment. I. Sweeney, Patrick J. II. Matthews, Michael D. III. Lester, Paul B.
  HD57.7.L43 2011
  658.4′092—dc23
                                  2011025667

19 18 17 16 15 14 13 12 11   9 8 7 6 5 4 3 2 1
First printing

*This book is dedicated to the men and women
who bravely and selflessly serve in harm's way for
the betterment of their communities and countries
and those of others. Your service uplifts and
helps make the world a better place in which to live.*

CONTENTS

Introduction

Section One: Enhancing One's Psychological Body Armor

ILLUSTRATIONS AND TABLES

Tables

FOREWORD

I have spent the better part of my life—the last forty years—working to protect the lives and property of the citizens of New York City. I have held every uniformed rank in the New York City Fire Department, and I have seen firsthand its best and its worst times.

The worst day in department history was September 11, 2001. That day, fire, police, and EMS personnel carried out acts of unflinching heroism and rescued thousands from the burning World Trade Center towers. Unfortunately, hundreds of first responders made the supreme sacrifice while fulfilling that mission. We mourn them to this day.

Leadership is crucial in all organizations. Unlike in civilian organizations, where consequences are not as extreme, in the military and other uniformed organizations, members of the leadership share in the risks taken by those working below them. That was made abundantly clear on September 11, when members from all ranks died, including chiefs and other high-ranking personnel.

In my forty years as a firefighter and an officer, I have seen firsthand how critical quality leadership is to emergency responders moving into harm's way. To risk their lives and safety, first responders must firmly believe in their leaders, know those leaders care for them, and have confidence that they can make good decisions quickly. This unique set of skills is called dangerous context leadership. Understanding how to operate and inspire in extreme circumstances greatly strengthens any organization, whether military or civilian. The contributions to *Leadership in Dangerous Situations* look at how to prepare leaders to fulfill their roles and how they motivate people to follow them, even in moments of extreme stress or danger.

This wonderful and unique book brings together dangerous context leaders and prominent scholars from around the world to explore the psychological, social, and organizational factors that influence leadership in critical situations. The first section focuses on how leaders can prepare themselves psychologically to handle the challenges they might face. It covers a range of topics, including building courage, managing stress, facilitating resiliency, mitigating post-traumatic stress disorder, promoting ethical awareness and reasoning, and finding meaning. The second section focuses on how to influence people who risk their lives to fulfill duties and examines such topics as trust, resilient teams, morale, influence, decision making, crisis leadership, and cross-cultural leadership. The third section addresses the organizational factors that facilitate leading in dangerous contexts, including developing a culture to operate under extreme conditions, recruiting and selection, and cultivating leaders.

Leadership in Dangerous Situations offers easily understandable guidance for leaders to prepare themselves and their organizations for the challenges of leadership and operating in dangerous environments. It has been written for the brave men and women who put themselves in harm's way every day to protect and serve. I strongly believe this definitive book will contribute to enhancing the effectiveness of dangerous context leaders.

SALVATORE J. CASSANO
Fire Commissioner, City of New York
March 2011

ACKNOWLEDGMENTS

We want to thank the fifty-eight contributors to this volume, who are collectively the top thinkers in the theory and practice of leading in dangerous contexts. All of us are grateful to the U.S. Military Academy for providing a supportive and intellectually stimulating forum for exploring and advancing new ideas. In closing, we extend our gratitude to Gretchen Bain Matthews, our technical editor, for her tireless assistance in reviewing drafts of the manuscripts and keeping the editorial team organized and on track.

LEADERSHIP IN
Dangerous
SITUATIONS

Introduction

CHAPTER 1

Leading in Dangerous Situations
An Overview of the Unique Challenges

Patrick J. Sweeney, Michael D. Matthews, and Paul B. Lester

The idea for *Leadership in Dangerous Situations: A Handbook for the Armed Forces, Emergency Services, and First Responders* evolved from the editors' collective experiences and research in dangerous contexts and from Patrick J. Sweeney's experience directing a course in combat leadership at the United States Military Academy, West Point. We discovered that the leadership literature lacked a comprehensive guide outlining how and why leadership is different in dangerous contexts; how to prepare oneself and followers for the unique challenges of operating in such contexts and how to recover following exposure to adversity; how to lead when group members face danger; and how to leverage organizational systems to facilitate group members' resilience in the face of and after adversities associated with dangerous contexts. The intent of *Leadership in Dangerous Situations* is to fill the gap in the leadership literature by providing the brave men and women who risk their lives to serve the public a comprehensive and easily understandable guide, backed by research, to prepare themselves and their units for the unique psychological, social, and organizational challenges of leading and operating in dangerous contexts.

This book is written for the practitioner, in practitioners' language. It teams international scholars with members of the military, law enforcement, and fire and rescue services to address the unique challenges faced by leaders in dangerous situations. Thus, each chapter integrates theory and research with practical experience to address the unique challenges leaders face while operating in dangerous environments. The blending of perspectives provides leaders with a clear understanding of and a guide to mastering the challenges of leading people when lives are in the balance.

WHO SHOULD READ THIS BOOK?

Whether you are a young leader preparing for war, a seasoned commander with multiple combat tours, a Special Weapons and Tactics (SWAT) team leader, emergency medical technician (EMT) supervisor, first-line supervisor of a law enforcement patrol unit, or a lieutenant responsible for a shift of fire-fighters, you are leading people in contexts in which life and death decisions are common. If a novice, you have likely asked, "How will leading in these situations be different from others I've faced." If a more experienced leader, you have likely asked, "Why is leading in these situations different?" With these questions in mind, our purpose here is to provide you—a leader—with a better understanding of what is required of you in dangerous contexts.

The contributing authors here delve into the psychological, social, and organizational factors that can impact your ability to lead, your followers' ability to perform, and your organization's ability to accomplish its mission. In the end, you should take away not only an understanding of how leading in dangerous contexts is different from leading in situations where lives are not at risk, but you should also have a deeper understanding of why it differs, where commonalities exist, and perhaps more important, how to prepare yourself to lead and your organization to perform in dangerous contexts.

DANGEROUS CONTEXTS

Dangerous contexts are highly dynamic and unpredictable environments where leaders and group members must routinely engage in actions that place their physical and psychological well-being at risk to accomplish the organization's objectives. In such situations, leaders and subordinates recognize that failure to perform their duties and accomplish the organization's objectives have the potential for catastrophic consequences not only for their organization, but also for the people it serves.[1] The group members perceive, experience, or expect a threat to their well-being while executing their duties. For instance, each time police officers respond to a call for assistance, they can reasonably expect a potential threat to their well-being. This is why most police forces require their officers to wear body armor at all times. Furthermore, if police officers fail to answer or properly handle calls for assistance, lawlessness will eventually ensue, and members of the community will be at greater risk.

Unique Leadership Demands

Leading in dangerous contexts is fundamentally the same, yet qualitatively different, from leading in non-dangerous contexts. The common fundamentals for leading in any context involve leaders possessing the key characteristics associated with competence, character, and caring; mutual influence exercised in and through leader–follower and peer–peer relationships; organizational factors, such as culture, policies, procedures, practices, and systems, that promote cooperation to achieve a common purpose; and the demands associated with the context. The demands of the context can exert a pervasive influence on leader and follower characteristics and skills; the nature of relationships within the group; and an organization's structure, operations, and systems. The unique psychological, social, and organizational demands that arise as a result of group members' perceptions of threat is what makes leading in dangerous contexts qualitatively different from leading in other contexts.

Psychological Demands

To handle the weighty responsibility for group members' well-being and lives and the potential catastrophic consequences of failure, dangerous contexts leaders must possess greater levels of credibility (trustworthiness) and psychological hardiness than leaders in other contexts. Leaders' trustworthiness is determined by followers' perceptions of their competence, character, and caring.[2] Psychological hardiness depends on how leaders frame events, their beliefs about influencing outcomes, finding purpose, and social support.

Competence. Dangerous context leaders need expertise in their domain, superb knowledge of the organization, outstanding stress management skills, and finely honed problem-solving skills that allow them to make quick, ethical decisions in dynamic, complex, and ambiguous circumstances. Leaders in other contexts are rarely faced with the challenge of managing the stress associated with having their lives in danger, and those of others, while at the same time being required to make quick decisions to accomplish the mission and minimize the risk to group members' well-being. Results from studies conducted in a combat environment indicate that soldiers placed the most importance on leader characteristics related to competence (decision making, technical knowledge, judgment) because they addressed their greatest dependencies by ensuring mission accomplishment with the least amount of risk.[3]

Dangerous context leaders must also possess a higher level of personal resilience to deal with the adversity and trauma inherent in these types of environments. An array of well-developed, positive coping strategies are necessary for leaders to understand, make sense of, and move forward to grow after adversity. In addition, these leaders have the responsibility of bolstering group members' resiliency through teaching and modeling positive coping strategies, shaping collective meaning-making, providing access to behavioral health specialists, and if necessary, managing the grieving process.[4] Other contexts do not require such high resilience capabilities from leaders because they do not operate in environments with a consistent risk of injury or death.

Physical fitness is another important competency that promotes psychological hardiness and contributes to personal effectiveness.[5] It helps build psychological hardiness in assisting with the management of stress by generally enhancing one's assessment of one's capabilities and providing a realistic perspective for assessing the demands of a situation. Most important, physical stamina influences members' strength of will to overcome fatigue, pain, and other obstacles to persevere to accomplish a mission and take care of teammates. In terms of effectiveness, physical fitness helps members maintain the high levels of thinking necessary to make quick and sound decisions in dynamic situations. Furthermore, physical stamina positively influences moral and ethical decision making and courageous behavior.[6]

Character. The life and death risks inherent in dangerous contexts prompts group members to place great importance on leaders' honesty and integrity. Followers are more apt to trust leaders who are true to their own and the organization's values and provide accurate information about the mission. Group members believe that leaders with integrity will make decisions and take actions based on positive values and also provide complete factual information about operations, which alleviates concerns about hidden agendas and directives requiring unnecessary risks.[7]

Another important character trait required to meet the unique demands of dangerous contexts is courage. Leaders must possess a high level of physical courage to overcome fears of being injured or killed to execute their duties and set an example for group members. Those found lacking in physical courage are likely to lose their credibility and followers' trust.[8] Furthermore, the risks associated with operating in dangerous environments prompts group members to place a premium on a leader's moral courage or willingness to take a stand to do what is right or protect followers' interests. Leaders with high moral courage are more likely to conduct operations in a moral and ethical manner and question directives that place their followers at unnecessary risk than are those of lesser moral fortitude. Demands of other contexts require leaders to possess some level of moral courage but not at the level required to lead in a dangerous context, and rarely do they need physical courage.

Caring. To effectively perform in dangerous environments, group members must believe that their leaders genuinely care about their welfare. The level of leader caring goes well beyond an interest in assisting them in performing their duties. Followers must believe that their leaders care about them as people and are interested in their personal as well as professional development. This includes leaders caring about, being interested in, and taking actions to promote the welfare of group members' families. Leaders that are genuinely concerned about their followers are more likely to be loyal, which includes looking out for group members' welfare during operations and willingly assuming risk to stand by and support them when they are vulnerable.[9] Demands associated with non-dangerous contexts do not require leaders to have such a deep and broad level of caring toward followers.

Psychological Hardiness

The threat of risk, being responsible for people's lives, and the potential traumatic consequences associated with fulfilling their duties, requires dangerous context leaders to have an exceptional level of psychological hardiness. They have to be able to regulate how they think about tasks and experiences in order to frame them in a positive manner that leads to growth. Furthermore, dangerous context leaders must possess a level of agency or belief that they can control their own and their organizations' destinies. Key to a sense of agency is the self-efficacy or confidence that comes with job competence, expertise, and coping skills. Feeling that they serve a higher purpose also assists leaders in maintaining motivation and finding meaning in their experiences. Dangerous context leaders also have a great need for social support networks to assist in managing stress and making meaning out their experiences.

SOCIAL DEMANDS

Studies conducted in combat consistently find that the quality of leader–follower relationships is higher in terms of psychological closeness, the degree of cooperation to achieve a common goal, and the extent of caring compared to non-dangerous areas.[10] Leaders achieve high-quality relationships with their group members by investing time to get to know them, seeking their input, caring about their training and development, and serving them and the organization in a selfless manner. A strong, quality relationship is functional in terms of ensuring mutual influence, open communications, and mutual concern for the mission and each other.[11]

Serving in dangerous contexts requires group members to form stronger psychological bonds with each other compared to members whose organizations do not operate in such situations. These strong bonds sustain their will and commitment to fellow members, the organization, and the mission.[12] They prompt group members to transcend self-interest to connect with and serve something greater than themselves. Cohesive bonds provide group members with confidence that all members of the organization are looking out for one another's best interest, and all are sacrificing to achieve the higher goal or purpose. Cohesion is important in helping members manage stress because it bolsters perceptions of collective efficacy. It is not only one individual facing danger, but a united group working together to meet a challenge. Thus, strong psychological bonds assist group members in meeting threats and provide them a sense of security.

Cohesion is also an important source of motivation for group members to fulfill their duties that in turn allows them to continue to bolster or maintain their status and connection with the group. Dangerous contexts leaders must constantly monitor and engage in activities to purposefully enhance the connections between group members. Cohesive bonds between them are the psychological links that bind members together in a collective force to accomplish their mission. These connections with others also serve to buffer the potential psychological impact of adversity and trauma.

Strong cohesive bonds between members serve to form an effective social support network within an organization. Support networks are important in assisting group members in managing stress because they provide a forum to voice concerns, receive guidance, and get information about how to more effectively manage problems. Thus, support networks enhance members' perceptions of their ability to handle dangerous situations and also to formulate realistic expectations of the demands involved, which helps members manage stress.

Furthermore, social support networks play a critical role in assisting organization members in making meaning, or understanding, of the adversity or trauma they might experience in performing their duties in dangerous contexts. Individuals are more apt to disclose their thoughts and feelings to members of their social network than to people with whom they do not have a strong psychological bond. This network provides members with a forum to safely express their thoughts and feelings and to hear other members express how they are making sense of the experience.[13] For instance, if a police officer has to shoot a suspect who is threatening citizens, that officer can turn to the social support network to voice her concerns about having injured another human being and attempt to resolve the conflict with her belief system. This sharing of views and experiences in the network broadens each member's perspective and also serves to shape collective meaning-making. Therefore, in essence, social support networks are learning communities that play a vital role in managing stress, promoting growth from adversity, and mitigating post-traumatic stress disorder (PTSD).

Leaders of organizations that operate in dangerous contexts also need to purposefully assist in shaping and ensuring the effectiveness of the social network among family members. These networks serve to socialize new members to the organization's culture, empower members to solve their own problems, serve as a sounding board for expressing concerns, learn new strategies to manage stress, meet each other's needs, and most important, support and uplift members if a loved one is injured or killed in the line of duty. Leaders must plan activities to encourage families to get together to start to build social bonds, keep them informed about organizational activities, demonstrate consideration for families by maintaining stability in work schedules when possible, and model concern for family members. Finally, leaders should consider providing family members the opportunity to voluntarily learn basic communication skills. Organizational members are more than likely to discuss adversities and trauma with their spouse or other loved ones, thus they too need the basic skills required to assist in the meaning-making process.

ORGANIZATIONAL DEMANDS

Dangerous contexts require organizations to have a strong and clearly articulated culture. In essence, culture defines the identity organization members need for the context and also serves to unite and synchronize members' efforts around a core purpose and vision. The organization's core values define the characteristics members need to possess to accomplish its mission. A review of dangerous context organizations' core values yields the following common values: service, courage, duty, integrity, and honor.

People who operate in dangerous contexts tend to find a higher purpose in serving others. Organization members who value service tend to transcend self-interest to serve the organization and the community, even at the risk of their own safety. Courage is an important value because it motivates members to face their fears and still perform their duties or take a stand for what is right. The value of duty ensures that members meet their responsibilities, especially when it is inconvenient or they must incur cost in terms of risking their safety. Integrity and honor serve as members' moral compass for determining the right way to execute their duties, especially when they require the application of lethal violence. Members who integrate these organizational values into their identities are more likely to possess the character necessary to fulfill their duties and to be resilient in dealing with the adversity and trauma they might experience.

Core purpose and vision unite members in their common quest to achieve a greater purpose that will have a positive impact on society. A worthy purpose can provide meaning to members' lives. They do not have a job; they have a calling or a profession that makes a difference in the world. A higher, noble purpose is worthy of sacrifice, including risking one's life.[14] Vision provides members with a common direction to work together to achieve the higher purpose in an effective manner. Therefore, core purpose and vision unite members in pursuit of a noble purpose and aligns them along a common direction. Operating in a dangerous context requires an organization's policies, procedures, practices, and systems to be geared toward achieving its core purpose in a hazardous environment. Leaders need to periodically review policies, procedures, practices, and systems to ensure they promote cooperation and cohesion and reinforce the organization's values and core purpose. For instance, if an organization has budgetary policies that pit sub-elements against each other as resource competitors, cohesion is likely to suffer in the group. Reward and evaluation systems deserve close scrutiny by leaders. As they review the reward system, leaders need to ensure it reinforces the organization's core values, teamwork, and training for mission readiness. Similarly, during an evaluation system review, leaders need to determine if the procedures assess core values, collective focus, teamwork, and mission readiness. Aligning organizational systems, policies, procedures, and practices assists in communicating and establishing a culture that prepares members for the psychological and social demands of operating in dangerous environments.

To summarize, leading in dangerous contexts is qualitatively different from leading in non-dangerous contexts because of the unique psychological, social, and organizational demands of such situations. Members of organizations that operate in dangerous environments require a greater degree of credibility and psychological hardiness to handle threats to safety and the adversity and trauma they might experience. To meet the unique psychological demands, leaders invest greater time in establishing high-quality relationships with followers that are characterized by mutual influence and trust. Leaders also take deliberate actions to build cohesive bonds among group members and to facilitate the creation of social networks for family members. Leaders also ensure that the organization's culture clearly articulates the core values that form the foundation of each member's identity and the noble purpose the organization serves. A higher purpose motivates members to transcend self-interest and to risk their lives to achieve it. Finally, leaders align the organization's systems, policies, procedures, and practices to facilitate mission readiness, psychological hardiness, cooperation, and cohesion throughout.

Thus, leading in dangerous contexts is, indeed, more complex, demanding, and dynamic than leading in safe contexts.

ABOUT THIS BOOK

The contributions to *Leadership in Dangerous Situations* are presented in three sections: Enhancing One's Psychological Body Armor, Influencing When People Are in Harm's Way, and Leveraging the Organization.

Section One: Enhancing One's Psychological Body Armor

The first section addresses the unique psychological skills and states leaders need to effectively function in dangerous, chaotic, and dynamic situations. Topics such as enhancing courage, managing stress, promoting resilience, assisting the group in handling trauma, mitigating stress-related pathologies, staying mindful of personal responsibilities, the ethics of applying lethal force, and the search for meaning and purpose are addressed in this section.

In Chapter 2, Paul Lester and Cynthia Pury introduce the concept of courage through the compelling story of Hugh Thompson's actions at and after the My Lai massacre. The authors discuss the components of courage and the various types of it using a variety of examples. The majority of the chapter focuses on simple actions leaders can take to build their own and their group members' courage to meet the fears and stressors of operating in dangerous environments. This chapter provides leaders with the means to turn lambs into lions.

James Ness' team, consisting of Denise Jablonski-Kaye, Isabell Obigt, and David Lam, provide a comprehensive review of stress and how it affects individual and team performance. In Chapter 3, they address the sources of stress in dangerous contexts and introduce models that illustrate how stress ensues and how various levels of it impact performance. The heart of this chapter is the enlightening discussion of techniques leaders can use to manage high levels of stress and still function effectively. These techniques are equally applicable for assisting group members in managing their stress. In addition, some mundane activities, such as good training, sleep, circadian rhythm management, healthy diet, and physical fitness, play key roles in successfully managing stress. The models introduced early on in the chapter assist leaders in understanding why and how various stress management techniques work, which greatly enhances leaders' abilities to create stress management plans.

In Chapter 4, Christopher Peterson, Michael Craw, Nansook Park, and Michael Erwin address how leaders can promote psychological resilience. They provide a helpful definition of resilience and discuss various techniques to promote it based on the concepts of positive psychology. The concept of post-traumatic growth is introduced, followed by a detailed discussion of how to assist organization members to grow from their traumatic and adverse experiences, instead of falling prey to stress-related illness. The authors also examine various techniques leaders can use to promote team and individual resilience. These authors propose that leaders try to mitigate post-operation psychological disorders by focusing on building group members' strengths to promote resilience prior to operating in dangerous contexts.

Joseph Geraci, Mike Baker, George Bonanno, Barend Tussenbroek, and Loree Sutton provide an enlightened and in-depth discussion in Chapter 5 on the concept of post-traumatic stress disorder, the factors that contribute to it, realistic expectations about probability of experiencing this disorder, and steps leaders can take to mitigate it. The essence of their analysis centers around a three-phase model leaders can implement to prepare themselves and followers for post-traumatic events and to mitigate the occurrence of PTSD.

In Chapter 6, George Mastroianni, Susann Kimmelman, Joe Doty, and Joseph Thomas provide an impactful discussion on obedience and personal responsibility when operating in dangerous contexts. The team addresses how individual, social, and organizational factors can work together to promote ethical behavior, but also how these same factors can conspire to prompt an individual to behave unethically. Invaluable is the discussion on what leaders can do to raise personal responsibility, manage social forces to promote ethical behavior, and establish organizational culture, policies, practices, and procedures to ensure ethical behavior in all circumstances, especially when operating in dangerous contexts.

C. Anthony Pfaff, Ted Reich, Walter Redman, and Michael Hurley address the ethics of applying lethal force. In Chapter 7, the team discusses ethics models from police and military perspectives for applying lethal force. The authors propose respect for humanity as the common moral grounding for applying such force. The concepts of discrimination, necessity, proportionality, immunity, and managing risk are introduced and applied to various scenarios to provide readers a thorough understanding of how to use lethal force in a moral manner. The authors provide leaders with a set of guiding principles to assist them in the moral application of lethal force to achieve an organization's mission. Understanding these ethics assists leaders and followers in making meaning out of injuring or killing another human in the execution of their duties and thus may help to mitigate PTSD.

David Barnes, C. Kevin Banks, Michael Albanese, and Michael Steger conclude this section with an exploration of the importance of meaning and purpose for people who serve in dangerous contexts. In Chapter 8, they offer a thought-provoking and thorough discussion about the importance of meaning-making and how leaders and group members go about understanding or making sense of their adverse or traumatic experiences. The authors discuss meaning-making from philosophical and psychological traditions and provide leaders with multiple perspectives to make sense out of their experiences or to assist their followers' meaning-making. Leaders play a key role in assisting collective meaning-making by sharing their perspective on traumatic events with subordinates and providing them the opportunity and encouraging them to share their understanding with each other. The ability to make meaning of and understand the purpose of traumatic and stressful experiences helps promote resilience and growth, and mitigates PTSD.

Section Two: Influencing When People Are in Harm's Way

The second section addresses the unique social and psychological challenges of leading in dangerous contexts. It exposes readers to theories and techniques for building strong teams, earning trust, exercising influence at a level that gets group members to step beyond individual needs to accomplish the mission and promote the welfare of the group. The contributions in this section highlight the importance of leaders investing in building good, quality relationships throughout their organization, genuinely caring for and protecting group members' welfare, seeking group members' input on decisions, and exercising values-based leadership. When peoples' lives and well-being are in the balance, relationships and leaders' credibility—competence, character, and care—assume far greater importance in the exercise of influence or leadership than in a non-dangerous context.

In Chapter 9, Patrick Sweeney, Kurt Dirks, David Sundberg, and Paul Lester provide a compelling discussion on trust development and the link between trust and influence. An elegant, easily understood, and empirically supported individual, relationship, organization, and context (IROC) model for trust development is presented with dialogue about techniques leaders can use to earn deep levels of trust. A leader's competence, character, and care (credibility) form the foundation upon which trust is built. Positive, cooperative relationships characterized by respect and empowerment facilitate the creation of trust. An organization's culture, policies, practices, and procedures also play a significant role in the development of trust throughout the group. The authors discuss how dangerous contexts influence the knowledge, skills, and abilities necessary for leaders and followers to earn credibility and how the characteristics of the social relationships within an organization must change to meet unique social demands. At the heart of this model is the proposition that trust is necessary and essential to influence group members to risk their lives to accomplish their mission. This chapter empowers leaders with the knowledge, model, and techniques to build trust at the high levels necessary to lead in dangerous contexts.

Stephen Zaccaro, Eric Weis, Rita Hilton, and Jack Jefferies address the techniques for building resilient teams to handle the unique social challenges of operating in dangerous contexts. In Chapter 10, they introduce the concept of team viability, defined as how strongly committed members are to working together and their sustained ability to do so effectively. Team viability is grounded in cohesion, trust, and collective efficacy. The concepts of social and task cohesion are examined and leaders are provided suggestions on how to enhance cohesion in their organizations. Techniques for building team trust are only briefly covered here because trust is discussed in detail in Chapter 9. Collective efficacy is defined and leaders are provided suggestions for building it in their teams. The second half of the chapter examines how leaders can build cognitive, social, and emotional resilience in their teams to meet the unique psychological and social demands associated with dangerous contexts. The chapter provides leaders with a detailed guide on how to build strong, resilient, and effective teams.

In Chapter 11 Brian Reed, Chris Midberry, Raymond Ortiz, James Redding, and Jason Toole address the essential intangible to a group's will to complete its mission, its resilience, and its effectiveness, which collectively represent its morale. Also known as esprit de corps, morale is the spirit of the unit and the indicator of its well-being. Morale infuses group members with the motivation to endure extreme hardships and overcome insurmountable odds to complete the organization's mission. When morale is good, group members develop a strong identification with the group, take pride in being part of something greater than themselves, and thus willingly step beyond self-interest for the needs of the group. The authors define the concept of morale, discuss how to assess it, and devote the majority of the chapter to providing leaders with suggestions on how to build this critical intangible.

Angela Karrasch, Alison Levine, and Thomas Kolditz provide a gripping and insightful discussion on how to influence when lives are on the line. Using evidence from research and compelling practical experience, the authors in Chapter 12 address sources of power and the most effective ways to influence people when they feel their lives and well-being depend on their leader's decisions. Leaders are provided a detailed discussion on skills, traits, and behaviors necessary to increase their ability to exercise influence in harm's way.

In Chapter 13, Joseph Pfeifer and James Merlo present a forceful discussion on intuitive decision making for dangerous contexts. They discuss several models for intuitive decision making and then propose their own model based on experiences from combat and firefighting. Moreover, the chapter provides an in-depth discussion on strategies to improve decision making in these circumstances. Dangerous contexts leaders will find this chapter invaluable for understanding how mortal stress affects decision making and will help prepare themselves and group members for making decisions under such conditions.

Michael Schuster, Lee Chartier, and John Chartier address the tenants of crisis leadership using the Station club fire in Rhode Island as a case study in Chapter 14. The authors use this compelling case to introduce leaders to L. Wooten and E. James' crisis leadership model, which identifies five phases of a crisis and outlines specific leader competencies associated with each of them. The authors use the gripping story of the 2003 Station club fire to discuss how competencies were either effectively or ineffectively employed and provide leaders with suggestions on how to apply them. Leaders are also presented a comprehensive framework to prepare themselves and their organizations for a crisis.

In Chapter 15, John Eggers, Rebecca Porter, and James Gray address leading and managing people in detention and those working with detainees and doing so in a way that promotes dignity and respect. The Abu Ghraib prison scandal illustrated to the world the importance of having clear and unambiguous procedures for the treatment of people in detention and the importance of leader presence. The authors discuss how leaders can leverage transformational and authentic leadership principles to develop and lead correction officers and inmates. The chapter provides a compelling glimpse into the leadership challenges associated with captive environments. The section on the psychology of inmates is powerful and insightful. The authors conclude with a discussion on how leaders can use principles of positive psychology to create a culture to promote growth and respect.

Closing out this section, in Chapter 16 Janice Laurence offers a thorough and impactful discussion on leading across cultures. In an era when military and civilian organizations are socially and culturally diverse, it is critical that leaders understand how diversity can enhance team performance and contribute to mission success. Various cultural views concerning leadership, the importance of emotional intelligence, and universal leadership traits and behaviors are addressed in this chapter. Leaders who treat people with respect and as valued members of their team, empower them, practice values-based leadership, and provide them a compelling vision are the ones best able to exercise effective leadership across all cultures.

Section Three: Leveraging the Organization

This section addresses how leaders can leverage an organization's structures and systems to prepare themselves and group members for the challenges of leading and operating in dangerous contexts. Leaders are provided techniques on how to build and assess the powerful influence mechanism of organizational culture. Also, leaders gain insights into the various methods law enforcement tactical teams and military Special Forces units use to recruit, assess, and select personnel. Choosing the right people is an important step toward building effective organizations that can operate well in dangerous environments. Another important step in building effective organizations is leader development. Readers are provided an in-depth discussion of targets and techniques for developing leaders to operate in stressful, dynamic, and dangerous environments.

Donald Horner, Luann Pannell, and Dennis Yates address the topic of creating an organizational culture for leading and performing in dangerous contexts in Chapter 17. Techniques for discovering and generating member commitment to the organization's core values and beliefs as well as establishing a compelling vision are discussed. The authors offer insights into establishing an effective socialization process to communicate the culture. Moreover, they examine ideas and techniques for shaping a professional identity centered on the organization's core values and beliefs. The authors also provide ideas on how to assess and align an organization's policies, procedures, and practices with the espoused culture.

In Chapter 18, Ole Boe, Kristin Woolley, and John Durkin explore recruitment and selection of leaders for dangerous contexts. The military, police and fire departments, and other high-threat organizations are turning more often to highly specialized units (SWAT, Special Forces, and so on) for precise and sometimes deadly responses to tactical situations. Members of elite teams tasked to these assignments must be stronger, faster, smarter, and more tactically proficient than the ordinary soldier, police officer, or firefighter. Hence, more care in the selection and training of team members is needed when forming these units. The authors provide readers a review and assessment of various selection models in a variety of high-threat occupational contexts.

Noel Palmer, Sean Hannah, and Daniel Sosnowik provide an insightful discussion on developing leaders for dangerous contexts in Chapter 19. Leader development starts with self-awareness and understanding how one makes meaning out of one's experiences. Personal insights are gained through seeking feedback and reflection on experiences and how one views leadership. Trigger or crucible experiences that put leaders outside their comfort zones by challenging skills or philosophies of leadership or life tend to lead to development. Various exercises are discussed to help leaders gain greater self-awareness and sense of agency. Leader development is a process of trial and error in which leaders take on and struggle through situations and then reflect on the experience. Mentors play an important role in assisting leaders in seeing their true selves, making meaning out of their experiences, sharing knowledge, suggesting challenging experiences, and prompting reflection. This chapter also presents a comprehensive model for understanding leader development.

CONCLUSION

In Chapter 20, the editors introduce a holistic development model for individuals and organizations to synthesize lessons learned and themes from *Leadership in Dangerous Situations* and to provide insight into developing people to operate in dangerous contexts. The holistic model provides a common framework and language that facilitates purposeful development. It addresses how to prepare people for the unique intrapersonal (individual), interpersonal (relationships), and organizational challenges of operating in dangerous contexts.

We wish you the best on your developmental journey and hope that leaders find this book helpful in preparing themselves and their organizations for the unique demands of leading in dangerous situations.

NOTES

1. Sean T. Hannah et al., "A Framework for Examining Leadership in Extreme Contexts," *Leadership Quarterly* 20 (2009): 2; and Donald J. Campbell et al., "Leadership in Military and Other Dangerous Contexts: Introduction to the Special Issue," *Military Psychology* 22, no. S1 (2010): S2.

2. Roger C. Mayer, James H. Davis, F. David Schoorman, "An Integrative Model of Organizational Trust," *Academy of Management Review* 20, no. 3 (1995): 709–734.

3. Patrick J. Sweeney, "Do Soldiers Reevaluate Trust in Their Leaders Prior to Combat Operations?" *Military Psychology* 22, no. S1 (2010): S82; and Patrick J. Sweeney, "Trust: The Key to Combat Leadership," in *Leadership Lessons from West Point*, ed. D. Crandall (San Francisco: Jossey-Bass, 2007), 252–277.

4. See Christopher Peterson et al., "Resilience and Leadership in Dangerous Contexts," chapter 4 in this volume.

5. Department of the Army, *Leaders' Manual for Combat Stress Control, FM 22-51* (Washington, D.C., 1994), E12–13.

6. Karl E. Friedl and David M. Penetar, "Resilience and Survival in Extreme Environments," in *Biobehavioral Resilience to Stress*, ed. B. Lukey and V. Tepe (Boca Raton, Fla.: CRC Press, 2008), 162–166.

7. Patrick J. Sweeney and Sean T. Hannah, "High Impact Military Leadership: The Positive Effects of Authentic Moral Leadership on Followers," in *Forging the Warrior's Character: Moral Precepts from the Cadet Prayer*, ed. D. Snider and L. Matthews (Boston: McGraw Hill, 2008), 91–115.

8. G. D. Mitchell, *Soldier in Battle* (Sydney: Angus and Robertson, 1940), 9.

9. Sweeney, "Trust: The Key to Combat Leadership," 258–259.

10. Samuel A. Stouffer et al., *The American Soldier: Combat and Its Aftermath*, vol. 2 (Princeton, N.J.: Princeton University Press, 1965), 118–131.

11. Patrick Sweeney, Vaida Thompson, and Hart Blanton, "Trust and Influence in Combat: An Interdependence Model," *Journal of Applied Social Psychology* 39 (2009): 235–264.

12. William Darryl Henderson, *Cohesion: The Human Element in Combat* (Washington, D.C.: National Defense University Press, 1985), 9–26.

13. Richard G. Tedeschi and Lawrence G. Calhoun, "Posttraumatic Growth: Conceptual Foundations and Empirical Evidence," *Psychological Inquiry* 15, no. 1 (2004): 1–18.

14. Patrick J. Sweeney, Sean T. Hannah, and Don M. Snider, "The Domain of the Human Spirit," in *Forging the Warrior's Character: Moral Precepts from the Cadet Prayer*, ed. D. Snider and L. Matthews (Boston: McGraw Hill, 2008), 55–99.

Enhancing One's Psychological Body Armor

CHAPTER 2

What Leaders Should Know about Courage

Paul B. Lester and Cynthia Pury

On the morning of March 16, 1968, Warrant Officer One Hugh Thompson Jr. flew above the hamlet of Son My, near the village of My Lai in the Republic of Vietnam, in support of U.S. Army ground operations. His mission was dangerous but routine—provide reconnaissance for a battalion task force searching for enemy forces. What he saw and did that day, however, would irrevocably change his life.

The My Lai massacre is a well-documented stain on American military history: An infantry company led by Captain Ernest Medina, Lieutenant William Calley, and others entered Son My and systematically murdered hundreds of Vietnamese civilians. Villagers were raped, bodies mutilated, children summarily executed in front of their parents. Seeing the carnage below, Thompson and his crew—Specialist Glenn Andreotta and Specialist Lawrence Colburn—placed their helicopter between American forces and the villagers. Thompson dismounted from his pilot's seat, then instructed his crew to cover him with machine-gun fire if the Americans began firing at the group of civilians he intended to help. He was aware that the order put him at risk of a court-martial or possible injury. Thompson coaxed several Vietnamese from a bunker and aboard evacuation helicopters and later evacuated a wounded young boy to a Vietnamese military hospital. Upon returning to base, he reported the massacre to his superiors, who immediately ordered an end to hostilities in Son My.

Commanders repeatedly tried to cover up the My Lai massacre. In a ploy to keep Thompson quiet, he was awarded the Distinguished Flying Cross for his actions that day, though he later threw away the bogus citation because it stated his heroism was a result of withstanding "intense crossfire" between friendly and enemy forces. This of course was a lie.

Subsequent investigations by the military and the media found that the villagers were unarmed, so there could have been no crossfire.

Thompson made his official report—he had witnessed American soldiers kill unarmed Vietnamese civilians—and he stuck by it despite intense pressure to recant. He repeatedly told his story to investigators and testified before the House Armed Services Committee. Committee members lambasted him for his actions, and Chairman Mendal Rivers of South Carolina stated that Thompson was the only person involved in the event who should be held accountable because he had turned his weapons against fellow Americans. Rivers even tried to have Thompson court-martialed, to no avail. Nevertheless, the damage was done, and Thompson received hate mail and death threats. Thompson's story, however, did not end with the investigation. He continued to fly in Vietnam and was shot down several times. He spent many months recovering in a hospital after breaking his back in a crash, but even that could not stop him. Thompson was commissioned and continued to fly in the Army, retiring in 1983 as a major. The immediate years following My Lai had been tough for him. He was constantly shunned by fellow officers, who considered him a turncoat.

The public's perception of Thompson began to change in the decades following My Lai. A letter-writing campaign gained traction, and he and his crew were eventually awarded the Soldier's Medal—the highest award for valor not involving enemy forces and a more poignant replacement of the Distinguished Flying Cross he had received during the attempted cover-up. He received numerous civilian honors for his actions at My Lai, including the Peace Abbey Courage of Conscience Award.

Thompson spoke of My Lai and battlefield ethics often and lectured at the United States Military, Naval, and Air Force Academies, though doing so took an emotional toll on him. Even after a diagnosis of terminal cancer, Thompson pressed on with his message: Common people can act with uncommon courage when necessary, and doing so can make a difference in the lives of many.

WHAT IS COURAGE?

Hugh Thompson's story is one of courage that went beyond placing himself between murderers and the civilians of My Lai. He not only placed himself in physical danger, but he later stood up for what was right, continuing to put forth his message even when doing so led to ostracism. Thompson acted courageously, but interestingly, he—like many people who exhibit courage—rarely if ever referred to his actions as courageous. Nevertheless, he acted, and we judge his actions to be courageous, but what exactly does it mean to be courageous?

In a series of carefully crafted studies of people's implicit theories, assumptions that people share about a topic, Christopher Rate and colleagues (Rate et al. 2007; Rate 2010) first looked at definitions of courage in a range of sources, including ancient philosophers, modern writers, psychologists, and others. They considered the commonalities and differences among the definitions and had a group of lay people and experts rate them based on shared features. They then incorporated these features into vignettes and found that people rated them as more courageous than others if they contained three features. First, the action must be freely chosen, that is, volitional. Second, the act must be in pursuit of a noble or worthwhile goal. Third, the actor must face significant personal risk from external circumstances. How does the presence or absence of each of these features change how courageous an action seems to be? Let's start with free choice.

Free Choice (Volition)

Volition is an act that is done willingly, voluntarily, deliberately, and freely (Rate et al. 2007). Unintentional actions do not qualify, and the possibility that an action was not intentional diminishes its courageousness. Hugh Thompson had multiple opportunities to choose an easier and less courageous path, such as continuing on his assigned mission, telling a different story about events, or letting his bogus citation stand.

The possibility that a person did not consciously decide to act can, conversely, reduce perceived courage. Marine sergeant Rafael Peralta was nominated for the Medal of Honor, the highest decoration in the U.S. military, following a firefight in Iraq in 2004. After being shot in the head, he pulled a live grenade toward himself, absorbing the fatal blast and saving six other Marines. Forensic scientists found that the bullet to his head likely led to instant brain damage, rendering Peralta incapable of intentional movements. Based in large part on this report, Peralta received a lesser, posthumous decoration (Zoepf 2010).

In one study, we asked participants to describe a time they had acted courageously, and then we followed up with multiple questions. The question "Why do you believe that your action was courageous?" was commonly (15 percent) answered by "the choice to take action." Unpublished data from the same study found that 243 of the 250 participants answered the question "How could you have responded to that situation in a NONcourageous manner?" by indicating that they could have taken a different action, (e.g., "I could have walked by and let the situation go on."). Thus, the vast majority of participants gave a clear description of an alternate and easier action open to them.

Most also indicated that the alternative action would have been easier than the action they actually took (Pury, Kowalski, and Spearman 2007).

Noble or Worthy Goal

For an action to be considered courageous, Rate and colleagues found that it must be taken in pursuit of a noble or otherwise worthwhile goal. If Hugh Thompson had taken his stand against the massacre to get discharged or to promote a book it would diminish our sense of his courage. Evel Knievel was largely perceived in the popular press as a fool after his failed attempt in 1974 to jump across the Snake River Canyon on a rocket-powered cycle. There was no noble goal, just high risk for money and more fame. Thus, pursuit of a worthwhile goal differentiates courage from risk-taking.

Evidence suggests people believe their own courageous actions are taken in pursuit of important goals. In a recent study Charles Starkey and colleagues asked 201 college students to describe a time when they had acted coura-geously, and then they followed up with an expanded and modified set of questions, including "What were you trying to accomplish with this action? What was your goal?" (Pury et al. 2009). Ninety-nine percent—all but two participants—provided a clearly articulated goal. Moreover, participants rated these goals as very strongly meaningful and important at the time. Indeed, on a scale of zero to ten, the most common answer to "How important was this goal to you at the time?" was ten.

Significant Personal Risk

Rate and colleagues (2007) also found that the action must take place despite threatening, dangerous, or other circumstances. Read most citations for cour-age and you will find extensive descriptions of risks faced by those decorated. Hugh Thompson's writing a report on My Lai can only be seen as coura-geous given the risks to his career. Steven Kurch was awarded his employer's Medal of Valor for stopping to help his colleagues climb up a steep hill. Under ordinary circumstances, this would likely seem to be courteous or collegial at most. Kurch and his fellow crew members, however, were working for the Los Angeles County Fire Department, extinguishing a hazardous brush fire in a dangerous, gas-filled canyon (County of Los Angeles Fire Department n.d.). That action alone, without the personal risk, would not be courageous.

Not all risks may be obvious to observers. Pury and colleagues describe personal courage, or the extent to which the action is courageous, as being in comparison to the actor's typical actions, not as compared to other people's action. Actions high in personal courage are those in which the person faces unique and personalized risks, such as confronting a fear of public speaking or dealing with a limitation that only he or she knows about. These personalized risks might or might not be accessible to outsiders. On the other hand, general courage—the extent to which an action is courageous compared to other people's typical actions—is related to more general risks (Pury, Kowalski, and Spearman 2007).

TYPES OF COURAGE

Although many different types of courage have been recognized, the most robust distinction is between physical courage and moral courage (Pury, Kowalski, and Spearman 2007). Physical courage typically involves taking a bodily risk, commonly to rescue others from that same risk, such as rescuing a drowning victim or saving a wounded comrade during a firefight. Moral courage, on the other hand, typically involves taking a social risk in support of one's beliefs, such as confronting a superior about misdeeds or challenging an unfair policy. This distinction may have come about because certain types of risks are more likely to co-occur with certain types of goals. Other courageous actions blur the line between physical and moral courage. Civil rights protesters marching after others were killed for similar actions or a wartime military recruit motivated by a love of country do not fit neatly into a single category, but are nonetheless courageous.

Philosopher Daniel Putman (2004, 2010) has proposed that philosophers and psychologists consider psychological courage, the willingness to face emotional instability to obtain one's goals, as a separate form of courageous action. Psychological courage is exemplified by the psychotherapy client who confronts internal demons to get well. It can also be seen in individuals who rock climb although they have a fear of heights or grieving family members who remain strong for others despite their own sadness (Pury, Kowalski, and Spearman 2007). A related construct, vital courage, involves mustering the strength needed to cope with physical illness or other impairments (Finfgeld 1999).

Is Fear a Necessary Part of Courage?

Obviously, being aware of personal risk might lead to fear. Many early psychological concepts of courage required the individual to feel fear. For example, Lord (1918) described courage as the sentiment of fear being overwhelmed by a more noble sentiment. More recently, Rachman (1990, 2010) described courage as experiencing the subjective or physiological components of fear (increased heart rate, sweaty palms, and so on) while not avoiding or fleeing the cause. Norton and Weiss (2009) introduce their paper-and-pencil measure of courage by defining it as "persistence or perseverance despite having fear. It takes courage to engage and persist in a terrifying activity. By definition, fear is necessary for someone to display courage" (p. 214). According to these definitions, one must have an emotional experience of fear to be considered courageous. Alternatively, it may be that courage requires awareness of risk rather than fear per se. For many people, awareness of personal risk leads quickly and directly to fear, but this may not be true for everyone.

If fear is a required element of courage, then many individuals and actions we might like to characterize as courageous fall short. Rachman asked decorated bomb disposal operators and other soldiers in a control group to discriminate between two different audio tones while hooked up to devices to measure their heart rate and skin conductance (to see how sweaty their palms became). An incorrect answer led to an electric shock. The tones became increasingly similar until they were identical. The decorated soldiers had lower subjective and physiological levels of fear than the non-decorated soldiers. Thus, if fear is a necessary part of courage, perhaps the group that was decorated for valor is better described as fearless rather than courageous (Rachman 1990, 2010; Cox et al. 1983; O'Connor, Hallam, and Rachman 1985).

Observers who view fear as integral to courage suggest that courage is a stepping-stone to fearlessness (Rachman 1990, 2010), or at the group level, to becoming a highly functional "quantum" organization (Kilmann, O'Hara, and Strauss 2010). One likely scenario is that fear may be part of courage as a process, that is, the way in which an individual goes about taking a (possibly) courageous action (Pury and Starkey 2010). The greater the subjective sense of risk and fear, the less likely the person is to take the action. Some people may have a higher threshold for experiencing fear, and thus may be more likely to perform well in extremely risky situations (Rachman 1990, 2010). Viewing oneself as someone who does not give in to fear may also lead to more courageous behavior (Norton and Weiss 2009).

Fear does not, however, seem to be a typical part of accolades for courage or the process by which observers perceive an action as more or less courageous. Those who thrive in dangerous working environments are typically seen as courageous by the civilian population, but research suggests that they have a lower than average level of fear (Rachman 1990, 2010). Citations for courage do not typically describe the fear experienced by the individual taking the action (Pury and Starkey 2010), but rather focus on the good that the person did and the risks he or she took to do it.

SUBJECTIVITY AND JUDGMENTS OF COURAGEOUSNESS

Two parts of courage—nobility of the goal and risk to the actor—are frequently subjective. That is not to say that there are not universals: Current research into the evolution of morality suggests that aiding others is likely to be seen as nearly universally noble (de Waal, Macedo, and Ober 2006). Simple physiology and mortality statistics tell us that physical danger should be seen as universally risky, while research into the history of humans as social animals suggests that we should all view the loss of social status as a threat (Nesse 1990). Other goals and risks might not be as universal.

This subjective quality can also be seen in a goal's value. Draft dodgers are seen as having more courage than soldiers by those with strong anti-war sentiments (O'Brian 1998). In a controlled empirical study, the perceived courageousness of pro-choice and anti-abortion protesters depended on the observer's opinion of both abortion and free speech (Pury and Starkey 2010). Certainly the House Armed Services Committee interviewing Hugh Thompson did not consider him courageous at the time. Such subjectivity means that an objective standard of courage for everyone and all actions is unlikely. Within an organization, shared norms based on mission, expertise, and social factors are likely to influence the perceived risk of specific actions and the perceived value of goals. Those working in physically dangerous environments will face elevated physical risks on the job compared to most other people. They also have the training, experience, and resources to handle such situations. Thus, taking on a certain level of risk to fulfill unit missions is expected rather than exceptional. As one police officer put it, if he disarms a criminal, that's just doing his job, but if an unarmed civilian disarms a criminal, that person is likely to be hailed as a hero.

Saying an action is courageous also implies the speaker agrees with the goal of the action (Breznican 2002; Pury and Starkey 2010). At a more basic level, citations for courage commonly make the case for the goodness of the action taken. Individuals involved in risky actions that cannot be publicly endorsed or perhaps even acknowledged thus might not be easily cited for valor.

GOAL ATTAINMENT AND JUDGMENTS OF COURAGE

The extent to which an action is successful can also influence its perceived courageousness. The Carnegie Hero Medal is most commonly awarded to individuals who saved the lives of others, not to those who merely attempted to save a life (Pury and Starkey 2010). When asked to describe a courageous action they have either performed or witnessed, the overwhelming majority of participants list an action that made the situation a good deal better and not at all worse, and, when asked to rate the courageousness of both successful and failed actions, participants rated successful actions as significantly more courageous than failed ones. This was true even when it was clear that the failure had nothing to do with the individual's action or limitations (Pury and Hensel 2010). Thus, when the goal of an action is not attained, people may discount the courage it took to make the attempt.

LEADERS: WHY BEING COURAGEOUS MATTERS

If you are reading this book, then you are likely a leader or someone who wants to become a leader, and the contexts in which you lead will, at times, be dangerous. Courage is that quality that allows someone to pursue valuable goals despite risks. Both the goals and the risks might be quite apparent in some contexts, for example, civilian and military rescues. They may be less obvious in the courage it takes to lead with integrity despite social and organizational pressure to do the wrong thing or in the courage it takes to admit that one needs counseling following a traumatic event. It also is a label applied after an action if it is seen as good and the dangers significant.

Given the complexities of leading in dangerous contexts, opportunities to act courageously will likely emerge. You may have the opportunity to save the baby from a burning building; you may uncover unethical behavior and blow the whistle; you may be wounded but choose to stay with your unit. In any event, most leaders find themselves orchestrating events toward mission completion. Stated another way, you—the leader—cannot be everywhere during a ground combat mission, during a four-alarm fire, or while executing a high-risk warrant on a fugitive. You must, therefore, rely on your followers to do what is required. Thus, a pressing question emerges: Are your followers prepared to act courageously in your absence? Even more pressing: What have you done to prepare your followers to act courageously?

Organizational Culture and Context

Preparing followers to be courageous starts with a leader's behavior and is reinforced by the organization. Organizational values and mission statements assist leaders in developing followers' courage. For example, courage is one of the seven values of the U.S. Army and a common value in other public safety or military organizations (Lester et al. 2010). These organizations publicly state that courage is "part of the job." From a practitioner perspective, a platoon leader or police sergeant may be able to leverage organizational culture to bolster courageous behavior in many ways. For example, he or she may recognize and reward a follower's physical courage during physical training or while performing drills, a subordinate leader's moral courage to stand up and support the best interest of soldiers or patrolmen, or a follower's psychological courage to seek help for stress symptoms.

Simply including courage as an organizational value, however, will not always result in courageous behavior. Acting courageously is a complex process, but including courage as a value is a signal of what is expected of members of the organization. Such signals can be an effective form of pressure that results in courageous behavior.

LEADER ACTIONS FOR FOSTERING COURAGE

Though history plays an important role in establishing organizational culture, leaders also help shape culture and set standards of behavior. At the individual and group levels, transformational leadership theory (Bass 1985) and authentic leadership theory (Avolio and Luthans 2006) both suggest leaders serve as role models and are emulated by followers. Additionally, Lester and colleagues (2010) have suggested that courage can be developed through a variety of structured approaches, one being mentorship relationships focused on courage development and discussion. Likewise, they point out that deliberate, repeated, challenging, and realistic training in military, police, firefighter, and other public service sectors results in behavior that observers would call courage. There are a number of ways leaders can promote courage.

Serve as a Role Model

Research on social learning and social cognitive theories has repeatedly shown that people learn by behavioral observation (Bandura 1977). These theories proffer three key concepts affecting courage development: learning behaviors through observational methods; learning that involves attention, retention, reproduction, and motivational processes; and learning through practice—or enactive mastery—role modeling, vicarious learning, social pressure and persuasion, and arousal.

Promote Learning through Observation. Bandura's (1977) research on social learning suggests that several pathways are required for effective observational learning. First, a stimulus must hold an individual's attention long enough for processing to occur and then to learn from it. Stated another way, simple exposure to an event may not be enough for learning to occur if the individual does not consider the event important or interesting. Second, individual differences matter greatly in social learning. In specific, people must be able to retain what they learn, suggesting the importance of factors such as intelligence matter. Likewise, they must be able to reproduce what they learn, indicating that individual skill sets or physical abilities may matter and that they must have the cognitive ability to transfer what they observe to their own behavior. Finally, individuals must be motivated to reproduce the observed behavior based on extrinsic rewards (e.g., money, recognition) or intrinsic rewards (e.g., personal satisfaction, such as knowing that the behavior was "the right thing to do"). Given these pathways, learning courage may be seen as the responsibility of the individual. While this may be true, leaders can enact other deliberate approaches for developing courage in followers.

Practice Being Courageous

Repeated practice, or mastery experiences, may lead to courage development. Indeed, research has consistently shown that past performance is one of the best predictors and enhancers of future performance (Bandura 1977, 1982, 1991). Here, it is proposed that a leader can deliberately create training environments that require courageous action and then provide trainees (followers) with structured feedback to assist with meaning making and to drive home the necessity of courage in certain contexts.

Promote Hands-On Practice. There are two forms of mastery—guided mastery and cognitive mastery modeling (Bandura 2000a, 2000b). Guided mastery consists of instructive modeling to transfer skills and knowledge (e.g., teaching), guided perfection of those skills (e.g., coaching and mentoring), and use of the skills and knowledge in a particular context (e.g., application). Leaders can leverage guided mastery pathways toward courage by providing resources followers need to be courageous (Hannah, Sweeney, and Lester 2007), reinforcing those resources with coaching or mentorship, and providing positive feedback. This drives home the necessity of deliberate (Lester et al. 2010), tough, and realistic training scenarios. As one would expect, research in high-stress contexts has shown that such practical training leads to more successful outcomes (Zohar and Luria 2003), possibly by reducing perceptions of risk or increasing the skills needed to perform despite risks.

Promote Mental Practice. While training event participation is ideal, time or resource constraints may make it impossible. When this is the case, cognitive mastery modeling serves as mental rehearsal, allowing individuals to think through behaviors prior to actual performance (Bandura 1996). Key to cognitive mastery is that an individual actually visualizes performance of a given task after observing a model performing the task. This type of cognitive rehearsal is common in a variety of contexts, such as sports and public speaking, because doing so helps establish scripts to be called upon during performance. Likewise, cognitive mastery modeling has direct application in contexts requiring courage. Hannah, Sweeney, and Lester (2007) propose that cognitive modeling can bolster a courageous mind-set by reducing fear when individuals are exposed to risk. Take, for example, a mountain climber about to begin a technically difficult climb involving out-of-reach handholds that will require explosive leaps. Simulating these moves, while possible, usually would not provide enough realism because the height, distance of the leap, and unique shape of the handhold cannot be fully replicated. Given this, the climber watches videos of other climbers successfully negotiating the section, and while doing so, the climber envisions himself doing the same thing. When the climber actually confronts that difficult section of the mountain, his fear is decreased because he cognitively rehearsed it, and he almost feels as though he has already climbed the section several times. Thus, realistic training is likely to reduce perception of risk and boost efficacy.

Promote Vicarious Learning. Similar to cognitive mastery modeling, vicarious learning is another method that a leader may employ to develop courage in followers. Although similar to informal role modeling, vicarious learning situations are deliberately constructed so that learners observe a role model performing the task and then replicate the task without rehearsal (Bandura 1997). Research by Bandura (1996, 1997) and Stajkovic and Luthans (1998) suggests that a similarity of task-specific attributes and context must exist between the observer and the role model performing the task, and portrayal of the task must be of high fidelity. Likewise, Bandura (1977) found that the role model must be credible, trustworthy, and important to the observer in order for the task to be salient enough for replication.

In dangerous contexts, leaders must be willing to put themselves at risk if they expect followers to do the same. This is not to say that leaders should unnecessarily place themselves or their followers at risk in a vain attempt to appear to be courageous. On the contrary, such behavior is foolhardy, or what Pury and Starkey (2010) refer to as foolish courage because the associated risk is too costly. Rather, the adage "be willing to do what you expect your followers to do" comes to mind. Though leaders must carefully balance placing themselves at risk to prove to followers that they can be courageous and serve in their particular role during a mission, leaders can still actively model physical and moral courage in training and operational environments.

For example, it is common practice for a Special Forces A Team leader to be the first man out of the aircraft on a high altitude–low opening (HALO) jump. Such behavior drives home the "follow me" attitude endemic in organizations that routinely place members at risk (Kolditz 2007; Lester et al. 2010). Conversely, a leader's failure to take such risk can have a debilitating effect on mission accomplishment. Imagine the A Team described here about to execute a high-risk HALO jump into a combat zone. As the aircraft ramp drops, the team leader moves to the edge, freezes up, and says "You know, I don't think I'm going to jump today . . . too dangerous!" If the team leader scratches the jump, he has set the new standard for unit member behavior (barring of course legitimate reasons for scratching). In other words, he transmitted a powerful message to his followers: It is OK to buckle under fear. What do you think might happen the next time the unit must jump in a high-risk setting and the leader isn't there? Will the leader's failure to act courageously in the past influence the group's future behavior?

The type of courage leaders are expected to show might depend on echelon or specific training. For example, senior strategic leaders in the Army must show moral courage, but they will never be found defusing a bomb, even if there are bomb disposal specialists in his division. A leader without the requisite skills to complete a particularly risky task safely will appear foolhardy rather than courageous. A worthwhile question to ask yourself if you are considering leading by vicarious learning is "Am I more qualified—or at least as qualified—as my followers to do X?" If the answer is no, you might not be modeling courage but rather modeling foolhardiness.

Use Social Persuasion and Feedback. Social persuasion, positive feedback, and other forms of coaching provide another route toward developing courage in followers. Verbal persuasion and feedback can lead to significant shifts in attitudes (Eagly and Chaiken 1993, 1998). As suggested in this chapter and by Lester and colleagues (2010), a systematic approach toward coaching and counseling that makes courage a central topic of discussion could increase self-efficacy and self-attributions toward courage. Here, the leader, serving as coach and counselor, has an opportunity to share experiences with the follower and discuss personal values as they relate to courage. Indeed, McGurk and Castro (2010) point out that the relationship between courage and values is not a new concept (e.g., Welton 1922), and researchers and philosophers alike believe that values play a central role in promoting courage by clarifying and aligning goals and effort (Lester et al. 2010; Goud 2005; Sandage and Hill 2001; Shepela et al. 1999).

Peer pressure and social comparison bolster social persuasion's impact on courage development. While some researchers (Darley and Latane 1968; Latane and Darley 1970) have shown that individuals in a group tend not to place themselves at risk, this bystander effect decreases when the threat increases (Fischer et al. 2006). Thus, individuals will act courageously for the group if the risk is great enough. Likewise, peer pressure and social comparisons can be leveraged toward courageous behavior, especially in organizations where courage is considered a social norm. Research in this area goes back several decades. Festinger's (1954) research on social comparisons and Tesser's (1988) work on self-evaluation maintenance suggest that self-esteem increases and decreases based on how one behaves in accordance with role model behavior and organizational norms. Therefore, followers may feel compelled to act courageously if they serve in organizations where courage is the norm, and they fear being ostracized by the group (Lester et al. 2010). Although the actions taken due to social pressure might not meet the requirements for process courage, they would for accolade courage, as the person has performed the externally desired action despite risk (Pury and Starkey 2010). For example, it is not hard to imagine a firefighter who, although afraid, still runs into a burning building. The firefighter does so for a multitude of reasons, but most germane to the current discussion are the likely outcomes if he does not. At best, failure to enter the building would likely result in his peers calling him a coward and potentially losing his job. At worst, his peers and the people they are trying to save could die in the fire.

Here again, the role of leadership linking social persuasion and feedback to courage development is clear. Over and above establishing courage as a central organizational value and norm, leaders must also serve as meaning maker, coach, and counselor for followers, driving home what is expected in situations calling for courage. The leader should not shrug off follower concerns about fear, on the contrary, such instances serve as critical "teachable moments" where the leader–follower bond could be strengthened by the leader explaining how he or she experiences fear and the tools needed to overcome it. In situ, the leader can also provide immediate, positive feedback when the follower performs courageously, which serves to reinforce the behavior and increases the likelihood of future courageous behavior.

The leader can and should tap into formal institutional rewards (e.g., medals and commendations) to acknowledge courageous actions. One perspective is that organizations should nominate members for medals following heroic acts because its members should be rewarded for such behavior. There is certainly some truth to this perspective, and there are organizational implications for doing so as well. Organizations should recognize courage because it sets a high standard that other members should strive to attain. Stated another way, it reinforces the value of an individual's behavior as a significant contribution toward mission completion, and the behavior should be emulated when the right context emerges.

Promote Positive and Optimal Stress. Most people who have played sports easily recognize the impact that physiological and emotional arousal can have on player performance: It's fourth down and twenty-five yards to the end zone with six seconds on the clock in the final football game of the season, before the state championship playoffs. You are the quarterback, and you can barely hear yourself think because every fan in the stadium is on their feet and screaming. You call the play and head to the line. The ball is snapped, you drop back, and you see two linebackers blitzing. Just as they pummel you, you spot your favorite wide receiver streaking toward the end zone. You reach back and let loose the strongest, tightest spiral pass of your career. Such performances are much more common than one might think.

Bandura (1997) and others have empirically shown a clear link between physiological and emotional arousal and increased performance. The psychology literature suggests that some people become energized by stress and subsequently perform better, but others crack under stress. Likewise, it is widely accepted that each person has an optimal stress limit that benefits performance. Crossing that limit may result in decreased performance, and such linkages have been made to courageous performance (Rachman 1983, 2010).

Use Referent Power and Inspirational Motivation

One final leader influence, beyond social learning theory, is that of inspirational motivation, where the follower has an emotional link to the leader. A leader's actions or words can spur courageous action by inciting followers to act. Martin Luther King's actions and speeches during the civil rights movement inspired an entire nation to change. An emotional link can also be a double-edged sword that could be abused. As suggested in attachment theory (Harms, in press; Bowlby 1982), individuals (followers) have a deep-seated desire to form strong bonds with attachment figures (leaders). Such a desire is often stronger when the attachment figure is charismatic (Shamir, House, and Arthur 1993), and may serve to explain why followers are willing to engage in foolhardy and often deadly behavior that serves no greater good (Graham 1991). For example, Reverend Jim Jones' followers drank and made their children drink poisonous Kool-Aid at his urging, leading to the death of more than nine hundred people (Tabor and Gallagher 1997). With this in mind, leaders must be mindful that physiological and emotional arousal can be taken too far, where behavior crosses from being courageous to being foolish.

CONCLUSION

Despite several thousand years of philosophical analysis, our understanding of courage and its development as a complex psychological phenomenon is only now emerging. As discussed in this chapter, there are three primary forms of courage recognized in the psychological literature—physical, moral, and psychological/vital—and how they function is as different as their conceptualizations. Where they conceptually converge, however, is that all three require deliberate risk taking toward some perceived noble cause, separating noble forms of courage from foolhardy behaviors and foolish courage (Pury and Starkey 2010). In line with Lester and coauthors, we propose in addition a social learning/social cognitive approach to developing courage in followers. We suggest that while leaders may be assisted in developing follower courage by the organization—after all, courage is a raison d'etre of many public safety and military organizations—it is the leader who can and must intervene to shepherd the courage development process along.

KEY TAKE-AWAY POINTS

1. Provide tough, realistic training for the duties your followers will need to perform, along with feedback that helps them internalize the idea of themselves as competent, courageous actors.

2. Share experiences with followers and explicitly discuss their relation to courage.

3. Role model the kind of behaviors you want your followers to emulate. This goes for courageous behavior, too.

4. When one of your followers acts courageously, provide immediate positive feedback. If he or she is eligible for an organizational commendation based on the action, take the time to complete the nomination promptly.

5. Consider what types of courage are recognized in your unit. Do you recognize and reward moral or vital courage? Courage is often rare, so ensure that you recognize it regardless of its form.

6. Be aware that both the value of the goal and the risks endured to pursue the goal have a subjective component. In other words, there is some truth in believing that courage is in the eye of the beholder. By praising actions

as courageous or dismissing them as not, you are sending a message to your followers about the relative value and danger of those situations. Be sure that you are sending the message that you want to send.

KEY REFERENCES

Hannah, Sean T., Patrick J. Sweeney, and Paul B. Lester. 2007. "Toward a Courageous Mindset: The Subjective Act and Experience of Courage." *Journal of Positive Psychology* 2:129–135.

Pury, Cynthia L. S., and Shane J. Lopez, eds. 2010. *The Psychology of Courage: Modern Research on an Ancient Virtue.* Washington, D.C.: American Psychological Association.

Rachman, S. Jack. 1990. *Fear and Courage.* 2nd ed. New York: W. H. Freeman, Times Books, Henry Holt & Co.

REFERENCES

Avolio, Bruce J., and Fred Luthans. 2006. *The High Impact Leader: Moments Matter in Accelerating Authentic Leadership Development.* New York: McGraw-Hill.

Bandura, Albert. 1977. *Social Learning Theory.* Englewood Cliffs, N.J.: Prentice-Hall.

———. 1982. "Self-Efficacy Mechanism in Human Agency." *American Psychologist* 37:122–147.

———. 1991. "Social Cognitive Theory of Self-Regulation." *Organizational Behavior and Human Decision Processes* 50:248–287.

———. 1996. "Ontological and Epistemological Terrains Revisited." *Journal of Behavioral Therapy and Experimental Psychology* 27:323–345.

———. 1997. *Self-Efficacy: The Exercise of Control.* New York: Freeman.

———. 2000a. "Cultivate Self-Efficacy for Personal and Organizational Effectiveness." In *Handbook of Principles of Organizational Behavior,* edited by Edwin A. Locke, 120–136. Oxford, UK: Blackwell.

———. 2000b. "Exercise of Human Agency through Collective Efficacy." *Current Directions in Psychological Science* 9:75–78.

Bass, Bernard M. 1985. *Leadership and Performance beyond Expectations.* New York: Free Press.

Bowlby, John. 1982. *Attachment and Loss.* Vol 1. *Attachment.* 2nd ed. New York: Basic Books.

Breznican, Anthony. 2002. "Bill Maher Tapes Final Episode of 'Politically Incorrect.'" Associated Press, June 27, 2002.

County of Los Angeles Fire Department. n.d. "Heroes in Action: Medal of Valor Awards Program." http://www.fire.lacounty.gov/Heroes/Heroes.asp.

Cox, D., R. Hallam, K. O'Connor, and S. J. Rachman. 1983. "An Experimental Analysis of Fearlessness and Courage." *British Journal of Psychology* 74:107–117.

Darley, John M., and Bibb Latane. 1968. "When Will People Help in a Crisis?" *Psychology Today* 2:54–57, 70–71.

de Waal, Frans, Stephen Macedo, and Josiah Ober. 2006. *Primates and Philosophers: How Morality Evolved*. Princeton, N.J.: Princeton University Press.

Eagly, Alice H., and Shelly Chaiken. 1993. *The Psychology of Attitudes*. Dallas: Harcourt, Brace, Jovanovich.

———. 1998. "Attitude Structure and Function." In *Handbook of Social Psychology*, edited by Daniel T. Gilbert, Susan T. Fiske, and Gardner Lindzey, 269–322. Boston: McGraw-Hill.

Festinger, Leon. 1954. "A Theory of Social Comparison Processes." *Human Relations* 7:117–140.

Finfgeld, Deborah L. 1999. "Courage as a Process of Pushing beyond the Struggle." *Qualitative Health Research* 9:803–814.

Fischer, Peter, Tobias Greitemeyer, Fabian Pollozek, and Dieter Frey. 2006. "The Unresponsive Bystander: Are Bystanders More Responsive in Dangerous Emergencies?" *European Journal of Social Psychology* 36:267–278.

Goud, Nelson H. 2005. "Courage: Its Nature and Development." *Journal of Humanistic Counseling, Education, and Development* 44:102–116.

Graham, Jill W. 1991. "Servant-Leadership in Organizations: Inspirational and Moral." *The Leadership Quarterly* 2:105–119.

Hannah, Sean T., Paul J. Sweeney, and Paul B. Lester. 2007. "Toward a Courageous Mindset: The Subjective Act and Experience of Courage." *Journal of Positive Psychology* 2:129–135.

Harms, P. D. In press. "Adult Attachment Styles in the Workplace." *Human Resource Management Review*.

Kilmann, Ralph H., Linda A. O'Hara, and Judy P. Strauss. 2010. "Developing and Validating a Quantitative Measure of Organizational Courage." *Journal of Business and Psychology* 25:15–23.

Kolditz, Thomas A. 2007. *The In Extremis Leader: Leading as Though Your Life Depended on It*. Hoboken, N.J.: John Wiley & Sons.

Latane, Bibb, and John M. Darley. 1970. *The Unresponsive Bystander: Why Doesn't He Help?* New York: Appleton-Century-Crofts.

Lester, Paul B., Gretchen R. Vogelgesang, Sean T. Hannah, and Ted Kimmey. 2010. "Developing Courage in Followers: Theoretical and Applied Perspectives." In *The Psychology of Courage: Modern Research on an Ancient Virtue*, edited by Cynthia L. S. Pury and Shane J. Lopez, 23–45. Washington, D.C.: American Psychological Association.

Lord, Herbert G. 1918. *The Psychology of Courage*. Boston: John W. Luce.

McGurk, Dennis, and Carl Castro. 2010. "Courage in Combat." In *The Psychology of Courage: Modern Research on an Ancient Virtue*, edited by Cynthia L. S. Pury and Shane J. Lopez, 91–107. Washington, D.C.: American Psychological Association.

Nesse, Randolph M. 1990. "Evolutionary Explanations of Emotions." *Human Nature* 1:261–289.

Norton, Peter J., and Brandon J. Weiss. 2009. "The Role of Courage on Behavioral Approach in a Fear-Eliciting Situation: A Proof-of-Concept Study." *Journal of Anxiety Disorders* 23:212–217.

O'Brian, Tim. 1998. *The Things They Carried.* New York: Broadway Books.

O'Connor, K., R. Hallam, and S. J. Rachman. 1985. "Fearlessness and Courage: A Replication Experiment." *British Journal of Psychology* 76:187–197.

Pury, Cynthia L. S., and Autumn Hensel. 2010. "Are Courageous Actions Successful Actions?" *Journal of Positive Psychology* 5:62–72.

Pury, Cynthia L. S., and Charles Starkey. 2010. "Is Courage an Accolade or a Process? A Fundamental Question for Courage Research." In *The Psychology of Courage: Modern Research on an Ancient Virtue,* edited by Cynthia L. S. Pury and Shane J. Lopez, 67–87. Washington, D.C.: American Psychological Association.

Pury, Cynthia L. S., Robin M. Kowalski, and M. Jana Spearman. 2007. "Distinctions between General and Personal Courage." *Journal of Positive Psychology* 2:99–114.

Pury, Cynthia L. S., Charles Starkey, Whitney Hawkins, Lindsay Weber, and Shawn Saylors. 2009. "A Cognitive Appraisal Model of Courage." Paper presented at the First World Congress on Positive Psychology. Philadelphia, June.

Putman, Daniel. 2004. *Psychological Courage.* Lanham, Md.: University Press of America.

———. 2010. "Philosophical Roots of the Concept of Courage." In *The Psychology of Courage: Modern Research on an Ancient Virtue,* edited by Cynthia L. S. Pury and Shane J. Lopez, 9–22. Washington, D.C.: American Psychological Association.

Rachman S. Jack. 1983. "Fear and Fearlessness among Trainee Parachutists." *Advances in Behavioral Theory* 4:153–160.

———. 1990. *Fear and Courage.* 2nd ed. New York: W. H. Freeman, Times Books, Henry Holt & Co.

———. 2010. "Courage: A Psychological Perspective." In *The Psychology of Courage: Modern Research on an Ancient Virtue,* edited by Cynthia L. S. Pury and Shane J. Lopez, 91–107. Washington, D.C.: American Psychological Association.

Rate, Christopher R. 2010. "Defining the Features of Courage: A Search for Meaning." In *The Psychology of Courage: Modern Research on an Ancient Virtue,* edited by Cynthia L. S. Pury and Shane J. Lopez, 47–66. Washington, D.C.: American Psychological Association.

Rate, Christopher R., Jennifer A. Clarke, Douglas R. Lindsay, and Robert J. Sternberg. 2007. "Implicit Theories of Courage." *Journal of Positive Psychology* 2:80–98.

Sandage, Steven J., and Peter C. Hill. 2001. "The Virtues of Positive Psychology: The Rapprochement and Challenges of an Affirmative Postmodern Perspective." 31:241–260.

Shamir, Boas, Robert J. House, and Michael B. Arthur. 1993. "The Motivational Effects of Charismatic Leadership: A Self-Concept Based Theory." *Organizational Science* 4:577–594.

Shepela, Sharon T., Jennifer Cook, Elizabeth Horlitz, Robin Leal, Sandra Luciano, Elizabeth Lutfy, Carolyn Miller, Grace Mitchell, and Emily Worden. 1999. "Courageous Resistance: A Special Case of Altruism." *Theory and Psychology* 9:787–805.

Stajkovic, Alexander D., and Fred Luthans. 1998. "Self-Efficacy and Work-Related Performance: A Meta-Analysis." *Psychological Bulletin* 124:240–261.

Tabor, James D., and Eugene V. Gallagher. 1997. *Why Waco?* Berkeley: University of California Press.

Tesser, Abraham. 1988. "Toward a Self-Evaluation Maintenance Model of Social Behavior." In *Advances in Experimental Social Psychology,* edited by Leonard Berkowitz, 21:181–227. New York: Academic Press.

Welton, James. 1922. *Groundwork of Ethics.* London: Clive.

Zoepf, Katherine. 2010. "What Happened to Valor?" *New York Times,* May 24 http://www.nytimes.com/2010/05/30/magazine/30medals-t.html.

Zohar, Dov, and Gil Luria. 2003. "Organizational Meta-Scripts as a Source of High Reliability: The Case of an Army Armored Brigade." *Journal of Organizational Behavior* 24:837–859.

CHAPTER 3

Understanding and Managing Stress

James Ness, Denise Jablonski-Kaye, Isabell Obigt, and David M. Lam

L eaders, particularly those who lead in dangerous contexts, are a powerful force in managing and alleviating the effects of stress. This chapter discusses how to leverage that force, describing stress management practices above and beyond the stalwarts of individual fitness, sleep, and good health habits. Theory along with the context of real-world cases are presented to make leaders aware of the nature and effects of the decisions to be made while preparing for or leading in dangerous situations and how to assess and respond to critical incidents. The main lesson is that leaders must know their people, know the crucible in which they operate, establish a culture of catharsis, and know that they are a principle source of resilience.

WHAT DOES STRESS ENTAIL?

The term "stress" derives from the Middle English word "stresse" and was originally used to convey physical hardship.[1] Although there are earlier, sporadic instances of the term being used in a psychological context, it did not assume a widely accepted psychological connotation until the work of Walter Cannon and Hans Selye in the late 1920s. As Selye's theory gained popularity, "stress" came to refer to an overall stressor or stress-response relationship.[2] More recently, the term has become more of a convenient semantic category accommodating an expanding family of behaviors, feelings, and experiences associated with psychological or physical complaints and life-related conditions. Although the term lacks the specificity required for scientific inquiry or diagnosis, its use in the general lexicon provides an opportunity to examine stress metaphors within an organization's culture to determine specific effects of the complaint and potential remedies.[3]

Examples of such metaphors include the complaints described in a case involving the symptoms of culture- and generation-bound syndromes.[4] In the mid-1970s, a U.S. Army clinic started seeing young healthy males who were withdrawing from life, hiding in their rooms and deteriorating in their performance. At the clinic, these individuals often were crying, screaming that they simply could not deal with the Army anymore, and shaking their limbs and bodies almost convulsively. Initial presentation involved complaints of limb numbness and tingling. Health care providers in the clinic came up with the usable, albeit catchall diagnosis "adjustment reaction of adult life." Upon further investigation, the condition's manifestations were found to be almost exclusively confined to a population of young (18-to-19-year-old) Puerto Rican males who had never been off their island and were involved in their first operational assignment. In discussing this with one of the unit's non-commissioned officers (NCO), who was also Puerto Rican, clinic staff were told that the men's reaction was a normal means of expressing stress on the island among this population group and that it was worse when they were not in contact with females (the implication being that Puerto Rican females, through social influence, modulate the response). The presentation was initially suspected to be some kind of group hysteria, but as explained, it was a culturally modified stress reaction. The clinic staff arranged for the NCO, his wife, and his wife's friends to meet with the soldiers individually. The problem did not recur, at least not to the knowledge of the clinic staff.[5]

Similar to cultures, organizations have means of expressing stress either as catharsis or as distress. Leaders of organizations should come to understand the language and manifestations unique to their organization to discern the cathartic nature of complaints, as happened in the above episode, from those indicating distress. As a leader, one must be mindful of the mannerisms and use of words among one's people. The reader is directed to the short video "The Ugly War."[6] In it, note the soldier's mannerisms and choice of words. In the end, the soldier, who is a medic, says that his mental health community "does not understand," referring to the difference between catharsis and distress. As with the young Puerto Rican males, in order to help, one must understand and be able to discern the difference between expressions of catharsis from those of distress.

COMMUNICATING HEALTH RISKS

Symptom clusters, associated with war, appear as "syndromes" with confounding etiologies.[7] E. Jones and colleagues researched British military pension files dating from 1872 through 1991 and found three varieties of post-combat disorder: a debility syndrome (involving weakness or loss of energy) without psychological or cognitive symptoms associated with wars fought before 1918; a somatic syndrome involving cardio-respiratory symptoms (e.g., rapid heartbeat, shortness of breath, fatigue) associated with World War I; and a neuropsychiatric syndrome (resulting in depression, anxiety, headaches) associated with World War II and conflicts through the 1991 Gulf War. There was no presentation of common symptoms across the various wars studied, though there were overlapping complaints. None of the syndromes identified could be linked to a definitive etiologic agent or uniquely identifiable trauma. This led researchers to implicate cultural factors as contributing to these unexplainable illnesses, thought to be precipitated by the aggregate stressors of deployment.[8] This is not to say that psychological trauma is not real; there is certainly a relationship between traumatic events and psychological sequelae.[9] Communicated complaints, however, are often confounded with a group's accepted cathartic expressions, preexisting conditions, common health fears of the time, reinforcing factors for expressing particular symptoms (compensation expectation), and trends in diagnostic labeling (post-traumatic stress disorder, PTSD, and mTBI, mild traumatic brain injury). This is not to diminish the complaints, but simply to ensure that other etiologic factors are not ignored or the complaints misinterpreted as being outside a range of normal.[10] Complaints must be taken seriously, but "syndromes" must be defined carefully, and any proposed causes must be continually evaluated. The lesson for a leader is to express caring and concern and help frame the complaints as a normal reaction to an extreme situation. This strategy is of course only applied if the person is not a threat to mission, themselves, or others.

Proper stress management planning takes note of the knowledge that health fears shape a person's attribution of reactions to dangerous contexts. Just as health fears can shape attribution, so can a leader shape attribution and improve resilience. A leader has two powerful tools for managing stress within an organization: the placebo and Hawthorne effects, referred to as caring and concern, respectively.[11]

Depression is frequently associated with dangerous context–related stress. Producing a placebo effect is one of the most effective treatments for mild to moderate depression.[12] A placebo is a harmless substance or procedure used for psychological benefit. Potential sources of such placebos include nutraceuticals, functional foods, and alternative medicines. Nutraceuticals are dietary supplements that may provide prevention and treatment of illness or disease. (In the United States, the federal Food and Drug Administration regulates health claims with the psychological benefit attested to by popular use.) A leader might suggest that a subordinate try an alternative practice, such as meditation, massage, yoga, and kneipp, to alleviate his or her symptoms. The recommendation here is not to promote a practice, but to offer potentially effective alternatives. A simple suggestion from an authority figure and a means for the individual to take control can have profound positive effects.[13] If the remedy does no harm, then an individual's faith in the practice should not be undermined.

The Hawthorne effect is the generation of positive responses that occurs because members of an organization feel that leaders care or are concerned about them.[14] An organization can leverage this effect through a number of organizational and individual-level programs and practices. These include but are not limited to establishing mentor relationships, integrating members into cohesive teams, and well-being and self-awareness programs.[15] In sum, the social and cognitive components that shape the manifestation of stress-related complaints lend themselves to remedies involving the tools of the placebo and Hawthorne effects, simply put, caring and concern, which a leader can use for effective stress management strategies.

STRESS THEORY

When a leader is confronted with a problem, he or she can neither act nor decide effectively upon a solution without first understanding the problem. The problem, in this case, is managing stress in dangerous contexts to maintain individual and unit well-being. As discussed above, however, the word "stress" is now a convenient semantic category used to attribute a cause to a range of health outcomes from transient moods to chronic ill health. To make sense of the collection of ideas engendered by stress, one can apply theory. Although not a law of nature, theory provides a systematic framework through which solutions to problems (as well as laws of nature) can be discerned.

Theories of stress can be nominally classified as emphasizing physiological homeostasis, cognition and memory, or managing stressors within the dangerous context. Each of the theories predicts and explains the relationship between antecedents and consequents of stress but with a different emphasis and set of presuppositions. The reason for the differences is, as with all theories, one seeks to balance prediction and explanation.[16] The dilemma that researchers, practitioners, and leaders face is how to organize observations and outcomes into a systematic body of knowledge to explain outcomes while avoiding contradictions in predictions, practice, and management. The only way to avoid this dilemma is to understand and consistently apply the presuppositions from which predictions and decisions are made.[17]

Physiological Homeostasis

The concept of homeostasis is rooted in the pre-Socratic philosophy of Hippocrates, in which health was equated to a balance of the elements and qualities of life.[18] Claude Bernard (in the mid-1800s) refined this concept of homeostasis defining the relatively narrow physiological limits within which the body operates.[19] He articulated the importance to the body of maintaining a relatively constant internal state (*milieu intérieur*) when being challenged with a constantly changing external environment. The idea of the *milieu intérieur* led to the concept of stress developed by Walter Cannon and furthered by Hans Selye: "stress is any challenge to the relative constant internal state."[20]

Cannon defined two states in response to stress: "rest/digest" and "fight/flight." A leader should remember that these states are adaptive in that the physiological cascade energizes the body to react to a threat through a well-modulated system that protects homeostasis. Some argue for modifying the cascade associated with the fight/flight response to improve post-critical incident well-being. The risk, however, is in rendering the individual ill-prepared to perform in or learn from a dangerous situation, thereby threatening mission success and individual survival.[21]

Since the work of Selye, the core meaning of stress has expanded to include psychological factors.[22] Selye proposed his general adaptation syndrome, arguing that the physiological response to stress is nonspecific and implicating the endocrine system as the principle system involved in resisting stress. Cannon focused on the relatively fast-acting neurotransmitters (noradrenaline) and the activation of the sympathetic division of the autonomic nervous system. Selye's contribution was to identify the hypothalamic-pituitary-adrenal nexus and the importance of the relatively slower-acting neuroendocrine response in resisting threats to the *milieu intérieur*. Although there is hormonal action in response to challenges, this hormonal response is complex and often misinterpreted.[23]

The general adaptation syndrome addresses chronic stress, whereas Cannon focused on acute exposure to stressors. For Selye, homeostasis is defended until chronic activation of defense mechanisms results in exhaustion of physiological resources resulting in increased risk for stress-related illness, such as heart disease. Stress plays a role in health, but the deleterious effect is not a result of exhausted physiological resources. In the case of heart disease, stress contributes to increasing the likelihood that circulating, low-density lipoproteins will adhere to injured blood vessel walls and occlude the vessel. The occlusion in turn causes further damage, perpetuating the cycle, which can ultimately result in a heart attack.

For nearly fifty years, Selye's theory predominated, until McEwen challenged Selye's assumption of a fixed, normal homeostatic internal state. McEwen introduced the concept of allostasis, approaching the environment as a reliable force to which the organism equilibrates physiological systems to a new, healthy homeostatic internal state. For example, a body's shift to the lower end of the core temperature range may not indicate succumbing to hypothermia because at the circadian nadir, core body temperatures of under-fed and fatigued soldiers sleeping outside can routinely drop to 35 degrees Celsius. This temperature is at the limit of thermoregulatory collapse. In this referenced case, however, physiological systems equilibrated in response to environmental loads and as a result reduced overall physiological strain and thus stress.[24]

Social variables are also reliable environmental forces that modulate the stress response. This recognition is important toward understanding the effects of unit cohesion on well-being. In a summarization of his work on aggression, R. Cairns concluded that contrary to widely held beliefs, the establishment of aggressive behavior does not require reinforcement or imitation or the experience of frustration or pain. Absences of social experiences are associated with aggression by the withdrawn or isolated individual, who is more reactive to stimuli.[25] Considering Cairn's finding of dysregulation, M. Hofer researched the physiological mechanisms modulated by the social environment, particularly those involved in separation and loss. He introduced the metaphor "homeostatically open system," which refers to the modulation of physiological and behavioral systems through the social environment.[26] Specific physiological and behavioral systems open to regulation stem from two independent phases: an acute protest phase and a chronic, slow-developing despair phase.

Changes associated with the acute phase of stress response manifest themselves immediately and include increases in agitation, heart rate, and glucocorticoid and catecholamine (e.g., norepinephrine) levels. This activation of the sympathetic response is similar to the symptoms reported by the young Puerto Rican men. The remedy was social contact with women from their culture. Changes associated with the despair phase are decreased and variable food intake, as well as decreased body weight, cardiac rate, growth hormone production, and T-cell activity. These symptoms are closely aligned to depression.

The negative effects of loss and separation, both realities of dangerous contexts, can be reduced through a network of camaraderie within an organization. The regulation of emotion through unit cohesion has also been suggested to help leaders control the violence that units must mete out during a mission, an inference corroborated by Cairns' stimulus reactivity finding.[27]

The homeostatic theories presented here only focus on the sympathetic division of the autonomic nervous system. Disease states may be a resultant of stress effects on the ability of the other division of the system, the parasympathetic nervous system, which is dominant during resting states, to modulate the actions of the sympathetic system stress response. This theory is called homeodynamics. It states that often what induces stress-related illness is not an overdriving sympathetic response, but an inability of the parasympathetic system to modulate sympathetic activation to return the autonomic nervous system to a rest and recovery state.[28] The message of homeodynamics and current thought to leaders: Quality sleep is a stalwart of any stress management program.

Cognition and Memory

I have a couple soldiers in my company that have had issues with PTSD. One claims the psychologists/psychiatrists he's seen have no other options for him. He was first diagnosed about three years ago, so he's had enough time to try a couple methods. He says the drugs help the depression, but nothing seems to get rid of the dreams, daydreaming, flashbacks, and such. I told him I'd try to find something a little unconventional, something he probably hasn't tried yet, but I'm really wary of trusting a "self-administered" treatment. I'm still trying to find some good articles, but I'm surprised at the low success of treatments. I am curious about one thing. Throughout the infantry, soldiers who have had PTSD problems, the few who can cope with it to the point where they consider themselves cured claim that the one thing that helped them the most was religion. I'm almost sure that no one involved in the psychological sector would ever dare to even take a statistical analysis to validate this or even accept it as plausible, but from my viewpoint, it's really working better than anything else.[29]

The captain who wrote this note makes several important observations. First, depression seems easily managed. Second, he is looking for alternatives but is cautious. Some individuals will try ill-advised supposed remedies (e.g., alcohol) or use prescription medication without medical guidance. An active campaign must be devised to prevent such practices and healthy alternatives offered. Third, the captain inquires about religion. Chaplains and other

Table 3.1 Qualities of Autobiographical, Flashbulb, and Trauma Memories

Quality	Autobiographical	Flashbulb	Trauma
Vivid	Not a reported quality	Detailed recollection for discovery context	Vivid sensory memory
Confidence in accuracy	Moderate	Strong	Strong
Recall	Conscious control	Conscious control	Involuntary and intrusive
Strength of emotion associated with memory	Neutral	Weak	Strong
Event	Neutral	Moderately emotionally arousing	Highly emotional, usually life threatening
Facts	Factual memories subject to forgetting	Discovery facts resistant to forgetting	Sparse, idiosyncratic facts resistant to forgetting
Quality of memory	Coherent in time and place	Coherent in time and place	Mainly sensory impressions
Time	Perceived as past event	Perceived as past event	"Here and now" quality

spiritual counselors can be effective. They develop and maintain strong communities of social support and safe places where soldiers can vent without the specter of the "medical record." A soldier's specific belief or practice is not important, only that there are culturally supported and communicated systems of empowering stories and exemplars through which to ascribe, make sense of, and manage intrusive memories.[30]

Table 3.1 summarizes the literature on memory quality and distinguishes the qualities of trauma memories from those of autobiographical and flashbulb memories.[31] Autobiographical memories include flashbulb memories and are characterized by specific, personal, long-lasting facts about oneself and one's experiences. These memories are not problematic. They are recounted as past events, are voluntary, subject to forgetting and restructuring, and organized in an apparent semantically associated network.[32]

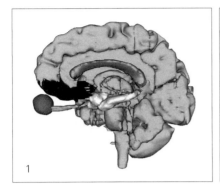
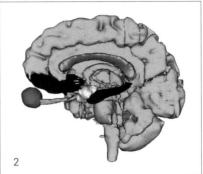

FIGURE 3.1 The temporal course of brain activity on the prefrontal cortex (left-most shaded structure), amygdala (middle shaded structure), and hippocampus (right-most

Trauma memories are qualitatively different from autobiographic and flashbulb memories and are formed from physiologically different mechanisms. Figure 3.1 summarizes the formation of trauma memories as described in the temporal dynamic model.[33] Immediately coincident with an emotional load, the amygdala increases activity, activates processes in the hippocampus, and suppresses function in the prefrontal lobe (Figure 3.1, panel 1). The effect on memory is an apparent enhancement making it the sole focus of attention (e.g., weapon focus) along with cues immediately preceding the event.[34] Contextual cues immediately coincident with the event are remembered, with many of the trigger stimuli having a temporal relationship with the event.

In the minutes following an event, only the amygdala is active, yielding memories of the gist of events and associated emotional valance (Figure 3.1, panel 2). The prefrontal cortex recovers as amygdala activity diminishes, with the recovery time dependent on the nature and intensity of the emotional load. Recovery usually occurs within several minutes (Figure 3.1, panel 3), but new memory formation is suppressed during the refractory period of the amygdala and hippocampus. Within hours to days, depending on the intensity of the emotional load, the hippocampus and amygdala recover function (Figure 3.1, panel 4).

Given the course of recovery, a leader should (1) give the affected individual at least twenty-four hours of rest so memory systems can resume normal function, (2) follow the steps outlined in Table 3.3, and (3) consult the organization's mental health support services. The memory is likely never to be forgotten, so the goal is to manage and master the memory of the traumatic event.[35] The following example shows how a trauma memory can form and

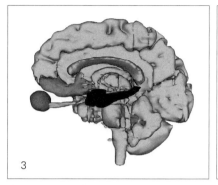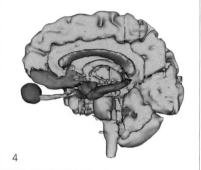

3   4

shaded structure) subsequent to a threatening event. White indicates heightened
activity, gray normal function, and black the refractory period.

---

how the actions of the paramedic team, leadership, and chaplain alleviated the
negative effects of the experience.

> A paramedic, who had responded to hundreds of calls of children in heat-
> induced seizure, prepared himself by reviewing and practicing the proper
> protocol for care. On one call, the facial features of the child struck him: it
> looked to be the identical twin of his own child. Although he knew that
> this was not his child, the paramedic was paralyzed by the close resem-
> blance. His peers noticed his hesitation and yelled at him to start per-
> forming his tasks. During the resuscitation of the child, the paramedic was
> visibly shaken by his inability to get past the physical resemblance. After
> the child was transported to the local hospital, the paramedic continued
> to have intrusive visual images of the lifeless child. His teammates noted
> his difficulties and contacted their captain. Shortly after the child was
> pronounced dead, a fire chaplain arrived to "take a walk" with the para-
> medic. The immediate response and opportunity to talk about the situation
> allowed the paramedic to deal with the images and his difficulty in func-
> tioning and remain confident in his abilities in the future.[36]

This incident illustrates that although stress reactions have a biological
basis, the stress response involves a process of cognitive evaluations of perceived demands on one's own person.[37] These evaluations can be influenced
as the individual continually reevaluates the event. There are many interventions, of which this is an example of an effective one. Effective interventions
are personal, voluntary, and continually offered by an experienced member of
the unit. There are however controversial techniques that a leader should dis-
courage, such as critical incident stress debriefing (CISD).[38] In concluding, it is

worth reinforcing the importance of unit-level tailored support as cautioned in the "Comments on 'A Study of Combat Stress, Korea, 1952,' *Technical Memorandum ORO-T-41 (FEC)*":

> It is true that experienced line and medical officers within the confines of their own unit, with knowledge of their personnel and of the particular situation confronting the group, can develop an operational formula specific for that time and group which is most useful. It is considered, however, that the formula for one group cannot be applied to the next, nor can it be taught to any specificity beyond the fact that it happens. Symptomatology of individuals under stress is most reactive to the patient's concept of what comprises useful symptomatology. If changes in overt behavior were specified and a matter of common knowledge, experience tends to show that the specified changes would occur with increasing frequency.[39]

Managing Stressors

The U.S. military augments deploying units with members from other units. The augmentees are fit, healthy, motivated, and professional, but they may not have experience with a deploying unit's operating procedures or equipment. This puts stress on the soldiers and can lead to accidents that negatively affect the unit. In one such case, a soldier was attached to a Stryker unit, although he was not trained on the Stryker. He was assigned as a gunner, whose duties included the operation of a laser dazzler, which is used to suppress threatening movements toward the convoy. He was briefly instructed on the use of the laser and told that the system worked. He was apparently not issued laser eye protection or was not instructed on the importance of wearing eye protection. Although laser beam characteristics at engagement ranges will not cause retinal injury, the beam is sufficiently powerful to damage the retina within a few meters of the exit port. During movement, the soldier was ordered to target a threatening vehicle. In slewing to engage he swept the beam across reflective surfaces on the Stryker and suffered a retinal lesion.[40] Such accidents are preventable, and when they occur, they are tragic for the individual and diminish unit morale.

Most stress-related symptom clusters correlated with operating in a dangerous context are not attributable to a critical incident. Thus, a complex of stimulus conditions within the context may constitute the stressor, which is an accumulation of events or situations outside the realm of routine that create a conflict in or a challenge or threat to the individual. Given the number of reported operation-related stress disorders, the greatest eroding effect on well-being may be the cumulative effect of the operational environment itself.[41] To alleviate the effects of the stressor, a leader should evaluate the context within which units are operating and manage the physical (e.g., safety, equipment, living conditions) and psychological (e.g., separation, perceived control, cohesion) aspects of the environment. One area for a leader's focus should be managing perceptions of the stressors by engendering attributions to help make sense of the circumstances.[42] Reframing the perceived stressful component helps reduce stress.[43] In particular, the leader can affect interpretations of stressors through education, cohesion, promoting coping strategies, and instilling a sense of commitment, control, and challenge.

Educate. It is important that a leader provide accurate information so team members can set appropriate expectations and be psychologically prepared. Information about the mission, rules of engagement, length of deployment, host nation, rival factions, and environment all proffer details for calculating the risks involved. Constant communication and updates maintain psychological preparedness, thus mitigating the unknown as a stressor.

Train without Interruption. Well-learned and practiced skills are less likely to be disrupted by stress than those that have not been perfected.[44] Realistic and mission-focused training builds confidence, improves cohesion, and prevents boredom. When an individual feels he or she is adequately prepared, trained, and equipped for any eventuality, personal stress reactions are minimized. For example, stress reduction–specific imagery and skills-training programs decrease subjective distress and physiological stress reactions.[45] In sum, stress inoculation training using realistic situations better prepares those operating in dangerous contexts for potential stressful situations.

Maintain Unit Cohesion. Unit cohesion is the bonding of members of an organization in such a way as to sustain their will and commitment to each other, the organization, and the mission. Cohesive, well-disciplined units are less susceptible to the influence of risk factors than those that are loose knit and lack appropriate discipline (Table 3.2). Cohesion encourages teamwork during tough or trying situations and assists with making sense of a crisis through grounding on comrades and leaders.

Establish a Culture of Catharsis. Jack, a friend of James Ness who fought in Vietnam, recounted this story of a firefight and of hearing a friend's call to shift fire. As Jack looked over in response to his friend's voice, he saw his friend's head separate from his body and roll past. Jack expressed how slow things seemed to move at the time. Later that week, the unit received a pallet of beer. Jack grabbed his weapon and a satchel of ammunition and sat on top of the pallet. He began drinking and threatening anyone who approached the beer. His unit let him be. A few days later, his unit headed out on patrol, and he

Table 3.2 Risk Factors for Stress Reactions

Soldiers and first responders are at risk for stress reactions just like any other individuals, no matter how seasoned or experienced. Risk factors are those conditions that increase the probability that stress exposure will turn into a serious mental health problem. Risk factors also make combat and operational stress reaction (COSR) more likely. The presence of risk factors does not automatically mean someone will become debilitated by stress, but it raises that risk. Many risk factors can be modified, reduced, or eliminated. The following risk factors have been associated with a stress reaction:

▸ Length of exposure to operational stress

▸ Severity of the operational stress experience

▸ History of previous traumatic events (war, child sexual abuse, assault) and the amount an individual personally relates to an event

▸ Previous mental health problems

▸ Alcohol abuse or dependence

▸ Lack of a support system or unit cohesion

was told that unless he sobered up, he could not go along. The thought of not being part of the team turned Jack around, and he went on patrol. The leaders of Jack's unit had built a cohesive unit and established a culture of catharsis. As a result, Jack's memory of the event, although vivid, was not intrusive or problematic. The lesson is, know one's people, know the crucible, set up a culture of catharsis, and know that leaders are a principle source of resilience.

Teach Coping Strategies. People develop patterns for coping with stress.[46] Having a sense of control is strongly associated with the mitigation of the progression of debilitating stress-related sequelae. Step 7 of the psychological first aid core actions suggests providing an affected individual with the tools needed to promote coping (see Table 3.3).

Numerous studies of people experiencing dangerous contexts indicate that individuals who feel that they are in control of their circumstances and their environment feel equipped to handle stress. Although exposure to life-threatening events is an obvious source of stress, the administrative and bureaucratic conditions within an organization can compound the experience and impair recovery.[47] Efforts must be made to de-stigmatize reporting, facilitate support, and eliminate administrative practices that make one feel controlled by the system.

Table 3.3 Psychological First Aid Core Actions

The following actions constitute the basic steps and objectives for a leader providing assistance to subordinates within days or weeks of their having experienced a threatening event. The amount of time spent on each goal will vary from person to person and depend on circumstances.

1. Contact and engage	Initiate contact with the individual in a non-intrusive, compassionate, and helpful manner
2. Provide safety and comfort	Provide immediate safety and emotional comfort
3. Stabilize (if needed)	Calm and orient emotionally overwhelmed and distraught individuals
4. Gather information on current needs and concerns	Identify immediate needs and concerns, gather additional information, and tailor psychological first aid interventions
5. Provide practical assistance	Offer help to the individual for addressing immediate needs and concerns
6. Connect with social supports	Establish brief or ongoing contacts with primary support persons, including unit members and friends, and other helpful resources
7. Inform about coping	Provide information and education about stress reactions and coping to reduce distress and promote adaptive functioning
8. Establish links with collaborative services	Connect individuals with needed services and inform them about available services that may be helpful in the future

Source: Adapted from *Psychological First Aid for First Responders* (Washington, D.C.: U.S. Department of Health and Human Services, 2005).

Commitment, Control, Challenge. Characteristics conducive to responding well to stress are a valuable asset. S. Kobasa studied executives under corporate stress and found that those who exhibit commitment, have a sense of control, and approach problems as challenges report less stress than those who do not exhibit these qualities.[48] (See Chapter 4, in this volume, for further discussion on how commitment, control, and challenge promote resilience.) With time, practice, and training, people can acquire these characteristics.

Commitment is the personal sense that one has a purpose and that one's contribution to a team is meaningful. Commitment to a mission and the importance of it allow people to feel that there is meaning to their lives. Leaders can facilitate commitment by integrating members into their team, giving them a role in it and a sense of control through freedom to act within that role.

There are two types of control: internal locus and external locus. Soldiers, police officers, firefighters, and first responders are well aware that there are many events over which they have absolutely no control. Although a particular event cannot be controlled, an individual's reactions and responses to it can be. Training prepares people operating in dangerous contexts for situations they may encounter, promoting an internal locus of control. Not all situations or scenarios can be anticipated, but using information from critical incidents to anticipate events is known to be effective in fostering an internal locus of control. In the scenario with the paramedic, he was prepared for responding to an unconscious child but was unprepared to be distracted by thoughts and feelings about his own child. With his internal locus of control temporarily disabled, he could not perform his duties. Restoring him to his normal level of functioning required that he believe that his child was safe and that he could overcome this experience.

An external locus of control is the belief people have about how much real or actual control they have over what happens to them. Operating in dangerous contexts is a delicate dance between what individuals control and what happens to them. Again, training is imperative for anticipating what might happen. Notwithstanding, leaders need to be able to respond to an unplanned situation within the framework of a plan, thus defusing the level of stress and increasing the sense of external control. People need to experience and perceive a sense of control over their destiny, even though they are in harm's way or battling to save a life. One way to expand external control is to frame an unexpected event as a challenge. Such a situation framed in this manner motivates those encountering the situation to meet the challenge and leaves a memory of honestly and honorably performing one's duty in the face of adversity.

CONCLUSION

The term "stress" has come to describe conditions ranging from minor to catastrophic, from mundane to traumatic, from tedious to high intensity. "Stress management" goes hand in hand with it as the panacea for its alleviation. In some ways, this manner of thinking is far too simplistic, but in others ways the simplicity of it, paying attention to the stress evoked in certain situations and circumstances, is just what is needed.

Simply put, beyond acknowledging the importance of the stalwarts of sleep, fitness, and good health habits, leaders should know their people, know the crucible, and establish a culture for catharsis. They should also be aware of the two forms of stress-producing experiences: the critical incident and the eroding effect of the dangerous context itself. A culture of catharsis is particularly important in the case of critical incidents; the leader and the unit members have the greatest positive effect on well-being, and they possess the best knowledge about the members of the unit and the incident. When Jack was allowed to have his beer and was then presented with the choice of remaining a part of the team, and when the paramedic took a walk with the chaplain, the positive agent of change was the unit, for which the leader had established a culture for catharsis and acted as the principle source of resiliency. A leader's stress management strategy should include educating, training without interruption, maintaining unit cohesion, implementing strategies of caring and concern, and framing the context to meet threatening situations as challenges.

NOTES

1. Online Etymology Dictionary, http://www.etymonline.com/index.php?term=stress; Wordnik, http://www.wordnik.com/words/stress.

2. T. C. Allbutt and H. D. Rolleston, *A System of Medicine* (London: Macmillan, 1910); C. Mazure and B. Druss, "A Historical Perspective on Stress as a Psychiatric Illness," in *Does Stress Cause Psychiatric Illness?* ed. C. Mazure (Washington, D.C.: American Psychiatric Press, 1995).

3. L. Kirmayer and A. Young, "Culture and Somatization: Clinical, Epidemiological, and Ethnographic Perspectives," *Psychosomatic Medicine* 60 (1998): 420–430.

4. R. D. Alarcón, "Culture, Cultural Factors and Psychiatric Diagnosis: Review and Projections," *World Psychiatry* 8 (2009): 131–139; and L. Payer, *Medicine and Culture* (New York: Henry Holt, 1996).

5. Personal communication, David Lam, M.D., an Army physician at the clinic, January 15, 2010.

6. For a vivid example see, J. D. McHugh et al., "The Ugly of War," GuardianFilms, September 8, 2008, http://www.guardian.co.uk/world/video/2008/sep/08/sixmonthsinafghanistan.afghanistan.

7. E. Jones et al., "Post-Combat Syndromes from the Boer War to the Gulf War: A Cluster Analysis of Their Nature and Attribution," *British Medical Journal* 324 (2002): 1–7; and J. Sartin, "Gulf War Illness: Causes and Controversies," *Mayo Clinic Proceedings* 75 (2000): 811–819.

8. Institute of Medicine, *Gulf War Veterans: Measuring Health,* ed. L. Hernandez et al. (Washington, D.C.: National Academy Press, 1999), http://www.nap.edu/catalog

.php?record_id=9636; E. Jones and S. Wessely, "War Syndromes: The Impact of Culture on Medically Unexplained Symptoms," *Medical History* 49 (2005): 55–78; and G. Gray, K. Kaiser et al., "Increased Postwar Symptoms and Psychological Morbidity among U.S. Navy Gulf War Veterans," *American Journal of Tropical Medicine and Hygiene* 60, no. 5 (1999): 758–766.

9. T. C. Smith et al., for the Millennium Cohort Study Team, "New Onset and Persistent Symptoms of Post-Traumatic Stress Disorder Self-Reported after Deployment and Combat Exposures: Prospective Population-Based US Military Cohort Study," *British Medical Journal* 336, no. 7640 (2008): 366–371.

10. C. Prine, "Problem Recruits Land in WTUs. Pentagon: Lowered Standards Led to Units with Drug Addicts, Criminals," *Stars and Stripes*, February 9, 2011, Mideast edition, 8(2), SS2011; M. Hotopf et al., "The Health of UK Military Personnel Who Deployed to the 2003 Iraq War," *Lancet* 367, no. 9524 (2006): 1731–1741; S. Inskeep and T. Bowman, "Army Documents Show Lower Recruiting Standards," Morning Edition, National Public Radio, April 17, 2008; and D. King, L. King, and D. Foy, "Prewar Factors in Combat-Related Posttraumatic Stress Disorder: Structural Equation Modeling with a National Sample of Female and Male Vietnam Veterans," *Journal of Consulting and Clinical Psychology* 64, no. 3 (1996): 520–531.

11. Payer, *Medicine and Culture*, xxiv.

12. A. Khan, N. Redding, and W. Brown, "The Persistence of the Placebo Response in Antidepressant Clinical Trials," *Journal of Psychiatric Research* 42, no. 10 (2008): 791–796; and J. C. Fournier et al., "Antidepressant Drug Effects and Depression Severity: A Patient-Level Meta-Analysis," *Journal of the American Medical Association* 303, no. 1 (2010): 47–53.

13. C. Douaud, "Consumers Look to Heal through Functional Foods," *Food Navigator-USA.com*, November 12, 2007; N. Shachtman, "Army's New PTSD Treatments: Yoga, Reiki, 'Bioenergy,'" *Wired*, March 25, 2008. Kneipp is a hydrotherapy common in Germany using contrasting, or alternating, hot and cold baths, referred to as "the cure"; R. Sapolsky, *Why Zebras Don't Get Ulcers*, 3rd ed. (New York: Henry Holt, 2004).

14. R. McCarney et al., "The Hawthorne Effect: A Randomised, Controlled Trial," *BMC Medical Research Methodology* 7 (2007): 30, doi:10.1186/1471–2288-7-30.

15. J. Ness et al., "Development and Implementation of the U.S. Army Leader Self-Development Portfolio," in *Handbook of Military Psychology* (Washington, D.C.: National Defense University Press, 2010).

16. J. Ness and V. Tepe, "Theoretical Assumptions and Scientific Architecture," in *The Science and Simulation of Human Performance*, ed. J. Ness, V. Tepe, and D. Ritzer (New York: Elsevier, 2004).

17. H. Reese and W. Overton, "Models of Development and Theories of Development," in *Life Span Developmental Psychology: Research and Theory*, ed. L. R. Goulet and P. B. Baltes (Hillsdale, N.J.: Lawrence Erlbaum Associates, 1970), 115–145.

18. T. D. Kontopoulou and S. G. Marketos, "Homeostasis: The Ancient Greek Origin of a Modern Scientific Principle," *Hormones* 1, no. 2 (2002): 124–125.

19. C. Gross, "Claude Bernard and the Constancy of the Internal Environment," *Neuroscientist* 4 (1998): 380–385.

20. J. Thayer and R. Lane, "Claude Bernard and the Heart–Brain Connection: Further Elaboration of a Model of Neurovisceral Integration," *Neuroscience and Biobehavior Reviews* 33, no. 2 (2009): 81–88, doi:10.1016/j.neubiorev.2008.08.004.

21. W. Cannon, "The James-Lange Theory of Emotion: A Critical Examination and an Alternate Theory," *American Journal of Psychology* 39 (1927): 106–124; M. Thompson, "America's Medicated Army," *Time*, 171(24), June 16, 2008, 38–42; J. Ness and S. Kornguth, *Technical Evaluation HFM-181 Symposium Human Performance Enhancement for NATO Military Operations (Science, Technology, and Ethics)* (Brussels: NATO Research and Technology Organisation, 2010), http://www.rta.nato.int/Pubs/RDP.asp?RDP=RTO-MP-HFM-181.

22. H. Selye, "The General Adaptation Syndrome and the Diseases of Adaptation," *Journal of Clinical Endocrinology* 6 (1946): 117–231, doi:10.1210/jcem-6-2-117.

23. R. Sapolsky, M. Romero, and A. Munck, "How Do Glucocorticoids Influence Stress Responses? Integrating Permissive, Suppressive, Stimulatory, and Preparative Actions," *Endocrine Reviews* 21, no. 1 (2000): 55–89.

24. B. McEwen, "Allostasis and Allostatic Load: Implications for Neuropsychopharmacology," *Neuropsychopharmacology* 22, no. 2 (2000): 108–124, doi:10.1016/S0893-133X(99)00129-3; A. Young et al., "Exertional Fatigue, Sleep Loss, and Negative Energy Balance Increases Susceptibility to Hypothermia," *Journal of Applied Physiology* 85, no. 4 (1998): 1210–1217; B. McEwen and J. C. Wingfield, "The Concept of Allostasis in Biology and Biomedicine," *Hormones and Behavior* 43, no. 1 (2003): 2–15.

25. R. Cairns, *Social Development: The Origins and Plasticity of Interchanges* (San Francisco: W. H. Freeman, 1979).

26. J. Ness, T. Marshall, and P. Aravich, "Effects of Rearing Condition on Activity-Induced Weight Loss," *Developmental Psychobiology* 28, no. 3 (1995): 165–173; B. Lickliter, "Theories of Attachment: The Long and Winding Road to an Integrative Developmental Science," *Integrative Psychological and Behavioral Sciences* 42, no. 4 (2008): 397–405; and M. Hofer, "Relationships as Regulators: A Psychobiologic Perspective of Bereavement," *Psychosomatic Medicine* 46 (1984): 183–197.

27. J. Griffith, "Further Considerations Concerning the Performance-Cohesion Relation in Military Settings," *Armed Forces and Society* 34 (2007): 138–147, http://afs.sagepub.com; Cairns, *Social Development.*

28. B. H. Friedman, "An Autonomic Flexibility-Neurovisceral Integration Model of Anxiety and Cardiac Vagal Tone," *Biological Psychology* 74 (2007): 185–199.

29. Personal communication, an Army captain to James Ness, August 2010.

30. J. Campbell, *Myths to Live By* (New York: Bantam, 1972).

31. A. Ehlers and D. Clark, "A Cognitive Model of Posttraumatic Stress Disorder: Invited Essay," *Behaviour Research and Therapy* 38 (2000): 319–345; E. Parker, L. Cahill, and J. McGaugh, "A Case of Unusual Autobiographical Remembering," *Neurocase* 12 (2006): 35–49; O. Luminet and A. Curci, eds., *Flashbulb Memories* (New York: Psychological Press, 2009).

32. A semantically associated network is a knowledge representation of facts related logically and by meaning.

33. D. Diamond et al., "The Temporal Dynamics of Emotional Memory Processing: A Synthesis on the Neurobiological Basis of Stress-Induced Amnesia, Flashbulb and

Traumatic Memories, and Yerkes-Dodson Law," *Neural Plasticity*, 2007, article ID 60803, 33 pages.

34. E. F. Loftus, G. R. Loftus, and J. Messo, "Some Facts about Weapon Focus," *Law and Human Behavior* 11 (1987): 55–62.

35. A. Ehlers et al., "Cognitive Therapy for Post-Traumatic Stress Disorder: Development and Evaluation," *Behaviour Research and Therapy* 43 (2005): 413–431.

36. Personal communication, Dr. Denise Jablonski-Kaye, assistant chief of mental health, Los Angeles Emergency Services, January 21, 2010.

37. R. S. Lazarus and R. Launier, *Stresskonzepte. Entwicklung von Rückkopplungsmodellen in der psychologischen Stressforschung* (Stress concepts. Development of feedback models in the psychological stress research) (Munich: Hampp, 1989).

38. National Institute of Mental Health, *Mental Health and Mass Violence: Evidence-Based Early Psychological Intervention for Victims/Survivors of Mass Violence. A Workshop to Reach Consensus on Best Practices*, NIH Publication no. 02–5138 (Washington, D.C.: Government Printing Office, 2002), 7.

39. Headquarter, United States Army Forces, Far East, "A Study of Combat Stress, Korea, 1952," *Technical Memorandum ORO-T-41 (FEC)*, Defense Technical Information Center (1952).

40. Bruce Stuck, personal communication to James Ness, August 12, 2009. Ness was completing work on a chapter based on his research for the book *Lasers on the Modern Battlefield*, edited by Stuck.

41. See the Millennium Cohort Study, 2010, http://www.millenniumcohort.org/presen tations.php; D. W. King et al., "Alternative Representations of War Zone Stressors: Relationships to Posttraumatic Stress Disorder in Male and Female Vietnam Veterans," *Journal of Abnormal Psychology* 104 (1995): 184–195; T. Tanielian and L. Jaycox, *Invisible Wounds of War: Summary and Recommendations for Addressing Psychological and Cognitive Injuries* (Santa Monica, Calif.: Rand Corporation, Center for Military Health Policy Research, 2008); R. Flannery and G. Everly, "Crisis Intervention: A Review," *International Journal of Emergency Mental Health* 2 (2000): 119–125; and Headquarters, Department of the Army, *Field Manual 8–51: Combat and Operational Stress Control. Tactics, Techniques and Procedures* (Washington, D.C.: Government Printing Office, 2003).

42. A. Bay, "Excerpt: Embrace the Suck," March 8, 2007, http://www.npr.org/templates/ story/story.php?storyId=7457988#idioms.

43. G. Everly, "Familial Psychotraumatology: An Analysis of the Impact of Traumatic Stress upon the Law Enforcement Family," in *Law Enforcement Families*, ed. J. T. Reese and E. Scrivner (Washington, D.C.: FBI, 1994), 177–184.

44. J. Dyer, "The Measurement of Individual and Unit Expertise," in *The Science and Simulation of Human Performance*, ed. J. Ness, V. Tepe, and D. Ritzer (New York: Elsevier, 2004).

45. B. Arnetz et al., "Trauma Resilience Training for Police: Psychophysiological and Performance Effects," *Journal of Police and Criminal Justice* 24 (2009): 1–9.

46. H. McCubbin, A. Thompson, and M. McCubbin, *Family Assessment: Resiliency, Coping and Adaptation* (Madison: University of Wisconsin, 1996), 49–55; U.S. Department of

Health and Human Services, *Psychological First Aid for First Responders* (Washington, D.C., 2005).

47. R. Bradstreet, "Cultural Hurdles to Healthy Police Families," in *Law Enforcement Families*, ed. J. T. Reese and E. Scrivner (Washington, D.C.: FBI, 1994), 19–26; and H. Toch, *Stress in Policing* (Washington, D.C.: American Psychological Association, 2002).

48. S. Kobasa, "Stressful Life Events, Personality, and Health: An Inquiry into Hardiness," *Journal of Personality and Social Psychology* 37 (1979): 1–11.

CHAPTER 4

Resilience and Leadership in Dangerous Contexts

Christopher Peterson, Michael J. Craw, Nansook Park, and
Michael S. Erwin

Daniel B. Cnossen was born and raised in Topeka, growing up on a small
farm. He spent his childhood reading, running, playing sports, and working on the farm. Cnossen enrolled in the United States Naval Academy
in 1998. He had never before seen the ocean and did not know how to
swim, but he asked his new friends at the academy to teach him; he would
often skip lunch to spend time in the pool. Cnossen joined the Navy tri-
athlon team to strengthen his swimming. By his senior year, he had been
elected captain of the team, which he helped lead to a national championship. After graduation, he headed to San Diego to undergo training as a
Navy SEAL.

Cnossen served several tours overseas. On September 6, 2009, less
than thirty-six hours on the ground in Kandahar, Afghanistan, he activated
a landmine, losing both legs and suffering internal injuries. Lieutenant
Cnossen is now back in the United States facing new challenges. He is
doing so with the same dedication and enthusiasm that he used to surmount previous challenges. He is positive and appreciative of his friends
and family, and he is happy to be alive.

Described by some as stoic, Cnossen is seen by those who know him
best as soft-spoken and humble. No one as full of curiosity, zest, and
humor as he is could be described as stoic. As Cnossen began his rehabilitation, he noted that now he would be able to do even more pull-ups.
While at the Walter Reed Army Medical Center, Cnossen and other troops
were visited by President Barack Obama. As the president was leaving,
he noticed a copy of *War and Peace* on Cnossen's bedside table. The two
men joked that merely lifting the book would be another form of physical therapy.

D angerous contexts pose not only the constant threat of injury or death, but also the likelihood of setbacks and failures.[1] They may be unpredictable and uncontrollable. How can those who lead in dangerous contexts help their subordinates navigate these inherent uncertainties and bounce back from obstacles encountered? Resilience is used to describe the characteristic of responding well to setbacks and failures, like Lieutenant Cnossen did; not only did he accept what had happened to him, but he moved on from it as well. Learned optimism and hardiness, two approaches to resilience, are the focus of this chapter.

WHAT IS RESILIENCE?

The term "resilience" is used to refer to reactions to adversity ranging from not being devastated after a loss to doing well in the wake of stress to being largely unaffected, and in some cases, to actually flourishing.[2] The range of definitions reflects the breadth of reactions people display in the face of adversity. In studies on resilience, some researchers neglect the details of the adversity of interest—that is, whether it is discrete versus chronic, specific versus diffuse, controllable versus uncontrollable. Some studies do not even establish that research participants actually experienced an adversity, only that they had a life event that seemed to be a bad one. One cannot speak of post-traumatic stress disorder or post-traumatic growth if no trauma occurred. Here are some definitions of possible responses to adversity (see Figure 4.1). First, however, what is resilience? In its original, non-psychological sense, resilience refers to the return to original form by an entity following a disturbance. A squeezed tennis ball resumes its original shape when the grip is released. In a psychological sense, resilience refers to the return to baseline functioning after a challenge, with respect to mood, performance, social engagement, and health. Resiliency refers to the qualities of an entity that lead to resilience.

Entities can break, depending on what happens to them. Tennis balls can be punctured or loose their bounce after repeated serves and volleys. Unless repaired, they stay broken. In psychological terms, a state of ongoing brokenness would be considered a chronic disorder requiring treatment. Traumatic events are a demonstrable risk factor for a variety of psychological disorders, as well as poor physical health.[3] Recent decades have seen particular interest in post-traumatic stress disorder (PTSD), a syndrome that can appear in the wake of life-threatening events.[4] Possible treatments of PTSD have proliferated.[5]

Invulnerability in the psychological literature refers to being unaffected by adversity or trauma. For example, children of mothers with active schizophrenia were considered to be invulnerable if they seemed normal.[6] A close look reveals that such children invariably had another adult (for example, a relative or teacher) in their lives who took on a care-giving role, an important reminder not to attribute resiliency solely to the individual, as if it were no more than a coating of psychological Teflon.

The philosopher Friedrich Nietzsche wrote, "That which does not kill us only makes us stronger." Growth refers to the condition whereby someone does better after an adversity than before it. Growth following a disturbance is akin to a squeezed tennis ball turning into a beach ball when released. In psychological terms, a person exhibits growth by having, for example, an enhanced appreciation of life, better relationships with people, and a greater sense of meaning and purpose than he or she had previously.[7]

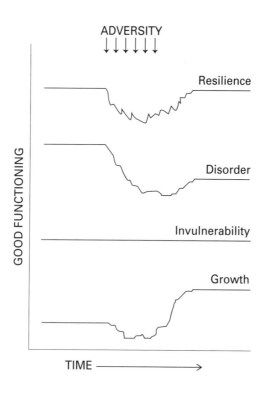

FIGURE 4.1 Possible reactions following a traumatic event

The possibility of post-traumatic growth (PTG) has captured the attention of psychologists but remains controversial. In relevant research, respondents have usually been primed by first being asked about trauma and then about its possible benefits. The validity of transparent self-reports, not only about post-trauma changes but also about trauma as a cause of these changes, has been questioned.[8] Many people tell a survivor story, drawing on a script framed in terms of redemption—that is, triumph after and over misfortune. The misfortune and its consequences may be exaggerated after the fact to fit a culturally appropriate script.[9]

One of the better demonstrations of growth is a study of character strengths that found elevations of certain strengths—religiousness, gratitude, kindness, hope, and bravery—following such events as assaults, natural disasters, and life-threatening illnesses.[10] It measured character strengths *before* trauma was mentioned. Priming was minimized, but the retrospective element was not ideal.

PTG is likely a real phenomenon and an important one. It serves as a reminder that permanent disorder is not the inevitable consequence of trauma or crisis.[11] That said, not enough is known about PTG. It is tempting to believe that growth after trauma is common, but available data are inconclusive. Furthermore, the reality of PTG does not mean that PTSD is fictional or created by a self-fulfilling prophecy. Even if PTG proves to be relatively frequent, one obviously would not welcome trauma because of the benefits that may follow.

The term "resiliency" is best used descriptively to refer to the return to "normal" following potential adversity. What is normal may or may not be all that positive, depending on where an individual starts. It also needs to be recognized that resilience is multidimensional; a person can bounce back in some domains but not others.

The relevant domains of functioning vary. Some research with the U.S. Army has focused on emotional fitness—positive mood, life satisfaction, freedom from depression, optimism, character strengths, and active coping styles; social fitness—engagement with, attachment to, and trust in friends and colleagues; family fitness—good relationships with spouses and children; and spiritual fitness—meaning and purpose in life that extends beyond the self.[12] Other domains, such as physical and financial fitness, are also important.

The length of time that passes before resilience is evident may vary, depending on the person and the domain. The same applies to growth or disorder. What may look like invulnerability in the short run may be something entirely different in the long term. The best research design would be ambitiously longitudinal, following individuals for years or even decades after traumatic events as they likely exhibit a variety of reactions to trauma as time passes.

Resilience only shows its worth when adversity is experienced. Take for example the 332nd Fighter Group of the U.S. Army Air Corps, also known as the Tuskegee Airmen, and the Japanese American 442nd Regimental Combat Team of the U.S. Army. These groups performed with distinction in World War II despite the personal and institutional discrimination their members faced because of their racial background. How was this possible? Perhaps because of their resilience at the group level and the role of their leaders in building and sustaining this quality. Resiliency is neither singular nor categorical. Rather, it covers a number of features, some internal and some external, existing along dimensions. An assessment of resiliency needs to measure its particular components and describe people and groups in terms of profiles. The cultivation of resiliency needs to target its components. Here the role of psychological theory becomes critical. This study focuses on the theories of learned optimism and hardiness to identify some of the critical features of resiliency.

LEARNED HELPLESSNESS AND LEARNED OPTIMISM

Helplessness refers to maladaptive passivity in situations where an active response can alleviate negative conditions or produce positive ones.[13] Helplessness entails a lack of motivation, aversive feelings, and difficulties in recognizing that certain behaviors influence outcomes. Helplessness has been explained from theoretical perspectives ranging from psychoanalytic accounts of symptom formation through sociological accounts of alienation, but its best-known contemporary explanation emerged from studies by psychologists of what has come to be known as learned helplessness. These studies investigated the causes and consequences of learned helplessness and led to effective strategies for treatment and prevention. More important, for the present contribution, theory and research on learned helplessness has led to an interest in those who are not helpless, that is, those who are resilient following challenge and crisis.[14]

Learned helplessness was first described by investigators studying animal learning.[15] Researchers immobilized a dog and exposed it to a series of electric shocks that it could not avoid or escape. Twenty-four hours later, the dog was placed in a situation in which the shocks could be terminated by a simple response. Rather than acting to end the shocks, the dog passively endured them. Dogs in a control group, however, reacted vigorously to the shock and quickly learned to turn it off.

The researchers proposed that the dog had learned to be helpless. When originally exposed to uncontrollable shocks, it learned that nothing it did mattered. The shocks came and went independently of behavior. Response-outcome independence was represented as an expectation of future helplessness that was generalized to new situations. The deficits that follow in the wake of uncontrollability are known as the learned helplessness phenomenon, and the associated cognitive explanation is referred to as the learned helplessness model.

Support for a cognitive interpretation of helplessness came from studies showing that an animal could be immunized against the debilitating effects of uncontrollability by first exposing it to controllable events. The animal learns during immunization that events can be controlled, and this expectation is sustained during exposure to uncontrollable events, precluding learned helplessness. In other studies, learned helplessness deficits were eliminated by exposing a helpless animal to the association between behavior and outcome. In these cases, the animal was compelled to make an appropriate response during the test task, by pushing or prodding the animal into action. After several trials, the animal noticed that escape was possible and began to act accordingly. Again, the process at work was cognitive. The animal's expectation of response-outcome independence was challenged during the therapy experience, and learning occurred.

Psychologists interested in human behavior were quick to see the parallels between learned helplessness as produced by uncontrollable events in the laboratory and maladaptive passivity in people. Thus, researchers began several lines of inquiry.[16] In one case, helplessness was produced in the laboratory by exposing people to uncontrollable events and observing the effects. Unsolvable problems were substituted for uncontrollable shocks, but the phenomenon of helplessness was still evident. In situations of uncontrollability, people show emotional, cognitive, and behavioral deficits. In other studies, researchers documented additional similarities between animal responses and those of humans in the laboratory, including immunization and therapy.

Assigning Causes

As research ensued, it became clear that the original learned helplessness explanation failed to account for the range of reactions that people display in response to uncontrollability. Some people show the hypothesized deficits that persist over time and are general across situations, whereas others do not. Furthermore, failures of adaptation that the learned helplessness model was supposed to explain, such as depression, are often characterized by a loss of self-esteem, about which the model is silent.

To explain the different responses among people, the helplessness model was revised and refined.[17] The variation in responses was explained by proposing that a person ask himself why uncontrollable (bad) events happen. The answer establishes the parameters for the subsequent helplessness. If the causal attribution is stable ("it's going to last forever"), the induced helplessness is considered to be long-lasting; if unstable ("my current situation is only temporary"), the helplessness is transient. If the causal attribution is global ("it's going to undermine everything"), the subsequent helplessness occurs across a variety of situations; if specific ("this cause only affects this one outcome"), it is circumscribed. If the causal attribution is internal ("it's all my fault"), the person's self-esteem drops; if external ("the cause has nothing to do with me or my character"), self-esteem is left intact.

These ideas comprise the attributional reformulation of helplessness theory. This newer theory left the original model in place, because uncontrollable events were still hypothesized to produce deficits when they gave rise to an expectation of future helplessness. Researchers' understanding of the nature of these deficits changed, however. They now thought it to be influenced by the causal attribution offered by the individual.

In some cases, the situation provides the explanation offered by the person. In others, the person relies on habitual ways of making sense of events that occur; this is referred to as the explanatory style.[18] People tend to offer similar explanations for disparate bad (or good) events. An explanatory style characterized by internal, stable, and global explanations for bad events is considered to be pessimistic, and the opposite style—external, unstable, and specific explanations for bad events—is labeled optimistic. Research has shown that people with an optimistic explanatory style are happier, healthier, more persistent, and more successful (at school, sports, and work) than their counterparts with a pessimistic explanatory style, especially in the wake of setbacks. Optimism is an important component of resiliency because it foreshadows resilience in a variety of important domains.[19]

Optimism as reflected in the explanatory style is not Pollyannaism. Rather, optimistic explanatory style is infused with a sense of personal competence and responsibility. "Things will be better because I can do things that will make them better." Optimistic explanatory style prevents people from thinking of themselves as victims.

Intervention

Negative reactions to adversity can be alleviated by changing the way people think about response-outcome relationships and how they explain the causes of bad events. Cognitive therapy for depression is effective because it changes these sorts of beliefs and provides clients with strategies for viewing future bad events in more optimistic ways.[20] Along these lines, helplessness and its consequences can be prevented by teaching clients cognitive-behavioral skills before problems develop. One protocol based on these tenets, designed for group administration, is the Penn Resiliency Program (PRP), a twelve-session curriculum taught by an expert trainer. It has two main components, one cognitive and the other based on social problem-solving techniques.[21]

In the cognitive component, core cognitive techniques are translated, through the use of scenarios and skits, into a language that clients can apply to their own lives. Group facilitators teach clients about the link between thoughts and feelings. Then clients learn how to evaluate their beliefs. Skits are used to help find differences between the beliefs of fictitious characters who are thriving and those who are not. Clients learn that "me" (it's my fault), "always" (it's going to be this way forever), and "everything" (it affects everything I do) beliefs about bad events are more likely than others to result in undesirable outcomes. Clients also learn to evaluate the accuracy of their first, and perhaps erroneous, belief. In addition, they participate in the "hot seat," a technique that helps transition the cognitive skills from the classroom into the real world by providing an opportunity for the rapid-fire challenging of negative beliefs.

Through the cognitive component, clients learn to evaluate the accuracy of their interpretations of the world. In the social problem-solving component, they learn skills—assertiveness, negotiation, relaxation, not procrastinating, social skills, decision making, and problem solving—that help them better interact and perform. The PRP was originally developed and tested among schoolchildren in the United States and China. Results indicate that prevention participants reported fewer depressive symptoms and were less likely to report symptoms during two years of follow-up.[22] The PRP has since been generalized to adults, including teachers in Australia and England and American soldiers.[23]

Role of the Leader

PRP is a "train the trainer" approach because the intent is not just to make direct recipients of the training more resilient, but also to impart to them strategies for teaching its lessons to those they instruct or lead. This strategy exponentially increases the number of people who eventually learn to be optimistic. In these interventions, the role of the leader, for example, teachers and drill sergeants, is made explicit: to instill optimistic thinking—one of the key ingredients of resiliency—in others. Leaders can also influence resiliency implicitly, through the way in which they speak to their followers as well as by the example that they set.

The way teachers criticize as well as praise their students influences their subsequent motivation to succeed.[24] If the feedback, praise or criticism, contains a message about student characteristics that cannot be changed (e.g., innate intelligence or ability), then motivation and performance suffer because a student perceives no control over what happens. In contrast, if the feedback contains a message about characteristics that can be changed (e.g., effort or practice), then motivation is sustained and even increased.

The components of resilience can be similarly discouraged or encouraged by how leaders speak to subordinates. "Good" feedback in this sense may or may not be positive, and it is not permissive. Especially for those who lead individuals at risk for injury and death, empty praise is dangerous. Criticism can be helpful if its intent is seen as improving performance, safety, and well-being. Research is also clear that being positive is, indeed, positive in its effects.[25] In productive work groups, positive messages outnumber negative ones,[26] and relationships are sustained when individuals take an active and positive interest in the successes of one another.[27] Leaders need to heed these lessons. A positive stance instills resiliency among those being led.[28]

Leaders who share hardships with subordinates can inspire them by their example, assuming that what they model is resilience and that trust exists between leaders and subordinates.[29] Here a fine line must be walked. Research on modeling shows that the model must be seen as similar by those who follow the model's example. If the leader is viewed in exalted terms, his or her example becomes too daunting to emulate.[30] So, the leader must reveal enough of his or her personal reactions to adversity and danger to appear similar to his or her subordinates ("yes, I'm afraid, too") while at the same time providing the appropriate example ("but we will prevail").

The practical implications of learned helplessness and its interventions are several. First, without denying the objective reality of difficult events, how one thinks about the events matters. To the degree that someone thinks about bad events and their causes in ways that are both realistic and hopeful, that person will be resilient. To the degree that someone believes future events can be controlled—that the future need not be the same as the past—that person will be resilient. Second, the leader of a group plays a crucial role not only in exemplifying resilient beliefs and attitudes but by building them among subordinates. The leader can speak to followers about their expectations and help them to frame them in optimistic ways, such as by pointing to past successes and instances of resilience by the group. Third, it is not sufficient to "think" resilience. One must also "do" resilience, and the best way to put optimistic beliefs into action is to have the requisite skills and resources to do so.

HARDINESS

Hardiness is another approach to resiliency identifying the psychological components of bouncing back from adversity and thriving in its wake.[31] Research on hardiness began decades ago, when researchers studied the health and well-being of executives at Illinois Bell Telephone during a restructuring of the company.[32] Some executives fared well, whereas others did not:

> Consider Chuck, an engineer by training who became a customs relations manager for Illinois Bell Telephone. As deregulation began, Chuck found his work difficult, but he redoubled his efforts to satisfy customers. Knowing that deregulation would lead to more competition, Chuck believed that good customer relations were essential to future success of the company and to his own role in it. On his own, he surveyed customers to find out what they liked about telephone services and what they wanted but did not have. He presented the results of his survey to his supervisors, but many of them were too preoccupied to consider his findings and their implications. Chuck persisted, until his plan was accepted and put into action. He was asked to take charge of its implementation. He did a good job, and Chuck became even more central to the company.[33]

Components

Executives who like Chuck were resilient displayed a constellation of attitudes identified as commitment, control, and challenge, which collectively were characterized as hardiness.

- *Commitment* means believing that life is worthwhile and deserving of one's engagement; it involves having a purpose in life and being involved with family, friends, faith, work, or community in ways that add meaning to one's life. Research links commitment to resilience in the wake of setbacks and failures and more generally to psychological and physical well-being.[34]

- *Control* refers to the belief that one can influence the important outcomes in life, especially those that are stressful. People with a sense of control are not helpless in the wake of challenge and difficulty.[35] Again, research shows perceived control to be linked to resilience.[36] Even if someone cannot literally change difficult events, control can still be exercised in how one chooses to interpret or react to them.[37]

- *Challenge* describes how people frame the events in which they are involved. It is evident when people see difficulties as opportunities to learn and grow. Positive framing of this sort is a powerful determinant of how people respond to difficult times. Approaching life's setbacks as a challenge does not entail denial.[38] Rather, it results in more active, effective, and creative problem solving, and resilience ensues.[39]

The executives with these attitudes were only 50 percent as likely as those without them to experience a stress-related health problem during the five-year study. They were not invulnerable to stress, but they did cope with it better, and thus by the parameters here, were more resilient.

Consequences

Hardiness research findings show that the constellation of commitment, control, and challenge predicts resilience not just among business executives but also students, athletes, nurses, lawyers, bus drivers, the elderly, and members of the military.[40] Outcomes predicted by hardiness include physical as well as psychological well-being.[41] Hardy individuals perceive difficult events as being less stressful than do less hardy people.[42] They also exhibit a reduced physiological stress response during challenges and a more vigorous immune response.[43] Like optimistic individuals, hardy individuals cope in active ways.[44]

It is not clear whether the three components of hardiness reflect a single underlying dimension—that is, hardiness—or are synergistic in their effects on well-being.[45] Studies usually combine the three components and do not test their separate or interactive effects. (The same criticism can be made of typical explanatory style research.) As argued, distinguishing the components of resilience is important, and to continue the argument, the components of these components must also be distinguished.

Intervention

HardiTraining is a program that increases hardiness.[46] It uses a variety of cognitive-behavioral techniques to produce the attitudes of commitment, control, and challenge. The PRP program overlaps with HardiTraining with respect to strategies for encouraging control and confronting challenges, but the unique contribution of hardiness training is its emphasis on commitment—that is, creating a sense of meaning and purpose. HardiTraining also addresses the importance of social support, good nutrition, relaxation, and physical activity. The goal of HardiTraining is to reduce an individual's stress response by encouraging different ways of thinking about adverse life events, in particular, by putting these events in a broader perspective. When effective, this process makes illness less likely. It also leads the individual to become a better problem solver.

HardiTraining consists of ninety-minute, small-group sessions led by an expert trainer and held once a week over ten weeks. The trainer emphasizes the attitudes that comprise hardiness and the skills needed to put these attitudes in action. Participants are given workbooks containing information about hardiness, examples of hardiness, and exercises. Assessment is ongoing, and the feedback from this assessment builds and sustains participant motivation. Several studies have compared participants in HardiTraining to people who did not take part in this intervention. HardiTraining is effective by self-reporting measures of hardiness, job satisfaction, anxiety, and depression and by objective measures of blood pressure and illness severity.

Role of the Leader

A leader can influence hardiness in direct and indirect ways among those being led.[47] Explicit instruction in how to adopt and use the attitudes of commitment, control, and challenge can be given. For example, "Try looking at things *this* way." A leader can also model what it means to be hardy. According to the hardy leader hypothesis, "Leaders who are high in hardiness themselves exert influence on their subordinates to interpret stressful experiences in ways characteristic of high-hardy persons."[48] This hypothesis has been confirmed in studies of military cadets being trained to become officers.[49] Those high in hardiness can lead others to perform well in dangerous contexts by imparting the beliefs that events can be controlled, that missions are worthwhile, and that mastery and growth can result from success against adversity.

It is recommended that leaders talk to those they lead, framing what they say in the language of hardiness. The hierarchical structure of organizations like the military and police and fire departments places leaders in positions of legitimized authority where they can exert considerable influence over subordinates in terms of how they make collective sense of stressful events.[50] Words are important, and effective leaders are skilled at crafting what they say so that it resonates with those who are led.[51]

> A police captain arrives at his new division for his first roll call. The division has existed for decades, and he is the new face in the crowd. He takes a seat in roll call in the middle of the room and pays attention to the officers as they assemble for assignments. He takes note of the players: Who is the jokester in the room, who is serious, who socializes with whom? When the watch commander asks the captain if he would like to address the troops, he declines. At the end of roll call, the officers assemble at the kit room to

pick up their equipment. The captain positions himself across the hall and watches quietly. When asked what he was doing, he replies, "Nothing."

This approach to leadership has been described as "watching the dance."[52] The leader engages in a form of mindful meditation, focusing on the here and now, including his or her own breathing or muscle tension, as well as what is going on in the external environment. A nonjudgmental attitude is important. By watching the natural ebb and flow of a work group, the leader can discern details that would otherwise be missed. Mindfulness short circuits the tendency to live in the future and allows one to see what is in the moment. This skill is commonly discussed with respect to stress management but is a useful addition to the leader's repertoire. This captain went on to develop a reputation as someone who cared for those under his command. His willingness to walk in others' shoes was repeatedly shown through compassionate acts.

Also important are the nonverbal messages and emotions the leader conveys. The captain described above is calm and confident, and his police officers "caught" his hardiness. In reframing adversity to place it in a larger context and remind followers of the meaning of what they do, an effective leader does not rely on abstractions. At least in the heat of combat, soldiers do not fight for flag or country. They fight for their comrades. A leader who reminds those led that all of them matter is going to be effective.

Emotional warmth on the part of the leader services this process.[53] Effective mentors and leaders are described by their students and followers as caring, a stance that helps those taught or led to define themselves in terms of what they can do as opposed to what they cannot. Contrast this with "gap analysis"—paying attention only to a worker's weaknesses—which is done routinely by too many supervisors. Negatively framed evaluations focusing on problems and mistakes only lead to negative goals—that is, avoiding further criticism—and certainly do not instill hardiness. Rather, cynicism and hopelessness are the more likely lessons learned. Leaders can further instill resilience through appropriate self-disclosure and genuineness in their emotional expressions, such as in the aftermath of tragedy.

A specialized police unit had experienced the line-of-duty death of one of its most senior members during a gun battle. The unit commander addressed the group several days after the incident. He recognized the need for the officers to acknowledge their loss and grief as he looked out over the sullen yet frozen faces in the room. He asked, "Am I the only one in this room who can't sleep, can't eat, has lost weight, and has had meltdowns that have taken me to the ground? Am I the only one that has experienced these?" One by one, the officers began raising their hands in agreement, and the group began to discuss their reactions to the event and the emotions they were feeling.

CONCLUSION

Although practical applications of research on learned optimism and hardiness started with different goals and proceeded rather independently, as the approaches took their current forms, their overall conclusions dovetailed. Both are accounts of bouncing back from adversity. As explained, "resiliency" subsumes the characteristics of the individual that allow him or her to do so. Both approaches hold that resiliency is multidimensional and that it can be learned. Furthermore, the components of resiliency can be instilled by leaders among their subordinates.

The discussion of resiliency here has treated it as a property of the individual. As noted, however, resiliency can also be a property of a group as a whole. It is unlikely this side of Hollywood that a highly resilient unit can be composed of thoroughly non-resilient individuals, but groups and individuals represent different levels of analysis. There are times when the group is greater than the sum of its parts as well as times when it is less.

As the attention of psychologists turns to the promotion of resilience, targets must include not only individuals but also the groups within which these individuals live and work.[54] Not only would group-level interventions be more efficient and likely more cost-effective than individual-level interventions, they might also be more powerful. It would be great if there were a "seven easy steps" formula for creating and sustaining resiliency, but there is not. The learned helplessness model and hardiness theory, however, specify some of the important components of resiliency and offer ways to bring them out using cognitive-behavioral strategies. Like any habit, resiliency is established through practice, feedback, calibration, and more practice. Leaders can play a critical role in modeling and training resiliency among those they lead.

NOTES

1. T. Kolditz, *In Extremis Leadership: Leading As If Your Life Depended On It* (San Francisco: Jossey-Bass, 2007).

2. S. S. Luthar, D. Cicchetti, and B. Becker, "The Construct of Resilience: A Critical Evaluation and Guidelines for Future Work," *Child Development* 71 (2000): 543–562.

3. B. A. Van der Kolk, A. C. McFarlane, and L. Weisaeth, eds., *Traumatic Stress: The Effects of Overwhelming Experience on Mind, Body, and Society* (New York: Guilford Press, 1996).

4. American Psychiatric Association, *Diagnostic and Statistical Manual of Mental Disorders,* 4th ed. (Washington, D.C.: American Psychiatric Association, 1994).

5. E. B. Foa et al., eds., *Effective Treatments for PTSD: Practice Guidelines from the International Society for Traumatic Stress Studies,* 2nd ed. (New York: Guilford Press, 2009).

6. E. J. Anthony and B. J. Cohler, eds., *The Invulnerable Child* (New York: Guilford, 1987).

7. R. G. Tedeschi and L. G. Calhoun, "The Posttraumatic Growth Inventory: Measuring the Positive Legacy of Trauma," *Journal of Traumatic Stress* 9 (1996): 455–471.

8. P. Frazier et al., "Does Self-Reported Posttraumatic Growth Reflect Genuine Positive Change?" *Psychological Science* 20 (2009): 912–919.

9. D. P. McAdams, *The Stories We Live By: Personal Myths and the Making of the Self* (New York: Guilford, 1993); and D. P. McAdams, *The Redemptive Self: Stories Americans Live By* (New York: Oxford University Press, 2005).

10. C. Peterson et al., "Strengths of Character and Posttraumatic Growth," *Journal of Traumatic Stress* 21 (2008): 214–217.

11. G. A. Bonanno, "Loss, Trauma, and Human Resilience: Have We Underestimated the Human Capacity to Thrive after Extremely Aversive Events?" *American Psychologist* 59 (2004): 20–28.

12. C. Peterson, N. Park, and C. A. Castro, "Assessment for the U.S. Army Comprehensive Soldier Fitness Program: The Global Assessment Tool," *American Psychologist* 66 (2011): 10–18.

13. C. Peterson, S. F. Maier, and M. E. P. Seligman, *Learned Helplessness: A Theory for the Age of Personal Control* (New York: Oxford University Press, 1993).

14. M. E. P. Seligman, *Learned Optimism* (New York: Knopf, 1991).

15. S. F. Maier and M. E. P. Seligman, "Learned Helplessness: Theory and Evidence," *Journal of Experimental Psychology: General* 105 (1976): 3–46.

16. Peterson, Maier, and Seligman, *Learned Helplessness.*

17. L. Y. Abramson, M. E. P. Seligman, and J. D. Teasdale, "Learned Helplessness in Humans: Critique and Reformulation," *Journal of Abnormal Psychology* 87 (1978): 49–74.

18. C. Peterson and M. E. P. Seligman, "Causal Explanations as a Risk Factor for Depression: Theory and Evidence," *Psychological Review* 91 (1984): 347–374.

19. C. Peterson, "The Future of Optimism," *American Psychologist* 55 (2000): 44–55.

20. M. E. P. Seligman et al., "Explanatory Style Change during Cognitive Therapy for Unipolar Depression," *Journal of Abnormal Psychology* 97 (1988): 13–18.

21. K. Reivich and A. Shatté, *The Resilience Factor: 7 Keys to Finding Your Inner Strengths and Overcoming Life's Hurdles* (New York: Broadway Books, 2002).

22. L. Jaycox et al., "Prevention of Depressive Symptoms in School Children," *Behaviour Research and Therapy* 32 (1994): 801–816; and J. Gillham et al., "Prevention of Depressive Symptoms in School Children: Two Year Follow Up," *Psychological Science* 6 (1995): 343–351.

23. A. Challen et al., "UK Resilience Programme Evaluation" (unpublished manuscript, London School of Economics, 2009).

24. C. S. Dweck, *Mindset* (New York: Random House, 2006).

25. B. J. West, J. L. Patera, and M. K. Carsten, "Team Level Positivity: Investigating Positive Psychological Capacities and Team Level Outcomes," *Journal of Organizational Behavior* 30 (2009): 249–267.

26. B. L. Fredrickson and M. F. Losada, "Positive Affect and the Complex Dynamics of Human Flourishing," *American Psychologist* 60 (2005): 678–686.

27. S. L. Gable et al., "What Do You Do When Things Go Right? The Intrapersonal and Interpersonal Benefits of Sharing Good Events," *Journal of Personality and Social Psychology* 87 (2004): 228–245.

28. J. Kuoppala, A. Lamminpää, J. Liira, and H. Vaino, "Leadership, Job Well-Being, and Health Effects—A Systematic Review and a Meta-Analysis," *Journal of Occupational and Environmental Medicine* 50 (2008): 904–915.

29. P. Sweeney, "Trust: The Key to Combat Leadership," in *Leadership Lessons from West Point*, ed. D. Crandall (San Francisco: Wiley, 2007), 252–277.

30. A. Bandura, *Social Learning through Imitation* (Lincoln: University of Nebraska Press, 1962); A. Bandura, *Social Foundations of Thought and Action: A Social Cognitive Theory* (Englewood Cliffs, N.J.: Prentice-Hall, 1986); A. Bandura, ed., *Psychological Modeling: Conflicting Theories* (New Brunswick, N.J.: Transaction Publishers, 2006).

31. S. R. Maddi, "The Story of Hardiness: Twenty Years of Theorizing, Research, and Practice," *Consulting Psychology Journal: Practice and Research* 54 (2002): 173–185; and S. R. Maddi, "Hardiness: The Courage to Grow from Stresses," *Journal of Positive Psychology* 1 (2006): 160–168.

32. S. C. Kobasa, S. R. Maddi, and S. Kahn, "Hardiness and Health: A Prospective Study," *Journal of Personality and Social Psychology* 42 (1982): 168–177.

33. S. R. Maddi and D. M. Khoshaba, *Resilience at Work* (New York: Amacom, 2005).

34. P. A. Boyle et al., "Purpose in Life Is Associated with Mortality among Community-Dwelling Older Persons," *Psychosomatic Medicine* 71 (2009): 574–579; N. Park, M. Park, and C. Peterson, "When Is the Search for Meaning Related to Life Satisfaction?" *Applied Psychology: Health and Well-Being* 2 (2010): 1–13; T. Sone et al., "Sense of Life Worth Living (*Ikigai*) and Mortality in Japan: Ohsaki Study," *Psychosomatic Medicine* 70 (2008): 709–715; and M. F. Steger et al., "Meaning in Life across the Life Span: Levels and Correlates of Meaning in Life from Emerging Adulthood to Older Adulthood," *Journal of Positive Psychology* 4 (2009): 43–52.

35. Peterson, Maier, and Seligman, *Learned Helplessness.*

36. C. Peterson and A. J. Stunkard, "Personal Control and Health Promotion," *Social Science and Medicine* 28 (1989): 819–828.

37. V. E. Frankl, "Postscript: The Case for a Tragic Optimism," in *Man's Search for Meaning* (Boston: Beacon Press, 1992; original date of publication, 1959), 137–154; and R. Rothbaum, J. R. Weisz, and S. S. Synder, "Changing the World and Changing the Self: A Two-Process Model of Perceived Control," *Journal of Personality and Social Psychology* 42 (1982): 5–37.

38. L. G. Aspinwall and S. M. Brunhart, "Distinguishing Optimism from Denial: Optimistic Beliefs Predict Attention to Health Threats," *Personality and Social Psychology Bulletin* 22 (1996): 993–1003; S. E. Taylor, "Adjustment to Threatening Events: A Theory of Cognitive Adaptation," *American Psychologist* 38 (1983):

1161–1173; S. E. Taylor and J. Brown, "Illusion and Well-Being: A Social Psychological Perspective on Mental Health," *Psychological Bulletin* 103 (1988): 193–210; and S. E. Taylor et al., "Psychological Resources, Positive Illusions, and Health," *American Psychologist* 55 (2000): 99–109.

39. C. S. Carver and M. H. Antoni, "Finding Benefit in Breast Cancer during the Year after Diagnosis Predicts Better Adjustment 5 to 8 Years after Diagnosis," *Health Psychology* 26 (2004): 595–598; and S. E. Taylor et al., "Maintaining Positive Illusions in the Face of Negative Information: Getting the Facts Without Letting Them Get to You," *Journal of Social and Clinical Psychology* 8 (1989): 114–129.

40. P. T. Bartone, "Predictors of Stress-Related Illness in City Bus Drivers," *Journal of Occupational Medicine* 31 (1989): 857–863; P. T. Bartone, "Hardiness Protects against War-Related Stress in Army Reserve Forces," *Consulting Psychology Journal* 51 (1999): 72–82; P. T. Bartone et al., "Psychological Hardiness Predicts Success in US Army Special Forces Candidates," *International Journal of Selection and Assessment* 16 (2008): 76–81; S. R. Maddi and M. Hess, "Hardiness and Basketball Performance," *International Journal of Sports Psychology* 23 (1992): 360–368; S. R. Maddi and D. M. Khoshaba, "Hardiness and Mental Health," *Journal of Personality Assessment* 63 (1994): 265–274; and M. Sheard, "Hardiness Commitment, Gender, and Age Differentiate University Academic Performance," *British Journal of Educational Psychology* 79 (2009): 189–204.

41. S. C. Kobasa, S. R. Maddi, and S. Courington, "Personality and Constitution as Mediators in the Stress–Illness Relationship," *Journal of Health and Social Behavior* 22 (1981): 368–387; see also Kobasa, Maddi, and Kahn, "Hardiness and Health"; and see Sheard, "Hardiness Commitment, Gender, and Age."

42. K. D. Allred and T. W. Smith, "The Hardy Personality: Cognitive and Physiological Responses to Evaluative Threat," *Journal of Personality and Social Psychology* 56 (1989): 257–266; and E. Rhodewalt and J. B. Zone, "Appraisal of Life Change, Depression, and Illness in Hardy and Nonhardy Women," *Journal of Personality and Social Psychology* 56 (1989): 81–88.

43. M. A. Okun, A. J. Zantra, and S. E. Robinson, "Hardiness and Health among Women with Rheumatoid Arthritis," *Personality and Individual Differences* 9 (1988): 101–107.

44. S. R. Maddi, S. Kahn, and K. L. Maddi, "The Effectiveness of Hardiness Training," *Consulting Psychology Journal: Practice and Research* 50 (1998): 78–86.

45. C. S. Carver, "How Should Multifaceted Personality Constructs Be Tested? Issues Illustrated by Self-Monitoring, Attributional Style, and Hardiness," *Journal of Personality and Social Psychology* 56 (1989): 577–585.

46. S. R. Maddi, "Hardiness Training at Illinois Bell Telephone," in *Health Promotion Evaluation,* ed. J. Opatz (Stephens Point, Wisc.: National Wellness Institute, 1987), 101–115; and see also Maddi, Kahn, and Maddi, "The Effectiveness of Hardiness Training."

47. S. R. Maddi, "Relevance of Hardiness Assessment and Training to the Military Context," *Military Psychology* 19 (2007): 61–70.

48. P. T. Bartone, "Resilience under Military Operational Stress: Can Leaders Influence Hardiness?" *Military Psychology* 18, no. S1 (2006): S131–S148, p. S139.

49. B. H. Johnson et al., "Predicting Transformational Leadership in Naval Cadets: Effects of Personality Hardiness and Training," *Journal of Applied Social Psychology* 39 (2009): 2213–2235.

50. J. Palus and W. Drath, *Evolving Leaders: A Model for Promoting Leadership Development in Programs* (Greensboro, N.C.: Center for Creative Leadership, 1995).

51. R. E. Boyatzis and A. McKee, *Resonant Leadership: Renewing Yourself and Connecting with Others through Mindfulness, Hope, and Compassion* (Boston: Harvard Business Press, 2005).

52. Ibid.

53. M. J. Burns, *Transforming Leadership: A New Pursuit of Happiness* (New York: Atlantic Monthly Press, 2003); and see also Boyatzis and McKee, *Resonant Leadership*.

54. A. Novotney, "Strong in Mind and Body," *Monitor on Psychology* 40, no. 11 (December 2009): 40–43; S. R. Maddi, D. M. Khoshaba, and A. Pammenter, "The Hardy Organization: Success by Turning Change to Advantage," *Consulting Psychology Journal* 51 (1999): 117–124.

CHAPTER 5

Understanding and Mitigating Post-Traumatic Stress Disorder

Joseph Geraci, Mike Baker, George Bonanno, Barend Tussenbroek, and Loree Sutton

First Sergeant Spock, in Afghanistan during his fourth deployment after 9/11, recalls a mission from June 2007 in Iraq. Improvised explosive devises (IEDs) had become the unsuspecting killer in his area, and his infantry platoon was on a mission to capture a key insurgent responsible for emplacing them. They had killed one of his soldiers and wounded eighteen other comrades. It was so likely that his platoon was going to hit an IED during the mission that his commander assigned a route clearance team (RCT) to his platoon.

The RCT gave Spock some comfort, but it quickly faded when he received word that an RCT vehicle had broken down. His platoon faced the dilemma of having to wait for mechanics to fix the vehicle and jeopardize the mission or to move on and run the risk of hitting an IED explosion. Spock describes how he knew that his decision might cost him his life and the lives of his fellow soldiers, but he knew the mission was too important to delay. If anyone was going to take the additional risk, it was going to be him, so with his heart racing, he looked at his driver with as much confidence as he could muster and said, "Take the lead. We are going to the objective." Spock recalls that his driver didn't show the slightest doubt or fear in his face. Without hesitation, his driver stepped on the gas and their vehicle raced to the objective, first in the order of movement. Fortunately, Spock's platoon captured its target, without injury, which greatly reduced the number of IEDs for the remainder of the deployment.

I f you are reading this, then the probability is high that you will face a similar situation as First Sergeant Spock in the future (or you already have) based on your chosen profession. The probability is also high that you will tell subordinates that you need them to perform a critical task that they may appraise as a potentially traumatic event (PTE), a threat to their physical or psychological health. Specific to leading in dangerous contexts, PTEs primarily consist of single or repeated experiences that may ultimately lead to death or serious injury for subordinates, their unit members, or a third party (i.e., a perpetrator, an innocent bystander, or an enemy).

A number of critical factors determine how PTEs affect psychological health. Two of them are discussed here. The first factor is how a subordinate cognitively appraises the PTE—that is, as a challenge or as a threat—and the second factor is the level of his or her coping flexibility, or ability to apply situation-appropriate coping styles after the event. When a subordinate appraises the PTE as a threat and then demonstrates coping inflexibility, post-traumatic stress disorder (PTSD) is a likely outcome. PTSD is a severe anxiety disorder that consists of persistent physiological, emotional, cognitive, and behavioral symptoms (related to facing a PTE) that cause significant distress or impairment in social, occupational, or other functional areas.[1] When a subordinate appraises the PTE as a challenge and is able to flexibly cope, then it is most probable that he or she will experience resilience. In such a case, the subordinate might have temporary reactions to the PTE, but these then return to baseline levels.[2]

One of the variables that helps determine how subordinates appraise PTEs and cope afterward is the strength of their "psychological body armor." This armor protects against PTSD and primarily depends on levels of social support, hardiness, and leadership. It is argued here that leadership is the most important component because leaders can greatly affect the social support and hardiness of subordinates. Thus it is essential that leaders understand how certain leadership behaviors can help minimize the number of subordinates on a PTSD trajectory and maximize those on a resilience trajectory. This is critical since researchers have recently associated PTSD with completed suicides and reduced health.[3] In addition, few would refute that PTSD negatively impacts the performance of small units that face the majority of trauma for their profession (i.e., the platoon level and below for most militaries, the shift or team level for the police, and company level and below for firefighters). Related to the opening scenario, it appears that the leadership behaviors of First Sergeant Spock before and during the PTE enabled his driver to view the situation as a challenge. The work to keep the driver on a resilience trajectory began after the PTE.

There is no perfect remedy for PTSD. Mitigating PTSD is extremely complex. More advances are needed before researchers can truly understand and alleviate PTSD in dangerous contexts. In the meantime, however, it is hoped that the framework presented here will help leaders improve the psychological health and performance levels of their units when PTEs occur.

PREVALENCE AND SYMPTOMS OF PTSD

Research conducted during the first decade of the 2000s on the prevalence of PTSD—determined by the number of individuals at the time experiencing it or who had experienced it within the year—found it among 16.7 percent of U.S. active-duty soldiers who had returned from Iraq,[4] 19 percent of police officers and 22 percent of firefighters who had worked in the aftermath of Hurricane Katrina,[5] and 25 percent of firefighters in Taiwan who had assisted with disasters.[6] Although accurately measuring PTSD is a difficult endeavor, the rate of prevalence for individuals working in dangerous contexts appears to be significantly higher than the average rates of 1.8 percent for American males in the general population and 0.5 percent for European males.[7] A plausible explanation for this disparity is that dangerous context professionals face more PTEs than civilians, and there is a positive relationship between the number of PTEs and resulting PTSD symptoms.[8] For example, N. Pole and colleagues found that cadets who had graduated from police academies in New York and California faced an average of seven PTEs during their first year of service.[9] This is compared to only 67 percent of European men who faced at least one PTE during their lifetime.[10] The same relationship was evident in a study that assigned soldiers to three exposure categories (low, middle, and high combat) and found that soldiers in the high group were 3.5 times more likely to screen positive for PTSD compared to the low group—that is, a prevalence rate of 28 percent versus 8 percent.[11] Since individuals in dangerous contexts face numerous PTEs that put them at greater risk for PTSD, it is important for leaders to be able to identify the symptoms of the disorder. It is natural for subordinates to temporarily experience PTSD symptoms, but leaders should become concerned when they experience them for more than thirty days after the PTE.[12]

Physical Symptoms

James Ness and colleagues highlight the adaptive nature of the body to return to homeostasis, or a stable state, in a discussion of allostatis (see Chapter 3 in this volume). As individuals face PTEs, they experience an inevitable imbalance

Table 5.1 Symptoms of Post-Traumatic Stress Disorder

Physical Symptoms	Cognitive and Emotional Symptoms	Behavioral Symptoms
▸ Difficulty breathing ▸ Profuse sweating ▸ Rapid heart rate ▸ Elevated blood pressure ▸ Migraines ▸ Exaggerated startle response ▸ Difficulty sleeping	▸ Easily agitated ▸ Trouble concentrating ▸ Negative expectations about oneself or distorted blame ▸ Inability to experience positive emotions ▸ Nightmares or flashbacks of the PTE with strong emotional response ▸ Feeling overwhelmed	▸ Avoidance of feelings, thoughts, people, places or events related to the PTE ▸ Being hyperalert ▸ Being detached and withdrawn ▸ Alcohol consumption ▸ Drug use ▸ Change in activities or loss of interest in hobbies ▸ Disciplinary issues

of hormones. If this imbalance persists for an extended period of time, physical symptoms can ensue. Some individuals may not be able to bring their bodies back to homeostasis for two inter-related reasons. First, fear conditioning occurs when the amygdala (which meditates the body's emotions) interprets neutral stimuli as threatening because the hippocampus (which plays a critical role in long-term memory) contains a memory of the neutral stimuli being paired with a threatening event. These threat-laden memories influence the amygdala's interpretation of these once-neutral stimuli as being the threatening PTE itself (for example, trash on the road paired with an IED).[13] Fear conditioning can be adaptive while dangerous contexts individuals perform their professional duties, but maladaptive in everyday life. Second, if the prefrontal cortex (which executes higher cognitive functions and regulates the body's responses) is unable to properly regulate an exaggerated response of the amygdala, physical symptoms can result.[14] Thus individuals with extensive fear conditioning and a diminished prefrontal cortex may experience an increased amount of physical symptoms of PTSD (see Table 5.1).

Cognitive and Emotional Symptoms

When people who have had a PTE experience physical symptoms from not being able to sleep at night, it is highly likely that they may become easily agitated or have trouble concentrating at work. They may also be struggling with strong emotions related to the PTE. When individuals cognitively appraise PTEs as threats, primary emotions, such as fear and anger, may be present. When they are not able to make meaning of the PTE or they experience a conflict between the consequences of the PTE and their existing belief systems, then secondary emotions, such as guilt, shame, and sadness, may result. Individuals might try to resolve this conflict by irrationally blaming themselves—"It's all my fault" or "I'm worthless." Although individuals may be able to avoid normal and everyday emotional experiences, secondary emotions cannot be easily avoided.[15] Therefore, images of the original PTE may emerge as flashbacks during the day or at night in the form of nightmares, thus resulting in the experience of strong cognitive and emotional symptoms (see Table 5.1).

Behavioral Symptoms

The symptoms of PTSD noted above can become intense and overwhelming, so individuals may believe that the only way to function in everyday life is to completely avoid things that might trigger them. This helps explain why sleep can be so difficult; it means giving up control and inevitably re-experiencing the PTE in dreams. So, from the perspective of someone suffering from PTSD, their options are don't sleep, sleep and face the nightmares, or drink enough alcohol or take enough drugs to shut down the brain to suppress dream states (see Table 5.1).

THE DEVELOPMENT OF PTSD

First Factor—Cognitive Appraisal

It appears that approximately 30 percent of subordinates may experience the symptoms of PTSD within a year after facing PTEs. It is important to note, however, that PTSD is not the only trajectory of psychological health and that most subordinates will experience a resilience trajectory. Two critical factors differentiate the two trajectories. The first factor is a person's "in the moment" reaction, or immediate psychological reaction, to the PTE as it is occurring. E. Ozer and colleagues found this to be the most robust factor in determining the later development of PTSD.[16] M. Olff and colleagues also concluded that the "in the moment" cognitive appraisal of the PTE is an important predictor of the later onset of PTSD.[17] Consistent with this research, V. Florian and colleagues found that Israeli soldiers who cognitively appraised their four-month basic military training as a threatening experience exhibited a significant decline in their psychological health by the end of the training.[18]

Although not involving dangerous contexts, the research of J. Blascovich and colleagues with collegiate athletes showed that an individual's reaction to a "threat appraisal" differs from a "challenge appraisal." In fact, a challenge appraisal predicted greater confidence in completing a task, greater energy mobilization, and better performance during a collegiate season. They found that individuals consider events to be a challenge or a threat based on a sequential appraisal of relevant demands and resources. In an initial demand appraisal, individuals assess the effort required of them to complete the task, the level of danger to themselves or others to complete the task, and the potential consequences of them completing or not completing the task. Next, individuals assess their resources—e.g., knowledge, skills, abilities, and the amount of external support available—to meet the demands of the situation. Based on this sequential appraisal, individuals perceive a challenge when evaluated resources meet or exceed demands, but a threat when demands exceed resources.[19]

The research presented here draws upon Patricia Resick's work with military veterans to add another variable to the threat-versus-challenge appraisal—the personal meaning that individuals take from the PTE. Resick points out that if a PTE is consistent with an individual's deeply held belief system, then he or she will quickly assimilate the consequences of the PTE into that system. In contrast, a PTE that shatters an existing belief system will cause an individual to see the PTE as a threat and increase the probability of following a PTSD trajectory.[20]

Second Factor—Coping Flexibility

Researchers contend that an individual's perceived ability to integrate certain coping styles after PTEs plays a crucial role in determining resulting trajectories of psychological health. They have attempted to identify the superior coping style for increasing psychological health but results have been inconsistent.[21] In response, G. Prati and colleagues posited that coping styles are not inherently good or bad, but their adaptive qualities depend on the contexts of specific situations.[22]

George Bonanno and colleagues concur with Prati and colleagues and introduced the construct of coping flexibility to identify individuals who are able to perceive themselves as flexible enough to engage in two different styles of coping based on the demands of the situation. The first style is forward focus coping, which emphasizes such means as maintaining goals and plans, attending to others, thinking optimistically, being able to laugh, reducing painful emotions, and remaining calm and serious. The second style of coping is emotional processing and consists of such means as fully experiencing the emotions related to the traumatic event and reflecting upon the meaning of it. In contrast to forward focus coping, emotional processing is more demanding and time consuming as individuals may need to temporarily suspend normal obligations to reflect upon and work through the traumatic experience. The researchers found that coping flexibility was related to reduced PTSD symptoms in American and Israeli college respondents, especially when the individuals had experienced high levels of trauma. In addition, they found that a perceived ability in only one of the coping styles predicted increased PTSD symptoms.[23] Acknowledging the limitations of research with college samples, some of the authors of this chapter are currently researching the impact of coping flexibility on the psychological health of soldiers in Afghanistan.

Trajectories Resulting from Cognitive Appraisal and Coping Flexibility

T. deRoon-Cassini and colleagues identified four distinct trajectories—PTSD, recovery, delayed PTSD, and resilience—of psychological health that result after individuals face a PTE.[24] Through introducing the two factors of cognitive appraisal and coping flexibility, it is proposed here that an interaction of these two factors contributes to subordinates experiencing one of the four trajectories. In particular, a cognitive appraisal of threat combined with coping inflexibility greatly contributes to the PTSD trajectory and detracts from optimal performance (e.g., inability to focus and concentrate on the task at hand) (see Figure 5.1). The recovery trajectory occurs when an individual experiences symptoms of PTSD for an extended period of time, from several months after the PTE or as long as one or two years. This occurs when individuals appraise an event as a threat but then later exhibit coping flexibility to ameliorate their situation. The delayed PTSD trajectory occurs when individuals experience minimal symptoms immediately after the PTE but the symptoms significantly worsen over time, which occurs when individuals appraise a PTE as a challenge and then experience coping inflexibility as they attempt to deal with the symptoms. DeRoon-Cassini and colleagues associate the resilience trajectory with individuals who may experience temporary symptoms of PTSD (e.g., several weeks of temporary preoccupation with the PTE or disturbance of sleep) but then are able to maintain relatively stable and healthy levels of psychological health. These individuals see PTEs as challenges and then employ coping flexibility after the event, which improves their performance during PTEs and gives them improved self-efficacy—an individual's feeling of confidence to execute intended actions—to face the next PTE.[25]

MITIGATING PTSD

Knowing the different trajectories that may result from an interaction of two key factors—cognitive appraisal and coping flexibility—what can leaders do to help subordinates appraise inevitable PTEs as challenges instead of threats and to integrate coping flexibility after the PTE to ensure that they follow a resilience trajectory? One important response is to strengthen the psychological body armor of subordinates, which consists of at least three protective components—social support, hardiness, and leadership. These components interact to strengthen the psychological body armor, which maximizes their appraisal of the resources available to them when they face PTEs and gives them the self-efficacy to flexibly cope after PTEs. As noted above, it is suggested here that leadership is the most important component because leaders can significantly impact the hardiness and social support of individuals in their units.

Social Support

Social support for subordinates is the perceived helpfulness of their social interactions within and outside their units. Researchers have found it to protect against PTSD.[26] In fact, Vietnam Veterans with high levels of social support were 180 percent less likely to develop PTSD than those with lower levels.[27] Lieutenant General Hal Moore (Ret.) captures the essence of social support after his experience as the commander for the 1st Battalion, 7th Cavalry, during the Vietnam War. In the Battle of Ia Drang, his unit was encircled by a numerically superior enemy. He later wrote that "we discovered in that depressing, hellish place, where death was our constant companion, that we loved each other."[28] These sentiments of social support are reminiscent of that conveyed by the Australian military term "mateship," which can be traced back to early settlers who endured the difficult conditions of the Outback and then to Australian servicemen in World War I who placed "more importance on 'not letting down their mates' than on their own well-being."[29]

Hardiness

Over the last thirty years, researchers have utilized the personality characteristic of hardiness to differentiate individuals—that is, Gulf War veterans, Israeli soldiers, Norwegian cadets, and Iraq and Afghan war veterans—with reduced levels of PTSD symptoms from those with elevated levels of PTSD symptoms. They define the construct of hardiness as a constellation of personality characteristics that function as a resistance resource as individuals face stressful life events. In addition, researchers have found that hardy individuals have a higher sense of commitment to such things as their work, activities, and relationships, gained from having a strong purpose in their lives; have a great sense of control over their surroundings, as well as their reactions to events; and appraise events as challenges (as already discussed).[30] (Please see Chapter 4 for a more in-depth discussion on hardiness.)

Leadership

At least since World War II, researchers have recognized the protective value of leadership and have found that units with good morale and leadership have fewer combat stress casualties than those without good morale and leadership.[31] Research confirms that this relationship also existed during the Iraq War: 20 percent of soldiers who rated their leaders as "high quality" screened positive for a psychological disorder in the high combat group, but among those high combat soldiers who rated their leaders as "low quality," 40 percent tested positive.[32]

D. Campbell and colleagues approach the component of leadership by describing it as a process of social influence that involves subordinates voluntarily accepting the influence of their leader and then willingly executing tasks that they otherwise might not have been inclined to do. This explains why First Sergeant Spock's driver did not show doubt or fear on his face. Leaders influence their subordinates not only through their observable personal characteristics (who they are) but also through their behaviors (what they do).[33] For more than forty years, researchers have reported that effective, or high quality, leaders influence subordinates primarily through task-oriented and relational-oriented behaviors.[34]

Task-oriented behaviors focus on accomplishing a mission and consist of such actions as leaders' defining tasks and work roles, ensuring that subordinates meet clearly established standards of task performance, and coordinating the efforts of subordinates in their unit. (Task-oriented behaviors are similar to transactional leadership behaviors.) Relational-oriented behaviors focus more on establishing supportive environments based on strong interpersonal relationships, such as showing concern and respect for subordinates, treating subordinates as equals, and focusing on the welfare of subordinates.[35] (Relational-oriented behaviors are similar to transformational leadership behaviors.) The execution of leadership can be complex. For example, dangerous context leaders must be able to shift between task- and relational-oriented leadership behaviors "depending on the phase of the mission and/or changing environmental demands."[36]

LEADERSHIP ACTIONS TO STRENGTHEN SUBORDINATES' PSYCHOLOGICAL BODY ARMOR

Preparation for PTEs

As noted above, a challenge appraisal results when individuals assess that their own resources (internal and external) will enable them to meet the demands of a PTE. Leaders help to increase this later assessment of resources by assisting individuals during the "preparation for PTEs" phase (see Figure 4.1). In this phase, leaders can improve subordinates' hardiness by utilizing task-oriented behaviors that increase their self-efficacy to successfully address the demands of PTEs. This occurs through leaders instilling discipline and providing rigorous training that replicates the dangerous context (e.g., elevated but safe levels of risk and stress). Such training enables individuals to hone their profession-specific skills and teaches them to appraise PTEs as challenges. A. Bandura refers to such experiences as mastery experiences and states that they enable individuals to "adopt strategies and courses of action designed to change hazardous environments into more benign ones."[37] For example, M. Perrin and colleagues found that emergency service workers less trained for the specific PTEs that they faced at the World Trade Center on 9/11 were more likely to later develop PTSD. Some of the highest rates of PTSD were among those who engaged in firefighting.[38]

Another benefit of rigorous and profession-specific training is that it provides an opportunity for leaders to demonstrate and improve their tactical competence levels (e.g., decision making and technical and tactical expertise), thus increasing subordinates' assessment of their external resources. This can occur through succeeding in difficult training exercises and through establishing and training on "battledrills" that capture and synchronize the actions of unit members in anticipation of the most threatening PTEs (i.e., dealing with an insurgent sniper attack for the military, confronting an armed and barricaded suspect for a police force, and being a firefighter injured in a burning building). P. Sweeney found that leaders in Iraq who had demonstrated competence during pre-combat operations enhanced the subsequent level of subordinates' trust in them during combat, while leaders who had failed to demonstrate competence did not engender as much trust.[39] As subordinates put their lives at risk to follow the orders of leaders, as First Sergeant Spock's driver did in the opening vignette, they watch their leaders closely and ask themselves, "Do I trust my leader with my life?" (The leader here is an external resource.) Sweeney's research suggests that part of the answer depends on the leader's tactical competence as demonstrated in the preparation phase. (See Chapter

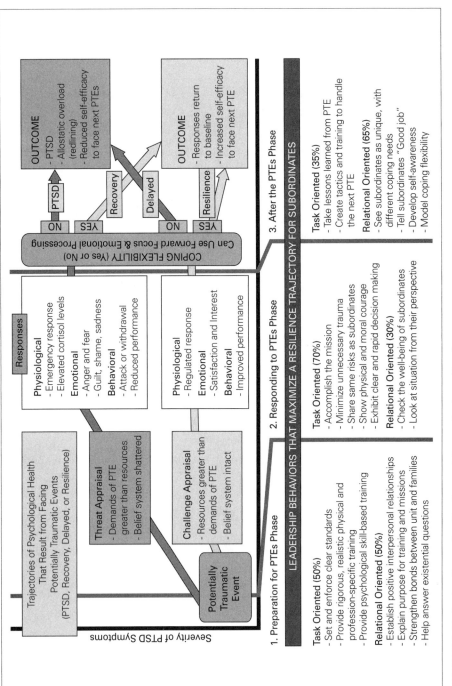

FIGURE 5.1 Understanding and mitigating post-traumatic stress disorder

9 for an in-depth discussion on how leaders can build trust among followers.) Other ways to help subordinates develop hardiness are through a rigorous and regular physical exercise program and in-depth psychological training focused on understanding and managing how the body responds to PTEs.[40]

An indirect effect of profession-specific training is that it can instill social support in units because it pushes individuals to their limits and forces them to pull together. This also enhances their assessment of their external resources. Through relational-oriented leadership behaviors, leaders can further develop this social support by establishing positive interpersonal relationships with their subordinates and learning about their lives, their families, and their aspirations. This will help to create a sense of family within the units and strengthen the bonds between the unit and subordinates' family members. (See Chapter 10 for more insight on how leaders can build strong teams.) Leaders can also utilize these relationships to help their subordinates reach their full potential to face PTEs through regular formal and informal counseling. Carl Rogers asserts that if dangerous contexts leaders are able to integrate three essential characteristics of positive interpersonal relationships—genuineness (being honest and real with subordinates), unconditional positive regard (loving every aspect of subordinates and being nonjudgmental), and empathy (taking on the worldview of subordinates to fully understand them)—then they will create subordinates who are "more self-responsible, more creative . . . and . . . better able to adapt to new problems."[41]

As part of subordinates' realistic and demanding training, it is recommended that leaders integrate the realism of PTEs by simulating wounded or injured subordinates and requiring other subordinates to provide them actual medical treatment (i.e., administer IVs as vehicles race to medical treatment facilitates). This training can save the lives of injured or wounded subordinates in the next phase and also help subordinates begin to answer such difficult and existential questions as "What would it be like if I was injured or if someone on my team died?" It is important for leaders to use their relational-oriented behaviors in this preparation phase to sit down, one-on-one, and help subordinates answer such questions and to explain the purpose of the training and of future missions. Leaders help to increase the hardiness of subordinates and their ability to make meaning out of the future consequences of PTEs when they help them to understand these purposes.

Leader competence in the preparation phase affects the level of trust that subordinates have in their leader in the "responding to PTEs" phase. Another critical component to this trust is a subordinate's evaluation of the level of care that he or she receives from the leader during this phase and that this evaluation is maximized when leaders establish positive interpersonal relationships with each subordinate. (See Chapter 9 in this volume.) Following a competent and caring leader who one trusts into the responding to PTEs phase can greatly increase subordinates' appraisal of the resources available to face the demands of PTEs. Given the importance of leadership behaviors during the preparation for PTEs phase, it is proposed that leaders can optimize the psychological body armor of subordinates when they establish a balance between task-oriented and relational-oriented behaviors. The comments below from First Sergeant Spock highlight this balance:

> As a leader on the back of a helicopter during Operation Anaconda, I was thinking tactically—"If this happens" or "If this happens." Then I asked myself, "Do my subordinates really trust me?" From that operation, I learned that the two most important things to help prepare your soldiers for such situations is training them and getting to know them. If you can do both, then you gain the soldiers' trust. It culminates to a point, even when you know that everyone is probably not going to come back okay, where they are still going to follow you. The soldier doesn't have a doubt in his mind about it. He just knows that I trust my leader.

Responding to PTEs

If leaders are able to successfully integrate both leadership behaviors during the preparation for PTEs phase, their subordinates will be more hardy, be more likely to perceive a strong sense of social support from their family and their unit, and be more trusting of their leader, because he or she had previously demonstrated competence and had established a positive interpersonal relationship with them. As a result, the leaders will have maximized the resources of their subordinates as they face the demands of PTEs in this phase, thus increasing the probability that they will see PTEs as challenges and experience a resilience trajectory. An absence of any of these protective components may create cracks in the psychological body armors of subordinates and place them at greater risk for appraising PTEs as threats and experiencing a PTSD trajectory. When discussing the leadership behaviors necessary during this phase, it is important to remember that dangerous contexts professionals provide key services for society, and it is their professional obligation to complete their profession-specific tasks. It is, therefore, critical for them to utilize task-oriented behaviors during this phase and accomplish their mission.

Given that PTEs can create situations that are time-sensitive, ambiguous, and potentially deadly, it is also important to utilize task-oriented behaviors to reduce the number of unnecessary and avoidable traumatic events that subordinates face during this phase. In addition, while responding to PTEs, subordinates anticipate their leaders to lead by example by sharing in the risks, exhibiting physical courage in the face of danger, and demonstrating their competence.[42] In these situations, there is considerable evidence to support the assumption that leaders speed up their decision-making process and that "a leader who can react quickly in emergencies will be judged better by followers than one who cannot."[43]

During PTEs, there is probably little time to integrate relational-oriented leader behaviors, thus necessitating that leaders rely on the positive interpersonal relationships built in the previous phase. These relationships will directly influence the level of social support and resulting assessment of resources available to subordinates as they deal with PTEs.[44] If there is time available, however, it may be beneficial for leaders to take a momentary pause and check on subordinates to assess their well-being and to see the situation from their perspective.

It is proposed that leaders continue to maximize the psychological body armor of subordinates during this phase by prioritizing task-oriented behaviors over relational-oriented behaviors (about 70 percent to 30 percent). This ratio is consistent with the work of Fiedler, who states that more task-oriented leadership behaviors are needed when situations are extremely ambiguous, dangerous, and unstructured.[45]

After the PTEs

To maximize the number of subordinates on a resilience trajectory, leaders are encouraged to facilitate coping flexibility in their units during this phase. Each individual is unique and will need different styles of coping after facing PTEs. Many subordinates may only need to integrate a forward focus coping style to continue on a resilience trajectory. Certain task-oriented leader behaviors, for instance, helping subordinates learn lessons from the responding to PTEs phase, may facilitate this; leaders can assist subordinates in developing new tactics and training to help the unit prepare for future PTEs. A shift leader for the German police who the authors interviewed in Afghanistan highlighted this point: "It is important to talk after a heavy duty or when a comrade is wounded. Talk about it and learn from it. Everyone has a right to say what went right and wrong. It is important for leaders to learn from mistakes."

One of the characteristics of PTEs is that they may "shatter" subordinates' beliefs about themselves, the world, or other people, thus requiring that they integrate an emotional processing coping style. As suggested by Resick, many of the initial symptoms of PTSD can be reduced if individuals are able to process and make meaning of secondary emotions and the consequences of facing PTEs.[46] In fact, research has shown that one form of psychotherapy, cognitive processing therapy (developed by Resick), significantly reduced PTSD symptoms among veterans compared to a control group.[47] To facilitate this emotional processing, the leadership style needed "in the heat of battle may be qualitatively different than that needed to help a unit psychologically recover from catastrophic losses after the battle ends."[48] Therefore, it is recommended that leaders utilize a leadership style in this phase that favors relational-oriented behaviors over task-oriented behaviors (about 65 percent to 35 percent), so they can address the individual needs of their subordinates. The following comments from a SWAT leader highlight this point: "I don't look at someone as a tool. They are individuals; each one of them is a unique person. For me, it is important to address the needs of the people. You have your 'human being' face on and you ask how they are doing. You need to be perceived as caring and sincere . . . believable. It is one of the duties and traits of a true leader."

As noted by the SWAT leader, it is important for leaders to create an environment that is nonjudgmental and safe for individuals to freely and flexibly cope. Leaders should talk one-on-one with subordinates in order to maintain the positive interpersonal relationships established with subordinates in the preparing for PTEs phase and strengthened in the "responding to PTE" phase. Leaders can educate subordinates about the different coping styles, as well as help them identify the one beneficial to them, and discuss things the leader can do to help them integrate these styles. Of course, some leaders will probably have subordinates who need to integrate a combination of the two coping styles.

Two of the most important ways for leaders to increase coping flexibility in their units is through developing their own self-awareness and modeling coping flexibility for their subordinates. This will be especially important for subordinates who might need to integrate the emotional processing coping style because the stigma against employing such a coping style is quite strong in dangerous contexts professions.[49] It is highly likely that if leaders enable themselves to utilize and demonstrate an emotional processing style, especially when it is not needed, then these leaders will greatly increase the coping flexibility available to their subordinates. Therefore, it may be helpful for leaders to discuss the impact of PTEs upon themselves and how they are flexibly coping with it. Such disclosures can "give permission" to subordinates to employ the full range of coping styles. The leader must also be able to flexibly transition back to forward focus coping in preparation for the next, inevitable PTE.

CONCLUSION

Dangerous contexts professionals will continue to face death given the nature of their work. As a result, they will experience elevated risks for developing PTSD compared to the general population. This does not mean, however, that they will inevitably experience a PTSD trajectory. In fact, strong psychological body armor can put them on a resilience trajectory by helping them cognitively appraise PTEs as challenges and to apply coping flexibility afterward. Leadership is the most important protective component of the body armor, and leaders can integrate specific leadership behaviors that maximize subordinates experiencing a resilience trajectory. In particular, leaders should establish a balance between task-oriented and relational-oriented behaviors in preparation for PTEs, prioritize task-oriented behaviors while responding to PTEs, and prioritize relational-oriented behaviors after the PTEs. Fortunately, for small-unit leaders—and those who train them—these leadership behaviors can be learned and developed.[50]

KEY TAKE-AWAY POINTS

1. Dangerous contexts professionals will continue to face PTEs, which increases their risk of developing PTSD. This elevated risk does not, however, mean that they will inevitably develop PTSD. In fact, most will experience resilience.

2. Leaders should be able to identify the physical, cognitive and emotional, and behavioral symptoms of PTSD in their subordinates and themselves.

3. Two of the critical factors that contribute to the resulting trajectories of psychological health (PTSD versus resilience) are the initial cognitive appraisal of PTEs and the coping flexibility individuals demonstrate afterward.

4. There are certain leadership behaviors that positively affect cognitive appraisal and coping flexibility, and the importance of these leadership behaviors (task- versus relational-oriented) vary based on the phase of PTEs: (1) preparation for PTEs, (2) responding to PTEs, and (3) after the PTEs.

KEY REFERENCES

Lukey, B., and V. Tepe. *Biobehavioral Resilience to Stress*. New York: Taylor and Francis, 2008.

North Atlantic Treaty Organization. "Psychological Support across the Deployment Cycle: A Leader's Guide." 2008. http://ftp.rta.nato.int/public//PubFullText/RTO/EN/RTO-EN-HFM-167///TR-HFM-081-ANN-G.pdf.

NOTES

1. American Psychiatric Association, *Diagnostic and Statistical Manual of Mental Disorders*, 4th ed. (Washington, D.C., 2000).

2. T. deRoon-Cassini et al., "Psychopathology and Resilience Following Traumatic Injury," *Rehabilitation Psychology* 55 (2010): 1–11.

3. J. Gradus et al., "Posttraumatic Stress Disorder and Completed Suicide," *American Journal of Epidemiology* 171 (2010): 721–727; I. Engelhard et al., "A Prospective Study of the Relation between Posttraumatic Stress and Physical Health Symptoms," *International Journal of Clinical and Health Psychology* 9 (2009): 365–372.

4. C. Milliken et al., "Longitudinal Assessment of Mental Health Problems among Active and Reserve Component Soldiers Returning from the Iraq War," *Journal of the American Medical Association* 298 (2007): 2141–2148.

5. B. Bernard and R. Driscoll, "Health Hazard Evaluation of Police Officers and Firefighters after Hurricane Katrina," *Morbidity and Mortality Weekly Report* 55, no. 16 (2006): 456–458.

6. C. Chang et al., "Posttraumatic Distress and Coping Strategies among Rescue Workers after an Earthquake," *Journal of Nervous and Mental Disorders* 191 (2003): 391–398.

7. R. Kessler et al., "Prevalence, Severity, and Comorbidity of 12-month DSM-IV Disorders in the National Comorbidity Survey Replication," *Archives of General Psychiatry* 62 (2005): 617–627; J. Darves-Bornoz et al., "Main Traumatic Events in Europe," *Journal of Traumatic Stress* 21 (2008): 455–462.

8. S. Booth-Kewley et al., "Correlates of Posttraumatic Stress Disorder Symptoms in Marines Back from War," *Journal of Traumatic Stress* 23 (2010): 69–77.

9. N. Pole et al., "Prospective Prediction of Posttraumatic Stress Disorder Symptoms Using Fear Potentiated Auditory Startle Responses," *Biological Psychiatry* 65 (2009): 235–240.

10. Darves-Bornoz et al., "Main Traumatic Events in Europe."

11. Mental Health Advisory Team, *Operation Iraqi Freedom 04: Final Report* (Washington, D.C.: Office of the Surgeon General, U.S. Army, 2006).

12. G. Bonanno et al., "Resilience to Loss and Potential Trauma," *Annual Review of Clinical Psychology* 7 (2011): 511–535.

13. E. Phelps et al., "Extinction Learning in Humans," *Neuron* 43 (2004): 897–905.

14. S. Rauch et al., "Neurocircuitry Models of Posttraumatic Stress Disorder and Extinction," *Biological Psychiatry* 60 (2006): 376–382.

15. P. A. Resick, *Stress and Trauma* (London: Psychology Press, 2001).

16. E. Ozer et al.,"Predictors of Posttraumatic Stress Disorder and Symptoms in Adults: A Meta-analysis,"*Psychological Bulletin* 129 (2003): 52–73.

17. M. Olff et al.,"The Psychobiology of PTSD: Coping with Trauma,"*Psychoneuroendocrinology* 30 (2005): 974–982.

18. V. Florian et al., "Does Hardiness Contribute to Mental Health during a Stressful Real-Life Situation?"*Journal of Personality and Social Psychology* 68 (1995): 687–695.

19. J. Blascovich et al.,"Predicting Athletic Performance from Cardiovascular Indicators of Challenge and Threat,"*Journal of Experimental Social Psychology* 40 (2004): 683–688.

20. Resick, *Stress and Trauma*.

21. C. Aldwin and L. Yancura, "Coping and Health," in *Physical Health Consequences of Exposure to Extreme Stress*, ed. P. P. Schnurr and B. L. Green (Washington D.C.: American Psychological Association, 2004), 99–126.

22. G. Prati et al.,"Coping Strategies and Professional Quality of Life among Emergency Workers,"*Australasian Journal of Disaster* 1 (2009): 1–12.

23. G. Bonanno et al.,"Coping Flexibility and Trauma,"*Psychological Trauma* (in press).

24. deRoon-Cassini et al.,"Psychopathology and Resilience."

25. A. Bandura, *Self-Efficacy: The Exercise of Control* (New York: Freeman, 1997).

26. R. Pietrzak et al., "Psychosocial Buffers of Traumatic Stress, Depressive Symptoms, and Psychosocial Difficulties in Veterans of OEF and OIF," *Journal of Affective Disorders* 120 (2010): 188–192.

27. J. Boscarino, "Post-traumatic Stress and Associated Disorders among Vietnam Veterans,"*Journal of Traumatic Stress* 8 (1995): 317–336.

28. H. Moore and J. Galloway, *We Were Soldiers Once—and Young: La Drang* (New York: Presidio Press Book, 1992), xviii.

29. K. Fisher et al., "The 'Bright' and 'Shadow' Aspects of In Extremis Leadership," *Military Psychology* 22 (2010): S89-S116, S97.

30. P. Bartone, "Resilience under Military Operational Stress," *Military Psychology* 18 (2006): 131–148.

31. S. Stouffer et al., *The American Soldier*, vol. 2 (Princeton, N.J.: Princeton University Press, 1949).

32. Mental Health Advisory Team, *Operation Iraqi Freedom 04*.

33. D. Campbell et al., "Resilience through Leadership," in *Biobehavioral Resilience to Stress*, ed. B. Lukey and V. Tepe (New York: Taylor and Francis, 2008), 57–90.

34. F. Fiedler, *A Theory of Leadership Effectiveness* (McGraw-Hill: Harper and Row Publishers, 1967).

35. D. DeRue et al.,"Trait and Behavioral Theories of Leadership: A Meta-analytic Test of Their Relative Validity,"*Personnel Psychology* 64 (2011): 7–52.

36. F. Yammarino et al., "Leadership and Team Dynamics for Dangerous Military Contexts,"*Military Psychology* 22 (2010): S15–S41, S19.

37. Bandura, *Self-Efficacy*, 141.

38. M. Perrin et al.,"Differences in PTSD Prevalence and Associated Risk Factors among World Trade Center Disaster Rescue and Recovery Workers," *American Journal of Psychiatry* 164 (2007): 1385–1394.

39. P. Sweeney, "Do Soldiers Reevaluate Trust in Their Leaders Prior to Combat Operations?" *Military Psychology* 22 (2010): S70–S88, S83.

40. M. Haglund et al., "Psychobiological Mechanisms of Resilience," *Development and Psychopathology* 19 (2007): 889–920; B. Arnetz et al., "Trauma Resilience Training for Police," *Journal of Police and Criminal Psychology* 24 (2009): 1–9.

41. C. Rogers, *On Becoming a Person* (Boston: Houghton Mifflin, 1995), 37.

42. T. Kolditz, *In Extremis Leadership: Leading As If Your Life Depended On It* (San Francisco: Jossey-Bass, 2007).

43. B. Bass and R. Stogdill, *Bass and Stogdill's Handbook of Leadership: Theory, Research, and Managerial Applications*, 3rd ed. (New York: Free Press, 1990), 684.

44. S. Hannah et al., "Advancing a Research Agenda for Leadership in Dangerous Contexts," *Military Psychology* 22 (2010): S157–S189.

45. Fiedler, *A Theory of Leadership Effectiveness*.

46. Resick, *Stress and Trauma*.

47. C. Monson et al., "Cognitive Processing Therapy for Veterans with Military-Related Posttraumatic Stress Disorder," *Journal of Consulting and Clinical Psychology* 74 (2006): 898–907.

48. Hannah et al., "Advancing a Research Agenda," S168.

49. Mental Health Advisory Team, *Operation Iraqi Freedom 04*.

50. DeRue et al., "Trait and Behavioral Theories of Leadership."

CHAPTER 6

Obedience and Personal Responsibility

George R. Mastroianni, Susann Kimmelman, Joe Doty, and
Joseph J. Thomas

D
angerous contexts are those in which the stakes are high and
where there may be little time to develop or discuss a course
of action. Unquestioning and immediate obedience may be
demanded precisely because deliberating or discussing might
delay responding and thereby increase danger or decrease chances of survival.
In some cases, there may be time for deliberation and discussion, even if there
is pressure to act quickly. Reaching the right conclusions when the chips are
down can be facilitated by having considered in advance one's obligation to
obey an order versus responsibility to oneself, one's values, and others who
may be affected by actions taken. This chapter considers legal constraints on
behavior and scientific evidence that helps frame thinking about the pressures
people may face and how to resist them. Two fictitious scenarios are used to
illustrate the application of these considerations in practice.

> You are a first-line leader responsible for a small detention facility in a
> remote area of a combat zone where detainees are housed for short peri-
> ods of time. The detainees are a mixed group who have been jailed for a
> variety of reasons and consist of a mixture of hard-core insurgents, inno-
> cent civilians, common criminals, and foreign fighters. Detainees are inter-
> rogated by intelligence personnel to determine whether they should be
> released or transferred to a larger facility. Your job is to administer the facil-
> ity, ensuring that the detainees are adequately provided with the necessi-
> ties of life, providing for internal and external security, and coordinating
> and cooperating with the intelligence personnel conducting interrogations
> to provide safe access to inmates as needed.

Your soldiers notice that detainees are returning from interrogations showing signs of physical abuse. The soldiers also report that some of the detainees have told them stories of abusive treatment during the interrogations. You approach your contact among the interrogators, the official to whom detainees are delivered for interrogation, and relay what you have heard. He says, "It's none of your business what goes on in the interrogations. Your job is to provide a safe environment to interrogate the detainees and to keep your mouth shut. The insurgents are trained to lie about their treatment, and by passing on their lies you are only helping the bad guys, who are killing your own soldiers."

For the next few days, you personally escort some of the detainees from interrogations and see firsthand the signs of abuse that the soldiers had reported. You approach your commander to report what you have seen. You tell him that you do not think your unit should be a party to abusive treatment and ask him to clarify with the intelligence authorities what is taking place during the interrogations. He responds that he has "no authority over the intelligence authorities," and even if he did, he would not tell them how to do their job. He adds, "The detainees are the same people who kill and wound our soldiers, and you should reconsider your priorities out here in the combat zone. If you care more about these scumbags than your own comrades, I have no use for you and will send you packing." He says you should "grow up, shut up and get back to work."

You are deeply conflicted about what to do. You do not think it is right to abuse detainees, especially when many of them may be innocent of any wrongdoing. You are pretty sure that the rules prohibit the kind of treatment you suspect the detainees are receiving, though the rules are complicated and this is not your area of specialty. You have also seen the results of insurgent activity and have lost soldiers to insurgent attacks, including a close friend who died the preceding week. You do not want to betray your comrades or dishonor the memory of your friend by being soft on detainees, none of whom seem to care much for you or your people anyway.

You think that you should tell your commander that you are going to report your suspicions up the chain of command despite his instruction to "shut up" and let the chips fall where they may. Your close friends in the unit tell you that you would only be sacrificing your own career and future for a bunch of people who would abuse you far worse if they had the chance. What do you do?

ABU GHRAIB, 2003

The above scenario is fictitious, but contains elements of realities that have played out many times in recent years. One real-world event, the abuses that took place at Abu Ghraib in fall 2003, has some important parallels with the fictitious scenario here. At Abu Ghraib, a military police unit was given the responsibility of administering a large prison outside Baghdad. This reserve unit was poorly trained, poorly equipped, and poorly supplied. Their living conditions and security were abysmal. The prison was overcrowded, leadership was largely absent or ineffective, and the chain of command and responsibility was convoluted.[1]

Into this situation stepped a cast of infamous characters: Specialist Charles Graner would become known as the ringleader of a group of soldiers whose degrading and disgusting treatment of detainees caused worldwide revulsion. Staff Sergeant Ivan Frederick, Specialist Megan Ambuhl, and Private First Class Lynndie England (among others) went along and participated in the abuse. Graner pushed them to cooperate in the abuse by convincing them that they were simply doing what intelligence personnel wanted them to do—"softening up" the detainees for interrogation. One soldier, Specialist Matt Wisdom, walked off the tier when he saw the abuses and immediately reported them to his sergeant. Another, Sergeant Joseph Darby, became aware of the abuses, could not reconcile them with his values and beliefs, and eventually reported them up the chain. Abu Ghraib became a symbol of all the things that were wrong with the Iraq War, a rallying cry for opposition to the war, and most significant, a recruiting tool for insurgents. Abu Ghraib was also only the latest incident in which soldiers accused of misconduct claimed that they were "only following orders."

SETTING THE STAGE: OBEDIENCE AND LEADERSHIP

Dangerous situations are ones in which, by definition, the stakes are high, and are also often situations in which there is not a great deal of time for reflection or discussion. Many assume that military culture requires unquestioning and immediate obedience to orders from above, and that a similar approach would be required in other dangerous situations outside the military. The reality is more complicated: wise leaders consult others as they develop their plans, and incorporate the advice and experience superiors, peers, and subordinates bring to the table.

Plan Inclusively, Discuss Openly and Honestly, Salute Smartly

Some outside military culture are surprised to learn that there is more to military life than simply transmitting orders up and down a chain of command and closely supervising their execution. Orders within the military are based on what is called the commander's intent. It comes from the senior leader and articulates the overall plan and end-state of a military operation. Before orders are issued, they are usually subjected to a great deal of discussion and sometimes quite lively debate. These discussions generally include individuals at various levels in the chain of command. This deliberative and reflective component to decision making is essential to ensure that the valuable experience of everyone is brought to bear on what are often life-or-death decisions.

The context in which this deliberation and reflection occur consists of a clear and formal hierarchy of relationships. As a result, it can be a challenge for military leaders to ensure that their subordinates feel comfortable expressing their views, especially when they differ from a superior's. This is, in principle, no different from what happens in nonmilitary contexts; it is simply more public. One important aspect of military culture is that once a course of action is decided upon, debate and discussion cease, and universal commitment to the successful execution of the plan is expected. It is at this point that the realities of military life most closely match widely held beliefs about it.

It Is Our Duty and Personal Responsibility to Disobey Unlawful Orders

During the execution of military operations, a legal obligation remains for service members to disobey orders under certain circumstances. Specifically, soldiers are required and expected to challenge and disobey unlawful orders and are morally obligated to do so by the terms of their oath. "I was only following orders" is not a valid defense for a military member charged with criminal conduct. This requirement places an immense burden on them. If a service member judges an order to be unlawful and disobeys it, and it is later determined that the order was lawful, he or she may be subject to severe sanctions (including court-martial), especially if the incident takes place under combat conditions. On the other hand, a soldier who obeys an unlawful order and commits a criminal act is subject to the full weight of the law for any offense committed, as if the order had never been given.[2]

Regardless of whether legal consequences ensue from following an unlawful order, soldiers often experience devastating psychological consequences as they confront doubt or guilt about their actions; such feelings sometimes haunt them for the rest of their lives. For example, in March 1968, Varnado Simpson took part in the My Lai massacre. "That day in My Lai, I was personally responsible for killing about 25 people. Personally. Men, women. From shooting them, to cutting their throats, scalping them, to . . . cutting off their hands and cutting out their tongue."[3] Since then, Simpson has suffered "chronic and very severe" emotional and psychological trauma. Although we can discuss these topics in a rational and dispassionate way, the fact is that real people may suffer real consequences as a result of their decisions and actions.

Model and Teach Professional Ethical Codes

These potentially conflicting obligations are perhaps more starkly apparent in military service than in other walks of life, but as John Kleinig argues in *The Ethics of Policing*,[4] the ethical tensions that exist in some professions are no different in principle from those in most people's everyday lives. These tensions often arise as universal moral obligations seemingly come into conflict with certain obligations assumed as professionals. Soldiers, firefighters, police officers, and medical professionals may have particular obligations that differ by the nature of their profession. Soldiers do not often worry about confidentiality issues, for example, while physicians may. Everyone, however, experiences conflicts from time to time and must be guided in their resolution by the requirements of law and the dictates of conscience. Complicating matters, law and conscience may not always coincide. For instance, medical professionals sometimes experience conflicts between professional ethical and personal religious obligations. The resolution of such conflicts depends on the priority individuals give to the competing obligations. In general, professionals agree to abide by the ethical code of their field. This can be problematic if the individual is new to the profession or is unfamiliar with the relevant code of conduct.

Loyalty to the Organization Comes before Loyalty to Peers

The attachments that form between and among those who share life-and-death experiences are emotionally and psychologically powerful, whether such events occur on the battlefield, in an urban back alley, or in a triage tent. These attachments complicate the purely rational processing of events and add a layer of complexity to the ethical decision making prominent in dangerous environments. Indeed, it has been said that soldiers do not fight for their country or for abstract ideals; rather they fight for one another.[5] Soldiers and leaders occupy organizational and social roles, and their inclinations as individuals may not always correspond with their inclinations as commanders or comrades. Exposure to common dangers and hardships binds people in ways that outsiders may not fully appreciate. Moreover, those bonds can become so strong that horizontal allegiances (those within the unit) may overpower or replace vertical allegiances to the overall organization or to superordinate entities, such as the society of which the organization is a part. In law enforcement, the popular term "blue wall of silence" refers to the unwritten rule that police officers protect one another from the consequences of improper or illegal activity. When such behavior occurs, it can corrode public trust and undermine effectiveness.

Commitment to organizational values is further complicated when members are expected to accept values that they may not endorse or may even oppose. There may well be political and ideological differences between most members of an organization and the society it serves. The case has been made by some that this is the situation with today's U.S. military. Duncan Hunter, a former congressional representative from California, has suggested that the military's "don't ask, don't tell" policy should not be repealed because the members of the military are generally conservative and should not have values with which they disagree imposed on them, even if they directly conflict with those of the broader society.[6] It is the leader's job to ensure that subordinates understand their obligations and are ready to live up to them even if they disagree with them or feel conflicting obligations to others around them. Leaders may, therefore, find themselves in the uncomfortable position of seemingly taking sides with "outsiders" against the members of his or her own unit. Leaders must ultimately remain focused on the society they agreed to serve.

The Law

The U.S. military justice system, the Uniform Code of Military Justice, is administered by service members who are all subject to the system and who can be expected to have experienced or to have knowledge of the very dilemmas and conflicts that confront individuals charged with unlawful conduct. Soldiers should thus expect that they will be judged by people who understand and can empathize with the challenges they face and the conditions under which important and morally ambiguous decisions must often be made. Military law comes down squarely on the side of personal accountability when obedience to orders may place a service member in jeopardy of committing criminal conduct. The reality for service members is thus far more complex than the view that simple unquestioning obedience is their only obligation. If only it were so simple.

Organizational Watchdog Agencies

These conflicting obligations similarly afflict police officers, firefighters, and medical personnel, where potential violations will be adjudicated in civil courts. Government entities generally have self-policing and enforcement mechanisms; for example, police departments have internal affairs bureaus that investigate allegations of corruption or misconduct by members. Those that do not have their own internal investigative groups will often rely on the district attorney's office or higher levels of government to perform this function. Inspector general offices have related responsibilities. Judgment is also sometimes sought through the courts. Challenges to the propriety of orders or refusing to follow orders can be decided through the judicial system, and compensation for right and wrong can be awarded through torts in civil courts.

The potential conflict between one's personal responsibility to the law and one's legal responsibility to obey orders is one which most service members will hopefully never experience. If, however, such a conflict arises, it is likely to be because of ambiguous circumstances, perhaps in a gray area with which the member may have no previous experience, often under conditions of extreme stress, fear, and fatigue and with little time to choose between right and wrong. These conditions are essentially those that the unlucky soldier in the opening scenario faced and also those with which the soldiers at Abu Ghraib had to contend.

When it comes to leadership in dangerous situations, the questions with which one must grapple with respect to obedience and personal responsibility are as follows: (1) How can one develop and sustain a leadership climate that encourages soldiers, police officers, and other first responders to think through the difficult moral and ethical challenges they may face? (2) What training and education can be provided to equip them for morally ambiguous situations in combat and elsewhere? (3) What special considerations, if any, do dangerous contexts compel one to consider when thinking about obedience and personal responsibility?

NEW HAVEN, 1961

Forty-two years before Abu Ghraib, in a psychology laboratory at Yale University in New Haven, Connecticut, an interesting scenario played out. Citizens answered an ad in a local newspaper to participate in a psychological experiment in return for a small payment. As instructed, they went to a laboratory at Yale University and were greeted by a scientist (the "experimenter") wearing a white lab coat. He told them that they would be participating in a learning study and that they would be the "teachers." They were introduced to a jolly, portly gentleman who was identified as the "learner." They were then taken to an adjacent room, where the learner was strapped into a chair, with one arm bound to a metal plate; the door was closed behind them. They then returned to the outer room, where they were seated in front of an ominous-looking console labeled "Shock Generator." Rows of toggle switches indicated voltage levels. The highest, labeled 450 volts, was marked "Danger: Severe Shock."

A teacher was instructed to read through a long list of word pairs, which the learner was supposed to memorize. When the teacher re-read the first word in the pair, the learner was supposed to provide the second one. If he failed, the teacher would deliver a shock. Each successive error raised the level of the shock. The "teachers" were actually the only subjects in the study; the "learner" received no shocks, but the teacher did not know this until the experiment was over.

Stanley Milgram, the psychologist who conducted this study, found that about two-thirds of the teachers (in the most well-known version of the study) administered the (supposedly) maximum and dangerously severe 450-volt shock to the learner, despite his (faked) screams, objections, medical complaints, and eventual apparent collapse. Many of the teachers were uncomfortable with what they were doing. They frequently turned to the experimenter for reassurance, often asserting that "they would not accept responsibility" for any harm done to the learner, sometimes requiring such gentle prodding from the experimenter as "The experiment requires that you continue." Nevertheless, under certain combinations of conditions, many of the subjects showed a kind of pathological obedience, obeying instructions they ought to have refused.[7]

From New Haven to the Nazis

The Milgram obedience study, as this experiment came to be known, occurred sixteen years after the end of World War II, at about the time Adolph Eichmann, a Nazi war criminal, was captured and subsequently prosecuted in Israel. Milgram, while reading Hannah Arendt's riveting account of the trial in *Eichmann in Jerusalem*, was struck by Eichmann's sheer ordinariness.[8] Arendt coined the term "banality of evil" to describe the completely unexceptional nature of people who nonetheless commit exceptional acts of what most would consider to be evil. Lieutenant William Calley, found guilty of personally murdering numerous defenseless civilians during the My Lai massacre, was judged by doctors and psychiatrists to be "normal" and capable of distinguishing between right and wrong.[9] The subjects in Milgram's study were also unexceptional people, who he showed were ready to apply dangerous shocks to perfect strangers merely on the say-so of a man in a lab coat. Although the Nazis were seen by many as evil, Milgram raised the possibility that they were really little different from anyone else.

As Milgram studied obedience in the laboratory more extensively and thoroughly, he began to uncover factors that systematically affected it. For example, he found that the closer in physical proximity a "teacher" was to a "learner," the less likely the teacher was to administer intense shocks; it is easier to harm someone from a distance than it is to harm someone nearby because one does not have to witness the victim's suffering. He also found that if the teacher is accompanied by other people who join him or her in resisting the experimenter's instructions to apply shocks, compliance with the orders is much reduced.

Milgram began to see an important, but disturbing implication: evil may not, as had been traditionally thought, be the result of bad individuals, but instead might be the product of bad situations. Any person thrust into such a circumstance might be induced by these forces to commit acts that he or she would otherwise condemn. This perspective turned on its head much of the conventional wisdom about human nature. Milgram's situationist perspective raised the possibility that people's self-described values might not have much to do with their actual behavior—that is, whatever people think about humans as moral beings, their conduct is heavily influenced and affected by external factors and contextual variables. As a result, it is up to individuals to be aware of these factors and resist them.[10]

Other researchers began studying these situational pressures in more detail, especially in the context of obedient behavior that unfolds over longer periods of time than the few hours it took for Milgram's subjects to be influenced. Milgram's systematic studies of obedience, coupled with extensive research by others in the years following the initial publication of the obedience studies, have produced a picture of the processes that can condition people who may think of themselves as compassionate and ethical to behave in ways that others might consider to be reprehensible. Researchers have identified such mechanisms as authorization, routinization, dehumanization, moral disengagement, bracketed morality, and transfer of responsibility to help explain how situational pressures can affect behavior toward others.[11]

Authorization is the perception that a particular behavior has been sanctioned or approved by a higher authority. At Abu Ghraib, for example, some of the soldiers who carried out the abuses reported that Graner had told them that he was acting on the instructions of military intelligence officials, who wanted him to "soften up"detainees for interrogation. Some of them had concerns and reservations about the abuses they were committing, but apparently convinced themselves that their behavior was acceptable because it had been authorized by higher-ups. Some careful thinking might have saved these soldiers a great deal of trouble.

Routinization occurs when people are gradually acculturated to commit abuses against others. For example, a soldier might arrive in a combat zone never having heard Middle Easterners referred to by any of the variety of pejorative terms soldiers sometimes use to refer to indigenous peoples in that part of the world. He or she may resist the use of such terms at first, but then hear them used so often that he or she may begin to use them as well. Increasingly routine behaviors can also escalate into abuse, often without conscious awareness of such a dramatic shift. Colonel H. R. McMaster, as commander of the 3rd Armored Cavalry Regiment in Iraq, prohibited his soldiers from using pejorative terms to refer to Iraqis in order to counter these kinds of effects.[12]

An important element in the process of acculturating someone to abuse others is dehumanization. Most people feel certain obligations toward other humans simply by virtue of their being human: people deserve respect and dignity and to be treated according to a set of more or less universal standards of respect. This commitment to respecting others must be overcome if abuse

FIGURE 6.1 A propaganda poster from World War I depicting German soldiers as inhuman, green-eyed monsters. Credit: F. Strothmann.

is to take place, and one way to do that is to categorize people as being something other than human. War propaganda throughout history has purposely dehumanized the enemy to facilitate their killing by armies composed of soldiers who may have little inclination to kill otherwise.[13]

Law enforcement personnel are not immune from these tendencies; referring to suspects as "perps" (perpetrators) and to the "perp walk" can have a dehumanizing effect, implying that perps are somehow different from the rest of us, and perhaps therefore making it easier to slip into disrespectful or even abusive behavior toward them. Prejudice is a preconceived evaluation, a judgment made without evidence. Such judgments are often applied to group members based solely on a perceived group identity, not on an assessment of the individual as an individual. Group prejudice is by its nature a categorical phenomenon, and anything that blinds one to individual characteristics and instead emphasizes group identity has the potential to lead to prejudice. Emergency medical personnel may sometimes use terms, such as "gomer" (Get Out Of My Emergency Room), to disparagingly refer to patients who they feel should not be receiving treatment or other terms that deflect attention away from the individual's particular needs and circumstances.

Albert Bandura theorized that individuals may slide into "wrong" or inappropriate behavior as a result of moral disengagement, which can be a by-product of physical, mental, or emotional exhaustion.[14] Moral disengagement may be related to the occurrence of so-called repressive coping, in which autonomic and emotional responses to stressful situations diverge.[15] When people are under a great deal of stress, their emotional response may shut down, making it harder for them to formulate good decisions, especially when their feelings or those of others are an important element of the decision-making process, as seems to be the case in ethical decision making.

"Bracketed morality" is a term that derives from an old military cliché: "What goes on TDY, stays on TDY" (temporary duty away from home). Some members of the military believe that they can (and should) act one way while at home station and act another way in a combat zone. This kind of compartmentalization is facilitated by dramatic differences in contextual cues that exist in different settings. These cues can be physical and environmental or social and organizational. Maintaining moral continuity with what was referred to during the Vietnam War as "the World" can be challenging.

The Milgram obedience study has had an immeasurable impact on the way researchers think about obedience. It was dramatic, and the results were shocking. Milgram's study was also important because its application of rigorous experimental methods to a problem that had previously been addressed mainly as a philosophical or ethical question powerfully influenced subsequent thinking about the behavior examined. The situationist perspective, perhaps best represented by this study, emphasizes the role of contextual factors in shaping behavior in ethically charged situations. This is not, however, the only theoretical framework through which one can consider these important issues.

PALO ALTO, 1971

Another example of the situationist perspective is the Stanford prison study. While this perspective adds little or nothing conceptually to Milgram's more rigorous and nuanced analysis, it is important to discuss because so much has been made of it in trying to explain the real-world abuses at Abu Ghraib (that resemble the opening scenario). The Stanford study, conducted by Phillip Zimbardo, was designed to demonstrate Zimbardo's view of what happens when people are given power but are not constrained in their exercise of it. Would people remain faithful to their values or would they succumb to the same kinds of behavior observed in the Milgram study, in which ordinary people quite readily acted to harm perfect strangers? Are there situations—as opposed to people—that can compel individuals, or at the very least tempt them, to behave badly? If so, what factors make them more likely to "obey"the dictates of the situation? What factors will help them resist those dictates?[16]

The Stanford prison study was ostensibly designed to simulate prison conditions. A group of college students were enrolled in the study and then randomly assigned to be either guards or prisoners. Those selected to be prisoners were picked up and brought to a simulated jail in the basement of the Stanford University psychology department building by Palo Alto police officers. Those assigned as guards were given free rein by the "warden," Professor Zimbardo.

The study was supposed to last weeks, but it was prematurely terminated after only a few days because the behavior of some of the participants quickly degenerated. Some of the guards became abusive, some of the prisoners became submissive, and the warden could not effectively exert influence to improve the situation; in fact, he may have perhaps exacerbated it. Some of the abuses devised by the guards included putting pillowcases over the heads of prisoners who were forced to wear hospital johnny coats, creating a visual effect that would bear a striking resemblance to some of the photos from Abu Ghraib. Zimbardo interpreted the results as showing that unrestrained authority inevitably leads to abuse and violence. For Zimbardo, evil does not arise because of bad individuals—a few "bad apples" in the much-abused metaphor but rather, evil arises because of "bad barrels."

In Zimbardo's view, it is the situation—prison and war are two such situations he identifies as "bad barrels"—that produces bad behavior, not the individuals. According to him, "The barrel corrupts anything it touches." This is the extreme situationist view, which denies any or much of a role for free will and sees behavior as largely determined by external forces.[17]

Unlike the Milgram obedience studies, which were carefully conducted experiments, the Stanford prison study was little more than a dramatic demonstration orchestrated by Zimbardo to illustrate his viewpoint on authority. Despite its lack of scientific rigor, the study has been relentlessly promoted and is well known to anyone who has taken an introductory psychology class. Zimbardo quickly seized on the superficial similarity between the Abu Ghraib photos and the photos from his study to claim that events at Abu Ghraib were an example of the kind of behavior he had observed. He offered an analysis intended to exculpate the soldiers who had committed the abuses and instead focused responsibility on high-level generals and government officials for having created the environment that led to the abuses. Zimbardo testified for the defense in the trial of Staff Sergeant Ivan Frederick, one of the soldiers accused of committing abuses, arguing that "the Army should be on trial," not Frederick. Ultimately, Frederick and others with a direct role in the criminal events at Abu Ghraib were convicted of crimes, while several higher-ranking officers (in one case, a brigadier general) were fined, reduced in rank, or subjected to career-ending administrative discipline. The excuse of "simply following orders" rang as hollow in the wake of Abu Ghraib as it had at Nuremberg.

BEYOND SITUATIONS

The Milgram and Zimbardo studies are often raised in discussions of real or suspected pathological obedience, where people obey instructions that others (and often the people involved, upon reflection) think should have been disobeyed. Mechanisms such as authorization, routinization, dehumanization, disqualification, moral disengagement, and bracketed morality can predispose soldiers in a unit toward pathological obedience or simply toward ethical lapses if they are present. Leaders must be aware of the situational pressures identified by Milgram and others in his tradition and must ensure that such conditions do not occur in their units.

Most people do not accept the idea that human behavior is primarily determined externally, by the situations encountered. Most think that thoughts, beliefs, and values guide individuals' actions. Those thoughts, beliefs, and values are a joint product of biological, psychological, and cultural and social factors. People have a lifetime to refine these thoughts and values, to develop cognitive schemas or internal scripts governing various situations and challenges. These internal, largely cognitive structures must still be translated into action, into behavior, at the moment of decision. Insofar as leaders need to help shape the internal discussion that soldiers have with themselves when confronted with difficult choices, they must understand and engage soldiers in a meaningful dialogue on these complicated issues, so that they have a set of internal structures that are likely to yield the "right" answer when queried. The leader must engage subordinates at the level of character; he or she must help others develop and refine their moral compass.

Leaders must also help ensure that appropriate impulses are the ones that get translated into action at the moment of decision. One way to think about this is to remember that situational factors are especially good at getting people to act "out of character," especially in unusual situations that they have not had time to reflect on or integrate into their cognitive schemas. Milgram's subjects were deeply conflicted even as they pressed the buttons to shock the learner. Staff Sergeant Frederick, reflecting on his actions at Abu Ghraib, thought that he "should have been stronger" and resisted Graner more effectively. Leaders must engage subordinates in the context of the situation, making them aware of the situational factors that can temporarily throw the needle of their moral compass out of whack.

DEVELOPING AND SUSTAINING THE RIGHT LEADERSHIP CLIMATE

Leaders at all levels have a responsibility to develop and build character in their subordinates. "Character" is a term that means different things to different people. Some consider it to be nothing more than a pattern of relatively consistent behavior across situations; for others, it represents a set of internal, mental, or cognitive attributes that we use to guide behavior. Whatever it "really" is, most think we know what it is when we see it, and we know that sometimes we do, or see others do, things that are "out of character." Whatever one thinks about "character," there are actions that leaders can take that will help members of an organization develop their own moral compass and follow the needle no matter what.

Education on Standards of Conduct

Leaders are not required to decide independently what behavior is good and what is bad. Military services, police and fire departments, and most other organizations have generally spent a great deal of effort spelling out in detail which behaviors are permitted, and which are not. Ensuring that subordinates are aware of the rules is the first step. In the military, there are requirements for periodic training on such topics as the Code of Conduct and the Law of Armed Conflict that offers opportunities to reinforce the normative foundation for correct behavior. The Law Enforcement Code of Ethics and the Hippocratic Oath spell out basic ethical standards in the fields of law enforcement and medicine, respectively.[18]

Be a Role Model and a Coach

If a particular eventuality can be anticipated and a correct response prescribed, then a leader needs simply to ensure that subordinates are aware of that response. Because organizations cannot anticipate every eventuality, however, they usually articulate general principles to govern conduct in novel or unique instances. The leader's role then becomes more challenging, as he or she must help the subordinate learn to apply these rules correctly to new sets of circumstances. Leaders are most effective at this when they function first as exemplars or role models, actually demonstrating the desired behaviors. Next they must encourage that type of behavior in subordinates by guiding them as mentors or coaches rather than as instructors passing on factual knowledge.

Train and Educate for Moral Ambiguity

As coaches, leaders can use so-called dilemma training to pose challenging scenarios that do not have a "school solution." By analyzing and evaluating the reasoning process applied by subordinates, leaders can help them hone their skills at recognizing the relevant features of scenarios and applying the principles correctly. Leaders can coach subordinates through different "lenses" (rules, outcomes, and values) in analyzing dilemmas. Many leaders are familiar with the concept of recognition-primed decision making.[19] Good decision making hinges on correctly perceiving a situation, because errors often take the form of doing the right thing at the wrong time—that is, thinking that one is in situation A, and applying response A, when one is really in situation B. The phrase "fog of war" captures this kind of confusion. Dilemma training can be an effective way to train people to look for and recognize the relevant features of situations, ignore distracting features that do not contribute to determining a correct solution, and respond quickly and correctly.

Character Development Requires Investment

Leaders must avoid a checklist or rote memory technique for developing character. Having people simply memorize and recite the seven Army Values or quizzing them on the Law Enforcement Code of Ethics or the Hippocratic

Oath is not an effective method of developing character.[20] This technique may even be counterproductive if the leader and the subordinate think they really are accomplishing something. Leaders must approach character development in a holistic manner with an understanding that a person's character is constantly being molded and shaped.

CHALLENGING ASPECTS OF DANGEROUS SITUATIONS

There are classes of people and situations to which the unusual conditions found in the Milgram studies are especially relevant. Military personnel are indeed people who may be exposed to situations not unlike the Milgram study. Abu Ghraib did contain some (though not all) of the elements of the Milgram situation. The night shift was isolated from the outside world, and the abuses asked of the soldiers were heinous and inhuman, but not fatal: detainees were not regularly subjected to extreme physical torture or killed. Graner served in the role of the experimenter, egging on the others, but even he had to invoke the unfamiliar authority of the military intelligence authorities to clinch the deal with some of the soldiers. Several of the soldiers involved referred to the social pressures to which they reluctantly succumbed.

In fact, the Milgram and Zimbardo studies both occurred in settings where the application of punishing stimuli to strangers was contextually reasonable: a prison in the one case, and a psychology lab, mysterious to the lay public, in the other. Military and policing settings also include these elements. They also are unusual in that they are generally isolated from others, and it is quite possible for a person to encounter someone he or she may not know but who nevertheless clearly has authority over that person by virtue of superior rank. These contextual variables are among those that may heighten the risk that someone will act out of character. When warning bells start to go off that perhaps one is starting down a bad path, run through a mental checklist and consult with others to see if the situation is one like Milgram has shown can degrade judgment.

There are also additional elements of potentially dangerous situations that go beyond those seen in the Milgram study to potentially degrade judgment still further. These include personal and environmental stressors and the nature of the individuals with whom one is likely to come into contact. Milgram's subjects were stressed by the study itself and the conflicts they experienced, but were otherwise not subjected to external stressors. Soldiers, firefighters, emergency medical personnel, and police officers may, on the other hand, be subjected to a wide range of intense stressors that often result in moral disengagement. These include the threat of injury or death, fatigue, sleep deprivation, lack of sanitation, exposure to temperature extremes, hunger or thirst, and many others. Research has shown that many of these stressors can impair specific kinds of cognitive performance, making it still more difficult for people to respond appropriately in difficult or confusing situations.

The teachers in the Milgram study had no reason to harbor any animosity against the learner; in fact, the learner was a particularly pleasant-seeming man. Soldiers and police officers are often dealing with people who actually want to harm them and who are far from the morally neutral actors the subjects of these psychological studies encountered. For this reason, soldiers and police officers may again be still more susceptible to the effects of Milgram-like conditions than were Milgram's subjects.

Just Fix the Problems

The following scenario is based on the kinds of events that occur daily in an American big-city police department. When improper or unethical behavior occurs, or is suspected or alleged, attention quickly turns to the question of responsibility: Who is to blame? In this scenario, consider the following questions: (1) Did the special operations lieutenant do anything wrong? (2) How would you evaluate the effectiveness of the leadership of the precinct commander, special operations lieutenant, and the sergeant in charge of the field training officers? (3) If you were the chief of this police department, what feedback would you give your subordinates about this series of events?

> A local precinct commander returned from a community council meeting that was well attended by influential people in the neighborhood. The commanding officer was asked to address a developing pattern of robberies as well as conditions at a local park where day laborers had begun gathering, consuming alcohol, urinating in public, and fighting with each other.
>
> The precinct commander calls in the special operations lieutenant, who is charged with handling anything in a precinct that is not addressed by patrol radio assignments. The precinct commander relays the events of the community council meeting and directs the special operations lieutenant to "fix the problems."
>
> The special operations lieutenant changes the tours of the anti-crime team (plain clothes officers) to the hours in which the robberies are occurring and moves the field training foot posts to cover pedestrian traffic routes. The anti-crime team and the foot posts are given the directive to increase Stop, Question and Frisk reports (stopping and questioning, as well as patting down individuals suspected of committing the robberies) and to increase the number of summonses issued for violations of the law.

The special operations lieutenant works with the anti-crime teams for one day and also checks the foot posts to ensure that everyone knows what is expected of them.

A newly promoted sergeant and a second group of field training officers are given the task of policing the two parks within the precinct. On three separate occasions within a week, the sergeant and officers enter the park where the day laborers are hanging around and conduct sweeps. All persons committing an infraction, violation, misdemeanor, or crime are summonsed or arrested. On the last two days of the week, the sergeant and the group of officers go to the second park in the precinct. There, they find high school–age children of local residents drinking alcohol, urinating in public, and smoking marijuana. The sergeant orders the officers to conduct the same sweeps as those done in the first park. The sergeant regularly reports to the special operations lieutenant with updates on the units' progress.

The special operations lieutenant contacts the precinct commander halfway through the effort to inform him of the steps taken and the progress made. The precinct commander says he really has no time to go over all the details; it is the special operations lieutenant's call, backed by the precinct commander's support.

At the next community council meeting, the same persons are in attendance. Although the robberies have stopped and arrests have been made, the attendees are upset with the commanding officer. The residents complain about being stopped, questioned, and frisked by officers, because they do not believe they look suspicious or fit the description of the persons who had committed the robberies. They are also upset because they travel the same routes daily, and the police still frisk them and issue them additional summonses. Even more infuriated are the parents of the teenagers in the park. They only wanted enforcement to be conducted against those whom they believed were from outside of their neighborhood. The residents also made phone calls to the mayor's office, resulting in calls to the police commissioner's office. The police commissioner's office then called the local precinct commander to determine what enforcement activity had been conducted and its purpose.

The precinct commander calls in the special operations lieutenant and berates him for the "terrible job" he had done in the precinct. He lets the lieutenant know in no uncertain terms that he thinks he had been overzealous in his planning, ineffective in his supervision, and directly responsible for a major flap between the police department and neighborhood leaders, with whom he had been trying to cultivate better relationships for years. The commander orders the lieutenant to attend the next community council meeting and personally apologize to the community leaders. He also says that he intends to make sure that the lieutenant's poor job performance is documented in his record.

Conflicts between obedience and personal responsibility to others, as in this scenario, can be difficult. The scenario also posits a conflict between obedience and responsibility to oneself as well as to an organization, which is even more trying. People who lead in dangerous environments are often quite comfortable with the idea of selfless service; self-sacrifice comes with the territory. For this reason, there may be a tendency for people like the special operations lieutenant to bite the bullet and take one for the team. Is this necessarily what is best?

The organizational climate in the scenario is extremely unhealthy. There are several features of the organization and its leadership that if unchanged could seemingly lead to serious ethical troubles. To begin with, the precinct commander failed to give the special operations lieutenant specific guidance. There is always a balance to be struck between micromanaging a subordinate and failing to manage a subordinate, but leaders need to make sure that the subordinate understands his or her intent and is aware of any boundaries or restrictions on execution that he or she has in mind. Furthermore, if there are any potential pitfalls or particular ways the effort could turn out badly, the leader should make the subordinate aware of them.

The precinct commander also failed to monitor execution adequately. When the special operations lieutenant reported to the commander after initiating the intervention, he received a lukewarm response and no face-to-face supervision. While leaders are always busy, there is no substitute for personal, hands-on involvement in day-to-day operations to ensure that policies and procedures are being followed, that subordinates understand what is expected of them, and that subordinates have the resources they need to succeed. Moreover, those actually doing the job are a rich source of insight about the approach being taken and potential improvements. By failing to engage subordinates in this way, the precinct commander may have inadvertently communicated that (a) the job did not matter to him all that much and (b) the particular approach taken was not that important.

The precinct commander also failed to show a level of integrity and professionalism commensurate with his position. The ultimate responsibility for the success or failure of the intervention must lie with the commander. By responding to the lieutenant's update by saying that he had his support, the precinct commander clearly implied that the responsibility for whatever happened lay at the top. When things went badly, however, the commander placed the blame on the lieutenant. The consequences of this unwillingness to accept the responsibility that comes with authority are likely to include resentment, anger, and reduced creativity and risk-taking on the part of the lieutenant in the future.

The special operations lieutenant was caught in the middle in this scenario; he was required to obey the precinct commander, but also had a responsibility to himself, others working on the intervention, and the organization to try to ensure that a good outcome for the department and the community would result. So who is personally responsible for the failure that occurred here?

In the military, the commander is responsible for everything that happens or fails to happen in his or her organization. Period. Regarding the scenario, the simple answer is that the precinct commander bears the primary responsibility for the failure, but if one assumes that this was not an isolated incident, and instead represents a pattern of performance that had developed over some time, one can begin to consider the role of organizational climate itself in promoting or inhibiting effective performance.

A healthy organizational climate is one in which members are aware of and committed to a common, clearly articulated set of values; leaders set the example by demonstrating personal behaviors consistent with those values; members are willing and able to communicate questions and concerns to others in the organization; and leaders are open and responsive to concerns raised by members. In the scenario above, the sergeants and the special operations lieutenant have a responsibility to refuse to accept blame they do not think they deserve; to do otherwise does nothing to improve the organization and reduce the likelihood of similar occurrences in the future. Their responsibility to the organization requires them to confront their immediate superior, and if this does not lead to a satisfactory result, to pursue the matter further, however uncomfortable or self-serving it may seem. Disobedience is easier to justify when one's actions stand to benefit someone else; by disobeying in these cases, the person takes the moral high ground. When disobedience—or something short of disobedience that questions and challenges the orders one is given—in hopes of changing them—might be perceived as benefiting oneself, the person may be more reluctant to act. It is often in just such cases that the organization loses out, however—when individual interests trump organizational obligations.

OBEDIENCE AND PERSONAL RESPONSIBILITY: LEADERSHIP DEVELOPMENT IMPLICATIONS

Should one work to make subordinates more obedient or more responsible? Which is more important? One answer might be that both are important and that the job is to properly balance these two things. It is argued here, however, that given the choice between a subordinate who is always responsible and one who is always obedient, one should always choose the more responsible person. Why? Because a subordinate who is properly responsible may sometimes be obedient and sometimes be disobedient, but will always be acting in the best interests of all concerned. A subordinate who is always obedient may or may not be acting for the common good.

Focusing on leader and leadership development should result in the cultivation of a sense of responsibility. If it is successful in building an appropriate sense of personal responsibility, there will be little else required in terms of fostering obedience. How does one build personal responsibility? By using the same principles that parents might use to build personal responsibility in their children. One can adapt and extend the same set of tools and techniques that parents use to develop good citizens of the world to develop good citizens of an organization. In the role of leadership developer, one must do the following:

1. *Show subordinates and developing leaders that they are genuinely cared for.*
   Trust and commitment are at the heart of responsibility. They cannot be purchased or acquired through mere exhortation. Trust and commitment arise when a relationship of mutual respect deepens during the course of repeated interactions in which each party treats the other fairly, compassionately, and consistently. Trust is a tenuous construct in any relationship; it develops slowly, but can be lost in a moment.

2. *Articulate and model a consistent set of values.*
   Values are where accountability begins. One must be accountable to a set of standards; values are the basis of those standards and must be clearly articulated. Values are subject to discussion, even adjustment, refinement, or replacement, but are not negotiable. All members of an organization must accept the values of the group; the organization must ensure that values are clear and understood and that policies are consistent with those values, in reality as in rhetoric.

3. *Provide developmental opportunities to succeed.*
   Learning takes place when actions are followed by consequences. When actions are followed by positive consequences, individuals recognize the effectiveness of their actions and are more likely to repeat them in the future. Leaders (and followers) learn best by doing, and the best way to learn to be responsible is to act responsibly and experience the positive feedback.

4. *Provide opportunities to fail.*
   Children who are not challenged enough in school—who are routinely successful at their work—may perform well but may also lack the capacity to stick with it when confronted with a problem they cannot immediately solve. Children who are challenged too much—who always confront difficult problems but rarely succeed—may develop learned helplessness; they may then stop trying. The best learning occurs when people are confronted not only with achievable problems, but also challenging ones that sometimes lead to failure. Failure, if it occurs in a supportive environment, is an effective driver of growth. Freedom to fail is more than a slogan; it is an essential characteristic of a healthy environment.

5. *Set and enforce high standards and apply them transparently and universally.*
   Nothing is more inimical to the development of a sense of responsibility among members of an organization than a perceived mismatch between what is said and what is done. People are exquisitely sensitive to issues of equity, and their willingness to hold themselves personally responsible for their behavior will not survive the perception that others fail to hold themselves to the same standards and yet escape the consequences of their behavior.

6. *Teach leaders to connect character to every action.*
   As has been discussed, circumstances sometimes make it difficult for people to behave as they ordinarily would. Leader developers must help subordinate leaders recognize circumstances that are likely to cause them to act out of character and to resist situational pressures that might lead them to behave in ways they might later regret.

KEY TAKE-AWAY POINTS

1. It is possible to be obedient but irresponsible. Being responsible sometimes means one must be disobedient. The starkest example of this is obeying an illegal order. Being responsible means saying, "I will not do that" to an illegal order.

2. The law is on a person's side when he or she disobeys illegal orders. It may or may not be when disobedience stems from judging orders to be *immoral,* insofar as that judgment goes beyond or even contradicts the legal obligations of respective ethical codes.

3. People have character, and character influences behavior over the long term. "Be more concerned with your character than your reputation. Character is what you really are. Reputation is what people say you are."[21]

4. Situations can also influence behavior in the short run. Being able to think about and reflect on contextual variables affecting oneself are skills (self-awareness and self-regulation) that can be taught and practiced.

5. In dangerous contexts, people are more likely to encounter situational pressures that might influence behavior than they are in more benign environments. This point highlights the need to develop and practice the ability to be self-aware and self-regulate in more benign environments so these skills are practiced automatically in dangerous environments.

6. Character can be developed and supported with the right kind of leadership, mentoring, and coaching. The development must be intentional, planned, practiced, and modeled.

7. Situations can be monitored and controlled to minimize negative influences. (See points three and four.)

8. Personal responsibility cannot flourish in an organization that fails to make consistent demands on all its members. Consistency builds trust, and trust is the basis of commitment.

9. When all is said and done, with all the research and theories about how and why people behave the way they do, the bottom line is that the individual is ultimately responsible for his or her behavior. We can blame Mom, Dad, the weather, the dog, my boss, the cat, my best buddy, the situation, etc., but at the end of the day "the Devil did not make you do it." You did it yourself.

NOTES

1. Taguba Report, Article 15-6 Investigation of the 800th Military Police Brigade, http://news.findlaw.com/hdocs/docs/iraq/tagubarpt.html.

2. Uniform Code of Military Justice, http://www.law.cornell.edu/uscode/10/stApIIch47.html.

3. M. Bilton and K. Sim, *Four Hours in My Lai* (New York: Penguin Group, 1992), 7.

4. J. Kleinig, *The Ethics of Policing* (Cambridge: Cambridge University Press, 1996), 52.

5. S. A. Stouffer et al., *The American Soldier: Combat and Its Aftermath* (Princeton, N.J.: Princeton University Press, 1949).

6. See "Updated: CNN Expunged 'Don't Ask, Don't Tell" Question and Answers in Rebroadcasts of Debate—without Disclosure," MediaMatters for America, http://mediamatters.org/research/200711290011.

7. S. Milgram, "Behavioral Study of Obedience," *Journal of Abnormal and Social Psychology* 67 (1963): 371–378; see also S. Milgram, *Obedience to Authority: An Experimental View* (New York: Harper Colophon Books, 1974).

8. H. Arendt, *Eichmann in Jerusalem* (New York: Viking Press, 1963).

9. Bilton and Sim, *Four Hours in My Lai.*

10. H. C. Kelman and V. L. Hamilton, *Crimes of Obedience: Toward a Social Psychology of Authority and Responsibility* (New York: Yale University Press, 1989); see also L. Ross and R. E. Nisbett, *The Person and the Situation: Perspectives of Social Psychology* (New York: McGraw-Hill, 1991).

11. Kelman and Hamilton, *Crimes of Obedience;* see also A. Bandura, "Moral Disengagement in the Perpetration of Inhumanities," *Personality and Social Psychology Review* 3 (1999): 193–209.

12. H. R. McMaster, personal communication, September 6, 2009.

13. See for example E. Staub, *The Roots of Evil: The Origins of Genocide and Other Group Violence* (Cambridge: Cambridge University Press, 1989).

14. Bandura, *Moral Disengagement.*

15. M. Westphal, G. A. Bonnano, and P. T. Bartone, "Resilience and Personality," in *Biobehavioral Resilience to Stress,* ed. B. J. Lukey and V. Tepe (Boca Raton, Fla.: CRC Press, 2008), 219–257.

16. C. Haney, W. C. Banks, and P. G. Zimbardo, "Interpersonal Dynamics in a Simulated Prison," *International Journal of Criminology and Penology* 1 (1973): 69–97.

17. P. G. Zimbardo, *The Lucifer Effect: Understanding How Good People Turn Evil* (New York: Random House, 2007).

18. The Uniform Code of Military Justice; the Hippocratic Oath, http://www.members.tripod.com/nktiuro/hippocra.htm.

19. G. A. Klein, *Sources of Power: How People Make Decisions* (Cambridge, Mass.: MIT Press, 1998).

20. Army Values, http://www.history.army.mil/lc/the%20mission/the_seven_army_values.htm.

21. J. Wooden and S. Jamison, *Wooden: A Lifetime of Observations and Reflections On and Off the Court* (Lincolnwood, Ill.: Contemporary Books, 1997), 28.

CHAPTER 7

Ethics in Dangerous Situations

C. Anthony Pfaff, Ted Reich, Walter Redman, and Michael Hurley

To protect soldiers repairing a vehicle on a road, a platoon leader in Iraq provided protection for them by positioning two manned vehicles along possible routes that other vehicles, potentially laden with explosives, could use. In doing so, he decided not to follow the platoon's standard operating procedure (SOP), which called for controlling traffic along the road by separating nonthreatening Iraqi vehicles from suspicious ones. He believed that he was being "paid to exercise judgment," so he broke from routine. Because he knew the enemy had used snipers against soldiers on this road in the past, he calculated that the risk of them doing so again far outweighed the potential of firing on nonthreatening Iraqi vehicles because of a failure to control the traffic.[1]

Soon after getting their vehicles in position, the soldiers saw a sedan speeding toward their position. As it got closer, the platoon leader ordered one of his soldiers to fire a warning shot, after which the sedan sped up. Thinking they were in imminent danger, the soldiers trained their fire on the sedan and braced for an explosion. The sedan skidded to a stop less than five meters from the soldiers, and they soon discovered that they had killed an elderly man with thick glasses and hearing aids in both ears. When the battalion executive officer reviewed the platoon's actions, he agreed with the lieutenant's decision to deviate from routine and not put soldiers on the road, affirmed that the soldiers "did the right thing," and called the killing of the elderly man a "terrible tragedy of war."[2]

ACCOMPLISHING MISSIONS WHILE MINIMIZING HARM

For the most part, the reason soldiers, police, and other crisis responders operate in dangerous situations is to make those situations safer
or to neutralize the danger altogether. Soldiers fight enemies, police
combat crime, and emergency workers rescue the distressed. Doing
so ethically requires them to balance the competing demands of accomplishing their mission, preserving lives, and minimizing harm to others and preserving personal safety. These competing needs can be categorized by levels
of risk: risk to mission, risk to others, and risk to self. Most societies create
and empower certain professional organizations—in particular, the military,
law enforcement, and emergency response outfits—to take risks, and in some
cases, even do harm in the name of protecting or restoring peace or order.
In doing so, they bestow a unique level of responsibility on the members of
these professions to manage the harm done in the course of their professional
duties. This dispensation is not afforded citizens at large.

In the military professions, whose purpose it is to fight and win wars,
members consciously accept the ultimate personal risk—death in battle—
along with the weighty responsibility of doing the ultimate harm—killing
others—if necessary to achieve victory. Law enforcement officers may face
death or injury in apprehending those who disrupt domestic peace by breaking the law, and they may use force, even lethal force under certain conditions, in trying to make an arrest.[3] Unlike soldiers, however, law enforcement
officers are not typically permitted to risk harm to bystanders while carrying
out their duties.[4]

The obligation to prevent harm significantly affects law-enforcement
operations. For example, when New York City police responded to a call
regarding a disturbed person at a homeless shelter, the suspect confronted an
officer with a knife. The officer tried to convince the man to drop the weapon,
and while talking to him, inched closer to get into a position to disarm the
man. Suddenly, the man lunged forward, stabbing the officer in the chest. The
officer fatally shot the disturbed man before dying himself.

This example, together with that of the platoon leader, illustrates the difference between military and law enforcement approaches to ethics in dangerous situations. In both cases, neither the soldiers nor the police were in
immediate danger, but both perceived differently the risks to themselves and
the corresponding permissibility of risks to others. In common, however, are
the respective decisions they made that affected to varying degrees the lives
and well-being of others, making this integral part of their professional duties
ethical decisions.[5]

To ensure that members act ethically in dangerous situations, their professions must educate and inspire them in understanding their codes of ethics and committing to upholding them. Doing the right thing in dangerous situations is more than simply following rules; it also requires sound judgment in order to understand and balance the competing risks involved. Such judgment stems from character, which is best developed through institutions and programs created and maintained by the professions. Strong character is a tremendous tonic in the face of the chaotic danger that these professionals often face, and it fosters resiliency in the face of the tension that comes from balancing competing ethical demands. (See Chapter 9 for a discussion on character traits of leaders who earn trust.) An understanding of the character required for professional emergency responders, soldiers, and police begins with an understanding of the common ethical principles each of their professions shares.

SETTING THE TERMS

The professional organizations that recruit, train, and deploy soldiers, police, and emergency responders, though their operating environments are often dramatically different, may all be called defenders, or in domestic situations, protectors of the peace because of the charters they are given by the institutions that empower them with these responsibilities. Since they willingly serve in these professions and accept their principles by virtue of oath and long-term membership, they are crisis professionals.

Respect as the Common Foundation

Concepts like necessary force, proportionality, human rights, and immunity from harm underpin the basic principles at play in moral arguments and subsequent judgments about crisis professionals' actions in dangerous situations. These concepts inform the principle of respect for basic human rights and the humanity of others (including potential and actual adversaries) that is foundational to the professional ethics of crisis professionals that guide them in their daily duties. Although the context of dangerous situations will vary, the common moral grounding for all of them is the basic respect for human rights that all of them engender. When crisis professionals are forced to make tough decisions about balancing risks, and those decisions result in harm, it is hoped that they can find strength in the power of these imperatives anchored in the moral worth of humanity.

Dangerous Situations Defined

Dangerous situations are essentially those that involve threats to the peace that are tantamount to actual or potential violations of rights. Their degree defines their meaning and prompts a contemplation of force as a response. At the international level, external threats are commonly referred to as acts of aggression, whereby nations or entities threaten the collective rights of others by actual or implied military force against an adversary's territory, people, or resources.[6] Domestic or internal threats occur when the aggression is personal rather than collective, with a personal rights violation at the heart of the wrong.[7] Here, the rights of individual persons are intentionally violated, often through personal coercion, for varying selfish motives, resulting in crime or the disruption of the common civic peace, which demands that police intervene, apprehend the suspected criminals, and restore a state of safety.

Though crimes might be isolated events, their frequent occurrence can create an uneasiness in a community that if left unaddressed could lead to reduced confidence in the rule of law and, over time, to increasing lawlessness. A central principle of law enforcement is that all citizens in a society bound by the rule of law are entitled to a peaceful existence, and most law enforcement departments' foundational codes begin with this basic premise. For example, the Los Angeles Police Department's (LAPD) vision statement begins with a commitment to serving the community while protecting the rights of all persons, and fundamental to these rights is the basic right to live in peace.[8]

Naturally occurring phenomena can also be dangerous and put citizens at risk. A natural disaster, like Hurricane Katrina in 2005, is an example of a situation where people's lives are in jeopardy, but without human aggressors. Other examples include traffic accidents or infrastructure fires, both potentially but not always caused by humans but not necessarily from aggressive motives.[9] Emergency responders, like firefighters and paramedics, restore peace by mitigating disruptive conditions through quick response and aid to those affected.

Fighting wars is different from fighting crime, and fighting crime is different from saving lives. The military defends states; police and other first responders defend individuals. Despite such differences, the desired result is a shared intent to restore the rights of those affected, whether they are a collection of individual rights in a state or the basic rights of individuals to life and freedom that civic violence, crime, or accident threatens. The perspectives of those who are professionally bound to face danger are varied, but the ethics behind their professional obligations are linked by their common inspiration from basic human rights.

MORAL STATUS OF ADVERSARIES AND NON-ADVERSARIES

Dangerous situations are most often made so by adversaries, who may be individuals or collections of individuals with motives to commit or threaten aggression. Crisis professionals are empowered to respond with deadly force, but the degree of response varies by their office, or alternatively, by the moral status of their respective adversaries. Comparing opposing soldiers in a war against criminals on the street yields some observations about the differences in moral status that exist between them.

In combat, when soldiers ambush opposing soldiers and kill them, they are not commonly judged as murderers. The label perhaps does not fit since killing for the sake of their nation's cause—and accepting that they could ulti-mately be killed while doing so—is what soldiers agree to do when they freely join the military. (From another perspective, one could argue that these soldiers knowingly surrender their rights to personal safety when they opt to become soldiers.) Change soldiers in the ambush example to police and opposing soldiers to suspected criminals, and one's intuition may not be so clear-cut. Ambushing and killing suspected lawbreakers seems harder to morally justify because somehow the tactic of ambushing does not seem to fit what police are supposed to do. Rather, it is beyond the scope of what society expects, and empowers, police to do. Ambushing is hunting with the goal of killing on sight, without questions. Soldiers expect to do this and to be targets of it in the course of their combat duties. It seems unlikely that police as well as the citizens they serve would share these expectations for law enforcement agents.

Why are expectations for soldiers and police different? The answer involves rights. Prominent military ethicist Michael Walzer puts it this way: Soldiers, if they serve freely, and they fight for a just cause, consciously accept that their basic rights to personal safety are secondary to their duty to risk their lives in fighting their nation's battles. Governments tacitly affirm this through the convention of supplying their militaries with weapons and personnel, all of whom swear an oath of allegiance as part of their entry into service. This process legitimizes the killing soldiers do in the course of battle, making it state-sanctioned, justified killing rather than murder.

Law enforcement officers on the other hand are not charged with fight-ing their state's wars; their scope is much narrower. They are empowered by regional and local governments to keep the domestic peace and safeguard the citizenry. This is a morally important difference. While soldiers typically fight to establish or reestablish order on a large scale, law enforcers preserve order on a much smaller one. They operate under a civil code ingrained with the basic concepts of rights-based rule of law and are bound to honor it even while apprehending those who are attempting to break it. This leads them to greatly restrain their lethality in order to maximize their chances of bringing suspected criminals to face justice. One can see these notions in the policies of law enforcement agencies, like the New York Police Department's (NYPD) imperative for its officers to use force to stop rather than kill.

The Management Principles of the LAPD further illustrate this point by prescribing the appropriate mind-set for its officers in the course of their duties: "a peace officer's enforcement should not be done in grudging adherence to the legal rights of the accused, but in a sincere spirit of seeking that every accused person is given all of his rights as far as it is within the powers of the police."[10] By urging its officers to be mindful of the principles that empower them, the LAPD seeks to maximize the preservation of the rights of those it also seeks to apprehend, as well as reinforce the ethics of its profession.

CHALLENGES TO THE WAR–LAW ENFORCEMENT PARADIGM

Terrorism and insurgency pose difficult challenges for crisis professionals because the tactics used by terrorists and insurgents often blur the distinction between criminals and enemy combatants. For military professionals, counterinsurgency doctrine overlays traditional combat tactics. For example, a unit might assume nontraditional tasks, like agricultural crop management and construction, while continuing to fight pitched battles against hostiles whose actions classify them as classic combatants one day but common criminals the next.

Law enforcement agents face similar challenges as terrorism and insurgency change the scope of their operations, often dramatically. On city streets, police increasingly find themselves "out-gunned" by drug traffickers and gangs. Overseas deployments are now a possibility for law enforcers, as national governments tap them to train foreign police agencies, often from scratch. In extreme cases, in regions like East Timor, where there is no commonly accepted rule of law, police trainers must assume full policing duties until a law enforcement system can be established, from the ground up. More and more, these types of situations are becoming the norm with soldiers policing and police officers soldiering.[11] Any ethical approach that seeks common ground for all types of crisis professionals must consider the ways in which their lines of duty continue to blur and blend.

COMMITTING HARM, DISCRIMINATION IN USE OF FORCE AND TARGETS, NECESSITY, AND PROPORTIONALITY

As noted earlier, soldiers killing other soldiers in war or police killing suspected lawbreakers in self-defense or defense of others is not considered murder. Though societies might later view such deaths as unfortunate, it is unlikely that minds will change about the moral justification if it is affirmed that the soldiers and police were acting in accordance with their duties. What grounds thinking, or moral intuition, here is the notion that in dangerous situations those who can defend against a threat should do so, even if it results in someone's death or injury, and it would be wrong if they did not act.[12]

Justified defense of self or others has limits, however. Both soldiers and police are obligated to discriminate in their use of force, selection of targets, and means of applying force. Just as soldiers may not intentionally kill or harm noncombatants, police must avoid incidental harm to bystanders and make every effort to warn suspects before they use deadly force against them. International laws as well as internal military regulations prohibit certain weapons and restrict the excessive use of force in conflicts just as domestic law and internal police policies prescribe limits on the use of force.

The crisis professionals' need to show restraint leads to a pronounced sense of tension when faced with the competing demand to accomplish whatever mission is required. Resolving this tension is the central ethical problem in dangerous situations. Perhaps the most common approach to this tension—and one that poses serious challenges to any principle-based professional ethic—is that of classic ends–means, or utilitarian, reasoning. Simply put, this line of thinking holds that the best decision is the one that results in the most good and the least bad for the most people. For those empowered to respond in times of crisis, the most good comes from accomplishing their profession's mission, even if it means in extreme cases committing some harm in order to do so, which in turn flies in the face of professional duties to minimize risk to themselves and others. The greater the perceived "good"or worth of the outcome, the lesser the value of the individual rights of persons affected by the crisis, and the stronger the pressure to violate them in order to secure the best outcome.

A natural offshoot of this reasoning is the concept of necessity and its cousin military necessity. Necessity is a powerful aspect of ends–means reasoning, and crisis professionals need to consider its entire scope and to what it commits them as they make decisions in dangerous situations. It follows from this line of thinking that the more good one thinks can be achieved, the more harm one should be willing to cause or accept in order to do it. Taken to extremes, this reasoning can lead to troubling actions by leaders under pressure to produce good outcomes.[13] A contemporary instance of this is illustrated in Lieutenant William Calley's closing remarks at his court-martial, where he was found guilty of orchestrating and participating in the murder of more than five hundred unarmed civilians in the village of My Lai in 1968 during the Vietnam War:

> If I have committed a crime, the only crime that I have committed is in judgment of my values. Apparently, I valued my troop's lives more than I did that of the enemy. When my troops were getting massacred and mauled by an enemy I couldn't see, I couldn't feel, and I couldn't touch, that nobody in the military system ever described as anything other than communism—they didn't give it a race, they didn't give it a sex, they didn't give it an age, they never let me believe it was just a philosophy in a man's mind and that was my enemy out there, and when it became between me and that enemy, I had to value the lives of my troops, and I feel that is the only crime I have committed.[14]

Calley's assertion that his troops' lives were worth more than his enemys' is clearly an attempted value-based justification for the murders in the village; coupled with his claim about the difficulty of identifying the enemy, his rationale for the slaughter becomes more apparent. Though killing a large number of people who appeared to be innocent was a near-term bad, there was a chance they could actually be or turn out to be the enemy, so killing them was in fact a larger good because it would prevent them from killing his soldiers. The duty for Calley to discriminate between friend or foe had less overall worth to him than the need to protect his soldiers. His actions reflect professional as well as ethical failures; he felt no tension because he perceived no boundaries to his judgment. As his example proves, such unrestrained reasoning in crisis can be extremely dangerous.

Central to the constraints inherent in the ethical codes of crisis response professions is the concept of proportionality, which translates in ends–means reasoning that prohibits actions whose outcomes result in more harm than good.[15] Thus, permissible actions are those in which the good achieved is proportional to or in balance with the bad incurred.[16] For example, professional military organizations must ensure their weapons are appropriate to the target type and avoid "squashing a squirrel with a tank,"[17] because doing so clearly overvalues destruction and undervalues the good produced by it. From a long-term perspective, protracted "squashing" or excessive use of force will threaten any claims of intentions to fight a just war, given that a primary objective of a

just war is the establishment of a better state of peace. The wanton pulveriza-
tion of an adversary seems hardly likely to produce such a goal.

Proportionality is also a critical component of law enforcement's professional ethic, as evident in the tenets of the Law Enforcement Code of Ethics,
an oath that every new law enforcement officer recites during graduation ceremonies or signs when joining a police department.[18] This oath, like all professional oaths, is thought to be morally binding throughout one's career of
service. The Law Enforcement Code of Ethics is particularly insightful in its
acknowledgment of the powerful emotions and tensions officers experience
in dangerous situations as they make decisions about risk and the use of
deadly force. Just as philosophers and religious thinkers have railed throughout the ages against rage, bloodlust, and "revengeful cruelty as unjust inspira-
tions for battle,"[19] the law enforcement code likewise implores its officers to
restrain their personal feelings and prevent them from influencing their decisions about risk and deadly force amid their pursuit of criminals. They must
enforce the law "courageously and appropriately without fear or favor, malice,
or ill will, [and] never employ unnecessary force or violence" in the process.[20]

Unnecessary force is understood here as force disproportionate to the
harm potentially being done. Such a use of force would be unprofessional and
unethical because it would violate the rights of those against whom the force
is directed. Even though a person or persons may be actively disrupting the
civic peace, they do not lose the right to be treated humanely as they are being
apprehended. Common ground on this point seems clear for both law enforcers and military professionals; force without constraint and discrimination is
unprofessional, unethical, and in the broadest sense, greatly undermines their
most common collective goal: a stable peace at any level.[21]

Proportionality properly considered at each level guides necessity in each
context; often, what's necessary for police in terms of violence is different from what's necessary for the military. The following example illustrates
this point: During the 1992 Los Angeles riots, a joint Marine–police patrol
responded to a domestic disturbance. The police readied to enter the room and
yelled to the Marines to provide them cover. The Marines responded by firing
approximately two hundred rounds through the door, the minimum volume
of fire necessary in their professional world to "suppress" a target and provide
cover for others moving forward in an assault. Fortunately for all, no one was
injured.[22] Though military and law enforcement organizations instruct their
members to use the least force necessary, this example shows they have very
different conceptions of what this means. In the policemen's view here, "cover"
probably meant aiming weapons at the door, and yelling "come out or we'll

shoot!" in order to gain time to understand the situation and consider whether nonviolent means could resolve the situation. As far as the Marines were concerned, however, "cover" meant suppressing the target even at the risk of others in the area.

These different reactions result in part from the way each profession perceives threats and trains to deal with them. For police, the threat is a lawbreaker who requires apprehension but still has a full complement of basic rights. Police emotions might run high, especially if the lawbreaker's offense is a horrible one, but their professional code demands apprehension and delivery to justice first, and deadly force only as a last resort. Members of the military on the other hand are professionally bound to defeat enemies. The focus of their training, resourced by their states, envisions the most extreme scenarios, in which all dimensions of military force (land power, sea power, air power) are brought to bear to completely destroy an enemy or cause it to surrender in order to restore peace. Thus, military professionals' first consideration is and must be the most force permissible.[23] This distinction means that any set of principles of necessity and proportionality meant to address all crisis professionals must be mindful of the rights that their professions are charged to respect and protect.

IMMUNITY FROM HARM AND THE ETHICS OF RISK

While the principles of necessity and proportionality restrain the use of force, they provide no guidance on how crisis professionals should aim or direct force. There are no restrictions on whom one may or may not target with force; rather, it is only important that the act be required to achieve success. In the absence of boundaries, these principles clash head-on with the notion of universal human rights, and for crisis professionals, represent clear contradictions to the codes they are sworn to follow.

A victory-at-all-costs mentality in a military context, for example, presents a clear challenge to the principles of human rights that most nations subscribe to either through their constitutions or through membership in the United Nations, whose charter clearly articulates human rights principles. In terms of killing, then, if all persons have a basic right to life, killing them would appear to be wrong or unjust unless they have done something to forfeit that right. As Walzer and others have pointed out, when conflicts occur, merely living near or within a group of aggressors does not automatically constitute a forfeiture of rights.[24] In a similar vein, just because one happens to be in the same building as a criminal, it does not mean he or she ought to be subjected to the same loss of rights that the criminal faces in the course of his apprehension. One could object to this by posing this question: When faced with a choice between defending myself and my colleagues or the members of a hostile population who also have rights, whom should I protect? Put another way, is it ever permissible to violate or even abandon the rights of others when the rights of your own people are also in jeopardy? These are fair questions.

Placing restrictions on the use of force can put friendly and innocent lives at risk as well as impede mission accomplishment. Thus, if such restraints exist, there need to be compelling reasons for them. Answers to the above questions begin by noting that while the ethics of dangerous situations center on balancing risks, the balancing process rests upon the fundamental and universal principle that all persons deserve to live their lives freely, not under threat of violence or oppression by others.[25] Because individuals have these rights, they are considered immune from harm and remain so unless they do something to warrant a loss of immunity. In the context of dangerous situations, this typically happens when persons threaten to harm or otherwise violate the universal rights of others.

Immunity protects non-harming persons from being intentionally targeted by lethal force during crisis response operations. If it can be thought of as morally enabling war fighting and policing, then it stands to reason that these same rights must also be preserved during the course of those activities, otherwise responders would undermine the moral purpose of taking action in the first place. In the United States, crisis professions draw inspiration and affirm allegiance to the Constitution, which codifies the universality of these rights and demands their defense. The UN Charter also serves the same function.

It follows then that to establish the principle of immunity, which states generally that a crisis professional when considering the use of lethal force must attempt to discriminate between legitimate and illegitimate targets as well as minimize the spillover of the effects of force on those not involved in the situation, law-enforcement professionals engaging criminals must avoid such spillover entirely because of their obligation to protect civilians from harm.[26]

Although the immunity principle obligates regular soldiers and police to refrain from directly targeting noncombatants or bystanders, what role, if any, does it play in today's complex "irregular" conflicts? Fights that pit combatants against combatants within clearly defined battle lines occur rarely in the context of the kinds of irregular wars U.S. forces find themselves in, thus introducing higher probabilities of noncombatant casualties. Moreover, as noted above, the roles of crisis professionals are increasingly becoming blended or blurred as some adversaries seek cover within noncombatant environments.

In these as well as domestic policing situations, crisis responders often find that their best and often only way to stop a violent act is by placing bystanders at risk, directly or indirectly. Imagine, for example, a police sniper tracking a person who is threatening to kill someone he is holding hostage. The officer sees him through a window of the building, but knows there are other people inside. A shot, if it ricochets, could injure or kill others, but it is the only way to stop the man from murdering his hostage. Does the sniper have an obligation to minimize or even avoid those casualties? If the commitment to the right to life is a serious one, the answer would appear to be yes. It is a truism about rights that if someone has a right, others should generally avoid violating it unless there is a compelling overriding reason. Dangerous situations do not override immunity so much as they recognize that because some situations make it impossible to avoid noncombatant casualties, it is similarly impossible to hold crisis professionals generally morally responsible for causing casualties if they do their reasonable best to avoid them. The best that can be done is to prescribe general limits, like proportionality and immunity, and hold these professionals responsible for complying with their oaths and charters.

MANAGING RISK

The more complex a dangerous environment is, the more difficult ethical decision making becomes. For crisis professionals to succeed in their missions in such environments, they must find and engage the enemy or criminal element discriminately within the population. To do so, they must delve into the population and find their targets, increasing their own vulnerability to attack as well as the probability of casualties, which would not only affect their units, but also potentially the overall popular will to carry on the fight.[27]

An alternative option to exacerbating vulnerabilities is to opt for weapons of greater standoff range, but these often decrease the ability to discriminate combatants from noncombatants. Adversaries who show no regard for the principle of immunity, and who kill wantonly, raise the pressure on principled leaders. Perhaps the truest test of leadership during crisis is for those in charge to inspire their subordinates to place themselves at great risk to preserve the rights and lives of innocents when their adversaries lack compunction about killing or harming in other ways. Yet, the subordinates must act, because doing so is part of the fiber of their professional lives. Moreover, because they receive training, equipment, and other resources to reduce their risk when fighting, it follows that they must accept some additional risk if it means preserving the lives of noncombatants, who by definition do not have these resources.[28]

Michael Ignatieff's *Virtual War,* about NATO's air campaign in its 1999 intervention in Kosovo, offers a good example of the extent of risk that crisis professionals are sometimes obliged to take. Describing this campaign as one with "high moral language of the cause" but "limited character," Ignatieff criticizes NATO's tactic of bombing from high altitudes to eliminate the risk of successful surface-to-air missile (SAM) attacks by Serbians.[29] By flying so high, the pilots could not clearly identify friend from foe as they searched for targets below. They made several widely publicized target identification errors that resulted in noncombatant casualties.[30]

Ignatieff's problem with this kind of "warfare of minimum risk" is that it willfully avoids personal combat risk while increasing the risk to innocents. He considers it patently immoral and unethical.[31] What makes this willingness to kill, but not risk dying unethical is that by transferring all the risk of combat to noncombatants, pilots—as well as their leaders who established their rules of engagement—completely void their moral responsibility to take due care in discriminating between combatants and noncombatants.[32]

As noted previously, rescue workers may take only limited risks when performing their duties, but this does not mean that they have no obligation to manage that risk. For them, managing risk is manifest in the investment in training and equipment for them so they are as well prepared as possible to conduct rescue operations as safely as possible. A parent is wrong to rush into a building to save his or her child in the presence of firefighters. It is right for the firefighters to do it because of their training and equipment, which greatly minimizes harm to them as well as to others. This does not suggest that rescue workers must eliminate the possibility of harm in dangerous situations; rather, they must eliminate the necessity of harm. Just as police may only undertake certain courses of action, like a high-speed chase, when harming bystanders is not a certain outcome, rescue workers may only attempt a rescue if they know that its success will not require harm to themselves or others not already at risk.

The requirement to eliminate the necessity of harm in large part distinguishes rescue workers from soldiers and police. Mission accomplishment usually entails soldiers and police employing force to defeat human adversaries who are also using force (and thus making the situation dangerous). The role of rescue workers, on the other hand, is to reduce the danger for everyone affected. Thus they do not accept the same risk experienced by the people they intend to rescue. For this reason, risk management for them entails reducing the overall harm possible rather than shifting the harm to the adversary.

FINDING COMMON GROUND

Though crisis professions vary in many ways, from the context of situations faced to the nature of adversaries, the generalized formulations below illustrate common ground between them with an eye toward the formulation of a unified crisis professional ethic:

- *Necessity:* Use lethal force and create risk for others and yourself only when there is no other way to accomplish your mission and restore peace or domestic order.

- *Proportionality:* Use as much force as is required to accomplish your professional mission but also preserve the rights of those affected by your mission. Accept a degree of risk to yourself and others that is commensurate with your professional obligations.

- *Immunity:* Those persons not directly engaged in threatening you, your colleagues, and others not involved in the situation in any meaningful way have the right to not be intentionally harmed as a result of your direct or indirect actions.

- *Discrimination:* When considering the use of deadly force, make every reasonable effort to distinguish those who threaten from those who do not, even if doing so means you and those who follow you must put yourselves at risk.

- *Respect:* Honor the basic human rights of all those affected by your professional mission and always consider them when making decisions in crisis situations.

CONCLUSION

Revisiting the introductory discussion of the decision made by the platoon leader, some judgments can be made from the perspective of the ethics of dangerous situations and some thoughts offered by way of judgment. First consider the professional identity of the platoon leader. It is clearly one of a crisis professional, commissioned by oath to his nation to lead soldiers to fight its battles. His oath commits him to assume risk to himself and his soldiers in the course of their duties, which include taking reasonable steps to distinguish friend from foe in battle. By forgoing his unit's SOP, one could argue that he fails to take those steps largely out of concern of putting his soldiers at risk of sniper attack. Yet, this failure somehow seems to discount the lieutenant's credibility in judging threats to his soldiers, which clearly matters in this case;

after all, he was there, so who better to decide what dangers really existed? Another objection, to the lieutenant's decision to open fire on the sedan, might be linked to the nature of the platoon's mission, arguing that it more closely resembles a law enforcement operation than a military mission, and therefore requires decision making about force and risk similar to those police officers make. (See Chapter 6 for a discussion on personal responsibility.)

One might then conclude that judgment might be better served by a consideration of this lieutenant's character. Is he honest? Does he truly embrace, through his words and demonstrated actions, the values of his profession? Does he truly care for his soldiers? Answers to these questions offer insight into what kind of person he is, which in turn could reveal something about his motivations for his decision to fire on the sedan and ultimately reveal the overall moral quality of his decisions.

From this admittedly brief analysis, the difficulty of ethical decision making for crisis professionals is apparent. These responders are required to win wars or keep the peace, protect the people they work with, and make every effort to protect those involved in the situations they respond to. This is difficult enough in clear-cut situations, where danger manifests itself in obvious ways, but the emergence of asymmetric enemy and criminal adversaries increases the complexity of these environments and inevitably raises pressure to make good decisions about harm and risk. Certain qualities unify crisis professionals across the spectrum of dangers that they face. Courage and resiliency will continue to underscore their collective character as they stand against the myriad of threats that exist to all levels of peace in society.

KEY TAKE-AWAY POINTS

1. Professions are organizations or groups whose members freely choose to serve through swearing or affirming acceptance to their codes of conduct or duties. In crisis professions, members' duties involve facing risk, often to extreme degrees, to protect others from danger or harm.

2. Though crisis professions vary by type and scope of duties, their individual codes of ethical conduct share certain general principles. The most fundamental of these principles is a respect for humanity and the basic rights to life and freedom.

3. Judgments about the ethical conduct of crisis professionals in complex and dangerous situations may rely on such principles as discrimination and proportionality, depending on the complexity of the situation, but in

the end they may come down to judgments about basic virtues like character and integrity.

KEY REFERENCES

Grant, J. Kevin. "Ethics and Law Enforcement." *FBI Law Enforcement Bulletin*, December 2002, http://findarticles.com/p/articles/mi_m2194/is_12_71/ai_96453523/pg_2/?tag=content;col1.

Walzer, Michael. *Just and Unjust Wars*. 2nd ed. New York: Basic Books, 1992.

NOTES

Special thanks to Captain Eamon Deery, Lieutenant Louis Caserma, Lieutenant Daniel Modell, Detective Darrell Corti, and Officer Joseph Agosto of the New York City Police Department for their efforts in this project.

1. Peter Kilner, Nate Allen, and Nate Self, eds., *A Platoon Leader's Tour* (New York: West Point Center for the Advancement of Leader Development and Organizational Learning, 2009), 66–67.

2. Ibid., 68.

3. New York City Police Department policy states, "Police officers shall not discharge their firearms to subdue a fleeing felon who presents no threat of imminent death or serious physical injury to themselves or another person present." *Manual of Use of Deadly Physical Force,* section 203–12.

4. The authors owe this point to Dr. Michael Matthews.

5. Louis P. Pojman, *Ethics: Discovering Right and Wrong* (Belmont, Calif.: Wadsworth Publishing, 1995), 1–3.

6. Brian Orend, *The Morality of War* (Petersborough, Ontario: Broadview Press, 2006), 3; and Michael Walzer, *Just and Unjust Wars*, 2nd ed. (New York: Basic Books, 1992), 51.

7. See Walzer, *Just and Unjust Wars*, 58–59.

8. LAPD, "Motto, Mission Statement, and Core Values," http://www.lapdonline.org/search_results/content_basic_view/842.

9. Aggressively motivated humans are those who intentionally seek to inflict harm on others or others' possessions. In the domestic sense, these are obviously criminals with motives like armed robbery, murder, arson, and so on. Accidental harm in the domestic sense would include instances where systems or conveyances fail for non-intentional reasons, like when an electrical appliance shorts and causes a fire or brakes fail on a car and cause a collision.

10. LAPD, "Management Principles of the LAPD," http://www.lapdonline.org/inside_the_lapd/content_basic_view/846.

11. Contracted security forces complicate this idea further because they are not bound to any kind of professional ethic in the same way crisis professionals are. Rather,

they are obligated to provide services only to the extent their contract identifies. With respect to risk, this causes them to differ from crisis professionals in morally significant ways.

12. Police may be liable legally as well as morally if they fail to make an arrest. For example, an officer who ignores a drunk driver may be held responsible for any harm later committed by the driver. The authors owe this point to Dr. Michael Matthews.

13. Walzer, *Just and Unjust Wars,* 130–132.

14. "Remember My Lai," PBS *Frontline,* transcript of original broadcast, May 23, 1989, http://www.pbs.org/wgbh/pages/frontline/programs/transcripts/714.html.

15. For an explanation of differing views of utility, see William Shaw, "The Consequentialist Perspective," in *Contemporary Debates in Moral Theory,* ed. James Dreier (Malden, Mass.: Blackwell Publishing, 2006), 10.

16. Proportionality is a notoriously difficult requirement to calculate, as one must measure harms that are not always commensurate as well as calculate the future harms one is trying to avoid.

17. Orend, *The Morality of War,* 119.

18. Kevin J. Grant, "Ethics and Law Enforcement," *FBI Law Enforcement Bulletin,* December 2002, 2, http://findarticles.com/p/articles/mi_m2194/is_12_71/ai_96453523/pg_2/?tag =content;col1.

19. See Orend, *The Morality of War,* 9–12.

20. Law Enforcement Code of Ethics, University of North Carolina Department of Public Safety, http://www.dps.unc.edu/DPS%20Policies%20&%20Procedures/Appe ndix/3LawEnforcementCodeofEthics.pdf.

21. The NYPD employs a concept known as the "scale of escalating force, force continuum" to manage the proportionality of force. This continuum identifies several levels of force, the lowest being an officer's mere presence and the highest being deadly physical force. The levels of force are based on the situation and can change as circumstances change. Officers are not required to start the application of force at the lowest level and exhaust all alternatives before progressing to the next level; where they start depends on the level of force a suspect employs. Officers in all instances are required to use the minimum amount of force, consistent with their personal safety, to accomplish the mission at hand. NYPD officers will often say based on this that the suspect determines what kind of force the officer will use; the officer merely reacts and responds.

22. James D. Delk, *Fires and Furies: The LA Riots* (Palm Springs, Calif.: ETC Publications, 1995), quoted in Christopher M. Schnaubelt, "Lessons in Command and Control from the Los Angeles Riots," *Parameters* 27 (1997): 88–109.

23. Tony Pfaff, "Military Ethics in Complex Contingencies," in *The Future of the Army Profession,* ed. Don M. Snider and Lloyd J. Matthews, 2nd ed. (New York: McGraw Hill, 2005), 412–414.

24. Walzer, *Just and Unjust Wars,* 146.

25. Walzer, *Just and Unjust Wars,* 53–54; also see Paul Christopher, *The Ethics of War and Peace: An Introduction to Legal and Moral Issues,* 2nd ed. (Trenton, N.J.: Prentice Hall, 1999), 164–166.

26. Paolo Tripoldi, "Peacekeepers, Moral Autonomy, and the Use of Force," *Journal of Military Ethics* 5, no. 3 (2006): 217.

27. Martin Shaw, *The Western Way of War* (Cambridge: Polity Press, 2005), 35.

28. James M. Dubik, "Human Rights, Command Responsibility, and Walzer's Just War Theory," *Philosophy and Public Affairs* 11, no. 4 (1982): 355.

29. Michael Ignatieff, *Virtual War: Kosovo and Beyond* (Toronto: Viking Inc., 2000), 110.

30. Their targeting mistakes included strikes on a refugee convoy, the home of an elderly Serb couple, a civilian train crossing a bridge, and the Chinese embassy in Belgrade. See Ignatieff, *Virtual War,* 103, 107.

31. Ignatieff, *Virtual War,* 110.

32. For a more complete discussion of obligations of combatants to take risks, see Don M. Snider, John A. Nagl, and Tony Pfaff, *Army Professionalism, Military Ethics, and Officership in the 21st Century* (Carlisle Barracks, Pa.: Army War College Strategic Studies Institute, 1999).

CHAPTER 8

Meaning-Making
The Search for Meaning in Dangerous Contexts

David M. Barnes, C. Kevin Banks, Michael Albanese, and
Michael F. Steger

On February 7, 2008, the first Los Angeles SWAT officer was killed in the line of duty after more than 4,500 high-risk SWAT operations since 1967. From a leadership perspective, this event tested one as a leader and clearly tested one's faith.

The incident involved a suspect who had shot three family members; the rescue of a pregnant hostage resulted in the death of one SWAT officer and the wounding of three others. In this case, the dead officer had iconic status within the police department. His character, intellect, physicality, and his heart to serve defined him. He was a man of enormous faith, who not only served the police department, but also spent his off-duty time selflessly serving in the inner city.

When an officer is killed in the line of duty, everything stops in the law enforcement community. The community, the media, and the department weigh in; for the most part, all grieve for the officer and his family. In this case, the media and community were captivated by the death of this particular officer. The incident dominated the news for days. More than 12,000 people and law enforcement officers from Alaska to New Hampshire attended the funeral. The community literally stopped for the day in reverence for this officer and the department.

"I felt that what I was standing on had given way, that I had no foundation to stand on . . . that I had nothing to live by."

—Tolstoy[1]

lthough Tolstoy's line seems overly pessimistic, his underlying uncertainty captures the perplexed emotions and often the confusion that could arise when an individual's passage through a dangerous context ends. During the event or the mission, the immediacy of the apparent conflicts between mission accomplishment and obligations to friends, combined with a strong desire for survival, generally block one's meaning-making of a particular action. Military operations, police actions, firefighting, and other assignments in so-called dangerous contexts have many characteristics in common, including danger, risk, and loss as well as the primacy of the moment. Conflicts often surface between the values and beliefs one has developed under ordinary circumstances and actions required in dangerous environments. Through this juxtaposition, experience in dangerous contexts can force one to question one's worldview. Maintaining the psychological welfare of followers is a central challenge of those who lead in dangerous contexts.

Depending on a number of factors, people may struggle to find a context that helps them understand and cope with their experiences. While most people at some point seek to find meaning in their existence, environment, and particular circumstances, those who find themselves operating in dangerous contexts come face-to-face with a reality that often seems wholly contrary to what they consider normal.

In the above SWAT scenario, making meaning of this death was a journey and remains a journey for those involved. The officer defined law enforcement professionalism and epitomized a servant's heart. Making meaning of his death ranged from the fatalistic—"it comes with the job"—to disbelief and struggles to answer the questions "Why him" and "Why now?" Because the officer was truly a man of faith, his death caused many to question their own faith; it made his death even more difficult and inexplicable. Overcoming these emotions and moving forward was a test of leadership, perseverance, and perspective. The struggle to identify, understand, and accept encounters with dangerous situations is called meaning-making. This chapter seeks to explain meaning-making and its particular relevance to people serving in dangerous operations, providing a model of how leaders can help their followers make adaptive, generative, and healthy meaning.

WHAT IS MEANING-MAKING?

"Meaning" can be defined as the interpretive framework through which individuals assign purpose and significance to their goals, actions, experiences, and contributions and to society, selves, and existence. One's meaning framework is derived from and linked to one's worldview, which entails one's core values and beliefs, assumptions on how the world operates, and what truth is. According to psychological theory, this framework is created through family, culture, political and economic environments, religion, experience, formal education, training, and personal makeup (personality, intelligence, talents, aspirations, and so on).[2] All people have a framework, whether explicit or implicit, well-defined or generic. Although it is always in flux to some degree, meaning serves to unite experience and determine peoples' courses of action, not only in terms of the objectives they are trying to attain and the options they consider, but also in terms of how they later interpret their decisions and actions. The outcomes of interpretation, decision, and action are incorporated into the framework itself. Optimally, experience matches the meaning framework and vice versa. Meaning-making is most often used in the context of adverse events, in which people must adjust either their initial appraisals of experiences to match their meaning framework or adjust their meaning framework to match experiences. The initiation and refinement of the meaning framework happens deliberately and passively, and either way, it is unavoidable.

PHILOSOPHICAL UNDERPINNING OF MEANING-MAKING

While meaning-making is generally considered to belong to the realm of psychology, its roots can be traced from Hellenistic Stoic theory through twentieth-century existentialism. In ancient Greece, Zeno, Epictetus, and other Stoics sought to define who we are as human beings, and what it means for us to live a flourishing life. The Stoics agreed with Aristotle that *eudemonia*, or flourishing, is the end that all humans ought to seek.[3] More recently, existentialists revitalized the tradition of questioning what it means to be human and how one sees oneself in the world. In order to answer questions of how we ought to live, these theorists sought first to address the essence of human existence and square human emotion and rational thought within an often-inhospitable environment. The Stoics' and the existentialists' ideas of what it means to be human when faced with adversity offer insight into how one prepares for dangerous contexts.

Stoics

According to the Stoics, the faculty of rational decision making is what makes us human beings. Reason, the Stoics believed, enables one to navigate the hazards in life and keeps one on the path to flourishing. Even Kant later noted that persons have intrinsic value just because of this faculty of reason.[4] According to the Stoics, life could be separated into two categories: that which we control and that which is outside of our control. Often, our lives swirl around us, and we find ourselves in situations we cannot influence directly. Epictetus wrote, "Some things are up to us and some are not. Our beliefs are a plus, our desires, our aversions, our attitudes. In short, whatever is our own doing."[5] Quite simply, then, we should only be concerned with the things over which we have control; trying to change things outside of our scope of control is irrational and is in fact what affects our well-being. Thus, when circumstances are difficult, we can succumb to helplessness or we can embrace life's demands and work on our own, controllable reactions instead.

"Difficulties are what show men's character," Epictetus reflects.[6] Furthermore, he wrote, "God gives you attributes, like magnanimity, courage, and endurance, to enable you to bear whatever happens. . . . He has put the whole matter under your control." Even in the most dire circumstances, we should be able to reason, and make meaning, to keep those things which we cannot control—our emotions, reactions, desires—at bay. However, this is not always the case. Sometimes the circumstances are too dire for people to make meaning, and often our occupations restrict the time needed to make meaning.

Consider the requirement for grief. Nancy Sherman notes that although the Army's former motto was an "Army of One," it should not entail that soldiers have to go it alone.[7] Like the Stoics, Sherman observes that the military has little time for, or institutional programs to, allow for a soldier's grieving. (Even memorial services, while allowing time for unit grief and closure, are insufficient for the full grieving process.) Cicero seems to capture the potential effects of not allowing for grief when he critiques the Stoics. He writes, "It is not within our power to forget or gloss over circumstances which we believe to be evil at the very moment they are piercing us. They tear at us, buffet us, goad us, scorch us, stifle us, and you Stoics tell us to forget about them?"[8] While Stoicism does offer a theory of human nature as well as an avenue for meaning-making in dangerous contexts, a Stoic solution may not be available or appropriate in every circumstance. Our emotions and reactions are part of who we are.

Existentialism

What seems missing in the Stoic account is the importance of interpersonal relationships to an individual's identity. Kierkegaard notes that "it is impossible to exist without passion,"[9] referring to the personal engagements that occupy us and allow us to develop our sense of identity. Through relationships, one can make sense of one's own life. Dangerous contexts, however, often isolate individuals.

Heidegger thought that one's engagements and goals also enable a person's identity development.[10] Like the Stoics, Heidegger observed that we often find ourselves in situations beyond our control, afflicted by things we did not choose. Furthermore, as human beings, we come to realize, especially in dangerous contexts, that we develop angst or the awareness of the precariousness of our lives when our values and goals are seemingly separated from our meaning framework.

One might also look at meaning-making in terms of Sartre's fundamental projects, where "projects" describes one's goals in life, with some projects being more valuable or fundamental to the individual. Fundamental projects act to unify one's actions, give meaning to motives, and connect the past to the present. This process is no different to the meaning we are trying to make. The project is fundamental; it literally "is my being."[11]

For Sartre, human freedom consists in being able to choose our fundamental projects. For example, when faced with a mountain in our path, our projects define our limits, not the mountain itself.[12] If our project is to climb the mountain, then the mountain is a liberating pathway. If our project involves merely seeing what is on the other side without obscuration, then the mountain is truly an obstacle. We cannot control the mountain, but we are free to choose our projects. Similarly, Sartre would argue that we are free to choose our emotions as well. He observes, "my fear *is* free and manifests my freedom; I have put all my freedom into my fear, and have chosen myself as fearful. . . . Under other circumstances I still exist as deliberate and courageous, and I shall have put all my freedom into my courage."[13] Therefore, we are free in a relevant sense to choose how our emotions affect us. Often dire circumstances appear to us as real limits to our freedom. Like the Stoics, however, Sartre notes that these circumstances are limiting only when we "confer upon [them] a coercive value . . . because of the weight [we] attached to it."[14] Death, for example, is an element of a dangerous context that one does not choose. One chooses, however, how to relate to death.

Consider the cases of prisoners held against their will. Sartre would argue that even in such seemingly hopeless situations, there is a fundamental way in which they remain free. Certainly, they are not free to escape, but they are free to choose their attitude to find purpose in the suffering. Sartre wrote, "[W]hatever [the prisoner's] condition may be, he can project his escape and learn the value of this project by undertaking some action."[15] For Sartre, we are what we choose ourselves to be; we make ourselves the individuals we are.

PSYCHOLOGICAL TRADITIONS

Frankl

Viktor Frankl argued that the "will to meaning," provides us with the capacity to endure—and potentially transcend—the seeming irrationality of suffering when the world seems meaningless. Nevertheless, hopefulness remains present even in the most hopeless of circumstances. Thus, the will to meaning is not some mere survival mechanism; rather, it is a constructive path to achieving a life of significance.

In *Man's Search for Meaning*, Frankl uses his experience in Auschwitz to describe meaningfulness and how one can surmount the existential vacuum that arises when a person's meaning becomes obstructed or seems to disappear. Even in the most absurd, painful and dehumanizing situation, life has potential meaning, and therefore, even suffering is meaningful. Thus, the act of surviving the harsh conditions of Auschwitz can make meaning. He wrote, "If the prisoner felt that he could no longer endure the realities of life, he found a way out in his mental life—an invaluable opportunity to dwell in the spiritual domain, the one that the SS were unable to destroy. Spiritual life strengthened the prisoner, helped him adapt, and thereby improved his chances of survival."[16]

Meaningfulness entails accepting one's freedom of choice in life and actively engaging the world. Each person lives uniquely in the world, creating parameters for the choices he or she makes. Within each of us, there is a desire and corresponding faculty to define meaning substantial enough to compel us to justify the life we lead. Despite external circumstances that can make us feel that we cannot justify our lives or see a path to the kind of meaningful life we desire, we must surmount those moments that erode hope. Accepting responsibility for determining our attitudes toward our lives is how we overcome despair in dire circumstances. Dangerous contexts present acute challenges to finding personally acceptable attitudes and choices, threatening people's sense of meaningfulness.

Frankl argued that we cannot solely rely upon others to make meaning. Doing so stunts our self-development. Thus, while leadership can provide guidance, support, and different perspectives to assist meaning-making for subordinates, the ultimate responsibility lies with the individual. It is the leader's job to help followers and provide the resources necessary to find meaning. Like the existentialists, Frankl felt that one way to establish or reestablish meaning in our lives is through the relationships we build with others. A shared collection of values actually helps individuals with their meaning-making when suffering a crisis. Although these relationships cannot direct (but only assist) one's meaning-making, relationships are the most commonly acknowledged source of meaning in people's lives.[17]

In dangerous contexts, the individual must transcend herself as an isolated unit and connect with others and with life in a fully meaningful way. Beyond the meaning-making power of relationships, Frankl described three additional pathways for this kind of self-actualization. First, meaning can be created when people identify at a deep, personal level with their work and accomplishments. Through work, we can also connect and identify with other members of our work teams, as well as with the importance of the mission. At the basic level of the fire team or patrol partner, through the squad-level and ladder crews, to the platoon or graveyard shift, the values and goals shared with one's team help define the self and how meaning is made from the dangers faced together.

Second, Frankl noted that one must be open and welcoming to what the world offers us. Dangerous contexts do not always offer easy-to-digest meaning, but they offer challenging circumstances that are a blend of highs and lows. Third, people must always be aware that the final choice of what we carry with us from situation to situation rests with us. Living authentically, in full appreciation of the weight and liberation of our choices, also extends to how we behave and how we endure circumstances beyond our control. Perhaps not every dangerous situation can be a source of meaning, but the way people comport themselves in those situations always can.

Antonovsky

Medical sociologist Aaron Antonovsky provides another view of meaning-making. He asserted that traditional medicine has missed the connections between health, stress, and coping. Antonovsky thought that even though stress is omnipresent, it does not always result in negative consequences. He sought to reformulate the relationship between stress, health, and coping so that practitioners consider the well-being of patients first as opposed to focusing solely on the ailment itself.

In *Health, Stress, and Coping* and *Unraveling the Mysteries of Health*, Antonovsky sought to explain how people survive, adapt, and overcome life stress experiences.[18] Why were certain people able to survive dire circumstances, or even excel, as other collapsed in despair? Those who were successful, Antonovsky theorized, had multiple generalized resistance resources (GRRs). GRRs refer to any coping resource—such as socioeconomic status, intelligence, ego-strength, and social support—that is effective in avoiding or combating psychosocial stressors. GRRs, he thought, enable individuals to make sense and manage life's experiences.[19] He argued that over time, in response to positive experiences provided by successful utilization of different GRRs, an individual develops an attitude that is in itself the essential tool for coping.

Antonovsky called this attitude, which links a person's own sense of being and the sense that life is meaningful, the sense of coherence, a formulation that provides a central explanation for the role of stress in human functioning.[20] Sense of coherence includes feeling that experiences are predictable and explainable, the perception that one has the resources necessary to cope, and the confidence that the challenges are worth confronting. Whether stress overwhelms one's sense of coherence is based upon how the stressor is perceived and the kind of response people marshal to cope with it.

From the different traditions discussed here, some common themes can be formulated. From the Stoics, we come to appreciate that there are certain things beyond our control, but how we face them is up to us. The existentialists add the importance of life goals and that our reactions in the face of dangerous contexts, together with our relationships, enable us to sustain these goals. Frankl points to how our goals and purposes can, in turn, sustain us, along with identifying with our work, building relationships, and welcoming the challenges of dangerous contexts. Antonovsky offers an explanation of essential stress coping GRRs, which help form one's meaning framework. Much of the contemporary work in meaning-making, such as Antonovsky's, focuses on areas of post-traumatic growth, cancer treatment, and terminal illness.[21] Unfortunately, for practitioners in dangerous contexts, existing research is lagging and provides few directly tested interventions or strategies.[22] The following case studies and examination of existing theories of meaning-making are an effort to help address this gap.

MEANING-MAKING IN DANGEROUS CONTEXTS

Those who serve in dangerous contexts often face considerable risk and self-sacrifice: physically, emotionally, relationally, and mentally. By definition, serving in dangerous contexts often entails risk to life, separation from support structures, and unclear understanding of the purpose of their service. Facing their own death, the death of those with whom they serve, the death of those they are duty bound to protect, or even those they are obligated to kill, forces people operating in dangerous contexts to question their identity, their projects, even their worldviews. Leaders must provide their subordinates with the means and skills needed to work through these issues in such a way that builds resilience of their whole person, so that they, too, can continue to contribute to the society they serve to protect.

Challenge of Meaning-Making

In the military, soldiers go through basic training—"mental programming" regarding killing, obedience, duty, and expected values—but currently this training is done without intentional regard to meaning-making. It is left to the soldier to find his own meaning. Similarly, law enforcement officer (LEO) trainees undergo indoctrination that focuses on the skills, rules and responsibilities, and fundamentals of law enforcement. Perhaps for the first time, they consider what it means to potentially take a life in the execution of their duties. Death and killing lie at the heart of these two professions.

Many new soldiers, rookies, and probies proceed in their duties, with little, if any, time, guidance, or training that addresses meaning-making. As they are promoted, they may carry unresolved questions and emotions—relating to death and injury or the failure to save a life or the duty to take life—that strike at the core of their being. Left unresolved, these leaders may provide uncertain guidance for new generations, leaving them to enter dangerous contexts with very little formal training or guidance in how to develop meaning frameworks to accommodate their extraordinary duties. The challenge is to overcome this glaring gap in current practice and provide a meaning-making mechanism.

Failure to Make Meaning

Consider the following imaginary, military illustration of how failure to make meaning affects personal resiliency. It is a worst-case scenario:

> John Doe enlists in the military due to patriotic feelings, family tradition, and religious beliefs. At basic training he is taught to kill. Army recruit Doe is afforded freedom of religious and philosophical reflection, but the

application of these is not required of him. He goes to worship services, enjoys watching *Band of Brothers* and *Boondock Saints*, and plays video games in which he is rewarded for indiscriminate killing. These experiences are tossed together, leaving him the job of creating a meaning framework that supports his idealistic view of his service.

Arriving to his first assignment, Private Doe finds most of his leadership embittered from their combat experience. He further finds that the Army Values he had heard about from the recruiter and that he had memorized at basic training are not emphasized in practice. In fact, some of his new leaders not only fail to conduct themselves according to these values, but they also fail to guide others in doing so. This is not the military his grandfather and father and the old men at church had talked about.

Since his arrival to his unit, Doe has been given no training or mentoring on how to use his framework of meaning to sort through these contradictions. He is left to rely on his seemingly distant family traditional values and the occasional interactions he has with his chaplain and other ethical leaders. This shock to his meaning framework creates a precarious instability.

Once in combat, the challenge of interpreting the chaos of war through a destabilized meaning framework begins. Slowly but surely, Doe's cumulative exposure to such issues as ethical breaches, questionable tactical decisions, extreme fatigue, broken relationships back home, killing of enemies, and loss of comrades begins to erode his framework. His meaning for service has changed from "I am doing this for my country, my family, and my convictions" to "I am only trying to keep my buddy and myself alive." This new, war-formed meaning framework might even deteriorate to an "anything goes" moral standard. Private Doe's fundamental projects themselves have changed.

Finally, when Private First Class Doe's initial deployment ends, he will be faced with the formative influences of his pre-combat meaning framework. This confrontation with his past self becomes another critical juncture in the reshaping of meaning. Doe will either face this reality and seek resolution and growth or hide from his pain through feigned indifference, perhaps by leaving the military, or through participation in harmful, risky behaviors, maybe even suicide. He also discovers how easy it is simply to immerse himself in his work to avoid self-confrontation.

Specialist Doe chooses the path of least resistance: he fails to make meaning but remains in the military. As a veteran leader, he may perpetuate this negative cycle through his influence on new recruits.

Success in Meaning-Making

This imaginary, worst-case scenario is clearly not the only outcome of dangerous contexts for soldiers, first responders, or LEOs. Even in the absence of a strong organizational guide for building robust meaning frameworks, most who serve carry positive, pre-service influences with them, allowing them to actively reason through, interpret, and integrate their experiences into a healthy, resilient meaning framework. Such people maintain their dignity, integrity, and sense of duty and purpose. They manage to grow through the successful implementation and maturation of their meaning framework.

In addition to those who never lose ground, there are those who experience failure yet seek growth and restoration, presumably through honest self-reflection and perseverance. Those who maintain effective meaning frameworks and those who grow from learning from their mistakes should be sought for retention, promotion, and leadership, where they can guide the moral, ethical, and meaning-making development of those who serve. These leaders may be able to influence the development of new operators and lead the way to a comprehensive strategy that enhances the social, spiritual, and psychological health and resiliency of those who serve in dangerous contexts.

HOW CAN LEADERS FACILITATE MEANING-MAKING?

We were assigned to guard an intersection along a rarely used rural road. The intersection was exposed to enemy indirect fire from a dense tree line across an impassible marsh. We regularly took indirect fire from the tree line with no effective unit strategy for retaliation or deterrence. This went on for at least a month, with enemy accuracy improving as they systematically plotted their impacts.

We made appeals to our leadership about the tactical soundness of guarding this intersection in the manner we were doing it, but they were unresponsive. The morale of my soldiers was at an all-time low. Our chaplain noticed the situation and encouraged me to try appealing the tactics on the basis of soldier morale. I took his advice and once again requested a justification for the mission, so I could encourage my team to persevere. The answer I got was to tell them to do it because they were ordered to do it.

Shortly thereafter, one of my soldiers was killed at that intersection by indirect fire from the tree line. Within a few days, the entry point mission was aborted without explanation. Our respect for our leaders and our confidence in our personal survival under their leadership was also aborted. This young American, my soldier, our buddy, had died for nothing apparently. Who would be next? Our morale never recovered from that incident;

we were filled with hate and just did what we thought we needed to do to stay alive. A number of men in our company went on to develop post-traumatic stress disorder (PTSD), and others chose to separate from the Army as soon as possible upon redeployment.

—Operation Iraqi Freedom leader's story

How could the leaders in this case help the unit make meaning? What can leaders do to facilitate meaning-making? They can approach it in three ways: (1) be the kind of leaders others are willing to follow into dangerous contexts; (2) provide an answer for the question "Why is this worth doing?"; and (3) develop a workable strategy to communicate and implement a meaning-based culture.

Developing the Foundations of a Unit Meaning-Making Structure: Leadership Prerequisites

Leaders can help provide the foundations for a meaning structure of people united by a common goal and ethos. The most important foundation a leader can lay, before any structure can be implemented, is, therefore, his own personal example and commitment. In most circumstances, the team's foundational values as well as its overall mission have been formally and clearly defined by superiors and the institution. The challenge of a unit leader will be to translate these imperatives into tangible personal motivators and commitments by the group as a whole and by the individuals comprising it. The leader must adopt a method of clear, timely, and believable communication. The ancient Greek ethos, pathos, logos pattern for public speaking applies here.[23] The Greeks realized that the power of influence and persuasion is essential to effective public leadership. The same is true for leaders in all organizations that practice in dangerous contexts.

Ethos. Ethos is trustworthiness earned via expertise, accomplishments, and character that is verifiable and meaningful to the group and pertinent to the situation. "Character" and "competence" are the watchwords here. Evan Offstein, in *Stand Your Ground*, his book on honorable leadership, describes the operative components and potential impacts of a leader's ethos. He borrows the Army's traditional Be-Know-Do leadership model to construct an ethos matrix to essentially show that there are varying degrees of a leader's knowledge and competence as well as levels of a leader's honor or sustained, proven moral character. Those who maximally embody character and competence, Offstein notes, lead from the "high ground."[24]

One who leads from the high ground is able to establish the kind of ethos needed to effectively instill a meaning-making framework within his organization and, thereby, set a tone that empowers the organizational pursuit of technical and ethical excellence from that foundation. Developing this high-ground ethos is always difficult for a new leader, but with time, determination, consistency, and an anti-zero-defect attitude toward self and others, he or she can attain this level of leadership influence.

Pathos. Pathos is the connection with the group via a believed and shared commitment to the mission and the welfare of the individuals involved. Taking care of one's subordinates seems straightforward, but it can be easily overlooked in a mission-oriented environment. The effective leader must make it a part of the mission to implement these care principles. Another expression of the principle of pathos is "Mission first, people always." Any hint that a leader is acting out of self-interest, self-glory, or self-promotion will result in a loss of influence, and, in dangerous contexts, such a loss is nearly impossible to recover. A subordinate can understand and forgive the occasional and small-scale failure, but will not tolerate lack of personal concern for himself and his comrades.

Logos. Logos is communication that supports ethos and pathos and simply and clearly articulates the vision, goals, principles, and methods to be used. Followers do not always arrive ready-made to connect deeply with the unit and its mission. Leaders must teach followers, using messages presented on the level of the audience.

LEADERSHIP GOALS

Trusted leaders help provide the foundations for the meaning framework of the team members united by a common goal and ethos. The need for meaning includes the purpose of the operation (What is this operation trying to achieve?), justification (Why is this effort necessary and why were we chosen?), self-worth (How does each individual contribute to the outcome?), and efficacy (How can we tell that we are achieving the desired outcome?).[25]

Purpose: What is this operation trying to achieve?

The leader must constantly strive to find ways to communicate macro- and micro-level purposes. In an ideal world, the meaning of every mission in dangerous contexts would fit within the parameters of societal ideals, specific unit objectives, or the codes of conduct that link generations of soldiers, LEOs, and first responders, as well as the leaders' intents. Leaders need not communicate the macro purposes at every mission, but these should be communicated at timely intervals to keep the chaos, sacrifice, and exhaustion in perspective.

Justification: Why is this effort necessary and why were we chosen?

Emergency situations do not allow time for leaders to explain everything. Frequently, when orders are given, execution must be immediate, without question. Lives and mission success depend on this process. The individual's willingness to endure this kind of trust in leadership can be enhanced by leaders taking the time to explain mission tasks and assumed risks whenever possible. If it is not possible to help followers see the justification for a course of action before the mission, then leaders can facilitate followers to make meaning afterward by helping them understand why what was done assists a broader mission. If failure to communicate mission and risk is persistent, followers will lose hope, and they may begin to suffer from feelings of personal uselessness and expendability.

Self-Worth: How does each individual contribute to the outcome?

When missions in dangerous situations are well planned and the objectives are clear, that each person has a role to play becomes manifest and should be rehearsed for the mission and discussed after it. The leader must bring the importance of each team member's respective role into all of his or her planning while reinforcing the fact that each must embrace his role as it applies to the overall mission and not compare his contribution to others.

Efficacy: How can we tell that we are achieving the desired outcome?

As events rapidly unfold in dangerous contexts, it can be difficult to identify concrete, immediately definable results. Cause and effect relationships are often immeasurable in the short term, and otherwise hard to quantify in the long term. How can one measure the results of arrests or patrols on the security of a neighborhood when acts of random violence can occur on any given day?

If in today's complex environments a leader tries to base the hopes of his subordinates on short term, surface-level success—e.g., enemy body counts, number of insurgents captured, patrols completed, lives saved, and so on—he will fail. His subordinates did not sign up to improve statistics and quotas; they want to make a difference. Thus, in the long-term fight to keep the peace, save lives, or win wars, those serving in dangerous contexts can find meaning via the honor intrinsic in voluntary service and the meaning held in the intentional sacrifice of personal freedoms, comforts, and safety, in order to make the public safer in their homes, neighborhoods, and abroad. In other words, every criminal taken off the street or every home saved is important. These are not mindless acts; they are meaning-based acts. The challenge of the leader in dangerous contexts is to make these abstract principles as concrete as possible.

LEADERSHIP STRATEGY

A leader who has patiently achieved the ethos, pathos, and logos prerequisites and who understands, affirms, and can articulate the goals of purpose, self-worth, justification, and efficacy, can then begin the process of planning and executing a strategy to infuse meaning-making effectively into unit culture. One such strategy used by an Army task force is called the Five Core Competencies of Combat Leadership (see Figure 8.1).

Even when one grasps the relevance of meaning-making and the important role of leaders in the meaning-making process, this kind of training might be perceived as impractical if not impossible. "To discuss such issues will be beyond a private's intelligence," some will say, or "This is irrelevant to his duties, not to mention that it's time- and resource-consuming." Yet, some still wonder why soldiers, LEOs, and first responders have difficulty with the repeated stress of operating in dangerous contexts. A systematic approach to meaning-making is required. Organizations that operate in dangerous contexts need an educational and implementation program to assist in the meaning process.

Through collaboration with certain specialists (e.g., religious advisors, mental health service providers, combat stress technicians, and so on), leaders must assist subordinates to think though the following tough questions prior to the mission: How would I make sense of taking another human life? How do I make sense out of giving an order that results in harm to my subordinates? How do I come to grips with the possibility of losing my life in the line of duty? The leader-specialist team can work together to reinforce the meaning-making (through purpose, self-worth, justification, and efficacy) using the following steps:

1. Requiring preoperational education and training focusing on preparing one to interpret upcoming experiences through the meaning framework.

2. Providing ongoing training and counseling or therapy during operations or immediately following a serious incident, reinforcing the meaning standard and assisting subordinates to work through issues.

3. Consulting with each other during operations regarding the moral, morale, and psychological status of the teams and the effect on leader policies and

Common Respect

- Motivate by pride, potential, tradition, success
- Use professional communication patterns
  - Abusive, profane language versus respectful language
  - Humiliation for failure versus instruction and coaching
  - Yelling versus assertive consistency
  - 5:1 ratio—5 deserved compliments : 1 needed criticism / correction
- Display, support, and enforce racial and religious tolerance
- Strive to be solution oriented rather than conflict oriented
- Do not play favorites
  - Fair and consistent discipline
  - Rotate difficult and unwanted duties
- Prevent petty harassment, AKA "Chicken Shit"

"Chicken Shit"—A term coined by the soldiers of WWII used to describe behavior by leaders that makes military life worse than it needs to be: petty harassment of the weak by the strong. . . . "Chicken Shit" is so-called . . . because it is small-minded and takes the trivial seriously. . . . [It] can be recognized immediately because it never has anything to do with winning the war."

— Paul Fussell, *Wartime*

In Summary: "Loyalty in the masses of men waxes strong to the degree that they are made to believe that real importance is attached to their work and to their ability to think about their work. It weakens at every point where they consider that there is a negative respect for their intelligence. . . . [What [a Soldier] thinks about his work will depend in a large measure upon the attitude of his superiors. . . . [One of the fundamental cause[s] of the breakdown of morale and discipline in the Army usually comes from this, that [leaders] transgress by treating men as if they were children or slaves instead of showing respect for their adulthood."

— S.L.A. Marshall, *Men against Fire*

Character and Competence

- Demonstrate a genuine desire and enlarging capacity to act consistently with organizational values. Soldiers have affirmed these as minimum character expectations for leaders (Sweeney and Hannah, *Forging the Warrior's Character*):
  - honesty / integrity
  - confidence and courage (moral and physical)
  - loyalty
  - fairness
  - sense of duty
  - self-control (composure under duress)

In Summary: "Honor is the foundation of truly great leadership. . . . [I]t is impossible to do other things well if you fail to put honor before leadership. Motivational techniques will be transactional. Communication will be . . . without rich meaning. Decision-making will be fundamentally flawed. The missing link in most leadership theory and practice is this very notion of honor. Honor must come first."

— Evan Offstein, *Stand Your Ground*

- Demonstrate a genuine desire and enlarging capacity to perform consistently with organizational standards. Soldiers have affirmed these as minimum competence expectations for leaders (Sweeney and Hannah, *Forging the Warrior's Character*):
  - tactical and technical knowledge and ability to execute / apply appropriately under duress
  - good communication and sharing of information
  - decision making and organizational skills
  - social skills and connection with subordinates

In Summary: "[The Soldier] will endure iron rations and the misery of outdoor living in foul weather for indefinite periods, provided that his tactical experience makes sense and he remains convinced of the general soundness of the operations. Once he loses that faith, it becomes very difficult to restore it. He will lose it very quickly when he sees that casualties are wasted on useless operations or when he begins to feel that he is in any respect the victim of bad planning or faulty concepts."

— S.L.A. Marshall, *Men against Fire*

Care for Soldiers and Families

- Excel at career management: Evaluations / awards / promotions / schools / Permanent Change of Station (PCS)
- Manage leave / pass time equitably
- Respect, protect, and facilitate personal and family worship / spiritual traditions
- Take swift action on family emergencies and needs
- Protect soldier personal time / sleep plan / Forward Operating Base rotation
- Attend to health concerns quickly and professionally
- Monitor soldier personal stress management techniques / Mentor these skills constantly
- Use stress diffusing techniques during mission debriefs
- Facilitate and encourage self-referral to chaplain, behavioral health, or medics
- Make formal or informal command referrals to chaplain, behavioral health, medics for stress triage and treatment (err on side of safety)
- Enforce attendance at scheduled appointments: medical, counseling, therapy, etc.

In Summary: "There is nothing more soul-less than a religion without good works, unless it be a patriotism which does not concern itself with the welfare and dignity of the individual."

— S.L.A. Marshall, *Men against Fire*

Cohesion and Morale

- Plan and implement unit / family social functions across the ranks
- Emphasize unit history, tradition, honor code, and accomplishment
- Build relationships of trust in a culture of honor and affirmation
- Give more rewards than administrative discipline
- Promote inclusion rather than ostracizing
- Pull subordinates up to next level of performance, rather than tearing down
- Prevent closing of ranks and blame shifting

In Summary: High morale and cohesion sustained by an environment of honor is a primary factor in mitigating long-term negative effects of combat stress.

— Concept adapted from Jonathan Shay, *Achilles in Vietnam*

Communication

- Implement, sustain, and frequently monitor a "need to know" information flow process through the chain of command
- Provide a clear task and purpose for every mission
- Maintain a clear connection between missions and overall national and operational goals, and demonstrate tangible evidence of progress frequently
- Strive to give subordinates 72 hours of predictability

In Summary: "[Accurate, timely, current] information is the soul of morale in combat.... [W]e strain our supply lines so that fresh eggs and oranges may be supplied in the front lines ... [yet] we have not found the means to assure an abundant flow of that most vital of all combat commodities — information."

— S.L.A. Marshall, *Men against Fire*

FIGURE 8.1 Five core competencies of combat leadership

decisions; helping subordinates understand their experiences by assisting them in working through their belief system and in sharing perspectives.

4. Assisting subordinates upon mission completion—via formal training requirements; individual interaction, counseling, and therapy; and leadership communication and example—to interpret their experiences based upon their prior meaning and helping them reformulate their meaning framework based upon this interpretation.

These ideas are not solely event driven, but can be worked into the very fabric of standard procedures, regulation, policy, and intentional, intense follow-ups upon mission completion. With this particular emphasis, the leadership becomes the formalized voice of meaning to the unit, increasing the probability of ethical action in dangerous contexts and the possibility of post-incident meaning-making and personal growth.

Meaning-Making for the Institution

A common discussion among those who lead in dangerous contexts surrounds the perception by many that American culture no longer has a meaning-making impulse that provides new military, LEO, and first responder candidates with a preexisting meaning framework comparable with the behaviors and values necessary in dangerous contexts. Word of mouth suggests that ethical failure in combat is happening more often than reported. Though such reports are unverified, a recent study revealed that a majority of soldiers and Marines would not report a comrade's ethical breach.[26] Could recent examples of dishonorable conduct be the tip of the iceberg?[27]

Leaders who can facilitate meaning-making to confront this challenge are critical. Institutionally, however, the armed forces and LEO agencies cannot afford to assume that their leaders are capable of providing this kind of leadership. Therefore, in addition to individual leadership initiative, there must also be an institutional response. Institutions should consider the following for meaning-making:

- Incorporate formal meaning-making training at every level throughout a career. The existential underpinnings that compel a person to form and apply meaning frameworks must be directly and clearly defined and developed. Committing tangible resources and time-allocation is critical.

- Implement creative and effective institutional meaning policies and training requirements at every unit level and include them as formal criteria for performance review. Create metrics for effectiveness of leadership in this area and then reward it.

- Set specific and measurable goals for institutional mind-set changes toward meaning-making in the organization.

- Identify and assist the restoration of hurting, dysfunctional leaders and refuse to promote those who resist such assistance or do not personally promote and exemplify institutional values, no matter their operational productivity.

The Army has made some recent progress in this area by launching a new soldier fitness program called Comprehensive Soldier Fitness. It is a first step in addressing the need to train the whole person, including the mind, spirit, and conscience, for combat experiences. It is only a first step, however. Institutions that operate in dangerous contexts must create an overall meaning-making culture.

MEASURING THE OUTCOMES OR MEANINGS MADE

Although this chapter has illustrated ways in which leaders and institutions can bolster effective meaning-making, meaning is nonetheless a personal experience. How can leaders recognize when meaning has been made? One possibility is to use psychological surveys. For example, the Meaning in Life questionnaire uses ten items to assess how meaningful people judge life to be and how much they are searching for meaning.[28] The stress-related growth scale assesses positive changes people perceive in themselves following traumatic events.[29] However, the words and deeds of those serving supply critical information, as well:

> A team of paramedics sit around a table with hot wings and beer, their after duty tradition, filled with fresh emotions of the day's tragedy. On their last response for the day, they were unable to revive a young child who had drowned in her neighbor's pond. It was a hard one. One team member reflects on the meaning-making training his unit had recently conducted. One exercise during the training had challenged them to think about tragedies that had contributed to shaping them into the first responders they had become. He remembered his uncle who had died in the World Trade Center towers on 9/11, and how he wanted to be like him. Perhaps, he thought, the family that had lost its child might adopt and bring a better life to an orphan. Perhaps the neighbor would invent a better gate lock, such things cannot be known. The potential for good exists, however, such as his own valiant efforts that day. He does not verbalize these thoughts that night, for fear of sounding out of touch, but he plans to talk about

them when he and the others get together at his house on Saturday for college game day.

Here are some suggestions for measuring meaning-making:

1. Listen for unit talk. Does it match the leadership's vision during routine operations and with resolution during times of trauma?
2. Watch for subordinate leaders' and subordinates' independent initiatives in accordance with this vision.
3. Monitor discipline, cohesion, and morale issues. Look for changes, such as higher retention, fewer psychological casualties, fewer breaches of conduct, and so on.
4. Consult with medics, religious advisors, mental health personnel, and subordinate leaders for trends.
5. Track grief responses and recovery patterns to the lowest level.
6. Conduct meaning-making reviews following traumatic events.

CONCLUSION

Dangerous context leadership requires the ability to motivate people to act contrary to their natural impulses of self-preservation and to do so in a way that maintains organizational standards and values. Many times these expectations create a seeming disconnect between one's values and the requirements of duty, eroding one's meaning framework. One might assume that the traditional compliance methodology provides sufficient control for leaders to guide their subordinates successfully in dangerous contexts and afterward.

We posit, however, that a compliance-only approach will not suffice. This chapter has attempted to demonstrate that leaving the value versus action disconnect unresolved may result not only in an individual's short-term degradation of psychological health, ethical resilience, and task accomplishment, but also in a long-term degradation of his or her ability to positively contribute to the organization and society. Employing institutional policies and leadership strategies that recognize intentional and appropriate meaning-making provides a promising way to foster the personal resilience necessary to achieve total mission success in dangerous contexts.

NOTES

1. Leo Tolstoy, "My Confession and Critique of Dogmatic Theology," in *The Complete Works of Count Tolstoy*, trans. Leo Wiener, vol. 13 (Boston: Dana Estes, 1904), 18.

2. Crystal L. Park, "Making Sense of the Meaning Literature: An Investigative Review of Meaning Making and Its Effects on Adjustment to Stressful Life Events," *Psychological Bulletin* 136 (2010): 257–301.

3. Aristotle, *Nicomachean Ethics*, 1095a15–22 in *Complete Works of Aristotle: The Revised Oxford Translation*, ed. J. Barnes, vol. 1 (Princeton, N.J.: Princeton University Press, 1984).

4. Immanuel Kant, *Groundwork of the Metaphysics of Morals*, 4:425–4:435, trans. Mary Gregor (Cambridge: Cambridge University Press, 1997).

5. Epictetus, *Enchiridion*, trans. George Long (Mineola, N.Y.: Courier Dover, 2004).

6. Epictetus, *The Discourses of Epictetus*, bk. 1, chap. 24, trans. W. A. Oldfather (New York: G. P. Putnam's Sons, 1925), 47.

7. Nancy Sherman, "Stoic Warriors: The Ancient Philosophy behind the Military Mind" (remarks at the Carnegie Council on Ethics and International Affairs, February 22, 2006), http://www.carnegiecouncil.org/resources/transcripts/5327.html.

8. Quoted in Sherman, "Stoic Warriors."

9. S. Kierkegaard, *Either/Or*, trans. Alastair Hannay (London: Penguin Classics, 1992).

10. M. Heidegger, *Being and Time*, trans. Joan Stambaugh (Albany: State University of New York Press, 1966).

11. Jean-Paul Sartre, *Being and Nothingness,* trans. Hazel Estella Barnes (New York: Simon and Shuster, 1995), 613.

12. Ibid., 620.

13. Ibid., 574.

14. Ibid., 672; cf. 680–707.

15. Ibid., 622.

16. Viktor E. Frankl, *Man's Search for Meaning*, 4th ed. (Boston: Beacon Press, 1992), 123.

17. Michael F. Steger, "Meaning in Life," in *Oxford Handbook of Positive Psychology*, 2nd ed., ed. S. J. Lopez (Oxford: Oxford University Press, 2009), 679–687.

18. A. Antonovsky, *Health, Stress and Coping* (San Francisco: Jossey-Bass, 1979), and *Unraveling the Mystery of Health* (San Francisco: Jossey-Bass, 1987).

19. Anotonovsky, *Unraveling the Mystery*, 19.

20. Ibid.

21. See C. L. Park et al., "Meaning Making and Psychological Adjustments Following Cancer: Mediating Roles of Growth, Life Meaning, and Restored Just World Beliefs," *Journal of Consulting and Clinical Psychology* 76 (2008): 863–875.

22. There have been, however, significant studies on why soldiers fight: Samuel Lyman Atwood Marshall, *Men against* Fire (Norman: University of Oklahoma Press, 2000), and Samuel A. Stouffer et al., *The American Soldier: Combat and Its Aftermath,* vol. 2 (Princeton, N.J.: Princeton University Press, 1949).

23. Stephen R. Covey, *The Seven Habits of Highly Effective People* (New York: Free Press, 2004), 255.

24. Headquarters, Department of the Army, *Field Manual FM 6–22: Army Leadership* (Washington, D.C.: Government Printing Office, 2005); Evan H. Offstein, *Stand Your Ground: Building Honorable Leaders the West Point Way* (Westport, Conn.: Greenwood Publishing, 2006).

25. Roy F. Baumeister, *Meanings of Life* (New York: Guilford, 1991).

26. See Department of Defense Mental Health Advisory Team (MHAT-IV) survey findings, http://www.armymedicine.army.mil/news/mhat/mhat.html. For a brief summary see http://www.defense.gov/releases/release.aspx?releaseid=10824.

27. Hal Bernton, "Stryker Soldiers Allegedly Plotted to Kill Afghan Civilians," *Seattle Times,* August 24, 2010, and Gene Johnson, "Grisly Photos Show U.S. Soldiers Posing with Afghan Corpses," *Chicago Sun-Times,* October 2, 2010, http://www.suntimes.com/news/nation/2764912,CST-NWS-afghan02.article.

28. M. F. Steger et al., "The Meaning in Life Questionnaire: Assessing the Presence of and Search for Meaning in Life," *Journal of Counseling Psychology* 53 (2006): 80–93.

29. C. L. Park, L. H. Cohen, and R. L. Murch, "Assessment and Prediction of Stress-Related Growth," *Journal of Personality* 64 (1996): 71–105.

Influencing When People Are in Harm's Way

CHAPTER 9

Trust
The Key to Leading When Lives Are on the Line

Patrick J. Sweeney, Kurt T. Dirks, David C. Sundberg, and Paul B. Lester

The Hostage Rescue Team (HRT) of the Federal Bureau of Investigation was called in to assist the bureau's Special Weapons and Tactics (SWAT) team in Memphis to apprehend a married couple wanted on drug trafficking charges. The fugitive couple and an adult son, all with criminal records, were believed to be living in trailers in a mountain valley where outsiders would be easily noticed. The fugitives were known to stockpile weapons and had vowed never to be taken alive by law enforcement. Thus the FBI considered them to be armed and extremely dangerous.

Two HRT snipers along with two SWAT snipers were given the mission of positively identifying the fugitives and providing security and containment for the assault force. The snipers would have to travel several kilometers through wooded, mountainous terrain using night vision goggles (NVGs). The SWAT snipers did not have nighttime, overland movement capability, which is why HRT was brought in.

The HRT leader and his partner, nicknamed Felix, had gone through HRT selection and had served together all around the world, in the process establishing complete trust in each other. They had never met the two SWAT snipers. The HRT leader, being familiar with SWAT training, believed that the SWAT snipers were expert marksman who would be highly effective once at the objective, but they lacked training in extended overland movement with NVGs. As a consequence, the HRT leader created two sniper teams, each consisting of one HRT and one SWAT sniper to mitigate the SWAT snipers' lack of NVG training and to promote teamwork.

The HRT leader knew that he needed to quickly earn the trust of the SWAT snipers because any hesitation in following directives during the mission could affect mission success and the safety of the team. The leader asked Felix to train the SWAT snipers on the use of NVGs and to give them a detailed mission brief to demonstrate the competence of the HRT members. The HRT leader encouraged the SWAT snipers to ask questions and offer suggestions concerning the mission.

The HRT leader's plan for the operation was to move by vehicle along the ridgeline above the valley where the fugitives lived and then move by foot with NVGs down the mountain to the fugitives' trailers. Once at the objective, the HRT-SWAT sniper teams would take up separate positions to have a 360-degree view of the objective area. Once the fugitives were positively identified, the HRT leader would notify the assault team, and the snipers would provide security and containment.

The HRT team pushed out from their staging area at midnight during a lightning storm that reduced visibility to just a few meters. The heavy rain made travel on the dirt trail leading to the ridge slow and hazardous. Several hundred meters from the top of the draw, the vehicles slid off the road into a swollen creek. The HRT leader gathered the men and equipment, made a change to the plan, and got the team moving again toward the draw. The leader placed Felix in the lead because he trusted his ability to navigate and control movement. The HRT leader traveled third in the file followed by his SWAT partner in the fourth position to provide rear security. Their movement was slow due to limited NVG visibility caused by the heavy rain.

From the top of the draw, the team descended the heavily wooded slope and NVG visibility deteriorated to only a few feet. The team's ability to see completely vanished during the lightning flashes. NVG movement under these conditions challenged the experienced HRT snipers and made it extremely difficult for the less-experienced SWAT snipers. The trees were so thick and visibility so low that Felix's SWAT partner had to place his hand on Felix's backpack so he did not lose his way.

HRT reached their objective rally point under the cover of darkness. The storm was still raging. The leader sent Felix and his SWAT partner forward to conduct reconnaissance of the objective and movement routes to final positions. They returned twice because flooding and deadfalls along the route prevented them from completing the reconnaissance. The team leader gave the SWAT snipers the mission of monitoring the satellite radio and providing security while he and Felix moved forward to locate the objective. After finding the objective, Felix and the leader returned to link up with the SWAT snipers just as it was starting to get light.

The team leader realized that it was not possible to move the sniper teams into the planned positions because the flooding and the sunrise greatly increased the chances of compromise. The leader had to quickly change the plan. Felix and his partner would move to the right side of the objective to provide cover and containment, and the leader and his partner would move to the rear of the objective to identify the fugitives. The new positions required the team members to assume additional risk because they were closer to the fugitives' trailers than originally planned. The leader's trust in his SWAT partner's training was justified when the sniper built a good, concealed position and set up effective observation of the target allowing the leader to focus on making additional changes to the plan if necessary and reporting to the operations center.

The dawn revealed a dismal rainy day. The fugitives started to move around after daybreak, relieving themselves outside their trailers. After three hours of intense observation, the team was able to positively identify all fugitives. The command post was notified and the assault team started maneuvering toward the objective.

The assault phase was a tense and critical part of the HRT mission because the sniper team had to keep the assault element informed about the location and activities of fugitives and be ready to take action if the assault element was compromised. The assault element stealthily moved their vehicles to the top of the drive leading onto the property. The assault team swept down on the objective while the HRT and SWAT snipers provided security. The fugitives were completely surprised and tried to run, but were quickly apprehended by the well-trained agents. The search of the trailers revealed assault rifles stacked by the doors. Fortunately, a well-planned and executed mission never gave the fugitives the opportunity to make a last stand.

TRUST AND LEADERSHIP

The sniper scenario highlights the important link between group members' trust in their leader and the leader's ability to influence them to willingly risk their lives to achieve the team's mission. Here "trust" means the willingness to assume vulnerability to the actions of another group member (leader, subordinate, or peer) based on a sense of confidence in that group member.[1] For example, during the sniper mission, the team members' trust in the HRT leader allowed them to follow him throughout the mission even when changes in the plan required them to assume additional risk. A study of soldiers serving in Iraq found that trust was necessary and essential for a leader to exercise influence in combat. Soldiers, who trusted their leaders, allowed them a greater degree of influence regarding their readiness to follow directives and motivation to perform duties to complete the mission.[2] This scenario and research point to trust being the psychological mechanism that provides group members with a sense of security to assume the risks associated with following leaders in dangerous contexts. Group members' willing acceptance of their leaders' influence represents true and impactful leadership, not mere compliance. Trust is a foundation of effective leadership across almost every type of organization and circumstance.[3]

Leaders tend to give trusted group members more opportunities to provide input about decisions and greater latitude to perform their duties.[4] For example, during the planning phase of the sniper mission, the HRT leader's trust in the SWAT members influenced him to seek their input. Group members who earn the trust of their peers possess a greater ability to exercise influence within the group. These trusted peers emerge as informal leaders who can significantly influence the morale, cohesion, and effectiveness of the group. Thus, to exercise influence within a group, one must first earn the trust of its members. Mutual trust between group members, especially leaders and subordinates, enhances mutual influence, which increases organizational effectiveness.[5]

Results from the aforementioned study conducted in Iraq also found that soldiers who did not trust their leaders would not willingly follow their directives, would question orders, and complied with orders only after taking actions to assume the absolute minimum risk. A lack of soldiers' faith in leaders' directives and elevated concern about personal safety put unit members' lives and mission accomplishment at risk. As one artillery gunner succinctly stated, "If you cannot trust your leader, you are going to have doubts about your safety as well as the safety of your fellow soldiers. You will not perform 100 percent for your leader if there is not trust."[6]

In a team, trust is the adhesive that bonds people, allowing them to work cooperatively to achieve a higher purpose or mission. The bonds of trust among group members fuel a commitment to stay connected, protect and promote the welfare of group members (even at the risk of personal cost, including one's life), and fulfill the group's purpose and mission.[7] Trust is a foundation on which cohesion and cooperation in organizations is built. One example of such cooperative action is when a soldier, firefighter, law enforcement officer, or medical professional risks his or her life to protect a fellow group member or complete a mission. To summarize, trust is important to leadership because it determines the amount of influence leaders exercise and also creates the bonds that encourage people to work cooperatively to achieve a common purpose or mission. In short, trust is necessary and essential for the exercise of influence within a group.

Assessing Trust

Although it is useful for leaders to accurately grasp the extent to which they are trusted, it can be difficult to ascertain in practice. There are a number of informal gauges and cues at the disposal of leaders for assessing the extent to which others willingly make themselves vulnerable to another's leadership. For example, one might consider the quality of communications, followers' desire for openness, and their willingness to exercise initiative.

Regarding communications, if followers trust their leader, they will provide him or her with candid, timely, and complete information that usually includes their personal thoughts and reactions.[8] Group members do not hesitate to share good and bad news, potential issues within the organization, and their candid input on the possible causes of problems and potential actions to resolve them. In such a relationship, the leader will not be blindsided by unresolved issues or group members' perceptions.

Followers are more likely to seek openness in their relationship with a leader when they trust that leader. For example, some followers take advantage of informal opportunities to engage their leader about work as well as non-work-related topics. During such interactions, followers are likely to share personal information (e.g., family history and activities, career goals, hobbies, and so on) and try to get to know the leaders as people. In leader-follower relationships characterized by trust, group members do not feel the need to rely on standard policies and procedures to protect themselves from their leaders' actions, so their relationships are more open and less formal.[9]

The willingness of followers to exercise initiative in performing their duties or bettering the organization is another potential indicator of their trust in leaders. Group members who trust their leader fulfill his or her directives without resistance and complete tasks beyond minimal expectations. Members feel safe in taking risks and making mistakes to exceed the leader's expectations or improve the organization because confident leaders use setbacks to facilitate growth.

THE IROC TRUST DEVELOPMENT MODEL

Trust develops through reciprocal cycles in which each person in the relationship acts in a cooperative and competent manner to reduce the other's anxiety or fear of exploitation and to reveal the potential rewards for staying in the relationship. The mechanism that drives the trust cycle is a person's willingness to assume some degree of risk related to the other's action. For instance, leaders who empower their followers with the freedom of action to do their jobs are assuming a degree of vulnerability, thus communicating to the group members their trust. If the followers perform their duties in a competent and cooperative manner, thus upholding the leader's expectation of their ability to complete their duties without much supervision, the leader is more likely to assume a greater degree of vulnerability in the future. Each time the leader and group members assume risk through dependence on one another and the choice is validated through results, the trust in the relationship deepens.[10]

We introduce here the IROC trust development model, which focuses on the influence of the individual, the relationship, the organization, and the context in creating and sustaining trust (Figure 9.1). The individual fac-

Credibility: The Foundation
- ▸ Competence
- ▸ Character
- ▸ Caring

Organization Systems
- ▸ Shared values, beliefs, and norms
- ▸ Structure, practices, policies, procedures, and systems

Relationships Matter
- ▸ Respect and Concern
- ▸ Open communication
- ▸ Cooperative interdependence to achieve common purpose and goals
- ▸ Willingness to trust and empower others

Context
- ▸ Change in dependencies
- ▸ Attributes, knowledge, skills, and abilities impacted
- ▸ Temporary team (swift trust)

FIGURE 9.1 The individual-relationship-organization-context (IROC) trust development model

tor addresses the knowledge, skills, abilities, and character traits leaders need to develop to fulfill their leadership duties. The relationship factor touches on leader actions needed to create the positive relationships required to function in dangerous contexts. The organization factor considers how unit culture, structure, policies, procedures, and practices set climate, which affects the individual and relationship factors. The context factor focuses on how environment can influence the nature of dependencies in relationships as well as members' psychological needs. The IROC trust development model assists leaders in organizing their thoughts about trust and provides them with a systematic means of creating interventions to enhance trust and a means for predicting how events or behaviors might impact trust.[11]

The Individual Factor

Followers place their trust in leaders based on the stable characteristics that define who the leaders are as people. Team members want leaders who are highly competent, display good character, and care about followers' and the group's well-being.[12] If group members can attribute leaders' competence, character, and caring to stable dispositional characteristics, then they have confidence in the leaders' ability to ensure future success of the group while at the same time protecting their welfare, which leads to trust. It is important that leaders possess these three attributes and that they find authentic ways for followers to recognize this.

Competence. In dangerous contexts, perceived leader competence is the dominant factor in the development of trust with group members because it plays a pivotal role in mission accomplishment and also in protecting members.[13] Competence entails a leader's decision-making abilities, domain and organizational knowledge, and stress-management skills. Group members must believe the leader possesses the necessary knowledge, skills, and abilities to accomplish the mission and protect their welfare.

The leader's primary function is to make decisions to ensure efficient use of resources to accomplish the unit's mission and to protect the followers' interests. Group members depend on their leaders' expertise and judgment to plan and execute operations that successfully complete the mission with the least possible risk to followers' lives. Thus, a dangerous context leader must have the intellect and domain expertise—understanding the capabilities of equipment and people and how best to employ them—to plan operations to efficiently accomplish assigned missions while anticipating possible contingencies and adaptations. For instance, in the sniper scenario, the team leader made quick adjustments to the movement plan when the insertion vehicle slid off the road prior to the designated insertion point.

One of the competencies unique to dangerous contexts is the importance of leaders' stress-management skills. Leaders' ability to effectively manage stress facilitates their ability to focus attention, process information, and make sound decisions in dynamic and dangerous situations. Equally important, leaders' composure under stress can bolster their followers' confidence that the group can effectively handle the situation, which reduces stress within group members.[14] For instance, in the sniper scenario, the leader's ability to handle the stress and stay composed while navigating difficult terrain in a torrential rainstorm that required a change in plans helped keep the team composed, confident, and focused on the mission.

Character. A leader's character entails factors such as honesty in word and deed (integrity), physical and moral courage, sense of duty, and loyalty. Integrity is important for the development of trust because it provides followers with a sense of confidence that regardless of the situation, leaders will act in accordance with their and the organization's values and also lead by example. Leaders should identify and take advantage of opportunities to communicate and model their values (e.g., relating decision rationale to values). Leaders who lead in accordance with their values serve as good role models and provide the organization with clear moral and ethical boundaries within which to accomplish missions. In dangerous contexts, especially when deadly force must be used to accomplish the mission, these boundaries validate group members' moral purpose and sustain their will to complete the mission.

Honesty in communication builds trust while simultaneously enhancing group effectiveness. Subordinates undertake risky actions based on the information leaders provide them, thus they demand honest and candid information about the purpose of the operation and the dangers involved. Candid information creates an atmosphere of transparency, providing leaders and group members with an enhanced sense of security because it assists in reducing perceptions of hidden agendas and opens channels of communication.

Furthermore, open communications fulfill group members' psychological need for knowledge about a situation and the true purpose and desired end-state of an operation (the why). This information reduces group members' uncertainty, allows them to assess feasibility, and also provides them a reason for risking their well-being.[15] Group members' understanding of the true purpose of an operation provides them a way to make meaning out of the trauma they might experience, which protects their mental health and fosters trust.[16] If the team does not understand the mission's purpose or thinks it is dubious, members expect their leaders to press higher authorities for clarification or modification of the operation. Any indications that leaders are hiding the true purpose or desired end-state of an operation would result in a decrease in group members' level of trust in their leaders and the motivation to accomplishment the mission.

Physical and moral courage are important elements in dangerous context leaders' character. Physical courage entails leaders perceiving risk, experiencing some level of fear, and willingly sharing the danger with group members while still performing their duties.[17] As highlighted in Chapter 2 leaders' physical courage provides followers with a sense of confidence that no matter how dangerous the situation becomes, the leaders will be with them carrying out their duties, thus bolstering trust. It is important to note that in dangerous contexts, group members understand that leaders will experience fear, however, they do not want them to show signs of it.[18] As one infantry company fire support officer stated, "[L]eader courage is [important because] if you show your fear, no one will want to follow you into a situation where you are putting your lives on the line."[19] Leaders behaving in a courageous manner tend to provide their subordinates with good examples to follow, serve as sources of strength, and instill a sense of confidence that the situation is not as bad as they think and they will get through it.[20]

Moral courage is important in earning trust because it provides leaders the strength of will to do the right thing, regardless of the situation and the cost they might incur. Put another way, moral courage is the willingness to incur risk in order to act in accordance with one's values and to uphold one's loyalty to followers and the unit by protecting their best interests. One example would be leaders' willingness to confront headquarters to request modifications to missions they feel put their organizations at unnecessary risk. Subordinates trust leaders with strong moral courage because they can depend upon them to act with integrity and to support them in the most vulnerable situations.

It is important to remember that once trust in a leader's character has been lost, it is difficult, if not impossible, to regain.[21] Followers tend to see a leader's character or integrity as being relatively stable over time. The stability of this perception and the fact that character is an assessment of the person's essence makes it a prominent factor in building and maintaining trust in all relationships.

Caring. Care for followers is the second most important leader attribute that influences the development of trust in the dangerous context of combat. Soldiers believe that leaders who care about them will plan and execute missions with the least possible risk to their lives. Also, soldiers think that caring leaders will support them by representing their needs and interests to higher authorities and fighting to obtain necessary resources. This type of bond with leaders seems to provide group members with a sense of security because it helps address followers' concerns about their safety.[22]

This category of behavior embodies a leader's concern for and desire to promote group members' well-being, even at the cost to his or her self-interest. Leaders' concern for group members' welfare forms the basis for building mutual cooperation in the leader-subordinate relationship, which is essential for the establishment of trust.[23] Situations in which leaders must sacrifice their own self-interest to promote the welfare of their followers tests and demonstrates the depth of care for group members. This sacrifice can be as simple as giving up a couple of hours on the weekend to visit a group member in the hospital or as complex as disobeying a directive in combat in order to protect the welfare of subordinates. The key is that the leader willingly incurs some cost to protect or promote the welfare of those that serve in the unit.

Where leaders spend their time indicates what they care about. Leaders who invest time in supporting, getting to know, listening to, and developing their group members are communicating to them that they are valued. One of the most powerful ways leaders can demonstrate their care for group members is to train them well. Tough, realistic training to standard, in which leaders participate, helps provide assurance that each individual and the group can accomplish assigned responsibilities. Other small investments of time leaders can leverage to demonstrate they care are writing thank you notes, conducting periodic counseling and mentoring sessions with members, publicly acknowledging and giving credit for group success to the members, walking around and visiting members daily to get to know them, sending them to school or for training even if it means a short-term decrement to the organization, helping them solve problems, and assisting them when they leave the organization.

To summarize, group members place trust in the characteristics of leaders that fall into the three categories of competence, character, and caring. Therefore, leaders should continuously strive to acquire domain knowledge and improve decision-making skills, develop their integrity by making daily decisions based on personal and organizational values, communicate the rationale behind decisions, and demonstrate care by investing their most precious resource, time, in the people they lead. These behaviors are associated with authentic and transformational leadership (individual consideration and idealized influence), which were discussed in Chapter 2.[24]

The Relationship Factor

Trust is placed in an individual based on competence, character, and caring, but it develops within a relationship. The quality of the relationship can either facilitate or hinder the development of trust. Relationships characterized by respect, concern, open and honest communication, common purpose, and dependence upon (or vulnerability to) another person facilitates the development of trust.[25] This is especially true in leader-subordinate relationships because the characteristics of a good, quality relationship tend to reduce the perceived hierarchical power differential between the leader and team members, thus reducing fear and uncertainty and promoting cooperation.[26]

Mutual Concern and Respect. As noted above, mutual concern and respect form the foundation for quality interpersonal relationships. From the leaders' perspective, the foundation for respect for followers rests in leaders' assumption that group members possess potential to enrich the unit. Leaders who care about and view their followers as valued team members set the conditions for subordinates to reciprocate care and respect. When leaders and group members care about each other's welfare and respect each other, cooperation begins to flourish because it is in the best interest of all parties. Mutual concern and respect also serve to facilitate open communication.

Open Communication. To establish a positive relationship with team members, leaders should start by clearly communicating their expectations of followers and providing followers with an opportunity to communicate their expectations of leaders. Clarifying expectations reduces the potential for future conflict in relationships and synchronizes members' efforts regarding responsibilities and priorities. Seeking subordinates' input on the operations of the unit is the surest way to open channels of communication. Leaders who seek follower input are communicating their respect for team members, trust in their competence, and a willingness to be vulnerable.

Furthermore, to foster a climate of transparency, leaders should make an extra effort to share information about the organization's activities, upcoming requirements, rationale for decisions that affect the group, and changes in priorities and policies. Keeping group members informed provides them insight into leaders' intentions, prevents rumors, provides opportunities to potentially influence group outcomes, and allows members to prepare for future operations. Thus, open communication facilitates the development of trust because it clarifies leaders' and members' goals and intentions, demonstrates respect, and provides members the opportunity to exercise potential influence on leader actions.

Mutual Dependence to Achieve a Common Purpose. Group members depending on each other to obtain a common purpose or goal facilitates trust and cooperation within the group.[27] Group members know that the most efficient way to achieve a common purpose is for everyone to perform their individual duties and to work cooperatively with others.

Leaders should create opportunities to discuss with group members how shared dependencies in the group make them into a stronger team. They should also discuss how each member's role impacts others and contributes to accomplishing the organization's mission. This technique helps members understand the role and importance of their individual contributions to the team and its purpose. Members who understand the dependencies within the team gain greater insight into how they can influence the team and how other team members influence them.[28] In a combat context, soldiers' desire to uphold fellow unit members' dependencies and maintain their status in the group are powerful motivating forces that encourage soldiers to face the dangers of combat and sustain them through the hardships of a tour.[29]

For dangerous context leaders, the best means of demonstrating that they accept dependence on group members is to share hardships and dangers with them. Leaders who willingly go into harm's way and place their safety in the hands of their teammates powerfully communicate the shared interdependence within the group and also their trust. Group members depend on leaders to make good decisions to accomplish their mission while protecting their welfare. Leaders who are out front sharing in the group's hardships and dangers are able to better understand the situational demands and capabilities of the team and thus can make well-informed decisions in adapting to the dynamic nature of a situation. Furthermore, sharing hardship and dangers with team members communicates the leaders' confidence in themselves and the members to complete the mission and highlights their mutual dependence.[30]

As an example of these points, in the sniper scenario the FBI SWAT snipers had to depend on the HRT leader to develop a plan to get them from the drop-off point to their watch positions safely and without compromise to achieve the common purpose of capturing the fugitive couple. The HRT leader had to depend on the SWAT snipers to provide security and surveillance for the assault element. The team leader was out front sharing the dangers of the movement in a lighting storm and the threat from the suspects at the objective. The willingness of the SWAT snipers and HRT leader to put their well-being in the hands of each other demonstrates the type of interdependence that facilitates cooperative behavior.

Willingness to Trust and Empower. To initiate the trust-building cycle with team members, leaders need to demonstrate their intention to trust followers.[31] A simple way to empower subordinates is to give them the trust and freedom to do their jobs without micromanaging them. This begins with the leaders' assumption that their team members are capable and motivated to do well. Leaders should encourage them to take the initiative to solve problems on their own and should be willing to view mistakes as developmental opportunities. A good empowering technique is to provide followers with mission-type directives, which clearly state what task needs to be done, the purpose of the task regarding its impact on the organization, and the desired effects of the task that need to be achieved in terms of time, space, terrain, and outcomes. Mission-type directives empower subordinates to determine how to accomplish an assigned task by providing them a broad, flexible decision-making framework within which to work and adapt to dynamic situations.[32] Also, group members' participation in decision making enhances their commitment to the decisions. Leaders will hear group members discuss decisions as "we have decided" or "our decision is" versus "the leader has decided."

In the sniper scenario, the officer in charge gave the HRT team leader two missions: to positively identify the fugitives before initiating the assault and to provide cover and containment for the assault team. In this situation, the sniper team leader was empowered to determine the best positions to accomplish the two missions, the movement plan, and the timetable. An understanding of the tasks (identify fugitives and provide cover and containment) and purposes (trigger to initiate assault and to protect assault members) provided the HRT sniper team leader the flexibility to adjust positions when the team encountered flooding at the objective.

To summarize, the quality of the relationship that leaders create with their followers matters in facilitating the development of trust. Therefore, dangerous context leaders are wise to invest time in developing quality relationships with each member of their team. Leaders should use authentic and transformational leadership (inspirational motivation and intellectual stimulation) behaviors to build quality relationships.[33]

The Organization Factor

Leaders should foster organizational behaviors and attributes that reinforce and support the characteristics of the relationship and individual factors.

Culture. An organization's culture influences the development of trust throughout the group. Shared values and beliefs provide members with guidelines indicating what they need to hold themselves and others accountable, how members should interact, and the characteristics that define the organization. Culture also serves as an agent that brings people together to strive to uphold common values and beliefs about the organization and its purpose.[34] Thus, the organization's culture has a powerful influence on members' expectations regarding others and their own behavior. For example, in the sniper scenario the HRT leader had never met the two SWAT snipers who were joining his team; however, being familiar with the culture and training of elite units, such as SWAT, the leader reasonably believed he would find in the new members levels of competence and values similar to HRT.

Leaders might use a vision-development process, such as the one outlined by James Collins and Jerry Porras, to assist members to collectively discover, define, or reaffirm the core values and beliefs that define their organization.[35] Examples of organizational core values that foster the development of trust throughout an organization include respect, caring for people, loyalty, honesty in word and deed (integrity), duty, courage, teamwork, and service to others. If all members of the organization support and hold themselves accountable to these values, then a peer, subordinate, or leader can reasonably expect that interactions with other members of the organization will be positive and within the framework of their values.

Structure, Policies, Procedures, and Practices. The systems used to run day-to-day operations can influence trust in relationships throughout an organization. The organization's structure, policies, procedures, and practices communicate the underlying assumptions about its values and members. Leaders should strive to ensure that organizational systems are congruent with espoused values and purpose, treat members fairly and with respect, and empower people to work cooperatively.

Leaders should strive to flatten the organizational structure as much as possible, clarify roles and scopes of authority, push decision making to the lowest level, reduce stovepipes that isolate elements, and ensure that subordinate elements do not have two bosses. Flat organizations, with unity of command and with multiple means for subordinate elements to share information, foster an open and cooperative climate that helps subordinate elements understand their dependencies on other elements, know what each one is doing to contribute to mission accomplishment, and coordinate efforts to create efficiencies, all of which serve to enhance trust within the organization.

Leaders should ensure that policies, procedures, and practices are fair, transparent, and promote cooperation. Indeed, fairness of procedures is one of the most powerful predictors of trust in leadership.[36] When making personnel assignments, leaders should consider existing unit cohesion and get input from subordinate leaders. The organization should have a socialization policy that assigns a sponsor to new personnel to assist them in integrating into the team. The criteria for promotions should be published and members counseled on their potential for advancement; all qualified members must be afforded equal opportunity. Organizations should use a collective reward system because individual reward systems tend to foster competition between group members that reduces cooperation and trust. A collective award system encourages members to work together to realize a common objective, which facilitates the development of trust.[37]

Procedures and rationales for allocating requirements and resources should be transparent and have a mechanism that allows for subordinate leaders' input. Transparency in the allocation of resources and requirements provides members with an organizational perspective and bolsters perceptions of fairness, which facilitates cooperation and trust. Leaders should review training policies to ensure that they maintain unit integrity as much as possible and also provide themselves the opportunity to participate in the actual training. Leaders should ensure that the organization has a system for sharing information and receiving feedback from group members on leaders' performance, the organization's performance, and ideas on how to improve both.

The Context Factor

The context within which a team operates will shape how the individual, relationship, and organization factors play out.

Changes in Dependencies. Dangerous contexts influence trust in relationships because they affect the nature of dependencies, which could impact members' psychological needs. Changes in dependencies in leader-subordinate relationships caused by the unique risks inherent in a dangerous context can trigger increased monitoring of and a shift in the importance individuals place on certain leader or follower characteristics perceived necessary to meet the new psychological needs, especially if one has no prior experience with the leader or group member in such a context.[38]

From the group members' perspective, operating in a dangerous context requires them to significantly increase their dependence on leaders to protect their physical and mental well-being while accomplishing the assigned mission. Therefore, group members place great importance on their leaders' behavior and seek to verify that they possess such characteristics as competence, character, and caring, which help ensure their safety during operations.[39] Results from studies conducted in combat found that soldiers placed the greatest importance on leaders' competence, loyalty (caring), integrity, and leadership by example. Soldiers also believed that (a) leader competence facilitated the accomplishment of the mission in the most efficient manner; (b) loyalty ensured all operations were planned and executed to protect soldiers' well-being; (c) integrity provided faith that information passed along about operations was honest regarding importance and risk; and (d) leaders sharing dangers and hardships ensured that leaders' and followers' outcomes were linked and communicated confidence, which reduced the threat to group members' lives and provided them a sense of security.[40]

From the leaders' perspective, the dangerous context increases their dependence on empowering subordinates to accomplish the mission and to provide timely and candid reports about the situation and their units' capabilities. Thus, leaders place great importance on follower characteristics of competence, honesty, and initiative, which help ensure mission completion with accurate and candid reporting. Results from a study conducted in combat to explore the attributes leaders looked for in trusted subordinates found that leaders believed (a) competence greatly enhanced the potential for mission completion, and thus was the most important characteristic; (b) honesty ensured candid and accurate reporting so leaders could plan future operations; (c) initiative, discipline, and perseverance provided units adaptability to complete missions in a dynamic environment; and (d) loyalty to the mission and unit contributed to mission accomplishment.[41]

Temporary Teams and Swift Trust. The sniper mission described at the beginning of this chapter provides a context that is often present in public safety and military sectors—a situation where several law enforcement organizations must come together and form a temporary team to accomplish a volatile task. Team members rarely know each other, and if they do, it is often based on reputation rather than actual interaction. Leaders in this situation must establish what is sometimes referred to as swift trust if they are to be able to exert influence.

While individuals may prefer to be able to observe how a team member performs in a situation before trusting, they do not have that luxury in temporary groups. As a consequence, they tend to rely on shortcuts, such as prototypes or mental models of what ideal team members may look like. The closer a person matches the individual's mental model, the greater the level of initial trust. As noted above, a study conducted in an Iraqi combat zone designed to map soldiers' mental model of the trusted combat leader found that such a person possessed the attributes of competence, loyalty, integrity, honesty, confidence, courage, composure, and leadership by example.[42]

Leaders can use the prototype of an "ideal" combat leader to assess themselves for self-development and also to create strategies to communicate possession of these attributes when taking charge of a temporary team or a new organization. Furthermore, organizations can use the prototype to tailor their leader-development programs so they are inculcating the necessary attributes. From the followers' perspective, they obviously need to be aware of their potential biases and ensure that they appropriately adjust their trust over time.

CONCLUSION

Mutual trust is essential to lead effectively, especially in dangerous contexts. The level of trust that group members have in their leader impacts the amount of influence the leader exercises, individual and organization performance, unit cohesion, and followers' job satisfaction.[43] The IROC trust development model provides dangerous context leaders with an easy, empirically supported, and systematic means for building and maintaining trust within their organization. Thus, when leaders hit the "trust point," they have what is necessary to lead effectively.

KEY TAKE-AWAY POINTS

1. Trust is the foundation of effective leadership across almost every type of organization and circumstance, but it is particularly critical when lives are on the line. People will focus on their personal safety instead of mission success when working with leaders and peers they do not trust.

2. Trust is built upon a leader's competence, character, and caring.

3. Leaders must invest time and energy to build positive, empowering relationships with their team members that are characterized by transparent communication, mutual influence, and cooperation to achieve common goals and purposes.

4. Leaders need to align and leverage the culture and systems of their organizations to promote cooperation and trust.

5. Dangerous contexts affect the dependencies in leader-follower relationships that can influence the importance members place on competence, character, and caring; the strength of social bonds (cohesion); and the organization's culture, policies, procedures, practices, and systems.

KEY REFERENCES

Dirks, Kurt, and Donald Ferrin. "Trust in Leadership: Meta-analytic Findings and Implications for Organizational Research." *Journal of Applied Psychology* 87 (2002): 611–628.

Sweeney, Patrick. "Trust: The Key to Combat Leadership." In *Leadership Lessons from West Point*, ed. Doug Crandall, 252–277. San Francisco: Jossey-Bass, 2007.

NOTES

1. Morton Deutsch, "Trust and Suspicion," *Journal of Conflict Resolution* 2, no. 4 (1958): 265–279; and Roger Mayer, James Davis, and F. David Schoorman, "An Integrative Model of Organizational Trust," *Academy of Management Review* 20, no. 3 (1995): 709–734.

2. Patrick Sweeney, Vaida Thompson, and Hart Blanton, "Trust and Influence in Combat: An Interdependence Model," *Journal of Applied Social Psychology* 39, no. 1 (2009): 235–264.

3. Kurt Dirks and Donald Ferrin, "Trust in Leadership: Meta-analytic Findings and Implications for Research and Practice," *Journal of Applied Psychology* 87, no. 4 (2002): 611–628.

4. John Gabarro, "The Development of Trust, Influence, and Expectations," in *Interpersonal Behavior: Communication and Understanding in Relationships,* ed. A. Athos and J. Gabarro (Englewood Cliffs, N.J.: Prentice Hall), 290–303.

5. Robert Golembiewski and Mark McConkie, "The Centrality of Interpersonal Trust in Group Processes," in *Theories of Group Processes,* ed. C. Cooper (London: John Wiley and Sons, 1975), 131–185.

6. Patrick Sweeney, "Trust: The Key to Combat Leadership," in *Leadership Lessons from West Point,* ed. D. Crandall (San Francisco: Jossey-Bass, 2007), 275–276.

7. Golembiewski and McConkie, "Centrality of Interpersonal Trust," 131–132; Darryl Henderson, *Cohesion: The Human Element in Combat* (Washington, D.C.: National Defense University Press), 9–26; and S. Bowles, "Group Competition, Reproductive Leveling, and the Evolution of Human Altruism," *Science* 314 (2006): 1569–1572.

8. Golembiewski and McConkie, "Centrality of Interpersonal Trust," 134–136.

9. Dale Zand, *The Leadership Triad* (New York: Oxford University Press, 1997), 93–97.

10. Harold Kelley and John Thibaut, *Interpersonal Relationships: A Theory of Interdependence* (New York: Wiley, 1978), 231–237.

11. Sweeney, Thompson, and Blanton, "Trust and Influence in Combat," 235–264.

12. Dirks and Ferrin, "Trust in Leadership," 611–628; and Mayer, Davis, and Schoorman, "An Integrative Model of Organization Trust," 717–720.

13. Yael Lapidot, Ronit Kark, and Boas Shamir, "The Impact of Situational Vulnerability on the Development and Erosion of Followers' Trust in Their Leader," *Leadership Quarterly* 18 (2007): 16–34; S. Stouffer et al., *The American Soldier: Combat and Its Aftermath,* vol. 2 (New York: John Wiley and Sons, 1965), 122–130; and Sweeney, Thompson, and Blanton, "Trust and Influence in Combat," 249–251.

14. Sweeney, "Trust: The Key to Combat Leadership," 263–265.

15. Ibid., 269–270.

16. Richard Tedeschi and Lawrence Calhoun, "Posttraumatic Growth: Conceptual Foundations and Empirical Evidence," *Psychological Inquiry* 15, no. 1 (2004): 1–18.

17. Sean Hannah, Patrick Sweeney, and Paul Lester, "Toward a Courageous Mindset: Subjective Influences on the Acts and Experiences of Courage," *Journal of Positive Psychology* 2, no. 2 (2008): 1–7.

18. G. D. Mitchell, *Soldier in Battle* (Sydney: Angus and Robertson Limited, 1940), 9–15.

19. Sweeney, "Trust: The Key to Combat Leadership," 266.

20. Ibid., 266–268; and Adolf Von Schell, *Battle Leadership* (Quantico, Va.: Marine Corps Association, 1999), 13–17.

21. P. H. Kim, K. T. Dirks, and C. D. Cooper, "The Repair of Trust: A Dynamic Bi-Lateral Perspective and Multi-Level Conceptualization," *Academy of Management Review* 34 (2009): 401–422.

22. Sweeney, "Trust: The Key to Combat Leadership," 258–259.

23. Morton Deutsch, "Cooperation and Trust: Some Theoretical Notes," in *Nebraska Symposium on Motivation,* ed. Marshall Jones, vol. 10 (Lincoln: University of Nebraska Press, 1962), 275–319.

24. Bill George, *Authentic Leadership: Rediscovering the Secret of Creating Lasting Value* (San Francisco: Jossey-Bass, 2003), 1–11; Bernard Bass and Bruce Avolio, "The Implications of Transactional and Transformational Leadership for Individual, Team, and Organization Development," *Research in Organizational Change and Development* 4 (1990): 231–272.

25. Deutsch, "Cooperation and Trust," 289–302.

26. John Thibaut and Harold Kelley, *The Social Psychology of Groups* (New Brunswick, N.J.: Transaction Inc., 1986), 100–125.

27. Ibid., 124–125.

28. Ibid., 100.

29. R. W. Little, "Buddy Relationships and Combat Performance," in *The New Military: Changing Patterns of Organization,* ed. M. Janowitz (New York: Russell Sage Foundation, 1964), 207; and Stouffer et al., "The American Soldier: Combat and Its Aftermath," 136.

30. Sweeney, "Trust: The Key to Combat Leadership," 261–263.

31. Deutsch, "Cooperation and Trust," 304–306; and Kelley and Thibaut, *Interpersonal Relationships,* 235–236.

32. Von Schell, "Battle Leadership," 17.

33. George, *Authentic Leadership,* 1–11; Bass and Avolio, "Implications of Transactional and Transformational Leadership," 231–272.

34. Edgar Schein, *Organizational Culture and Leadership,* 3rd ed. (San Francisco: Jossey-Bass, 2004), 25–37.

35. James Collins and Jerry Porras, "Building Your Company's Vision," *Harvard Business Review,* September–October 1996, 39–51.

36. Dirks and Ferrin, "Trust in Leadership," 614.

37. Deutsch, "Cooperation and Trust: Some Theoretical Notes," 279–285; and Craig L. Pearce, "The Future of Leadership: Combining Vertical and Shared Leadership to Transform Knowledge Work," *Academy of Management Executive* 18, no. 1 (2004): 51–52.

38. Thibaut and Kelley, "The Social Psychology of Groups," 100–125.

39. Patrick Sweeney, "Do Soldiers Reevaluate Trust in Their Leaders Prior to Combat Operations?" *Military Psychology,* suppl. 1, 22 (2010): S70–S88.

40. Gregory Belenky, Shabti Noy, and Zahava Solomon, "Battle Stress: The Israeli Experience," *Military Review,* July 1985, 11–19; and Sweeney, "Trust: The Key to Combat Leadership," 252–277.

41. Sweeney, "Trust: The Key to Combat Leadership," 252–277.

42. Ibid., 253–275.

43. Dirks and Ferrin, "Trust in Leadership," 623; and Sweeney, Thompson, and Hart Blanton, "Trust and Influence in Combat," 258.

CHAPTER 10

Building Resilient Teams

Stephen J. Zaccaro, Eric J. Weis, Rita M. Hilton, and Jack Jefferies

T eams that do well in routine and normal circumstances can easily fall apart when confronted with *in extremis* conditions. The qualities that promote team success under normal contexts are different from those that help teams continue to succeed when their operational circumstances turn tumultuous and dangerous. Researchers use the term "viability" to define those teams in which members can work together effectively in most normal contexts (Sundstrom, DeMeuse, and Futrell 1990). Team viability is a fundamental condition for team effectiveness, but while it is necessary, it alone is insufficient for team success within *in extremis* contexts. Team effectiveness in dangerous conditions requires not only viability, but also team resilience—the collective ability of team members to continue to perform effectively as conditions turn more arduous, dangerous, and challenging. Team resilience emerges from (a) focused team-building and team-training interventions that strengthen the individual and team factors—contributing to team viability; (b) shared operational experiences that nurture team viability into team resilience; and (c) leadership processes that operate in team training and team operational experiences to facilitate team growth and cohesiveness. Cohesion, trust, and collective efficacy—the three main elements of team viability—are discussed here along with cognitive, social, and emotional components of team resilience. Figure 10.1, below, summarizes the elements of team viability and team resilience.

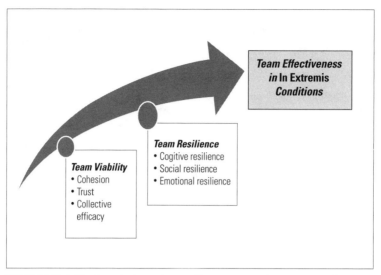

FIGURE 10.1 The foundations of team effectiveness in *in extremis* conditions

TEAM RESILIENCY: AN ILLUSTRATION

On the morning of August 11, 2007, the soldiers and leaders of a mechanized infantry task force in a rural area of Iraq found themselves in contact with a highly skilled and elusive guerrilla-type enemy that could strike and kill with great efficiency. As part of the "surge brigade" strategy, the battalion had not replaced a departing unit; there was no theater-provided equipment or mature sector for the battalion to inherit. Their area of operation, just southeast of Baghdad in the Tigris River Valley, had been void of coalition forces or Iraqi security forces since late 2005 and was one of the last strongholds of al-Qaeda in Iraq (AQI) in the country. Numerous irrigation and drainage canals severely restricted friendly freedom of movement and were augmented by a dense mixture of pressure-plated improvised explosive devices (PPIEDs), command-wire improvised explosive devices (CWIEDs), and house-borne improvised explosive devices (HBIEDs).

August 11 started like any other—another twenty-four hours of combat duty utilizing a combination of static route presence (on previously cleared roads) and dynamic dismounted clearance in sector due to the mounted IED threat. As the element farthest south in the battalion's area of operation, this particular infantry platoon was conducting a presence patrol along the southern high-speed avenue of approach with Bradley Fighting Vehicles (BFV) and up-armored Humvees while its dismounted element was busy conducting a controlled burn of high reeds and vegetation on the edge of the road in order to reduce concealed routes up to the road, provide better fields of fire, and uncover potential weapon storage caches.

A single enemy sniper shot rang out in the early morning air, instantly killing the driver of the southernmost BFV. The platoon sergeant began immediate casualty evacuation procedures. The remainder of the platoon leadership directed a defensive posture to report the contact, assess the threat, ascertain where the shot came from, and determine the next course of action. While the battalion tactical operation center coordinated for casualty evacuation and immediate attack aviation support, the company commander directed a reinforcing platoon into the sector and a subsequent cautious clearance to the south in order to prevent the sniper from successfully egressing the area.

The remainder of the platoon, led by a second lieutenant infantry officer, began a systematic clearance of buildings in the area. After no enemy contact in the first two multilevel buildings, a four-man element consisting of a squad leader, two team leaders, and a rifleman entered the final building. As the first man moved toward the inner stairwell, he inadvertently triggered what an explosive ordinance detection team would later reveal to be a pressure-plated IED, which caused the entire building to explode. The sound was deafening and could be heard in the battalion tactical operation center more than two miles away. Within the span of approximately two hours, the infantry platoon lost five soldiers. The clearance operation understandably stalled. The platoon leader directed a tighter defensive posture in order to conduct the mass-casualty evacuation once the fire in the building was under control. The sniper was never caught.

After the platoon leader conducted a relief-in-place briefing with his sister element, the platoon was directed back to the battalion's patrol base, a relatively safe area to recover and reflect on the day's deadly consequences. Although early into their tour, this unit had already experienced enough casualties to be wholly familiar with the grieving and recovery process. Chaplains, grief counselors, combat stress elements, and leadership from higher headquarters surged to the patrol base to serve as outlets for the soldiers and leaders attempting to deal with the traumatic event. After-action reviews were conducted at all levels to glean as much from the experience as possible. New tactics, techniques, and procedures were quickly developed, disseminated, and practiced horizontally and vertically throughout the organization.

Leaders and soldiers were consoled and allowed time to mourn the loss of their friends and comrades. After cross-attaching new leadership from internal and external sources to assume empty squad- and team-leader positions and allowing them to acclimatize to the unit and area of operation, the platoon was reinserted into the line-of-fire following a two-day stand down period. This unfortunate event was neither the first nor the

last to be experienced by this unit. In early July, the company lost two soldiers to a PPIED triggered in a driveway. There were many similar bad days
to come in their long, fifteen-month deployment.

In total, the battalion task force suffered fifteen killed-in-action and
ninety-seven wounded-in-action. However, there was no immediate or
enduring decrement in the performance of its soldiers and leaders. They
were able to rapidly and rationally deal with the complex and chaotic situation. They carried both the literal and figurative scars expected from such
a traumatic event but were able to successively go on with their mission.
In fact, only one month later, the company served as the task force's main
effort element as it extended the battalion's footprint deeper south into
AQI-controlled territory in order to establish a reinforced company-sized
patrol base that still stands today.

This episode took place in an extreme environment characterized by several
stressors, including hot weather, rough terrain, and an exhaustive, twenty-
four-hour patrol cycle. Confronted by a particularly deadly situation involving
traditional and homemade improvised explosive devices, the task force members proved to be a resilient unit. How do group members acquire and maintain their hardiness as a unit in the face of such mortal threat and challenge
(Bartone 2006)? What are the roles and responsibilities of team leaders in fostering this resilience?

Teams begin to become a sustainable reality when members perceive that
working together will result in greater goal accomplishment than if working
separately (Thibaut and Kelley 1959). Dangerous contexts can create forces
and perceptions that hinder this process if unaddressed by the leader and
team members early in the team's developmental cycle. Team developmental
processes and leadership actions can counter such negative dynamics by facilitating the emergence and maintenance of team viability and resilience. This is
a progressive process, with viability established first, followed by key qualities
that promote resilience. In the next section, we further describe the separate
viability and resilient components that facilitate this building process, as illustrated in Figure 10.1.

THE ELEMENTS OF TEAM VIABILITY

Team viability refers to how strongly members are committed to working
together in close coordination and to their sustained ability to do so effectively
(Barrick et al. 1998; Sundstrom, De Meuse, and Futrell 1990). The three key
elements of team viability are cohesion (Sundstrom et al. 1990), trust, and collective efficacy—all of which can be influenced by the leader.

Cohesion

Cohesion refers to the strengths of attraction or attachment members have to the team—that is, their willingness to serve within the team (Festinger 1950). Researchers have described three main sources for the attachments and bonds that exist in cohesive groups (Back 1950; Festinger 1950). The first, social cohesion, refers to the degree of interpersonal attraction among team members, in other words, the extent to which they like each other (Carron 1982). Members can commit to other members and to the team as a whole, simply because they like them. The second source, task cohesion, refers to the degree of interest members have for the tasks and mission of the team and the extent to which they like them (Carron 1982). This attraction can flow from the intrinsic nature of the task or from the extrinsic rewards and outcomes that they derive from task accomplishment. The third source of cohesion is a sense of pride engendered by group membership (Festinger 1950). Some groups possess a long and prestigious tradition, and admission to such groups may be limited and difficult to attain. Special Weapons and Tactics (SWAT) teams, specialized firefighter units, and Army Special Forces are examples of these kinds of teams. The bonding of members in these groups may follow not only from task and social ties, but also from loyalty to each other as members of an elite unit.

Building Team Cohesion. Each source of cohesion can follow from different antecedents. Research has shown that interpersonal attraction derives from several factors, including similarity (Byrne 1961) and familiarity (Zajonc 1968). As team members discover shared backgrounds, interests, attitudes, beliefs and values, they increase their fondness for one another (Byrne and Nelson 1965). Also, as team members spend more time together, their liking of one another grows, as long as initial interactions are not negative (Swap 1977). This happens because the uncertainty common to meeting strangers typically gives way to more positive reactions; with repeated interactions, members learn more about one another and typically discover little ground for any possible initial wariness (Lee 2001).

These findings suggest that leaders can build social cohesion by providing new team members opportunities to (a) become familiar with one another and (b) discover similarities among themselves. Thus, early in a team's formation, leaders might have members engage in social activities that they determine most if not all of the members would enjoy. They can also simply ensure frequent interactions among members to foster greater familiarity. Given the deleterious effects of early negative interactions, leaders need to intervene quickly in such events so that they do not derail emerging social cohesion.

Task cohesion emerges when team members value and commit to the unit's work. Hackman and Oldham (1975) have defined five core elements of jobs that make them intrinsically interesting: significance (the importance of the work), variety (greater range in the different skills required to do the work), identity (involvement in all aspects of the work being completed), autonomy (decision-making freedom provided by the work), and feedback (knowing how one is performing). For many of the kinds of teams discussed here—military and first responder units working in dangerous environments—these elements are often a given. Their work typically is of great significance, whether responding to a threat to the nation or to a catastrophe in a community. Members of such units typically need to use a range of skills in completing their mission and will participate at all stages of the mission, whose desired outcome is often self-evident.

To build group cohesion around the work of the team, leaders need to foster the shared belief that only by collaborating effectively can team members gain the benefits of task accomplishment. Thus, leaders should emphasize to team members that they can realize more significant teamwork effects by working together (Sweeney, Thompson, and Blanton 2009; Thibaut and Kelley 1959). This interdependence of action is often truer in dangerous conditions, as effective collective action will save the most lives. The threat of personal danger, however, can result in members forgetting this connectivity. Thus, leaders need to continually reinforce the notion that remaining a cohesive group when confronted with extreme danger provides the best chance for survival.

Although not highlighted in the Iraq vignette, there were many actions the leaders and soldiers engaged in during their mission preparation that assisted in developing critical social and task cohesion. The shared hardships of countless iterations of intense, realistic training created a climate that fostered confidence in individual tactical skills that translated into subsequent trust and faith in each other and their leadership as a collective unit (see similar examples in Sweeney 2007; Sweeney, Thompson, and Blanton 2009). They also had sufficient time to interact with one another in more relaxed settings and develop the kinds of social and friendship bonds that promote social cohesion.

Trust

Mature and viable teams have members that trust one another. Research suggests that team trust reflects several beliefs that members have about one another. First, members have confidence in the skills and abilities of their fellow members to successfully complete their part of the team's mission (Cook and Wall 1980; McAllister 1995). This assumed reliability exists even when missions become complex and difficult. Second, members believe that their teammates' behavior will consistently match their word, implying dependability and indicating that members will honor commitments they make to one another (Bromiley and Harris 2006; Cummings and Bromiley 1996). Third, team members have communication and interactions that are honest and open (ibid.); there is no expectation or reality of hidden agendas among members. Fourth, members assume a common goodwill toward one another, and more important, mutual care and emotional support (McAllister 1995). This element reflects perhaps the deepest level of team trust and is particularly important for teams operating in dangerous environments.

The resilient team in Iraq demonstrates the importance of these elements of trust. When the driver of the BFV was killed by the sniper, the unit engaged in activities to evacuate casualties, locate and track the sniper, and clear surrounding buildings. To work effectively as a unit under the circumstances, team members needed to trust absolutely in the competency and reliability of one another, to believe that each person knew what had to be done and how to do it. More important, especially after the triggering of the HBIED, members needed to rely on one another for emotional support, to trust that they could display strong emotions and grief to one another and knowing that they would be consoled and nurtured without judgment. Emotional trust contributes greatly to the resilience of a team.

Building Team Trust. Assumed reliability, verbal dependability, mutual honesty, and mutual emotional support are aspects of team trust discovered through research. What can leaders do to facilitate the development of cognitive and emotional trust in team members? Jarvenpaa and Leidner (1999) found in a study of geographically distant teams that early task communication fosters reliability. In addition, early social communication through which members get to know about one another lays the foundation for later emotional trust. Leaders of newly formed groups should encourage and provide opportunities for such information exchanges. Leaders need to ensure that role and normative expectations are clear to all members (Mayerson, Weick, and Kramer 1996). Such communication contributes to assumed reliability, allowing members to have faith in the competence of their fellow teammates. This perceived reliability will often develop quickly in military units and first responder teams that go into dangerous environments because they typically receive intensive task training before joining or being accepted to the team. Thus, the assumption at group formation is that members assigned to the team have high minimum levels of competence.

Leaders can also foster team trust by insisting on verbal dependability—that is, following through on stated commitments—as a strong norm in the group. This means that leaders must "walk the talk" as well, keeping their word to the team and leading by example. They do so by embedding with the team in whatever dangerous context, sharing the threat equally with their subordinates. In addition, leaders contribute to development of team trust by promoting an atmosphere of openness and judgment-free communication. In essence, they stress that members are not allowed to censor one another's well-intentioned and honest communications, creating what Edmondson (1999) calls an environment of psychological safety. Leaders set norms that lead to feelings of safety and trust by (a) indicating that inputs are needed from all members, (b) listening to members' concerns, (c) being receptive and encouraging members to listen to others' ideas, and (d) modeling psychological safety by engaging in appropriate self disclosure (Edmondson 2003).

Collective Efficacy

Collective efficacy has been defined as "a sense of collective competence shared among individuals when allocating, coordinating, and integrating their resources in a successful concerted response to specific situational demands" (Zaccaro et al. 1995, 309; see also Bandura 1986). This definition emphasizes the shared belief among team members that they can work well together—that is, they have "coordination capabilities" (Zaccaro et al. 1995, 311). For *in extremis* contexts, collective efficacy means the team members have a shared belief that they can meet the threats and dangers confronting them.

Collective efficacy contributes to team effectiveness in several important ways, particularly in dangerous circumstances. Members of efficacious groups are more likely to work harder on behalf of the group, set more challenging goals, and persist in the face of difficulties and obstacles (Zaccaro et al. 1995). Also, as members gain confidence in the team's collective competence, group cohesion grows stronger. Such perceptions are strongly related to the assumed reliability elements of team trust. Thus, collective efficacy buttresses the two other elements of team viability.

Building Collective Efficacy. Belief in one's own efficacy or that of a team tends to emerge from consistent patterns of successful past performance (Bandura 1986; Tasa, Taggar, and Seijts 2007). Collective efficacy can also derive from patterns of constructive feedback that allow the team to determine reasons for specific failures and develop corrective measures (Zaccaro et al. 1995). Also, leaders who encourage their teams to work hard, help members enhance their skills, model effective task and teamwork behaviors, and carry out certain leadership functions effectively increase the collective competence beliefs of their subordinates (Kane et al. 2002; Zaccaro, Rittman, and Marks 2001).

Table 10.1 Summary of Leader Actions That Facilitate Components of Team Viability

Element	Contextual Definition	Facilitating Actions by Team Leaders
Cohesion • Social • Task Pride	Strength of attachment members have to the team • Social cohesion: degree of interpersonal attraction among members • Task cohesion: degree of interest members have in mission tasks • Pride: sense of fulfillment members derive from social identification with the unit	• Maximize opportunities to become familiar with each other and discover similarities • Address task significance, variety of tasks and missions, emphasize identity and levels of autonomy, and provide feedback • Emphasize interdependence of outcomes • Accentuate and highlight salience of proud traditions
Trust • Assumed reliability • Verbal dependability • Mutual honesty • Mutual emotional support	Possessing confidence in the skills and abilities of fellow team members and leaders, leading to bonding and open communication and genuine caring	• Encourage opportunities to engage in frequent task and social communications early in the team's formation • Establish clear roles and normative expectations; insist on verbal dependability as a norm • Lead by example • Share experiences in hard, realistic training events • Reflect on reliability and dependability of teammate and leader actions • Encourage sharing of open and honest assessments of skill level, values, beliefs, and emotions
Collective efficacy	Sense of shared confidence among members that they can work effectively as a team in response to specific challenges	• Provide constructive feedback to address gaps in individual and collective skills and abilities • Build upon success with multiple and increasingly difficult drills to develop patterns of success • Model effective task and teamwork behaviors

To build collective efficacy, a leader needs to provide opportunities for team members to work together in ways that develop a record of success. This can be done most easily through training exercises, where members focus on learning and rehearsing effective teamwork. One key is to provide team members opportunities to see their teammates exhibiting teamwork behaviors. Leaders should make use of feedback in these exercises after team performance missions to help members understand (a) that any failures are not a consequence of team incompetence, but correctable mistakes, and (b) helping devise team strategies for avoiding such mistakes on future missions. Throughout team-training exercises and missions, leaders need to assure members that they have the ability to perform the tasks at hand (Zaccaro, Rittman, and Marks 2001). They also need to model effective teamwork. From such experience, team collective efficacy develops and contributes to team viability. The leader actions that facilitate team viability are illustrated in Table 10.1.

MOVING FROM TEAM VIABILITY TO TEAM RESILIENCY

Team viability or maturity is an important prerequisite for team resilience, but while team maturity is necessary for team resilience, it is not alone sufficient. Teams also need to develop certain norms and procedures that help them cope with the extraordinary cognitive and emotional demands of highly dangerous missions. There are a number of suggestions on how team resiliency can be maintained and strengthened before, during, and after dangerous events (see Table 10.2).

Strategies for Building Team Resilience

Dangerous events can influence three sets of processes in lesser resilient teams. First, the severity of danger can impair how team members think and process information. Second, imminent threat can disrupt the cohesion of the unit. Third, the possibility of dying, and its actual occurrence (or near miss), can raise strong emotions that disrupt interactions among remaining team members. Building team resilience requires interventions that counter the influences of threat and danger on team cognition, social bonds, and emotional dynamics. These interventions go beyond building team viability to focus on helping teams perform effectively and maintain viability when in danger. A number of strategies are necessary to foster team cognitive, social, and emotional resiliency.

Building Cognitive Resiliency. Threat and danger narrow the cognitive focus of a team and impair individual and collective information processing (Staw, Sandelands, and Dutton 1984; Weick 1993). Leaders can help their teams become more cognitively resilient through four types of interventions: overtraining of routine but critical drills, rehearsals and contingency planning, establishment of information communication norms, and after-action reviews.

Table 10.2 Summary of Leader Actions That Facilitate Components of Team Resilience

Element	Contextual Definition	Facilitating Actions by Team Leaders
Cognitive resilience	Ability to focus cognitive resources on necessary adaptive and non-typical actions as conditions of threat impair information-processing capacity	• Overtraining of routine but critical drills; cross-training • Rehearsals and contingency planning • Establishment of norms for communicating information • After-action reviews
Social resilience	Maintenance of cohesion among team members under conditions of high threat; grounded in the understanding that members are more likely to survive and be successful in the face of danger if they maintain their team bond and work together as a group	• Intensive team training to encourage collective efficacy, trust, and confidence
Emotional resilience	Capacity to manage one's own and others' emotions under conditions of threat	• Pre-event: conducting emotional rehearsals and simulations during training and mission preparation • During: modeling calmness prior, during, and after traumatic events • Post-event: honest reviewing of event for sensemaking; sharing emotional responsibility; providing emotional coping support

In the course of a dangerous mission, when unit members are engaged in the most critical and threatening part of an operation (e.g., when under attack), there are many "routine" actions and maneuvers that need to occur in addition to any necessary adaptive and non-typical responses. For example, in the Iraq scenario, after the sniper had killed the BFV driver, the unit needed to (a) begin casualty evacuation procedures, (b) set up a defensive posture, (c) develop a plan to try to prevent the sniper from escaping, and (d) undertake a building clearing operation. If these activities were not already well-rehearsed by unit members, precious cognitive resources would need to be spent on trying to conduct them instead of tending to the adaptive actions necessary to succeed in the crisis. Such typical activities should be "overtrained" (Schendel and Hagman 1982) to the point where members collectively conduct them automatically, without much if any need for conscious processing. This approach applies not only to physical tasks, but also to cognitive ones, such as information retention. Thus, team leaders need to ensure that all members have been trained to this standard and use refresher training whenever possible to reinforce it (Schendel and Hagman 1982). Such training becomes even more important when new people join the team; refresher training facilitates the team continuing to act automatically after acquiring new members.

In his description of a unit's failure in the Mann Gulch fire disaster, a wildfire in Montana's Helena National Forest that claimed the lives of thirteen firefighters during 1949, Weick (1993) notes that the rigid adherence to their formally-defined role structure was a significant factor in the collapse of sensemaking for the unit and points out the failure of most members to take on new roles as team members become separated, lost, or killed. Role substitutability can be promoted through cross-training, the "instructional strategy in which each team member is trained in the duties of his or her teammates" (Volpe et al. 1996, 87). Cross-training can entail having members describe their tasks and roles to other team members, model their role for other members, or engage in exercises in which they perform different roles (Blickensderfer, Cannon-Bowers, and Salas 1998). This training strategy produces a shared understanding of how individual roles are integrated in team action and consequently leads to better team coordination and performance (Marks et al. 2002). Thus, to foster team resiliency, team leaders should combine overtraining strategies with cross-training interventions.

What strategies foster cognitive adaptability in dangerous missions? Tucker and Gunther (2009) interviewed Army leaders who had served in Iraq and Afghanistan and twenty-four Joint Readiness Training Center facilitators and found that adaptability occurred when team leaders and members engaged in contingency planning that entailed "thinking through alternative scenarios that could occur along a predetermined route prior to the mission, such as enemy contact and interactions with civilians" (p. 323). They suggested developing alternative strategies for missions, defining multiple possible outcomes, and engaging in adversarial thinking (taking the perspective of the enemy) as cognitive approaches to foster adaptive performance. These strategies likely help leaders anticipate possible changes in their environment and prepare them to adapt quickly to their occurrence. Leaders are advised here to use these strategies in their mission planning or in the transition phase of team operations (Marks, Mathieu, and Zaccaro 2001). Also, time permitting, they should rehearse alternative strategies and scenarios in which leaders are killed requiring team members to assume new roles (Tucker and Gunther 2009).

In the chaos of crisis situations, information exchange and continual situational awareness can be among the first processes to break down among non-resilient individuals and teams (Weick 1993). To counter such an occurrence, leaders need to foster strong norms in team members to keep communicating vital information throughout crisis episodes (Baran and Scott 2010). They can use simulations and war gaming to help enforce these behaviors (Paton 2006). Leaders also need to model information communication in crises, including asking specific members for specific information. Klann (2003) notes that in a crisis, leaders should inform their followers about "what they know has occurred, explaining what is being done about it now (and what steps are being taken so it won't happen again), and, when possible, describing implications" (pp. 44–45). It should be added that such actions are likely to further team members' trust in the leader.

Team leaders need to make effective use of after-action reviews to examine the information processing and decision making that occurred in the mission. Most important, from a cognitive standpoint, is to determine how shared understandings among team members should be adjusted to accommodate enemy tactics or unanticipated events in a disaster. Note how in the Iraqi vignette, after-action reviews were conducted to gain as much insight from the experience as possible. Based on this knowledge, new tactics and operating procedures were quickly developed, disseminated, and practiced throughout the organization. The unit did not allow the emotionality generated by the loss of comrades to interfere with this crucial cognitive endeavor. Such actions help resilient teams respond more effectively in future missions.

Building Social Resiliency. One particular danger to a group in a moment of disaster or mortal threat is that members will start to worry more about self-preservation than collective survival. In accordance, they begin to act as individuals rather than a team. To avoid such disintegration, team leaders need to establish early on in team training the firm belief that individual survival is maximized when the team acts together. For example, the unit in Iraq developed critical social cohesion through countless hours of personal interaction during mission preparation and training. The collective interdependence of tasks and mission created a sense of team unity and trust and faith in each other. This cohesion can translate into a strong commitment to each other in action—a mentality of "Don't worry. I got your back"—especially when the team is in danger. In operation, such team members experience a shift from a focus on individual, self-preservation to a collective sense of others; that is, the team remains more important than the individual.

Although fear and anxiety are key characteristics in *in extremis* environments, team members' sense of affiliation with the group helps mitigate these elements' debilitating effects. In dangerous environments, soldiers often engage in acts of self-sacrifice to protect their buddies. The Army reinforces this conduct through what is perhaps its strongest norm—no soldier is to be left behind—and by touting as its bravest soldiers those who risk or sacrifice their lives to save their comrades, among them, for example, Medal of Honor recipients (Collier 2006). The Army stresses selfless service as one of its core values.

Prominent among the strategies noted here for reinforcing team cognitive resilience is extensive training as a team. Such an exercise fosters cognitive resilience by routinizing interactions necessary in a crisis and developing shared understandings needed for team adaptation. This type of training potentially has other effects contributing to social resilience. First, as noted earlier, repeated interactions as a team within training scenarios can boost the collective efficacy of the group; this in turn can enhance cohesion. Second, such training can redound in trust in the leader. As teams train with their leaders, they gain confidence in their competence, a key element in subordinate trust (Sweeney 2010). Thus, many of the strategies suggested here for cognitive resilience will likely have ancillary effects for team cohesion, trust, and efficacy (see Cacioppo, Reis, and Zautra 2011 for another perspective of social resilience).

Building Emotional Resiliency. The core challenge to teams in *in extremis* conditions is managing the strong emotional turmoil triggered by individual and collective mortality salience. In the case of such turmoil, team emotional resilience can emerge from three processes: the team leader modeling calmness throughout traumatic events; emotional rehearsals during team training and mission-planning processes; and emotion regulation processes in post-action phases of a mission. The Iraq example illustrates the first process, in that a young and relatively unseasoned junior officer is subjected to a chaotic environment few can scarcely imagine. Rather than freezing during this intense situation, the repetitive nature of the realistic training and extensive contingency planning the unit had completed helped the platoon leader take immediate and effective action.

The leader's demeanor had a calming and direct effect on the unit's psyche, although internally he may have been the opposite of calm. It was not mentioned explicitly in the vignette, but the unit had verbally and physically rehearsed what types of tragedies could occur on a battlefield (such as being wounded- or killed-in-action). Despite a possible desire to stop and administer comfort to a fallen comrade, the threat had to first be eliminated. However, all were assured that aid would be administered and that team members would not be left behind. This trust and faith helped bridge the visual and traumatic chaos team members experienced and greatly assisted later when the unit was able to reflect on the day's events.

When teams encounter *in extremis* conditions, they look to their leaders to make sense of the situation and to provide behavioral guidance (Yammarino et al. 2010). At a minimum, leaders need to display a sense of calm—an unruffled, cool, and consistent exterior demeanor—that models how team members should respond. The failure to do so could result in a form of emotional contagion (Hatfield, Cacioppo, and Rapson 1994) whereby panic shown by the leader permeates the rest of the team. Researchers have identified two leader attributes possibly contributing to impression of a sense of calm. The first, mental toughness, stems from the sports psychology literature and consists of an ability to display calmness, despite inner turmoil (Mack and Ragan 2008; Loehr 1986). The second attribute is hardiness (Bartone 2006; Maddi 2007), which reflects the belief that people can "control . . . the events of their experience," a deep commitment to one's life activities, and the perception of both positive and negative changes as learning opportunities (Kobasa 1979, 3; see also Bonanno 2004). Perceptions of control and an approach to negative effects as learning experiences help hardy individuals tamper feelings of threat in *in extremis* conditions better than the less hardy (Bonnano 2004).

Mental toughness and hardiness are often viewed as stable individual attributes. Building emotional team resilience may depend upon selecting team leaders that possess these attributes. Maddi and colleaques have developed training programs that have demonstrated success in fostering hardiness in adults (Maddi 2007; Maddi, Kahn, and Maddi 1998). This line of research suggests that such training be part of building team resilience. Indeed, with the goal of reducing post-traumatic stress disorder, depression, and anxiety associated with combat trauma, the Army introduced the Comprehensive Soldier Fitness (CSF) program in 2009 to assess the status of its 1.1 million active duty, reservist, and National Guard soldiers and enhance their coping strategies (Cornum, Matthews, and Seligman 2011; U.S. Army n.d.).

Emotional rehearsals represent another mechanism for building team emotional resilience. These involve leaders and trainers increasing soldiers' awareness about the emotional dimensions of combat. Along this line, Paton (2006) argues that training simulations for police officers should reflect the psychological demands and challenges likely to be confronted by individuals in dangerous circumstances. He notes that such training can "help increase knowledge of stress reactions and provide opportunities for officers to rehearse strategies to deal with them" (p. 3). Increasing awareness of possible emotional reactions may also be effective as part of mission planning. Unit leaders can remind unit members, especially those who have never been in combat, of the emotional demands they are likely to encounter and to be prepared with recommended coping responses.

The value of these mental rehearsals of emotional events derives from the literature about inoculation and forewarning effects on resistance to persuasion (McGuire 1964). As members experience a degree of psychological threat in training and simulations, they may begin to build emotional defenses and coping mechanisms; likewise, when forewarned in mission planning about combat stressors, they may increase their readiness to activate such mechanisms.

Perhaps the most important contribution to building team resilience lies in post-combat processes engaged in by the team. Post-operation briefings play crucial roles in emotional resilience. First, in missions that did not achieve full success, analyzing the causes of events helps build a sense of collective responsibility and a clearer understanding of how to cope with such events in future missions (Hannah, Campbell, and Matthews 2010). Resilient teams are ones that thrive at dissecting their failures because they realize that the investigation of particular issues or problems are not necessarily a direct reflection of their personal failure but rather a more critical assessment of what was supposed to happen, what did happen, why (contributing factors to faulty decision or action), and what they need to do or change in order to prevent a repeat of the outcome. The exceptional leaders and teams are those that do not follow-up one mistake (making it during an action or performance episode) with another (by not acknowledging the mistake and thus failing to fully understand it and learn from it). The value of problem-focused coping to emotional resilience lies in the sense of control it engenders in team members, lessening the likelihood of feelings of helpless in such situations.

The second role of post-traumatic-event processes is to help team members confront as honestly and openly as possible the emotional consequences of experiencing *in extremis* events. This emotion-focused coping may take the form of an active action, such as sharing the burden of teammates lost, or a passive one, in which the leader and team recognize that they need space and time to deal with losses. A crucial element is the provision of support from outside the team, because all members of a traumatized unit may need support, rendering internal provisioning of emotional support difficult (Paton and Violanti 2007). Along this line, the unit described in the Iraq scenario received substantial outside support as "chaplains, grief counselors, combat stress elements, and leadership from higher headquarters surged to the patrol base to serve as outlets for the soldiers and leaders attempting to deal with the traumatic event." As evidenced by the unit's ability to recover rapidly, re-set, and return to the field of battle, the combination of problem-focused and emotion-focused coping in after-action reviews of traumatic operations can substantially assist the team in building and maintaining emotional resilience.

CONCLUSION

Since the al-Qaeda attacks on the September 11, 2001, the United States had to confront various national security challenges in addition to the panoply of natural and human-manufactured disasters. In these endeavors, the work of first responders and the military became more vital than ever. Such work most often involves teams. National security as well as disaster responses hinge on the effectiveness of teamwork. Team effectiveness in these instances depends in part on how viable the team is and whether it can maintain its viability when environmental and contextual challenges increase in threat, danger, and stress. Team viability depends upon high levels of cohesion, trust, and efficacy. *In extremis* conditions can impair team cognitive, social, and emotional processes, which in turn can negatively affect cohesion, trust, and efficacy. Leaders have several ideas and strategies at their disposal to help them build team viability and foster cognitive, social, and emotional team resiliency in dangerous circumstances.

REFERENCES

Back, K. 1950. "The Exertion of Influence through Social Communication." In *Theory and Experiment in Social Communication,* edited by L. Festinger, K. Back, S. Schachter, H. H. Kelley, and J. Thibaut, 21–36. Ann Arbor, Mich.: Edwards Bros.

Bandura, A. 1986. *The Social Foundations of Thought and Action.* Englewood Cliffs, N.J.: Prentice-Hall.

Baran, B. E., and C. W. Scott. 2010. "Organizing Ambiguity: A Grounded Theory of Leadership and Sensemaking within Dangerous Contexts." *Military Psychology* 22: S42–S69.

Barrick, M. R., G. L. Stewart, M. J. Neubert, and M. K. Mount. 1998. "Relating Member Ability and Personality to Work-Team Processes and Team Effectiveness." *Journal of Applied Psychology* 83:377–391.

Bartone, P. T. 2006. "Resilience under Military Operational Stress: Can Leaders Influence Hardiness?" *Military Psychology* 18:S131–S148.

Blickensderfer, E., J. A. Cannon-Bowers, and E. Salas. 1998. "Cross-Training and Team Performance." In *Making Decisions under Stress: Implications for Individual and Team Training,* edited by J. A. Cannon-Bowers and E. Salas, 299–311. Washington, D.C.: American Psychological Association.

Bonanno, G. A. 2004. "Loss, Trauma, and Human Resilience: Have We Underestimated the Human Capacity to Thrive after Extremely Aversive Events?" *American Psychologist* 59:20–28.

Bromiley, P., and J. Harris. 2006. "Trust, Transaction Cost Economics, and Mechanisms." In *Handbook of Trust Research*, edited by R. Bachmann and A. Zaheer, 124–143. Northampton, Mass: Edward Elgar.

Byrne, D. 1961. "Interpersonal Attraction and Attitude Similarity." *Journal of Abnormal and Social Psychology* 62:713–715.

Byrne, D., and D. Nelson. 1965. "Attraction as a Linear Function of Proportion of Positive Reinforcements." *Journal of Personality and Social Psychology* 1:659–663.

Cacioppo, J. T., H. T. Reis, and A. J. Zautra. 2011. "Social Resilience: The Value of Social Fitness with an Application to the Military." *American Psychologist* 66: 43–51.

Carron, A. V. 1982. "Cohesiveness in Sport Groups: Interpretations and Considerations." *Journal of Sport Psychology* 4:123–138.

Collier, P. 2006. *Medal of Honor: Portraits of Valor beyond the Call of Duty*. New York: Artisian.

Cook, J., and T. Wall. 1980. "New Work Attitude Measures of Trust, Organizational Commitment, and Personal Need Nonfulfillment." *Journal of Occupational Psychology* 53:39–52.

Cornum, R., M. D. Matthews, and M. E. P. Seligman. 2011. "Comprehensive Soldier Fitness: Building Resilience in a Challenging Institutional Context." *American Psychologist* 66: 4–9.

Cummings, L. L., and P. Bromiley. 1996. "The Organizational Trust Inventory (OTI): Development and Validation." In *Trust in Organizations: Frontiers of Theory and Research*, edited by R. M. Kramer and T. R. Tyler, 68–89. Thousand Oaks, Calif.: Sage.

Edmondson, A. 1999. "Psychological Safety and Learning Behavior in Work Teams." *Administrative Science Quarterly* 44:350–383.

Edmondson, A. 2003. "Speaking Up in the Operating Room: How Team Leaders Promote Learning in Interdisciplinary Action Teams." *Journal of Management Studies* 40:1419–1452.

Festinger, L. 1950. "Informal Social Communication." *Psychological Review* 57:271–282.

Hackman, J. R., and G. R. Oldham. 1975. "Development of the Job Diagnostic Survey." *Journal of Applied Psychology* 60:159–170.

Hannah, S. T., D. J. Campbell, and M. D. Matthews. 2010. "Advancing a Research Agenda for Leadership in Dangerous Contexts." *Military Psychology* 22:S157–S189.

Hatfield, E., J. T. Cacioppo, and R. L. Rapson. 1994. *Emotional Contagion*. New York: Cambridge University Press.

Jarvenpaa, S. L., and D. E. Leidner. 1999. "Communication and Trust in Global Virtual Teams." *Organizational Science* 10 (6):791–815.

Kane, T. D., S. J. Zaccaro, T. Tremble, and A. D. Masuda. 2002. "An Examination of the Leader's Regulation of Groups." *Small Group Research* 33:65–120.

Klann, G. 2003. *Crisis Leadership: Using Military Lessons, Organizational Experiences, and the Power of Influence to Lessen the Impact of Chaos on the People You Lead*. Greensboro, N.C.: Center for Creative Leadership.

Kobasa, S. C. 1979. "Stressful Life Events, Personality, and Health: An Inquiry into Hardiness." *Journal of Personality and Social Psychology* 37:1–11.

Lee, Y. T. 2001. "The Mere Exposure Effect: An Uncertainty Reduction Explanation Revisited." *Personality and Social Psychology Bulletin* 27:1255–1266.

Loehr, J. E. 1986. *Mental Toughness Training for Sports: Achieving Athletic Excellence.* Lexington, Mass.: Stephen Greene Press.

Mack, M. G., and B. G. Ragan. 2008. "Development of the Mental, Emotional, and Bodily Toughness Inventory in Collegiate Athletes and Nonathletes." *Journal of Athletic Training* 43:125–132.

Maddi, S. R. 2007. "Relevance of Hardiness Assessment and Training to the Military Context." *Military Psychology* 19:61–70.

Maddi, S. R., S. Kahn, and K. L. Maddi. 1998. "The Effectiveness of Hardiness Training." *Consulting Psychology Journal: Practice and Research* 50:78–86.

Marks, M. A., J. Mathieu, and S. J. Zaccaro. 2001. "A Temporally Based Framework and Taxonomy of Team Processes." *Academy of Management Review* 26:356–376.

Marks, M. A., M. J. Sabella, C. A. Burke, and S. J. Zaccaro. 2002. "The Impact of Cross-Training on Team Effectiveness." *Journal of Applied Psychology* 87:3–13.

Mayerson, D., K. E. Weick, and R. M. Kramer. 1996. "Early Trust and Temporary Groups." In *Trust in Organizations: Frontiers of Theory and Research,* edited by R. M. Kramer and T. R. Tyler, 166–195. Thousand Oaks, Calif.: Sage.

McAllister, D. J. 1995. "Affect- and Cognitive-Based Trust as Foundations for Interpersonal Cooperation in Organizations." *Academy of Management Journal* 38:24–59.

McGuire, W. J. 1964. "Inducing Resistance to Persuasion: Some Contemporary Approaches." In *Advances in Experimental Social Psychology,* edited by L. Berkowitz, 1:192–229. New York: Academic Press.

Paton, D. 2006. "Critical Incident Stress Risk in Police Officers: Managing Resilience and Vulnerability." *Traumatology* 23:1–9.

Paton, D., and J. M. Violanti. 2007. "Terrorism Stress Risk Assessment and Management." In *Psychology of Terrorism,* edited by B. Bongar, L. M. Brown, L. E. Beutler, J. N. Brecjkenridge, and P. G. Zimbardo. New York: Oxford University Press.

Schendel, J. D., and J. D. Hagman. 1982. "On Sustaining Procedural Skills over a Prolonged Retention Interval." *Journal of Applied Psychology* 67:605–610.

Staw, B. M., L. E. Sandelands, and J. E. Dutton. 1984. "Threat-Rigidity Effects in Organizational Behavior: A Multilevel Analysis." *Administrative Science Quarterly* 26:501–524.

Sundstrom, E., K. DeMeuse, and D. Futrell. 1990. "Work Teams: Applications and Effectiveness." *American Psychologist* 45 (2): 120–133.

Swap, W. C. 1977. "Interpersonal Attraction and Repeated Exposure to Rewarders and Punishers." *Personality and Social Psychology Bulletin* 3:248–251.

Sweeney, P. 2007. "Trust: The Key to Combat Leadership." In *Leadership Lessons from West Point,* edited by D. Crandall, 252–277. San Francisco: Wiley.

Sweeney, P. 2010. "Do Soldiers Re-evaluate Trust in Their Leaders Prior to Combat Operations?" *Military Psychology* 22:S70–S88.

Sweeney, P., V. Thompson, and H. Blanton. 2009. "Trust and Influence in Combat: An Interdependence Model." *Journal of Applied Social Psychology* 39 (1): 235–264.

Tasa, K., S. Tagger, and G. H. Seijts. 2007. "The Development of Collective Efficacy in Teams: A Multilevel and Longitudinal Perspective." *Journal of Applied Psychology* 92:17–27.

Thibaut, J. W., and H. H. Kelley. 1959. *The Social Psychology of Groups.* New York: Wiley.

Tucker, J. S., and K. M. Gunther. 2009. "The Application of a Model of Adaptive Performance to Army Leader Behaviors." *Military Psychology* 21:315–333.

U.S. Army. n.d. "U.S. Army's Comprehensive Soldier Fitness Program." http://www.army.mil/csf/.

Volpe, C. E., J. A. Cannon-Bowers, E. Salas, and P. E. Spector. 1996. "The Impact of Cross-Training on Team Functioning: An Empirical Investigation." *Human Factors* 38:87–100.

Weick, K. E. 1993. "The Collapse of Sensemaking in Organizations: The Mann Gulch Disaster." *Administrative Science Quarterly* 38:628–652.

Yammarino, F. J., M. D. Mumford, M. S. Connelly, and S. D. Dionne. 2010. "Leadership and Team Dynamics for Dangerous Military Contexts." *Military Psychology* 22:S15–S41.

Zaccaro, S. J., A. L. Rittman, and M.A. Marks. 2001. "Team Leadership." *Leadership Quarterly* 12:451–83.

Zaccaro, S. J., V. Blair, C. Peterson, and M. Zazanis. 1995. "Collective Efficacy." In *Self-Efficacy, Adaptation, and Adjustment: Theory, Research, and Application,* edited by J. Maddux, 305–330. New York: Plenum.

Zajonc, R. B. 1968. "Attitudinal Effects of Mere Exposure." *Journal of Personality and Social Psychology* 9:1–27.

CHAPTER 11

Morale
The Essential Intangible

Brian Reed, Chris Midberry, Raymond Ortiz, James Redding, and
Jason Toole

We knew going into Ramadi that it was going to be a gunfight. Weekly
updates and reports from Ramadi painted a picture of tough days for units
in the city. Although the city was small and densely populated (500,000), it
was all two battalions—one Army in the east and one Marine in the west—
could do to conduct offensive operations.[1] Hotel Company was tasked to
provide a mobile unit for security as the battalion commander circulated
the battlefield. Because we were the forward command post (CP) during
battalion operations, our call sign was "Blade Jump" or as we called ourselves, "The Jump."

Morale was high in The Jump. We were a highly trained and experienced organization. Hand selected for the task, our mission was important
and relevant. As a group, we had been together for several months and had
forged bonds and a sense of togetherness through the crucible of training for combat and combat itself. Individually and collectively, our will and
spirit was far above that of the average unit.

Throughout the deployment we did many things typical of other companies in the battalion; however, because of the operational tempo and our
requirement to circulate throughout the entire city, we became very good
at identifying and destroying improvised explosive devices (IEDs). We were
so good that we became the asset of choice for the explosive ordnance
disposal (EOD) team's escort and route clearance when high-level general officers or State Department officials would visit our area of operations. I must admit that even with practice, this skill, which we never took
for granted, took time to develop. In fact, early in the deployment we were
more lucky than good. On a few occasions we were hit by an IED planted

only a few feet from us. With one exception, when a Marine in the gun tur-
ret had his hand ripped in half, we never received a serious casualty. Our
success can be attributed to high morale, tough vehicles, a thorough turnover from the battalion we relieved, and our ability to capitalize and learn
quickly from mistakes, thus ensuring we never made the same mistake
twice. As good as we were at identifying IEDs, we never became complacent because we knew the enemy was always getting better and training
to kill us.

Current research on morale points to an important and defining
characteristic of this phenomenon that is especially critical to those
who find themselves in organizations operating in a high-threat
environment. Specifically, morale has been found to be motivating, leading to perseverance and presumably success at group tasks, especially
under trying circumstances.[2] Morale is potent in the face of external challenges, defined by difficulties, danger, high stress, and adversity. The defining
characteristic of morale is that it is a "force multiplier"—that is, high morale
has a positive impact on performance, and low morale has a negative effect on
performance. The Marine unit in the opening vignette was good at their job,
in fact very good. What allowed it to be successful was its members' superb
equipment, meaningful mission, ability to learn from and adapt to the environment (enemy, people, and terrain), and their high level of mutual trust and
confidence in themselves. Quite simply, they had high morale.

In World War II, the combat flying personnel in the Army Air Corps possessed unusually high levels of morale. Their duty entailed some of the highest risks of death, even higher than that for ground troops. Their bombing runs
against the German war machine, often initiated from England, required missions across enemy-controlled territory within enemy-controlled air space,
oftentimes in daylight. The crews that flew these missions knew that their
chance of survival was miniscule, yet they continued to fly and continued
to have high morale. These results contradict perceptions of common sense.
Unlike in some other Army elements, the soldiers in the Air Corps volunteered
for this service once they were in the force. They tended to be more educated
overall and viewed their unit as elite and their missions as directly contributing to the war effort. Others viewed them as superior because of their selection and skills training.[3] While all of the above were contributing factors to the
overall success of the mission, it was their morale that allowed them to fly day
after day with incredible results.

Each aircrew was unique, and the relationships within the crews were
special, allowing them to handle the dangers, stress, and adversity of repetitive daytime bombing missions into enemy territory. Similar to The Jump, the

bomber crews were a highly trained and experienced group. As volunteers, they were self-selected for their task (unlike the hand-selected Marines in The Jump), and their mission was relevant, purposeful, and important. Morale was high and had a positive impact on the crews' positive performance.

Implicit in the notion of morale, particularly as the term has been used in military organizations, is the idea that high-morale groups are especially likely to perform more effectively than low-morale groups when confronted with severe obstacles and adverse conditions.[4] The current nature of war indicates that units operating outside the large forward operating bases (or "outside the wire") are the only forces capable of causing soldiers to expose themselves consistently to enemy fire. The same can be said for police, fire, and other paramilitary organizations in their relevant contexts. The confusion, danger, hardship, and isolation of the modern battlefield have exacerbated reliance on the small groups to which soldiers belong. Although there is no ironclad framework for asserting the importance of one factor over another in assessing the individual and unit performance of these groups, the impact of morale on group effectiveness in terms of courage, discipline, enthusiasm, and willingness to endure hardship is clear.[5] It is impossible for the military to function, particularly during highly stressful and demanding missions, without support, trust, unity, and esprit de corps at the small-unit level.[6] No doubt, there are many reasons why a unit or organization performs well (or poorly) under stress. Undeniable, though, is the importance of morale as a key variable that influences both motivation and performance. Put simply, morale matters.

WHAT IS MORALE?

What is morale? On the surface, this seems like a question with a simple answer. There are, however, differing perspectives based on a vast amount of research and the extensive literature of the different disciplines of the social sciences. Although behavioral scientists have long used the term "morale," there is little agreement about what exactly it does or should mean. Morale, as described by military authors, seems to be a complex construct that includes an array of attitudinal, motivational, and social predispositions. It is more general than the concepts of motivation and satisfaction in the psychology literature but encompasses major elements of both concepts as well as the notion of group cohesiveness.[7] The word "morale" is of French origin and entered English common usage in the mid-1700s. Originally indicating morality or good conduct, the word soon came to mean confidence and was applied in particular to military forces.[8]

As used today, morale is defined as a cognitive, emotional, and motivational stance toward goals and tasks. It encompasses confidence, optimism, enthusiasm, and loyalty. In group situations, the focus here, it also includes a sense of common purpose. In organizations, morale entails how one thinks and feels about the group's task, mission, and purpose, which greatly affect the group's motivation to perform, especially in dangerous environments. Morale is both an indicator of group and individual well-being.[9] Although an individual's morale is certainly relevant to the overall morale of a unit or organization, in a high-threat environment the larger issue is how group (two or more people) morale affects organizational effectiveness. Most sizable groups can sustain good morale with a handful of alienated or disgruntled members.[10]

The components of morale are multifaceted and include confidence, enthusiasm, optimism, capability, resilience, leadership, mutual trust and respect, loyalty, social cohesion, common purpose, devotion, sacrifice (selfless service), compelling history, honor, and moral rightness. These elements exist · on a continuum of degrees. They are desirable in their own right, but they are also valued because of their presumed consequences—perseverance, courage, resilience, and, of course, success—for the group and its members.[11] The Marines in the opening vignette clearly exhibited these characteristics: they were successful, persevered in difficult situations, were courageous under fire, and resilient in spite of setbacks. The Jump was not your typical Marine infantry unit, comprised solely of infantry specialists. Instead, it also consisted of Marines specializing in supply, communications, and motor transportation. This configuration could be cause for concern to those outside of the unit, but to Marines, who they are and what they represent, that is, warriors is what matters. True to the warrior ethos, The Jump organized, trained, and fought as such. Because of the diverse specialty backgrounds of each Marine in the unit, the motto "Every Marine a Rifleman" resonated more with them than in typical Marine outfits.

The Marines in The Jump were hand-selected for the unit and given the toughest and most important missions; they were elite. They had a swagger that spoke to the confidence and pride that came from their being well-trained and having a compelling mission and purpose so strong that others were attracted by it and wanted to be part of something as great. The bonds of trust forged through shared hardships during tough, demanding, realistic training and other perilous, real-life situations enabled The Jump to not merely survive, but to thrive. The individual Marines knew that the company commander was in charge, but more importantly they knew and believed in each other and what they were doing. They held each other in high regard, with mutual respect and trust. During the events described in the vignette, young privates stood with the more senior sergeants, corporals stood with captains, and none was more safe or less at risk than the other. Success bred success, which in turn contributed to high morale and effective unit performance, as evidenced by the unit's success in locating and destroying IEDs or as the unit of choice for high-visibility missions. Each component of morale was manifest in this group, thereby resulting in very high morale and increased group effectiveness.[12] Table 11.1 summarizes the key factors that affect morale.

Table 11.1 Factors Affecting Morale

Trust between leaders and members	Member selection
Respect	Mission clarity, purpose, and moral rightness (task cohesion)
Tough, realistic training to enhance capabilities, which boosts confidence	Sufficient material resources
Past successes; emphasizing the organization's past history	Positive, caring leadership
Strong social relationships based on respect and loyalty (social cohesion)	Sacrifice for the good of the group (selfless service)
Honorable performance of duty	Optimism about the future
Commitment to excellence	Devotion to the cause

CULTURE AND MORALE

I took command of a mechanized infantry company in East Baghdad in September 2005. At the time, my battalion was about two-thirds of the way through a twelve-month deployment and my initial concern was that morale was low, and even worse, complacency was high. It had been a frustrating deployment in that we were not finding and killing the enemy. My battalion task force was assigned a sector in east Baghdad just south of Sadr City and during the year had seen the rise and proliferation of the explosively formed penetrator (EFP). The EFP had been the cause of several KIAs [killed-in-action] and WIAs [wounded-in-action] in my battalion, and frustrations were high because we were not finding and killing the IED builders, financers, and emplacers. Instead, soldiers in my company were responsible for securing portions of a main supply route (Route Plutos), which at the time had been a fertile route for placing IEDs to kill U.S. troops.

I knew I was taking command of my company at a critical point in the deployment. Soldiers had less time remaining in Iraq than they had already spent in theater and my greatest fear was complacency causing the death or serious injury of any of my soldiers. On my first day of command, I walked around the company just trying to soak things in and see what I was getting myself into. What I saw only concerned me more. I saw soldiers walking around in mismatched uniforms and many walking around the company area in civilian clothes. The general cleanliness of the company CP and adjacent living area was a complete mess. Overall standards and discipline in the company seemed to be low. I sensed a level of fraternization between the NCOs and junior enlisted soldiers when I overheard privates calling their sergeants by their first names. The outgoing company commander and company executive officer had the filthiest rooms in the company. My initial assessment of patrol orders and pre-combat inspections conducted prior to going outside the wire was that these vital processes were being "finger-drilled." Soldiers felt like they had gone on too many patrols to remember and consequently they knew what they needed to do without having to use a checklist or spot-check subordinates.

My concern was what I called "creeping complacency," which was complacency starting out as something small and then turning into something large with the potential to cause the death or injury of one of my soldiers. For example, seemingly small uniform violations or minor lapses in standards and discipline were to me indicative of greater problems to come. I knew that something needed to change and this change needed to happen fast!

According to renowned social psychologist Edgar H. Schein's classic definition, and those of other theorists, culture may be said to refer to the structure of organizations rooted in the prevailing assumptions, norms, values, customs, and traditions that collectively, over time, have created shared individual expectations among the members. The culture's meaning is established through socialization of the identity groups that converge in the operations of the organization. Culture includes attitudes and behavior about what is right, what is good, and what is important and is often manifested in shared heroes, stories, and rituals that promote bonding among the organization's members. Culture is, in short, the "glue" that makes an organization a distinctive source of identity and experience. Thus, a strong culture exists when a clear set of norms and expectations—usually a function of leadership—permeates the entire organization. It is essentially "how we do things around here."[13] In the end, morale is rooted at the core of organizational culture. In order to assess and affect morale, leaders need to begin with an understanding of the immediate climate and long-term culture of the group they are leading.

High or low morale can often be traced to the strength of the culture of a unit. In order for a positive morale to be internalized and ingrained in the unit's fabric, the culture of the organization needs to be one that promotes, promulgates, and supports a high-morale environment. Before a leader can influence the unit morale or the personal morale of its members, he or she first needs to assess the organization. In the vignette above, the new commander recognized that he needed to immediately address some issues in his unit because tangible indicators pointed to a culture in which indiscipline and low morale had become problematic. A high-morale environment, as it relates to the preceding story, would be a unit where leaders set the example and support the parent organization's goals and values. In a high-morale unit, subordinates identify and internalize the unit goals and values, such as discipline, mission readiness, and high performance and conduct.

All three levels of culture—artifacts, espoused beliefs and values, and underlying assumptions—must be congruent and consistent with respect to what the institution is promoting.[14] In evaluating culture, on the first (or surface) level lie artifacts, that is, all the phenomena that one sees, hears, and feels when encountering a group with an unfamiliar culture. Artifacts include the visible products of the group, such as the architecture of its physical environment; its language; its technology and products; its artistic creations; its style, as embodied in clothing, manners of address, displays of emotion, and myths and stories told about the organization; its published list of values; its observable rituals and ceremonies and so on. The important point about this level of culture is that it is easy to observe and difficult to decipher. In the case of the new commander, the artifacts—lack of orderliness and cleanliness of the CP and living areas, soldiers in mismatched uniforms and civilian clothes, privates calling sergeants by their first names—paint a picture of an ill-disciplined and complacent unit. The commander could interpret these artifacts to mean that the soldiers in the company were tired from months of long, repeated missions or that unit morale and overall satisfaction with the mission was low.

At the second level of organizational culture are the espoused beliefs and values of the organization. High-morale units espouse beliefs and values that stress loyalty, competence, affiliation with the primary group, discipline, and trust.[15] All group learning ultimately reflects someone's beliefs and values, the sense of what ought to be, as distinct from what is. Beliefs and values at this conscious level will predict much of the behavior that can be observed at the artifact level. If the beliefs and values are not based on prior learning, however, they may also only reflect espoused theories, which predict well enough what people will say in a variety of situations but may be out of line with what they will actually do in situations in which those beliefs and values should, in fact, be operating. If espoused beliefs and values are reasonably congruent with the underlying assumptions, then the articulation of those values into a philosophy of operating can be helpful in bringing the group together, serving as a source of identity and core mission.

As the new commander began to "peel back the onion" with respect to the company's culture, the observed artifacts revealed an unhealthy organization where the espoused beliefs and values were not congruent with the parent (battalion) organization or what the members knew to be right (as learned through basic training, unit training, and other forms of institutional and organizational socialization). The vignette portrays an organization with potentially incongruent espoused beliefs and values and likely low morale. In an Army that teaches and values loyalty, duty, respect, selfless service, honor, integrity, and personal courage, the artifacts indicate that this is a company that has lapsed into indiscipline, individuality, carelessness, and selfishness, thus fostering a culture of low morale.

To get at the deepest level of cultural understanding and to predict future behavior correctly, one must understand the level of basic underlying assumptions. When a solution to a problem works repeatedly, it comes to be taken for granted. What was once a hypothesis, supported only by a hunch or a value, gradually comes to be treated as a reality; people believe that nature works that way. When basic assumptions are taken for granted in an organization, one finds little variation within the group. This degree of consensus results from repeated success in implementing certain beliefs and values. In fact, if a basic assumption comes to be strongly held in a group, members will find behavior based on any other premise inconceivable. Therefore, basic assumptions can be thought of as the implicit, core assumptions that guide behavior, that tell group members how to perceive, think about, and feel about things.

Basic assumptions tend to be non-debatable, and hence are extremely difficult to change. To learn something new in this realm requires reexamining and reconstructing existing paradigms. The role of leadership is especially critical to a successful reexamination and reconfiguring of basic assumptions, and therefore, to the overall morale of the unit. In the vignette above, it is essential that the new commander determine whether the basic underlying assumptions of his organization are functional or dysfunctional. Because the artifacts appear to paint a picture of dysfunctional espoused beliefs and values, it is vital that he quickly determine whether this cultural dysfunction has permeated the organization to the point where its underlying assumptions have become misaligned with the parent organization's.[16]

Culture is to a group what personality or character is to an individual. Closely associated with an organization's culture is its climate. In contrast to culture, climate refers to environmental interactions or behaviors rooted in the organization's value system, such as rewards and punishments, communications flow, and operations tempo, which determine individual and team perceptions about the quality of working conditions. It is essentially "how one feels about this organization." Climate is often considered to be alterable in the near term and largely limited to those aspects of the organizational environment of which members are aware.

Unit culture allows for high morale to exist. Good unit culture creates the conditions for good unit morale, and vice versa. In the opening vignette, there are several key indicators that highlight the low morale in this unit (see Table 11.2).

Table 11.2 Indications of Poor Morale

Factor	Indicator
Loss of mission clarity and purpose	"[The] battalion was about two-thirds of the way through a twelve-month deployment and . . . had less time remaining in Iraq than they had already spent in theater and my greatest fear was complacency."
Lack of past success	"It had been a frustrating deployment in that we were not finding and killing the enemy."
Lack of mutual respect	"I sensed a level of fraternization between the NCOs and junior enlisted soldiers when I overheard privates calling their sergeants by their first names."
Poor leadership	"The outgoing company commander and company executive officer had the filthiest rooms in the company."

To clarify the role of culture and morale, consider the indicator for the lack of respect, that is, the use of first names by the privates when referring to their NCOs. This is an artifact, a visible product of the group. An espoused belief and value associated with this artifact is that it is an acceptable norm to call the company leadership by something other than their military rank. Through socialization and prior learning at entry training and time spent in more disciplined units, the average soldier knows that the use of a first name when addressing a superior is not acceptable and that anything other than this is dysfunctional. Because the informality has likely occurred for most of the deployment, the basic underlying assumption is that the privates do not respect their NCOs and, therefore, the implicit, core assumption that guides the behavior of the privates is to dismiss their NCOs as superiors and think of them instead as equals. The impact of such general lack of respect rooted in the culture of a unit can be catastrophic. Disrespect for unit leadership breeds a lack of trust and sows the seeds for insubordination and indiscipline. At a minimum, undisciplined organizations in high-stress environments are unsuccessful in mission completion; at worst, the death or injury of organizational members may result because of such indiscipline.

Table 11.3 Assessing Morale

A member identifies strongly with his or her unit when the unit satisfies major physical, security, and social needs. A high-morale unit:
▸ provides adequate food, water, medical support, rest, and essential supplies and weapons.
▸ is the primary social group for the individual and controls his or her day-to-day behavior.
▸ provides the major source of esteem and recognition.
▸ provides a strong sense of mutual affection and attraction among unit members.
▸ provides the member a sense of influence over events in his or her immediate unit.
▸ causes the member to identify strongly with immediate unit leaders at squad, section, platoon, and company levels.

When assessing the morale of an organization, Table 11.1, highlighting the factors affecting morale is a good place to start. There are some intuitive indicators in a unit that will lend themselves to these factors and whether morale is high or low. Table 11.3 offers another perspective on assessing unit morale and focuses on basic member needs and one's sense of belonging to a group.[17]

BUILDING HIGH MORALE

Early in my career [as a police officer], while on patrol during a hot summer night, a 10–13 [officer needs immediate assistance] came over the patrol radio. Several men armed with handguns and automatic weapons were being pursued by patrol officers; shots had been fired. Arriving upon a dangerous and chaotic scene, I looked for guidance from one of the more experienced officers and was absolutely shocked when no one came forward. Unsure, I sought cover and waited for direction, as my partner and I were rookies. Shortly thereafter, an experienced officer arrived on the scene and loudly began to issue directions and make sense of the mayhem. I personally felt reassured; this veteran had returned a sense of control to this high-threat situation. I remember feeling there must be a competent leader to give direction and inspire the troops in the field. This veteran officer's clear competence and concern for a safe and timely resolution to the crisis was obvious.

As an officer on patrol, I have learned that through the daily danger, I must remain focused, calm, and always ready to take charge while motivating my squad to excel. I have always made it a habit to mentally rehearse each possible dangerous situation my squad may find themselves in. I consider tactics, personnel deployment, maneuvers, and how to best use the resources at my disposal. It is critical that the squad leader is knowledgeable and confident while making tactical decisions in the field. I once worked for a commanding officer (CO) who liked to respond to high-threat locations to lend a steadying presence. For example, there was a call for an armed robbery in progress at a bank. As I responded to the location, the CO had arrived there first, disarmed the perpetrator, and placed him in custody. As word spread through the command, we all knew exactly what was expected by his example. In my experience the competence of the leader establishes a benchmark for the performance of a department. This trust in his ability cannot be earned overnight but is the product of repeated positive examples and demonstrated caring for the well-being of his subordinates and organization.

In organizations that customarily operate in dangerous environments, good morale is influenced by extensive training, sufficient material resources, and the sheer nature of the threat or scope of the task. Also contributing to military morale are good leadership, mutual trust and respect among group members, clarity of mission, perceived public support, past combat success (unit history), and low casualty rates. Military units with low turnover rates tend to have higher morale, as do units where members expect to serve a lengthy time in the unit.[18] Those in the military do not fight for their flag or their country as much as for their brothers and sisters who share a trench with them.[19]

The actions of the New York City police officer who took charge in the preceding vignette illustrate the affect on morale generated by the actions of the leader; they cannot be underestimated. In fact, most research suggests that morale is best predicted by variables suggesting engagement in meaningful work and confidence in unit functioning and leadership.[20] In the

Israel Defense Forces (IDF), morale is sometimes referred to as their "secret weapon." Historically, a high level of morale has been found in every IDF soldier surveys since its early years.[21] How do units and organizations achieve this level of morale, which in turn allows them to be successful in environments characterized by stress, uncertainty, and danger?

In the IDF, two variables were found to be most strongly associated with personal levels of morale and perceived company morale: perceived unit togetherness and relationships with commanders.[22] With respect to the former, collective efficacy is the belief that individuals hold concerning the ability of their group to successfully perform its tasks. Collective efficacy is considered a compilation of a soldier's experience; the leader's tenure, competence, and experience; the leader's confidence in the group, unit discipline; and members' identification with the unit.[23] Of these characteristics tested within the IDF, the strongest predictor of perceived combat readiness was the unit member's identification with his company. A strong sense of belonging and shared beliefs and attitudes reinforced the trust members placed in each other and their

Table 11.4 Factors and Leader Actions That Build Morale

Factor	Leader Action
Trust in one another and confidence in unit leaders	Continuously improve competence, demonstrate honesty and integrity, protect and promote group members' welfare, share hardships and experiences, conduct tough, demanding, and realistic training, and create opportunities for social and team-building events
Experience of leaders and subordinates	Provide a holistic training program involving physical, mental, and skill-specific elements
Discipline	Establish and enforce high standards, ensure that leaders model the standards at all times, and communicate to group members why it is important to adhere to the standards
Identification with the unit and its history	Instill pride in the unit and a sense of history about those who preceded the current members
Positive, cooperative, and interdependent relationships among group members	Trust and empower group members, share information, and promote participative decision making

leaders. Additionally, the tenure of the leaders and the experience of the soldiers increased perceptions of readiness, as did the level of discipline in a unit. Experienced formations have confidence in their skills and abilities. Leaders understand the value of discipline and the impact it has upon readiness and resultant morale. Therefore, the greater one's belief in the unit's ability to conduct the mission, the higher one's individual and unit morale. This belief is positively affected by a member's identification with his or her unit. Table 11.4 outlines factors that influence and actions leaders can take to build morale.

For the IDF, individual morale and the perceived unit morale were significantly correlated with the degree of confidence in the battalion commanding officer and in the company commanding officer.[24] In high-threat environments, the soldier finds that his or her survival depends mainly on the actions of the more immediate leaders. Other factors that directly affect morale (as influenced by the leader) are confidence in oneself, team, and weapons. For the Israeli soldier, his combat team, his weapon, and his sense of competence may frequently be determinants of his survival on the battlefield; the higher his confidence in these factors, the higher his morale, hence his combat readiness. In general, individual morale is characterized by "a sense of well-being based on confidence in self and in primary groups."[25] It follows that the impact on group morale is positive.

Table 11.5 Leader Behaviors for Building and Sustaining Morale in a Dangerous Environment

Take charge	Remain calm to make good decisions
Project a sense of control	Remain focused
Give direction	Be a steadying presence (model confidence)
Inspire subordinates	Exhibit optimism
Share leadership (empowerment and participation)	Be loyal and attentive to group members' safety
Maintain unit integrity on missions	Provide resources needed for success
Share dangers and hardships by leading from the front	Perform missions in a moral and ethical manner
Ensure the organization continues to learn and improve	Be honest and transparent with group members
Communicate, explain, and live the shared values	Engage in selfless service

The group leader is directly responsible for developing the self-confidence of his or her subordinates, as well as fostering the subordinates' confidence in the leadership. A leader can take specific steps to build such confidence. Training, shared hardships, developmental exercises, and the like are a handful of examples. Equally critical, if not more important, is the leader's direct role in high-threat situations. The commanding officer in the NYPD earned the confidence and trust of his subordinates via his actions at the decisive moment of a high-stress event. In turn, he built and created an environment of high morale and a benchmark for better performance in the department. Table 11.5 notes behaviors most relevant for leaders in a dangerous situation.

CONCLUSION

Morale matters, especially in environments characterized by volatility, uncertainty, complexity, and ambiguity. Morale is a "force multiplier"—high morale has a positive impact on an organization's performance, especially in a high-threat environment. As the essential intangible, leaders can harness this so-called X Factor to better ensure effective unit performance. Unit organizational culture, through the actions of leaders, directly affects unit performance in high-threat environments. Leaders have a responsibility and imperative to build high morale by developing their own proficiency and displaying confidence in themselves and others. A detailed knowledge of potentialities and the current mission is also critical. Individual expertise and the promotion of strong unit cohesion couples with these characteristics in the formation of high unit morale. A unit organizational culture that fosters high morale may result in high levels of unit performance in high-threat environments.

KEY TAKE-AWAY POINTS

1. Morale is embedded in the very culture of an organization. An organizational culture that fosters a positive, values-based framework will facilitate high unit morale.

2. Leaders have a direct role in assessing and building morale. Leadership is absolutely critical in creating the conditions for high morale, both prior to immersion in a hostile environment and in the hostile environment itself.

3. In a high-threat situation, leaders can affect morale by their actions during the crisis. There is no substitute for the positive, direct actions of the leader.

KEY REFERENCES

Ender, Morten G. *American Soldiers in Iraq: McSoldiers or Innovative Professionals?* New York: Routledge, 2009.

Gal, Reuven. *A Portrait of the Israeli Soldier*. New York: Greenwood Press, 1986.

Henderson, W. D. *Cohesion: The Human Element in Combat*. Washington, D.C.: National Defense University Press, 1986.

Peterson, C., N. Park, and P. Sweeney. "Group Well Being: Morale from a Positive Psychology Perspective." *Applied Psychology* 57 (2008): 19–36.

Schein, Edgar H. *Organizational Culture and Leadership*. 3rd ed. San Francisco: Jossey-Bass, 2004.

Shamir, B., E. Brainin, E. Zakay, and M. Popper. "Perceived Combat Readiness as Collective Efficacy: Individual and Group Level Analysis." *Military Psychology* 12 (2000): 105–119.

NOTES

1. A battalion consists of approximately 600 to 700 soldiers or Marines and accompanying equipment, vehicles, and weapons.

2. C. Peterson, N. Park, and P. Sweeney, "Group Well Being: Morale from a Positive Psychology Perspective," *Applied Psychology* 57 (2008): 19–36.

3. Morten G. Ender, *American Soldiers in Iraq: McSoldiers or Innovative Professionals?* (New York: Routledge, 2009).

4. S. J. Motowidlo and W. C. Borman, "Behaviorally Anchored Scales for Measuring Morale in Military Units," *Journal of Applied Psychology* 62 (1977): 177–183.

5. W. D. Henderson, *Cohesion: The Human Element in Combat* (Washington, D.C.: National Defense University Press, 1986).

6. S. Maguen and B. T. Litz, "Predictors of Morale in U.S. Peacekeepers," *Journal of Applied Social Psychology* 36 (2006): 820–836.

7. Ibid.

8. Peterson, Park, and Sweeney, "Group Well Being."

9. Ibid.

10. Ibid.

11. Ibid.

12. Moral rightness is the least obvious component in this vignette. It is exemplified in the Marines' belief in the goodness of their mission and what they were doing.

13. Don M. Snider, "An Uninformed Debate on Military Culture," *Orbis* 43 (1999): 11–16.

14. Edgar H. Schein, *Organization Culture and Leadership*, 3rd ed. (San Francisco: Jossey-Bass, 2004).

15. Reuven Gal, *A Portrait of the Israeli Soldier* (New York: Greenwood Press, 1986).

16. While the artifacts and the espoused values and beliefs indicate dysfunction, this does not necessarily imply that the basic assumptions are consistent with these. It

is critical for the new commander to make this determination as soon as possible by looking at artifacts and espoused beliefs across the company. What is described in the vignette may be isolated to a handful of units, not representative of the entire company. If representative, it is understood that complacency, substandard performance, and half efforts are accepted means of behavior.

17. Henderson, *Cohesion.*

18. Peterson, Park, and Sweeney, "Group Well Being."

19. Henderson, *Cohesion.*

20. T. W. Britt et al., "Correlates and Consequences of Morale versus Depression under Stressful Conditions," *Journal of Occupational Health Psychology* 12 (2007): 34–37.

21. Gal, *Portrait of the Israeli Soldier.*

22. Ibid.

23. B. Shamir et al., "Perceived Combat Readiness as Collective Efficacy: Individual and Group Level Analysis," *Military Psychology* 12 (2000): 105–119.

24. Gal, *Portrait of the Israeli Soldier.*

25. Ibid.

CHAPTER 12

Leadership When It Matters Most
Lessons on Influence from
In Extremis *Contexts*

Angela Karrasch, Alison Levine, and Thomas Kolditz

N one of us would study or read about leadership if we did not think that leadership is important to people. Assuming that leadership is, indeed, important to people, it then follows that it is most important when people's lives are at risk. This chapter is a discussion of the most important niche in leadership thinking and analysis—leader influence in dangerous contexts.

There is social benefit to such a discussion. When one adds up the publicly released figures for numbers of active duty military personnel, law enforcement officers, and firefighters—all people who live and work in dangerous contexts—the total is in the millions. Adding mountain climbers, skydivers, and other extreme sports enthusiasts to the list swells this figure. Not to be overlooked are ordinary individuals suddenly and unexpectedly thrust into a dangerous circumstance (for example, shootings, floods, mine disasters, airline incidents) where leadership matters or could have mattered. Dangerous contexts are ubiquitous, and leadership during them can make a difference.

Dangerous contexts are among the most difficult subjects to study, because they are inhospitable to researchers and hard to define. Those interested in discussing or studying such contexts may be tempted to simply define danger as actual physical threat. Such an approach falsely assumes that danger is merely the quality of an environment. True, there are certain environments that are easier to negotiate than others, but what is dangerous to one person may not be to another, even in rather extreme environments. For example, a dangerous climb for a novice adventurer may pose little actual risk for an expert climber; the former may be terrified while the latter remains completely unconcerned. Was the environment itself dangerous? No. Danger is created only when a person interacts with the environment. Danger is what we label circumstances when an individual is in an environment that he or she cannot adequately control without the threat of negative consequence. It makes no sense to attempt to define dangerous contexts by focusing on the environment itself.

To study leadership in dangerous contexts, it would be empirically sound to define a measurable interaction between individuals and their perceptions of the environment. One way to do this is to measure or assess beliefs. For example, one may define a dangerous context as one where followers believe that a leader's behavior could affect their physical well-being or survival.[1] Beliefs are easily measured and have a relationship to behavior. This chapter focuses on the perceptions and beliefs of followers and how they relate to leader influence.

A CASE OF *IN EXTREMIS* LEADERSHIP: POLAR EXPLORATION

Alison Levine is an avid adventurer and explorer who has traveled to some of the world's most remote regions, many of them inhospitable and dangerous. She has climbed peaks on every continent and in 2002 served as the team captain of the first American Women's Everest Expedition. This is her firsthand account of how she was influenced by an *in extremis* leader:

> In December 2007 I found myself embarking upon one of my most physically demanding, mentally challenging adventures—a ski traverse across west Antarctica to the South Pole. I was a part of an international team of adventurers, led by Eric Phillips, who had been awarded the Medal of the Order of Australia for achievements in polar exploration. Physically, Eric wasn't the largest person on the team, but pound for pound he was the strongest of us all, and his experience level earned him our respect.
>
> This adventure entailed six weeks of skiing across 600 miles of the coldest, windiest, harshest environment on the planet, while each hauling 150 pounds of gear and supplies in sleds harnessed to our waists. Our route was a remote one that few people had ever followed because of the considerable amount of crevasse danger and challenging terrain. The skiing often required maneuvering over and around mounds of ice that could be up to a meter high—making the surface conditions exhausting and treacherous. Frostbite, malnutrition and incapacitating exhaustion were constant threats. In addition to the physical risks involved in this type of extreme journey, polar explorers face mental challenges that are unique to

the Antarctic environment. Because everything is white and there is relatively little visual stimulation, on cloudy days it is impossible to determine where the ground stops and where the sky starts, and this causes mental confusion and dizziness. And because there is 24 hours of sunlight in the summertime it can be very difficult to sleep. Lawrence Palinkas and Peter Suedfeld published a paper several years ago that defined a condition known as "polar madness," where people on polar expeditions or working at polar research stations deteriorate psychologically because of the lack of visual stimulation, sleep deprivation, and physical and mental exhaustion. People become increasingly irritable, agitated and depressed. Palinkas' paper mentions examples of polar expeditions that ended in disaster because of psychological stress, including a scientific expedition in the 1880s that led to suicide and cannibalism.

In order to avoid some of the pitfalls and disasters that had plagued previous polar expeditions, Eric urged us to show up prepared, both physically and mentally. Once we were out on the ice Eric required us to rotate tent partners each night so that everyone spent time with everyone else and got to know each other. This created loyalty and cohesion amongst expedition members. And throughout the journey Eric continually stressed the importance of teamwork because in order to get to the Pole, everybody had to be willing to share various responsibilities, including navigating the route, making critical decisions, organizing camps and sharing the workload.[2]

LEADING TEAMS *IN EXTREMIS*

People who view a leader as increasing the likelihood of their physical well-being or survival may find themselves in such a context without intending to be in such circumstances. Often, however, as in Alison Levine's example, groups of people willingly go into harm's way to achieve a goal. When a team voluntarily puts themselves in potentially dangerous situations to achieve goals, its members are committed. This represents an opportunity for an *in extremis* leader to go beyond using influence to change behavior, attitudes, or beliefs. Rather, the leader can use influence to maintain the teams' commitment to a shared goal when extreme and dangerous conditions would have them change. The *in extremis* leader uses competence, credibility, and trustworthiness to maintain the high level of commitment from the team.

Influence Process

Three types of influence processes—instrumental compliance, identification, and internalization—take into account different motives and perceptions on the part of the person being influenced.[3] While these processes are separate and distinct, more than one process may occur at the same time. Instrumental compliance occurs when the follower (the person being influenced) accepts influence from another in order to attain a reward or to avoid punishment. In this case, the leader (the person attempting to influence another) has power that stems from controlling rewards and punishments. In many jobs, the follower's performance will depend partly on surveillance by the leader. Many people hold jobs for the paycheck and find no intrinsic value in the work itself, but a leader can provide rewards (paycheck or bonus) or punishments (dock pay, fire) depending on performance. If no surveillance were in place, the follower's compliance with the task (performance) would drop off, because he simply does not care about the work; he only cares about the rewards and avoiding punishment. In a dangerous environment, a leader cannot afford to be constantly monitoring team members' compliance with their assigned tasks, roles, and responsibilities. The leader in dangerous situations must be assured of rapid compliance or commitment regardless of surveillance. Instrumental compliance will not suffice as the main process of influence in dangerous situations.

Personal identification occurs when the follower imitates the leader's behavior or adopts the same attitudes in order to gain acceptance and esteem and to maintain a relationship with the leader. This relationship may help the follower's need for esteem from others, and becoming more like the leader improves the follower's self-image. The source of power that makes the leader attractive may be status, esteem, or resources. Compliance or commitment by the follower depends on the salience of his relationship to the leader. The more closely a follower personally identifies with the leader, the more likely it is that he will take on the leader's mission as his own.

The U.S. Army employs security force advisers that it embeds with foreign militaries to promote and support security in other nations. These advisers use their expertise and resources to support and train foreign militaries. Reports from American foreign security force (FSF) advisers indicate that Iraqi and Afghan soldiers, in their respective countries, would emulate their behaviors in order to gain status among their units and with the advisers, but often without understanding. Advisers quickly recognized that the Iraqi and Afghan soldiers consistently desired to simply be "seen with" coalition forces. Knowing that their actions would be emulated, FSF advisers took their responsibilities as role models quite seriously and were able to use role modeling as an effective influence strategy. Of course, this is true within the U.S. Army as well. Junior leaders watch and emulate senior leaders, and senior leaders are aware of their responsibilities and the power associated with being a role model.[4]

Internalization occurs when the follower accepts the leader's influence because there is consistency between what the leader proposes and the follower's values, beliefs, and self-image. The follower is committed to the ideas of the leader, not to the leader. The source of the leader's power stems from credibility. The leader is a credible prototype of the group's shared values and beliefs. Transformational leadership is associated with inspiring followers to internalize values that promote group interest over self-interest.[5] Alison Levine's story reflects this type of influence process. Her team members all valued exploration, and their passion for learning and their beliefs and need for survival aligned with the leader's beliefs and needs. Eric consistently demonstrated these values and competence, which gave him the credibility he needed to sustain their commitment.

Gaining Influence

The social exchange theory is useful in understanding how power is acquired.[6] Essentially, this theory proposes, the team members assess the relative potential contributions of others and then attribute status and power to a leader based on that assessment. So, if someone repeatedly demonstrates competence and integrity, she will be afforded power or the ability to influence the behavior of group members. As long as the leader produces such things as resources, solutions, and vital information, the team will grant her power. They exchange power for the security provided by the leader. In the example of the arctic explorers, the team members recognized Eric's ability to survive multiple polar expeditions, which gave him credibility in their eyes. Because of his ability, they placed their confidence in him, giving him the power to make decisions about the route, logistics, and communications. Social exchange theory applies to leaders in both safe and dangerous situations. It is likely, however, that fewer mistakes are forgiven in the dangerous context, because followers may be more "tuned in" to leader performance; their survival depends on it.

The transformational leadership theory suggests that leaders gain influence by using individual consideration (attention to needs, aspirations, and abilities), intellectual stimulation (promoting new ideas and relevant mindsets), and charismatic or inspirational leadership (energizing motivation). The expedition group knew that their leader understood basic needs for climbing, but what maintained their trust in him are instances when he recognized individual needs and worked to address these needs. In one instance, he saw a lack of strength due to dehydration, so he removed weight from that member's pack and carried it himself. In taking care to help the team member regain strength, Eric served as a role model for teamwork.

Trust and Expertise

In dangerous contexts, leadership is a product of today's actions and yesterday's groundwork. When leaders ask followers to change current practice, it is their leadership not just at that moment, but also previous experiences with their followers that will determine whether they maintain power or lose it. In August 1949, the U.S. Fire Service sent sixteen smoke jumpers into the Gates of the Mountains region in Montana to put out a fire.[7] Wagner Dodge led the group of jumpers. Dodge was a man of few words, but he had the technical expertise to lead this type of mission. The team members had not trained with him or with each other.

Dodge scouted a safe landing zone. At first glance, the fire seemed nothing out of the ordinary, but Dodge recognized the fire was far more dangerous than he had estimated from his aerial reconnaissance, so he instructed his men to move toward the mouth of a gorge. This made sense because he wanted to get his crew between the fire and the river. If the fire forced them into the river, they could swim out until the fire swept by. As they moved toward the mouth of the gorge, Dodge saw that fiery eddies had closed the escape route, so he reversed course, without saying anything to his men. Within minutes Dodge passed word for the men to drop all their equipment and move as fast as they possibly could. When a fire fighter drops his equipment, he is no longer a fire fighter, and his mission turns to simple survival. The men began to run.

The region they were in was a transition zone, where mountains turn to grassy plains. Dodge realized he and his crew would not be able to outrun the fire, which was consuming the shoulder-high, dry dense grass. He stopped, lit a match, and threw it into the grass in front of him. His crew had never seen anything like it and didn't understand when he jumped across the blazing ring and moved to the smoldering center. They thought maybe he was lighting a backfire, which would make sense in some cases, such as when there is thought to be some time before becoming engulfed. Dodge, however, was not thinking about a backfire. He could not be heard over the roaring flames but was waving frantically for them to join him. At this point, the men didn't understand how this could possibly save them; they thought he had gone crazy. They ran past his smoldering ring of fire and up a hill. Thirteen men died that day.

Dodge's instinct to create a safety zone by burning potential fuel for the main fire has become an accepted practice in firefighting, and after the incident, a board of review concluded that all of his men would have survived if they had heeded Dodge's efforts to get them into the escape-fire area. The innovative tactic that firefighters now practice as a lifesaving measure was not accepted by Dodge's crew because he had lost his ability to influence them. The crew had not personally worked with Dodge before this incident, so they did not have a sense that he knew or cared for them. They did not know Dodge. There was no bond of trust between them to carry them through a situation that did not make sense to them. They were only willing to follow as long as they saw the benefit or could make sense of what Dodge was doing. He had a quiet nature, and although he provided specific and direct instructions, he offered no rationale for his decisions. The nature of the fire caused Dodge to continually change course and revise previous instructions. According to the social exchange theory, followers will concede power only as long as they believe the leader will provide some form of security. According to transformational theory, group members follow leaders who communicate openly and demonstrate care.

If conditions for survival change drastically, power can shift dynamically. Team members may recognize that competence in one area is no longer relevant. They will reassess the type of expertise needed to address the new conditions and shift power to the leader that meets the new requirements. This happens in the competitive corporate world as well as within the military. General Stanley McChrystal replaced General David McKiernan in overall command of NATO forces in Afghanistan because of a need for "new thinking." McChrystal had spent most of his career specializing in counterinsurgency (COIN), which requires a different way of thinking than high-intensity combat does. Although McChrystal had the appropriate competence, some of his actions led the president and coalition members to lose trust in him; hence he was replaced by General David Petraeus. McChrystal's rise and fall highlight the criticality of both competence and character in maintaining influence.

Regardless of whether a leader works at a strategic or tactical level, followers need to know that the person with the most relevant capability is in charge. On one particular FSF adviser team, the chief was a major with an infantry background. Infantry are very disciplined, and legitimate authority is key to mission accomplishment. Infantry traditionally relied heavily on positional power, inspiration, and strict compliance for influence. As team chief, this major was frustrated by the lack of influence he had within his team and among Iraqis. He did not modify his leadership approach; he had legitimate power by rank and assumed that he could rely on it. The team realized early on, however, that their effectiveness, and indeed their survival, depended on building relationships with the local populace and by gathering intelligence from them. Many of the traditional infantry competencies and leadership techniques would not be relevant in this type of mission. The team looked to the one other major on the team, whose background was in the military police. This major knew how to talk to locals, he had experience "reading people" and asking questions to get good intelligence for raids and general security purposes, and his leadership style was less authoritarian. The formal leader with legitimate authority lost power within his team, because he could not adapt fast enough. Kolditz's research with *in extremis* leaders indicated the importance of "learning" above all other leader competencies.[8]

Mutual Influence

With highly committed members like the polar explorers described above, a team can be highly effective through reciprocal influence, that is, although the leader has a strong influence, he or she listens to and empowers the team members. They participate in critical decisions that empower them and promote their commitment. Reciprocal influence also allows the leader to get a good sense of how team members think and what motivates them. In one FSF adviser team in Iraq, the team leader had to tell team members that his job was their job too. This team used main supply routes (MSRs) that were known to be dangerous due to improvised explosive devices (IEDs) planted by insurgents. Insurgents changed tactics at a rapid-fire pace, making it hard to keep up through counter-IED strategies. The team leader felt responsible for bringing his guys home alive, so he required every member on the team to contribute intelligence every day on what they had seen and heard in the area of operations. Some team members did not think they had the experience or the credibility to speak about suspicious behaviors on the MSRs. The leader told them that even if it was "out of their lane," he wanted them to participate in collecting information and proposing solutions. The team recognized that this leader had their best interests in mind and respected his commitment to gathering as much information as possible to increase their chances of survival. Thus the leader maintained his ability to influence the group.

This example is a case in which a leader relinquishes some power to a team that is highly committed to survival. Contrast this leader with the infantry officer who refused to relinquish any control and attempted to maintain power through rank. Research indicates that effective leaders in "safe" conditions also create relationships in which they have strong influence but remain receptive to influence from subordinates. They empower team members to discover and implement new and better ways of achieving goals in order to stay competitive.

SOURCES OF POWER AND INFLUENCE

Broadly speaking, sources of power can be conceptualized along two lines.[9] One source is power derived from the authority that comes with one's job, role, or status. This type of power is referred to as positional power. It includes potential influence derived from control over information, resources, rewards, punishment, and things like the physical work environment. Given an *in extremis* condition, this type of power to influence will fall short. Followers who face a real possibility of death or dismemberment are not concerned about rewards or punishments; they only care about survival.

The other source of power is personal power, which may stem from a person's expertise or competence, character, integrity, friendship, loyalty, or other attributes that make the person attractive. Referent power, a subtype of personal power, is typically acquired easily by someone who is attractive, charismatic, charming, friendly, and trustworthy. Authentic leaders increase their power to influence by showing care and concern for other's needs and developing trust within their organization. When leaders promote trust they create a bond that allows for cooperative and committed work as a team. (See Chapter 9, in this volume, for an in-depth discussion of trust development.)

A second subtype of personal power is expert power, which is influence gained from knowledge or competence that is needed by others to perform well or survive. The more rare and important the competence is to the group, the more power the group will concede to the leader. More research is necessary to determine how important competence is compared to trust and integrity when people face *in extremis* conditions.

A survey of upper-middle and executive level leaders by the Center for Creative Leadership identified the top three sources of power as the power of expertise, the power of information, and the power of relationships.[10] Participants in the study reported that the power of relationships would become the most important source in the next five years. The least popular source of power was the power to punish. Given extreme conditions, it is hard to imagine that the power to punish would in any way be effective when followers are faced with survival. *In extremis* leaders must develop the relationships that promote trust and commitment.

Understanding Those Whom You Wish to Influence

A dangerous context leader should understand the motivation of team members. Kurt Lewin describes a common psychological phenomenon called approach/avoidance motivation.[11] In essence, people act out of desire for something or fear of something. To create motivation to act, a leader can heighten a follower's desire for something, lower the follower's fear, or both. Leading in extreme conditions often involves the strong emotions of fear. FSF advisers found that Iraqi soldiers could be inspired to participate in dangerous operations when they focused them on the vision of a secure neighborhood for their children to play and attend school in, that is, something the soldiers desired. They also found that driving the Taliban out of villages in Afghanistan (i.e., lowering fear) was effective in gaining locals' cooperation in rebuilding communities. *In extremis* leaders can use transformational leadership to develop an understanding of followers' needs, fears, and values. This caring quality supports leaders' ability to determine the most influential actions they can take to help their followers and accomplish missions.

Leader and Leadership Development Implications

An *in extremis* leader is only effective because followers maintain trust and want him or her to be their leader; the dangerous context strips away the validity of other sources of leader authority and power. An understanding of why followers choose to concede power improves the leaders' ability to assess the most effective means of influence. A leader should ask, "Is the follower motivated by rewards and avoiding punishment, or does the follower want to be like me, or even believe as I do?" The answers inform the leader about the follower's level of commitment. They also provide insight into appropriate influence techniques. For example, if the follower only seeks reward, a leader knows that positional power is at play and that in a crisis, this follower may not comply with requests. In situations when lives are on the line, the power that comes from positional authority often will be insufficient to influence followers. In this case, the leader needs to get to know the follower better so he or she can determine how to build commitment. Personal authority that comes from competence, trust, and credibility with followers may be more influential than positional power. Ironically, the same principle likely holds true for ordinary circumstances, where there is no danger, yet leaders in quiet contexts may lean on their positional authority like a crutch. This sets the conditions for leaders to suddenly lose the ability to influence when an unforeseen crisis raises the stakes. This may explain why the concept of crisis leadership has gained in popularity in recent times as nations struggle through the challenges of economic downturn, terrorist threats, and natural disasters. Leaders in all contexts need to engage in interactions with followers that demonstrate care and build relationships and eventually gain commitment.

It is also important for a leader to understand how to use reciprocal power while also maintaining power. In today's complex environments, it is unlikely that one leader will have all the answers to volatile, uncertain, and chaotic challenges. A leader must, therefore, be humble enough to empower others to develop solutions and be confident enough to execute the best solutions regardless of the source.

The most fundamental lesson from dangerous contexts is recognizing that the emergence of a perceived threat—when followers believe that a leader's behavior will profoundly influence their well-being—is a game changer. Leaders in all contexts struggle constantly to maintain influence and give purpose, motivation, and direction to their group, but a perceived threat to that group may require a shift in influence strategies. The ability to gauge followers' needs and apply the right strategies to influence their perceptions of one's leadership and the context is a ubiquitous ability, suited not merely to the dramatic circumstances presented by danger, but in all circumstances where people look to a leader for direction and purpose. The focus of studying *in extremis* leadership is not merely to understand leadership in dangerous contexts. It is to better understand leaders in all contexts. As put so aptly by Jack Bovender, the CEO of Hospital Corporations of America during the successful evacuation of the Tulane Hospital during Hurricane Katrina, "I couldn't become in 30 minutes what I hadn't been in 30 years."[12] None of us can.

KEY TAKE-AWAY POINTS

1. Leaders in dangerous contexts need to gain influence based on competence, character, and trust prior to asking followers to engage in life-threatening duties.

2. Commitment from followers is earned by knowing their needs, values, fears, and capabilities, and by being willing and able to put their interests first, and by inspiring group members to do the same for each other.

3. Commitment from followers is hard won, but much more effective than attempting to impose compliance in *in extremis* conditions.

4. Every interaction with followers should build the leader's influence and build the relationship with them so that when a leader has to expend influence, it is there to use.

5. Influence strategies should be aligned with the leader's source of power, the follower's needs, and the situation.

KEY REFERENCES

Kelman, H. C. "Interests, Relationships, Identities: Three Central Issues for Individuals and Groups in Negotiating Their Social Environment." *Annual Review of Psychology* 57 (2006): 1–26.

Kolditz, T. *In Extremis Leadership: Leading As If Your Life Depended On It.* San Francisco: Jossey-Bass, 2007.

Yukl, G. *Leadership in Organizations.* 6th ed. Upper Saddle River, N.J.: Pearson Education International, 2006.

NOTES

1. T. Kolditz, *In Extremis Leadership: Leading As If Your Life Depended On It* (San Francisco: Jossey-Bass, 2007); Thomas A. Kolditz and Donna M. Brazil, "Authentic Leadership in *In Extremis* Settings: A Concept for Extraordinary Leaders in Exceptional Situations," in *Authentic Leadership Theory and Practice: Origins, Effects and Development,* ed. William Gardner, Bruce Avolio, and Fred Walumbwa, Monographs in Leadership and Management, vol. 3 (Oxford: Elsevier, 2005), 345–356.

2. On polar madness, see L. Palinkas and P. Suedfeld, "Psychological Effects of Polar Expeditions," *Lancet* 371 (9607) (2008): 153–163.

3. H. C. Kelman, "Interests, Relationships, Identities: Three Central Issues for Individuals and Groups in Negotiating Their Social Environment," *Annual Review of Psychology* 57 (2006): 1–26.

4. A. I. Karrasch, "Indirect Influence: Foreign Security Force Adviser's Lesson Learned" (paper presented at the Joint Center for International Security Force Advisor Conference, Quantico, Va., October 26, 2008).

5. J. M. Burns, *Leadership* (New York: Harper and Row, 1978).

6. E. P. Hollander, "Leadership and Social Exchange Processes," in *Social Exchange: Advances in Theory and Research,* ed. K. Gregen, M. S. Greenberg, and R. H. Willis (New York: Winston-Wiley, 1979).

7. M. Useem, *The Leadership Moment* (New York: Times Books, 2006).

8. Kolditz, *In Extremis Leadership.*

9. G. Yukl, *Leadership in Organizations,* 6th ed. (Upper Saddle River, N.J.: Pearson Education International, 2006).

10. V. Bal et al., *The Role of Power in Effective Leadership* (Colorado Springs: Center for Creative Leadership, 2008).

11. K. Lewin, *A Dynamic Theory of Personality* (New York: McGraw-Hill, 1935).

12. Kolditz, *In Extremis Leadership,* 44.

CHAPTER 13

The Decisive Moment
The Science of Decision Making under Stress

Joseph W. Pfeifer and James L. Merlo

I n January 2009, US Airways Flight 1549 performed an emergency landing in the Hudson River after hitting a flock of birds and losing thrust in
all engines. Decisions made by the pilot not to return to the airport of the
flight's origin or to attempt to land at surrounding airports, but instead to
bring the aircraft down in the icy cold waters between New York City and New
Jersey, saved all 155 people on board. A few years earlier, on September 11,
2001, another plane had flown down the Hudson River, this time intentionally
crashing into the North Tower of the World Trade Center. Seventeen minutes
later, hijackers flew a second plane into the upper floors of the South Tower.
On that fateful morning, there were two other deliberate plane crashes, one
into the Pentagon and the other into a field in Pennsylvania. People around
the world watched intently as firefighters and other emergency responders
made critical decisions in their efforts to rescue some 20,000 people thought to
have been in the towers that day. Subsequently, in Afghanistan and Iraq, military commanders made life and death decisions on battlefields. Through the
use of mass media, people around the world are often eyewitnesses in near
real time to the decisive moment when leadership is on the line and critical
decisions are made to adapt to the danger of extreme events. Those watching
the decision makers have infinite time to second-guess after the fact, free of
the stress and personal drama that surround these decisions.

Many who operate and lead in dangerous contexts have stories of decisive moments of exercising their leadership. The *in extremis* (dangerous) core of
decision making, however, is one of the least studied elements of the human

dimension.[1] The physical realities of professionals undertaking decisions in dangerous contexts, like firefighting and military operations, make this one of the most difficult environments for the application of science. Few researchers have endured the risk or unpredictability of studying human processes in the presence of danger, preferring instead less meaningful post hoc strategies. Nonetheless, understanding decision making in dynamic, complex situations where people's lives are at stake provides important insights into leadership in dangerous contexts.

Part of decision making involves when to employ which method to increase the odds of succeeding when leading in a dangerous context. To demystify this process, decision-making research will be applied here to personal experiences while peering inside the World Trade Center on September 11, visiting the battlefield, and going inside a cockpit during an emergency landing to see what it is like to make decisions when it counts the most. Examining the decisive moments for firefighters, soldiers, and airline pilots provides unique insight into how decisions are made under the stress and pressure of extreme events. Knowledge gained about decision making in dangerous environments can be applied to a broad range of businesses, governmental and nongovernmental services, or wherever leadership is expected to make critical decisions in a crisis.

THE ELEMENTS OF COMMAND AND DECISION MAKING

Extreme events require leaders to make critical decisions under a haze of uncertainty and perform complex organizational tasks, usually under tremendous stress. These leaders are asked to act decisively, yet remain flexible to a changing threat environment. The actual unpacking of decision making is a monumental task because researchers define the term in different ways, such as in relation to strategic thinking, psychology, neuroscience, and so on. In the nineteenth century, the military strategist Carl von Clausewitz wrote that during pre-battle evaluations, great commanders, such as Napoleon Bonaparte, saw how to win a battle in a "glance." Clausewitz uses the French expression coup d'oeil, which he describes as "the rapid discovery of a truth that to the ordinary mind is either not visible at all or only becomes so after long examination and reflection."[2] This "glance" is the moment during which commanders make sense of a situation and quickly envision a plausible course of action. Having this capability is the first element of command.

The second element of command is having the resolve to carry through with one's strategic intuition despite surrounding uncertainty. A simple plan vigorously executed in a timely manner is almost always better than a complicated plan performed too late.[3] The third element is having the "presence of mind" not to ignore uncertainty but to remain flexible to the unexpected, which may require analytical thinking. Clausewitz discovered that great commanders first see what needs to be done and then resolve to follow their insights while adapting to the unexpected. These three elements of command are also seen today during emergency and military operations. Examples of the three elements can be seen in the actions of firefighters in New York City following the al-Qaeda attacks of September 11.

> On September 11, 2001, at 8:46 a.m., while operating in the street at a gas emergency in Lower Manhattan, a group of firefighters heard the roar of a low-flying commercial airliner accelerating as it flew down the Hudson River. Suddenly, the plane appeared, then aimed and crashed into the North Tower of the World Trade Center. No one could believe that on a perfectly clear day, a plane would crash into New York's tallest building. In an instant we knew that we were going to the biggest fire of our lives. I remembered trying to comprehend what took place and at the same time take command. My first order was a direct command: "Go to the World Trade Center." This was followed by a brief description on fire dispatch radio that a plane has crashed into the World Trade Center and to transmit a second alarm. Based on past experience at major fires, I knew I had to give concise orders to maintain command and control. These orders were given almost automatically, within seconds of impact and without fully understanding the magnitude of the event. Without hesitation, firefighters immediately mounted their fire trucks. With flashing lights and blasting sirens, we raced to the World Trade Center. The fire and the smoke coming from the upper floors of the World Trade Center fit the pattern of a high-rise building fire. But this was no routine fire.
>
> The World Trade Center attack was a novel and complex event. Never before had a commercial plane deliberately crashed into a modern skyscraper. It did not match anything from our firefighting experience and was quit different from the accounts of a much smaller military B-25 plane crashing into the Empire State Building on July 28, 1945. As we responded to the World Trade Center, I remember telling myself that I had to slow my thoughts down and deliberately think of what I had to do next. There were tens of thousands of people that needed to be evacuated or rescued. I forced myself to remain calm.
>
> Within a minute of my first radio transmission, I gave additional orders very precisely and deliberately over the Manhattan fire dispatch radio: "Battalion One to Manhattan, we have a number of floors on fire. It looked like the plane was aiming for the building. Transmit a third alarm. Have the second alarm report to the North Tower and have the third alarm stage at

Vesey and West Street." This message began with an intuitive statement of the plane aiming for the building, denoting a terrorist attack, and an analytical order envisioning the initial resources needed and where to deploy these units. Over the next 100 minutes after this transmission, dramatic events of rescue and building collapse unfolded rapidly requiring critical decisions that combined intuition and analysis.

In a crisis, leaders are expected to not only use intuitive, gut feelings but also to apply rational thinking when making critical decisions. Each mode of decision making uses different parts of the brain, with one mode outperforming the other depending on the task that needs to be accomplished. The key to good decision making in dangerous situations is knowing when to rely on which mode of thinking and when to use both. The battlefield is replete with examples of commanders constantly switching from one mode to another or sometimes applying a hybrid approach. For example, on April 5, 2003, less than two weeks after ground forces started moving north into the country of Iraq, U.S. military forces conducted raids through the center of the Iraqi capital, Baghdad. Three battalions, fewer than a thousand combat soldiers, had launched an aggressive thrust of Abrams tanks and Bradley fighting vehicles into the heart of the city, and in three days of bloody combat ended the initial phases of the Iraq War. The surprise assault on Baghdad, spearheaded by the Spartan Brigade commander, Colonel David Perkins, who led the 2nd Brigade of the 3rd Infantry Division (Mechanized), is an illustration of one leader's intuition that a single armored brigade would be able to successfully penetrate and literally capture a city defended by one of the world's largest armies.

Using a combination of intuition (I have sufficient combat strength to accomplish the mission) and analytical thinking (my logistics can support this initiative), Perkins declared on April 7, "If I can spend a night in Baghdad, then this war is over." Organized resistance by defenders of the regime of Saddam Hussein essentially ended after this commander's bold action. Thus, a decision by a commander on the ground potentially saved lives by ending the immediate armed resistance. Some of the highest officers in the U.S. military command found out about Perkins' tactical exploitation of the enemy only after seeing media coverage of it. The operation exceeded their expectations. The critical combination of intuition and analytical thinking were paramount. The decisive moment in dangerous situations requires the ability to switch and combine the different modes of thinking.[4]

INTUITIVE THINKING VERSUS ANALYTICAL THINKING

The most widely accepted rational model for decision making derives from the work of I. L. Janis and L. Mann, who define decision making as a process of comparing a range of options, evaluating them, reexamining their positive and negative consequences, rating them, and then determining the best option.[5] The difficulty is that rational decision making has limited application in a dangerous situation, where leaders are forced to act quickly and without comprehensive information. Rational decision making works well with simple events or even complicated ones when there is sufficient time to analyze and compare the facts; this, however, is not how firefighters, soldiers, or pilots operate at the scene of complex or dangerous incidents, where fire or bullets are flying or a plane has no power. Those confronted with such situations depend heavily upon their intuition in deciding what actions to take. Yet, analytical decision making is also called upon during emergencies to craft creative solutions for novel events. Problems might arise from a lack of guidance regarding when best to use intuition and when to switch to rational analysis. To fully comprehend decision making, one should examine research on it in the psychology and neuroscience literature.

The psychologist Gary Klein has done extensive research on the decision making of firefighters and combat soldiers. Based on his analysis, they make decisions by using cues to recognize a situation as typical (or atypical) and to decide a course of action by relating it to their experience.[6] Developing a quick course of action benefits from pattern matching and envisioning how actions will be carried out while also adapting to the evolving situation. This means that firefighters and soldiers do not compare all possible options, but choose the solution most likely to work based on prior experience.[7] These experiences are rooted in past events or training or are vicariously experienced through the study of after action reviews and history. If an option is not working, it is immediately customized or abandoned and a new solution created. This permits firefighters and soldiers to adapt quickly and avoid being paralyzed by evaluating endless possibilities. These types of decisions are further defined by A. Dijksterhuis and L. F. Nordgren as a gut feeling and by the popular writer Malcolm Gladwell as decisions that occur in "blink."[8] Here, researchers believe that intuition, which is recognizing what to do without fully being conscious of why one has this knowledge, plays a critical role in decision making.

To explain intuition, J. Lehrer explores the inner working of the brain. He argues that emotions that trigger intuitive insight occur when the neural transmitter dopamine is released. Dopamine automatically detects subtle patterns based on experiences that are not consciously noticed.[9] The more experience and knowledge one has, the more likely a new incident will match a pattern from the past. Intuition or the emotional brain is especially useful in making immediate decisions in life-threatening situations. It is the supercomputer of the brain, rapidly scanning past experience to find relevant information that matches the current condition.[10]

Another example of high-stakes decision making with lives on the line occurred on January 15, 2009. After taking off from New York's LaGuardia Airport, US Airways Flight 1549 struck a flock of geese, which caused the plane to lose thrust in both engines. Captain Chesley "Sully" Sullenberger radioed a Mayday message, stating that the plane had lost power and was turning back toward LaGuardia. The air traffic controller suggested runway 13. Sullenberger "knew intuitively and quickly that the Hudson River might be [the] only option, and so articulated it." He responded to the controller, saying, "We're unable; we may end up in the Hudson."[11] Sullenberger next, however, considered Teterboro Airport, in nearby New Jersey. After being told by the air traffic controller that he was cleared for an emergency landing on runway 1, Sullenberger said, "We can't do it." Not wanting to believe the gravity of the situation, the air traffic controller again asked Sullenberger which runway he would like at Teterboro. Sullenberger immediately replied, "We're gonna be in the Hudson."

Desperate to come up with another option, the air traffic controller suggested Newark International Airport, which was a few miles away, but the decision was already made. Captain Sullenberger then narrowed his focus to concentrating on landing the aircraft in the icy Hudson. The airplane skidded along the surface of the water and turned slightly left before it came to a stop near the Intrepid Air and Sea Museum. Sullenberger, realizing that the airplane was in danger of sinking, opened the cockpit door and gave a single order: "Evacuate."

During three critical minutes of flight, Captain Sullenberger did not try to compare all of his options before determining the best choice, but instead considered one at a time that he thought might work. He later wrote that there was not enough time to calculate the plane's rate of decent. Instead, he created a "three-dimensional mental model" of the situation to determine if his choice could be executed.[12] This type of decision making fits Klein's recognition-primed decision-making model. As each of Sullenberger's mental simulations failed in his search for the likely option that might work, he came to realize the best option was the Hudson River.[13] Making decisions in dangerous circumstances requires the intuitive brain to size up the situation and form the initial impulse about what to do.[14] The analytical brain then can be used to process the mental simulations to see if the option will work. Pilots often refer to the skill to think during a crisis as creating a "deliberate calm," which blends intuitive pattern matching with analytical thinking. Analytical thinking occurs in the prefrontal cortex of the brain.[15] It is where calculations are computed, logical sequences processed, and rational thinking takes place. This part of the brain also can turn off impulses, which is what Sullenberger did when he decided not to act on his first thought—to return to LaGuardia— but decided instead to land in the Hudson River.

COMBINING INTUITION AND ANALYSIS TO MANAGE DANGEROUS SITUATIONS

Intuition is good for matching patterns based on experience, but when someone encounters a novel problem that does not match his or her experience, and dopamine secretions fail to generate the desired neuronal connections, it is essential, Lehrer argues, to remain calm and analyze the situation to generate a flash of insight.[16]

On September 11, 2001, even the smallest decision was the difference between life and death. As events rapidly evolved, it was essential that emergency responders blend intuition with analytical thinking. Upon arriving at the World Trade Center, firefighters initiated rescue operations by evacuating people from the buildings and trying to rescue those trapped by the raging inferno. Firefighters carried heavy rescue equipment and self-contained breathing apparatus as they ascended the narrow stairs. Along the way they encouraged people not to stop to rest, but to keep moving down the stairs and to exit the buildings. Little did anyone know that the fires were weakening the structural integrity of each building, and time was running out.

> At 9:59 a.m., we heard a load roar and felt the building rumble. Unbeknown to us in the North Tower, this was the sound of the collapsing South Tower. In a fraction of a second, we knew something was seriously wrong and quickly moved a few meters from the lobby command post to a passageway leading up to a pedestrian walkway over six lanes of traffic on West Street. This gut feeling or intuition was generated not by knowledge of the collapsing South Tower, but by matching the loud roar to the experience of similar sounds of structural collapse. Immediately we interpreted this sound as a dangerous condition to us in the lobby and looked for shelter. This took place within an instant, without any analysis or second thought. I knew we had to move quickly from where we were standing. Seconds later, we were covered with choking dust and complete darkness, making it difficult to breath and impossible to see the hand in front of your face.

Many firefighters, without consciously understanding what was taking place, made this intuitive decision, which saved them from being killed by flying debris. J. LeDoux proffers that intuition or gut feeling buys time while rational thought searches for a solution to a novel event.[17] In the example above, instead of spending time analyzing what was happening, the intuitive part of the firefighters' brains quickly processed information and came up with the idea to leave the lobby. Firefighters and soldiers often use this type of decision making in times of danger. Klein also suggests that intuition precedes analysis.[18] People with expertise know what to look for when sampling environmental stimuli. L. Shattuck, J. Merlo, and J. Graham found that more experienced military leaders, based on time in service and rank, tend to ask for less information when making decisions than do officers with less experience.[19] Their study of military leaders' decision making, which they termed "cognitive integration," suggests that experienced leaders' intuition allows them to sample a small number of sources, ignoring those they deem not worthy of consideration. Less-experienced officers sample all sources of information available and usually as much of each as allowed.[20]

> Switching from intuitive thought to rational analysis is even more difficult under dangerous and high-stress conditions. Immediately after the loud rumbling stopped (later we learned the sound was from crashing steel and concrete), some of the Chiefs continued to use their intuition to issue orders that "we have to get out of here." Certainly, this was a good idea and a major concern when you do not know how to get out of the building. But this was a building that I was very familiar with and I had been to hundreds of times. Even in total darkness I had a good idea on how to get out. My experience and knowledge of the World Trade Center complex allowed me a few seconds to switch my thinking from intuition to analyze. Here I was able to focus on the next most important action to take, besides our own escape. It was clear that if we could no longer command from the lobby of the North Tower (Tower 1), we had to withdraw the firefighters from the building. I depressed the transmission button on my portable radio and gave the following firm order, "Command to all units in Tower 1, evacuate the building."[21]

While this may sound like an obvious decision for those watching broadcasts of events on September 11, it was not that obvious for those at the World Trade Center who did not have the same information, that is, that the South Tower had collapsed. Those in command at the North Tower had to overcome cognitive biases to continue rescue operations and instead to make a decision that had never been made in the history of the New York City Fire Department—abandon a burning building with hundreds of people still trapped inside. The novelty of the 9/11 attacks did not allow the firefighters to match their experience to past patterns of commanding and follow standard procedures. Instead, it forced them to become creative in the decisions they made. A. Howitt and H. Leonard note that emergency responders need to improvise when confronted with novel events.[22] Many of the people that were saved on September 11 owe their lives to improvisational thinking.

Lehrer points out that emotions are adept at finding patterns based on experience, but when someone encounters an event never before experienced, he or she needs to deliberately analyze the situation to devise innovative solutions.[23] On 9/11, instead of responding to the gut feeling to get out of the North Tower, the firefighters there concentrated on continuing to command. The prefrontal cortex is uniquely designed to manage emotions, filter out extraneous information, and search for creative solutions to complex problems. Switching from intuitive to analytical thinking allowed emergency responders to focus on commanding, which led to the flash of insight to evacuate firefighters from the North Tower.

In immediately dangerous contexts, people act first and then try to make sense of the situation.[24] In complex contexts, however, leadership involves probing first, making sense of the situation, and then responding.[25] Leaders allow new patterns to emerge. The decision making in the North Tower of the World Trade Center is an example of this blending of intuition and cognition. Intuition gave the firefighters the extra seconds needed to conduct more analytical reasoning to adapt to the novelty of the situation.

> After giving the evacuation order and finding our way out, we stood under the north pedestrian bridge over West Street, connecting the World Trade Center to the World Financial Center. The street was covered with paper and the air filled with a brownish-gray dust. The Marriott hotel that was between the North and South Towers was heavily damaged and the incident command post, overseeing command of rescue operations in both towers, was abandoned. This critical situation with novel sensory information made little sense. Even standing in the street, we never received word that a 110-story office building just collapsed nor could we see the collapsed South Tower because of the dust. I remember forcing myself to comprehend what possibly could have taken place. The more I tried to analyze the situation, the longer it took to make a decision on what to do next. Little did we know that the North Tower was about to collapse and crush the overpass we were standing underneath. My intuition could not match what I was seeing to any experience and my analysis failed to make sense of the scene.
>
> Then suddenly, I felt this cold chill running down my spine that this was a bad place to stand. Immediately, I acted quickly to lead the group

I was with out from under the pedestrian bridge and north to the corner of West and Vesey Streets. Key to this decision was the ability to have the presence of mind to switch between the two modes of thinking and not be paralyzed by too much analytical thinking.

Adaptability in dangerous contexts requires the ability to oscillate between intuitive and analytical modes of thinking for decision making.

BARRIERS TO DECISION MAKING

Dangerous conditions demand that personnel who perform in such contexts prevail over physical, cognitive, and organizational limitations to carry out their mission. In extreme danger, these limitations become barriers for leaders to overcome in their decision making.

Physical Limitations

Warriors and emergency responders operate in conditions that can and do impose significant demands on the senses, limiting the ability to communicate through normal auditory and visual pathways. Noise (e.g., vehicle engines, power tools and gushing water, weapons fire) and murky conditions (e.g., smoke, sandstorms) can hinder the ability to communicate critical information. Under high stress, an attentional narrowing of the senses occurs that can, for example, reduce one's peripheral vision.[26] This affects perception by the senses as outlined in the above example of the environmental factors present at ground zero. These physical challenges make it extremely difficult to scan, focus, make decisions, and act. Heat, cold, exhaustion, and a host of other stressors can have debilitating effects on the long-term and working memory.[27]

Cognitive Limitations

Many military strategists emphasize that the strength needed to win future wars will be more cognitively based than kinetically based.[28] This assertion rings true for emergency responders as well. Early tactical decisions made in the handling of dangerous emergencies will have significant operational-level effects on outcome. In such situations, leaders will need to overcome their cognitive biases to increase the quality of their decisions when lives are involved.

Decision makers constantly try to make sense of context. M. Endsley points out that sensemaking is backward focused, finding reasons for past events, while situation awareness is typically forward looking, projecting what is likely to happen in order to inform effective decision-making processes.[29] Decision making relies on seeing what has happened and anticipating what

Table 13.1 Common Decision Making and Behavioral Biases

Automation bias	The tendency to trust information provided via electronic information systems over intuition or humans; accepting information derived from the use of automation as a "best guess" instead of vigilant information seeking and processing
Bandwagon effect	The tendency to do (or believe) things because other people do, with the goal of gaining in popularity or being on the winning side
Confirmation bias	The tendency to search for or interpret information in a way that confirms one's preconceptions or course of action.
Professional deformation	The tendency to look at things according to the conventions of one's profession, ignoring broader points of view
Denial	The tendency to disbelieve or discount an unpleasant fact or situation
Expectation bias	The tendency to believe or certify results or analysis that agree with one's expectations of an outcome and to disbelieve, discard, or downgrade corresponding weightings for information that appears to conflict with those expectations
Extreme aversion	The tendency to avoid extremes, being more likely to choose an option if it is the intermediate choice
Framing effect	The drawing of different conclusions based on how data are presented
Illusion of control	The tendency to believe that one can control or at least influence outcomes that one clearly cannot
Information bias	The tendency to seek information even when it cannot affect action
Loss aversion	The disutility of giving up an object is greater than the utility associated with acquiring it
Normalcy bias	The tendency to discount novelty and to respond to such events with only routine procedures
Neglect of probability	The tendency to completely disregard probability when making a decision under uncertainty
Not invented here	The tendency to ignore that a product or solution already exists because its source is seen as an adversary
Reactance	The urge to do the opposite of what someone wants one to do out of a need to resist a perceived attempt to constrain one's freedom of choice
Selective perception	The tendency for expectations to affect perception
Unit bias	The tendency to want to finish a given unit of a task or an item often resulting in sequential behavior limiting simultaneous tasks
Wishful thinking	The formation of beliefs and making decisions according to what might be pleasing to imagine instead of by appealing to evidence or rationality
Zero-risk bias	Preference for reducing a small risk to zero instead of a greater reduction in a larger risk

might happen. So, how does an expert process information? Along with understanding context and noticing information, cues, and data in the environment, or the lack of certain cues, an expert often also has the ability to tune out unnecessary information. Sometimes leaders can successfully employ cognitive shortcuts by utilizing heuristics, or rules of thumb. These tactics and techniques, however, cannot alone be relied upon.

Instructing leaders on the dangers and benefits of types of cognitive shortcuts or strategies that are used consciously and unconsciously will potentially make a better decision maker, or at least a more informed one, especially under extreme conditions, when physical and cognitive resources are potentially at their limits. The benefits of shortcuts for decision making are self-evident, for example, deciding which exit of a plane one would choose in an emergency or formulating an escape route when searching an apartment on fire. The pitfalls of certain heuristics and biases are, however, well known, from the framing of decisions to the readiness to use what is available to the memory, or the availability heuristic.[30]

Cognitive biases are essentially mental errors caused by simplified information-processing strategies. It is important to distinguish cognitive bias from other forms of bias, such as cultural bias, organizational bias, or bias that results from one's own self-interest. In other words, a cognitive bias is not necessarily the result of an emotional or intellectual predisposition toward a certain judgment, but rather of subconscious mental procedures for processing information.[31] One of the ways to avoid the pitfalls and shortcomings associated with cognitive heuristics and biases is to be aware of them and to use simulations to practice overcoming them. Table 1 lists some common decision-making and behavioral biases of which all decision makers should be aware.

Organizational Limitations

While cognitive bias may blind individuals to emerging threats, organizational factors may prevent the integration of information until it is too late.[32] As events move from routine to complex, emergency responders and members of the military tend to "segregate" functional tasks. What was once a convenient division of labor mutates into specialized fiefdoms, with little contact or communication between people performing one task and those performing another.[33] This separation creates organizational blind spots in decision making. There is a natural tendency for people with similar backgrounds to form homogeneous groups and provide more information to members of their own group and less to members outside the group. The organizational behavior of separating and providing information only within a certain group is known as organizational bias.[34] In some businesses, such behavior is necessary for maintaining a competitive advantage over the competition. In dangerous contexts, however, such behavior potentially limits situational awareness, which creates barriers for decision making and commanding.

The propensity of similar individuals to migrate to each other is called homophily.[35] Evidence has been found that as the stress and complexity of a crisis increase, people tend to narrow their focus on aspects they judge to be most important to them.[36] In extreme danger, they often feel little obligation to share valuable information with those outside their group, since responsibility for acting is diffused across the in-group. In most cases, people think that someone else in their organization will share the information. In social psychology this concept is referred to as a diffusion of responsibility and is what often leads to the well-known bystander effect.

NOVELTY AND COMPLEXITY POINTS TO INTERDEPENDENCE

Fire chiefs, military commanders, and airline pilots dominate the examples cited here, but most professionals who regularly operate in dangerous contexts have the authority and often the experience to deal with critical situations—until perhaps they are faced with novel and complex events. These events by their very nature are characterized as having interagency dependencies for collaborative intelligence, requiring decisive leadership to overcome cognitive and organizational biases. A failure to address biases will result in a lack of situational awareness and poor decision making, which places leaders and managers at a disadvantage in handling crises. During complex and novel events, incident management does not rest with a single person; rather, leaders should increase the rate of information exchange and foster collaboration to generate new tactics and ideas. The key issue for decision makers is often not the ability to acquire more knowledge, but the ability to harness the knowledge of others.

On May 1, 2010, emergency responders had to overcome cognitive and organizational biases when they were called to a possible vehicle fire in New York's Times Square. When firefighters arrived, they noticed that something "did not seem right." The owner of the SUV was nowhere to be found, and there was white smoke coming from the car rather than black smoke. A handheld thermal camera showed no sign of fire, and an odor of fireworks emanated from the rear of the vehicle. Firefighters exchanged this information with police and asked them to run the license plates. The plates did not match the car. The fire lieutenant had to quickly process all these pieces of information.

It would have been easy for the lieutenant to have fallen victim to a number of cognitive biases and treat the incident as a routine car fire. Instead, he concluded that they had a car bomb on their hands. He avoided organizational bias by collaborating with police throughout the process, which led to a decision to evacuate people from the area. Combining intuition with analysis and overcoming biases to recognize interdependencies of information were critical for safety. It was later determined that the SUV had the potential to be a lethal bomb.

IMPROVING DECISION MAKING

An ongoing effort exists to find technological answers to address the physical dangers, cognitive puzzles, and organizational challenges that push leaders to their limits. The New York City Fire Department has developed an electronic command board (ECB) system to assist chiefs in decision making at fires and emergencies. ECBs are touch-screen computers for a network that displays such information as unit deployment, emergency distress signals, and digital blueprints of floors and other building information. Large (32-inch) ECB displays are used for major fires, but there are also smaller (10-inch) tablets, both of which graphically present essential information for decision making. As an incident increases in complexity, incident commanders are forced to remember dozens of unit names and locations within a building, while still managing the fire (or fires). Trying to manage too much information can overload the brain's working memory, adding to the stress of command and limiting one's ability to concentrate on critical aspects of incident management. The ECB frees the brain from memorizing facts by displaying them in easy-to-grasp pictures. This prevents chiefs from being overwhelmed by information occupying valuable cognitive space, and instead to concentrate on managing the incident, which requires the brain to blend intuitive and analytical decisions. ECB is part of a wireless decision-support system that can share information with other first responders at the scene and emergency operation centers elsewhere, thus creating a common operational picture and collaborative decision-making environment.

The military strategist Clausewitz states that war is influenced primarily by human beings rather than technology or bureaucracy, although technology advancements indeed change the tactics, techniques, and procedures used. Exercising leadership in dangerous contexts is not only about individual decisions, but also about getting others to adapt to a new threat environment. In extreme events, such as those terrorist attacks, military conflicts, and aviation emergencies, decision making is an interdependent activity, requiring collaborative intelligence. The challenge is to design a response system able to support and adjust readily to the urgent demands of events.

Providing decision makers with access to information from within and outside their agencies that normally would not be available can now be done through networks. Such networks have the emergent property of the whole being greater than the sum of its part because of the interaction and interconnection of their members.[37] This fact was acknowledged through the Goldwater Nicholas Act of 1986 and by the 9/11 Commission by requiring and reiterating that military and emergency responders must operate together in a unified system to be as effective as possible.

Initiatives are under way to develop means to allow military and emergency responders to accumulate life experiences through the use of virtual simulations. These simulations should be designed to adapt and respond to decision makers in an intelligent manner and portray cognitively, culturally, and intellectually accurate and challenging scenarios focused on identifying, developing, improving, and assessing intuitive and analytical decision-making skills. The development of such simulators will provide leaders with the chance to learn and train through scenarios that replicate life experiences, repetitiously and with low overhead and little risk.

Human factors—the cognitive, cultural, and intellectual aspects of conflict—are proving increasingly to be the vital elements determining success on the battlefield. It is the proper application of technology to aid the human, that is, engineered with the human in mind, that will leverage human capabilities and enhance human performance. For example, a well-designed interface that elicits personal interaction could lead to a self-referent memory approach by a trainee, potentially improving accurate recall when a similar situation arises.[38] This type of interaction with a simulator supports the theory of recognition-primed decision-making.[39] If properly exploited through interfaces it could promote perceptual learning in the areas of intentional weighting, stimulus imprinting, differentiation, and unitization.[40] These facets of cognitive psychology and learning are addressed in flight simulators, while military and law enforcement organizations try to do the same with firearm and gunnery simulators and fire departments with high-rise building fire and flashover simulators.

While a positive transfer of training is expected from virtual experiences, a host of other benefits can be realized with a well-made decision trainer. One can build crisis decision-making proficiencies—the deliberate practicing of skills—using dynamic scenarios for use on tabletops as well as devising full-scale exercises that promote intuitive and analytical decision making under stress, teaching leaders to blend reason with emotions. These simulators could be used to assist the development of individual and collaborative decision making.

Instructional methods for developing expertise must couple new technologies with seasoned experts, allowing simulations to compress experience into efficient repetition. The simulations should challenge trainees to adapt to novelty as well as act reflexively based on a strong grounding from what has happened in the past. Because time will not stop, and junior leaders require skills immediately upon entering high-risk occupations, it is necessary to accelerate the development of expertise by forming a cognitive apprenticeship with leaders recognized as being successful. Effective instructional methods provide mental schemas, allowing the organization of learning so leaders can match solutions to past or ongoing problems and create innovative courses of action for tomorrow's new problems. This type of approach should aim to improve long-term memory for ready recall in dealing with future extreme situations. Training needs to support guided discovery using the experiences of veteran leaders and include learning from errors through naturalistic feedback. Leaders must be given time to reflect individually as well as collaboratively with peers and coaches on how to use the two modes of decision making to adapt to threat environments or crises.

LEADERSHIP IMPLICATIONS

Extreme events require leaders to place people in dangerous situations to contain and mitigate hazard. Using their understanding of decision making and behavioral biases, and with the help of simulations and repetitive training, successful leaders employ a blend of intuition and analytical decision making. Although technology continues to influence decision makers at all levels, tactics, techniques, and procedures only change as a direct result of the coupling of humans with the technology. The skillful integration of human and machine results in improved performance, which in the end can save lives.

In stressful situations, leaders overcome ever-changing physical, cognitive, and organizational environments to make critical decisions by producing a deliberate calm. The professionals who make leadership decisions under such extreme conditions exhibit remarkable fortitude and resilience. Those who operate in dangerous conditions have chosen a lifestyle that embraces challenges. They not only aim to survive harsh environments, but they thrive in them as well. Effective decision making under stress requires a balance between cognitive intuition and analysis. The stirring stories of 9/11, military battles in Iraq, and the emergency landing in the Hudson River illustrate the need to be armed with the knowledge of human cognitive capabilities and the understanding of strengths and weaknesses of the modes of decision making.

Decision making in a crisis becomes more difficult with increased complexity and the need for rapid solutions. Not only will firefighters, military, and pilots face decisive moments in their careers, executives will also find themselves making critical leadership decisions in business. Supplementing the individual decision making skills discussed in this chapter, collaborative decision making is the next inescapable leadership challenge and thus necessitates further research.

NOTES

Joseph Pfeifer of the New York City Fire Department served as a battalion chief on September 11, 2001. He was the first chief on the scene and directed part of the operations that day. The firsthand accounts in this chapter are his.

1. T. Kolditz, *In Extremis Leadership: Leading As If Your Life Depended on It* (San Francisco: Jossey-Bass, 2007).

2. C. von Clausewitz, *On War* (London: Penguin, 1968; original work published 1832), 142.

3. R. Marshal, ed., *Infantry in Battle* (Washington, D.C.: Marine Corps Association, 1982).

4. D. Zucchino, *Thunder Run: The Armored Strike to Capture Baghdad* (New York: Grove, 2004).

5. I. L. Janis and L. Mann, *Decision Making: A Psychological Analysis of Conflict, Choice and Commitment* (New York: Free Press, 1977).

6. G. A. Klein, *Sources of Power: How People Make Decisions* (Cambridge, Mass.: MIT Press, 1998).

7. G. A. Klein and D. MacGregor, *Knowledge Elicitation of Recognition-Primed Decision Making* (Fairborn, Ohio: Klein Associates, 1987). Report under contract MDA903–86-C-0170 for the U.S. Army Research Institute Field Unit, Ft. Leavenworth, Kansas.

8. A. Dijksterhuis and L. F. Nordgren, "A Theory of Unconscious Thought," *Perspectives on Psychological Science* 1 (2006): 95–109; M. Gladwell, *Blink: The Power of Thinking Without Thinking* (New York: Little, Brown, 2004).

9. J. Lehrer, *How We Decide* (New York: Houghton Mifflin, 2009), 48.

10. Ibid., 248.

11. C. Sullenberger, with J. Zaslow, *Highest Duty: My Search for What Really Matters* (New York: Harper Collins, 2009), 223.

12. Ibid., 223–224.

13. G. A. Klein, *Streetlights and Shadows* (Cambridge, Mass.: MIT Press, 2009), 92.

14. Ibid., 94.

15. Lehrer, *How We Decide*.

16. Ibid., 128.

17. J. E. LeDoux, *The Emotional Brain* (New York: Simon and Schuster, 1996), 175.

18. Klein, *Sources of Power*.

19. L. G. Shattuck, J. L. Merlo, and J. Graham, "Cognitive Integration: Exploring Performance Differences across Varying Types of Military Operations," in *Proceedings from the Fifth Annual Federated Laboratory Symposium on Advanced Displays and Interactive Display* (College Park, Md.: Army Research Laboratory, 2001).

20. Ibid.

21. National Commission on Terrorist Attacks Upon the United States, *The 9/11 Commission Report: Final Report of the National Commission on Terrorist Attacks Upon the United States* (New York: W. W. Norton, 2004), 306.

22. A. M. Howitt and H. B. Leonard, eds., with David Giles, *Managing Crisis: Response to Large-Scale Emergencies* (Washington, D.C.: CQ Press, 2009).

23. Lehrer, *How We Decide,* 128.

24. Ibid.

25. D. J. Snowden and M. E. Boone, "A Leader's Framework for Decision Making," *Harvard Business Review*, November 2007, http://hbr.org/magazine.

26. C. M. Janelle, R. N. Singer, and A. M. Williams, "External Distraction and Attentional Narrowing: Visual Search Evidence," *Journal of Sport and Exercise Psychology* 21 (1999): 70–91.

27. W. C. Harris, P. A. Hancock, and S. C. Harris, "Information Processing Changes Following Extended Stress," *Military Psychology* 17 (2005): 115–128.

28. R. H. Scales, "Clausewitz and World War IV," *Armed Forces Journal*, July 2006, http://www.armedforcesjournal.com/2006/07/1866019.

29. M. R. Endsley, "Situation Awareness: Progress and Directions," in *A Cognitive Approach to Situation Awareness: Theory, Measurement and Application,* ed. S. Banbury and S. Tremblay (Aldershot, UK: Ashgate, 2004), 317–341.

30. A. Tversky and D. Kahneman, "The Framing of Decisions and the Psychology of Choice," *Science* 211 (1981): 453–458; D. Kahneman, P. Slovic, and A. Tversky, *Judgment under Uncertainty: Heuristics and Biases* (New York: Cambridge University Press, 1982).

31. D. Kahneman and G. Klein, "Conditions for Intuitive Expertise: A Failure to Disagree," *American Psychologist* 64 (2009): 515–526.

32. M. H. Bazerman and M. D. Watkins, *Predictable Surprises* (Boston: Harvard Business School Press, 2004).

33. P. M. Senge, *The Fifth Discipline* (New York: Doubleday, 2006), 24.

34. J. W. Pfeifer, "Understanding How Organizational Bias Influenced First Responders at the World Trade Center," in *Psychology of Terrorism,* ed. B. Bongar et al. (New York: Oxford University Press, 2007), 207–215.

35. M. McPherson, L. Smith-Lovin, and J. M. Cook, "Birds of a Feather: Homophily in Social Networks," *Annual Review of Sociology* 27 (2001): 415–444.

36. K. E. Weick, *Sensemaking in Organizations* (London: Sage, 1995).

37. N. A. Christakis and J. H. Fowler, *Connected: The Surprising Power of Our Social Networks and How They Shape Our Lives* (New York: Little, Brown and Company, 2009), 26.

38. T. B. Rogers, N. A. Kuiper, and W. S. Kirker, "Self-Reference and the Encoding of Personal Information," *Journal of Personality and Social Psychology* 35 (1977): 677–688.

39. G. A. Klein, "Recognition-Primed Decision," *Advances in Man-Machine Systems Research* 5 (1989): 47–92.

40. R. L. Goldstone, "Perceptual Learning," *Annual Review of Psychology* 49 (1998): 585–612.

CHAPTER 14

Crisis Leadership
The Station Club Fire

Michael H. Schuster, Lee M. Chartier, and John E. Chartier

O n the evening of February 20, 2003, the rock band Great White had just begun to play to an overcapacity crowd at the Station nightclub in West Warwick, Rhode Island, when at 11:07 p.m., the band's tour manager set off pyrotechnic displays. Sound insulation in the ceiling ignited, followed by the wood paneling on the walls. A flash fire engulfed the building within five and a half minutes. Ninety-six people died in the club, and four more died at local hospitals. Many of the 230 injured received such severe burns that they required multiple surgeries and months of rehabilitation. Only the 132 people who exited in the first 250 seconds were unharmed.

Organizational crises are low-probability, high-consequence events typically also involving ambiguity.[1] Crises can be grouped into four categories: accidents, such as Alaska Airline Flight 261, which crashed off the California coast, killing eighty-three passengers and five crew members;[2] scandals, such as the 2002 crisis at Tyco in which the CEO and CFO were convicted of stealing $170 million in unauthorized compensation;[3] product safety and health incidents, such as the Firestone/Ford recall of defective tires on the Ford Explorer in 2000;[4] and employee-centered crises, like the 2004 crisis at Abercrombie & Fitch in which a race-based class action discrimination suit was filed against the company.[5]

Leadership crises occur infrequently, usually unpredictably, and in the case of accidents, with no prior warning. They arise with limited frequency, because organizations have built-in processes to minimize their occurrence and effectively expedite a return to equilibrium.[6] Research on crisis management and leadership is difficult, always retrospective, and usually results in suggestions for crisis training.[7] Rarely does a crisis affect an entire state and have national implications, as did the Station club fire in 2003, the fourth deadliest night-club fire in U.S. history. This chapter uses this fire to assess leadership competencies in crisis. The descriptions of an authentic leader developed by Lynn P. Wooten and Erika H. James and Thomas A. Kolditz and Donna M. Brazil are used to examine and illustrate the leadership skills, abilities, and traits needed for effective crisis leadership.

CRISIS MANAGEMENT VERSUS CRISIS LEADERSHIP

Crisis management relates primarily to the operational issues associated with an event. In contrast, crisis leadership refers to how leaders handle the human responses to the incident or crisis, including their own, during and after the event.[8] Most research on crisis management has focused on internal and external communication.

Wooten and James note that crisis leadership requires the application and integration of skills, abilities, and traits to facilitate planning, responding, and learning from the crisis while under public scrutiny. In the case of the Station club, fire response planning had been part of prior training and existing procedures. None of the responders, however, had ever experienced a crisis of this magnitude. Public scrutiny of the manner in which the Station club crisis was handled was high due to its magnitude. In a best-case scenario, the manner in which a crisis is handled should result in an organization being "better off after a crisis than it was before,"[9] as a result of individuals and the organization learning from their experiences.

The research presented here parallels many of the attributes identified in Kolditz's research on authenticity in extreme situations.[10] Authentic leaders are described as "confident, optimistic leaders of high moral values . . . aware of their own thoughts, behaviors, abilities and values . . . attentive to these characteristics in others and the situational context in which they operate."[11] *In extremis* leadership occurs in situations where the risk of death is present. Kolditz asserts that the success of *in extremis* leaders is measured in "units of authentic leadership—moral character, trust, hope, optimism, and positive emotionality"—behavior the authors also believe to be indicative of authentic leadership. In these situations, followers seek to be led by individuals with these characteristics.[12] Leaders and followers who work in *in extremis* situations are generally not compensated at higher levels than those who do not. They choose their profession "inspired by their role in society and by leaders who have a strong mission and beliefs about the value of their activities."[13] Firefighters, for example, display many of these characteristics in their work.

CRISIS PHASES AND LEADERSHIP COMPETENCIES

Wooten and James, in summarizing the literature on crisis management, identify five phases of a crisis:

1. Signal detection: recognize early warning signs of a crisis
2. Prevention and preparation: avert a crisis or prepare should a crisis occur
3. Containment and damage control: keep the crisis from expanding
4. Organization recovery: resume normal operations
5. Learning and reflection: examine critical lessons from the crisis[14]

Although accidents are unpredictable, in the Station club's case it could have been expected that the initial crisis (the fire) would set in motion additional crises, such as the recovery of victims and subsequent issues. Following is an examination of the leadership competencies used to resolve and contain the crisis.

In their work on crisis leadership, Wooten and James identified eleven leadership competencies across the five phases listed above (Table 14.1). We provide here supporting evidence for each competency from our study of the fire and have also identified additional competencies (not included in their analysis) that characterize authentic leadership in *in extremis* situations.[15]

Following a brief description of our methodology, this chapter provides background on the Station club crisis; its origins; the incident (the fire), which ended quickly (albeit tragically); and the recovery of victims. The analysis was developed from fire to recovery to the immediate aftermath. The detailed description of the event and all that it encompassed is necessary to highlight the leadership competencies under discussion. There have been extensive criminal and civil proceedings as well as national analysis of the fire. The focus here is on the leadership issues that arose during the first days of the crisis. The findings and implications of this research are presented in the context of the theoretical models.

METHODOLOGY

This research uses a methodology developed by Wooten and James in their study of twenty business crises. They selected secondary sources that were then subjected to ethnographic content analysis, which involves analyzing numeric and narrative data, often generated by the media, to shed additional light on an issue. We had access to official government documents on the facts surrounding the Station club fire and many of the leaders involved in

Table 14.1 Wooten and James' Leadership Competencies by Phases of a Crisis

Crisis Phase	Leadership Competencies
Signal detection	Sensemaking ▶ Turning circumstances into a situation that is comprehended and that serves as a springboard for action
	Perspective-taking ▶ Ensuring the well-being of those affected by the crisis, to act in the best interests of those involved
Prevention and preparation	Issue-selling ▶ Directing attention to and understanding important issues that would be immediately recognized
	Organizational agility ▶ Having full knowledge of the organization and working cross-functionally (organizational functions, departments, silos) to fulfill the task
	Creativity ▶ Identifying problems and solutions that go beyond traditional thinking
Containment and damage control	Decision making under pressure ▶ Making sound and rapid decisions under pressure, particularly when time pressures and limited information exist; in situations such as the Station club fire, physiological, emotional, and cognitive constraints can interfere with decision making
	Communicating effectively ▶ Connecting emotionally and psychologically with the audience to create a favorable view of the organization
	Risk-taking ▶ Using risks can be associated with creativity and innovation; avoidance of risk narrows the ability to respond
Organization recovery	Promoting organizational resilience ▶ Producing a new view of an organization's possibilities; resiliency in the "maintenance of positive adjustment under challenging conditions"
	Acting with integrity ▶ Acting ethically in decision making and behavior is essential for trust and organization integrity; trust is important during a crisis to avoid a perception of betrayal by the stakeholders
Learning and reflection	Learning orientation ▶ Including post-crisis assessment based on reflection and learning for exceptional crisis management

Source: L. P. Wooten and E. H. James, "Linking Crisis Management and Leadership Competencies: The Role of Human Resource Development," *Advances in Developing Human Resources* 10 (2008): 352–359.

Note: For more, see K. Weick, K. Sutcliffe, and D. Obstfeld, "Organizing and the Process of Sense-Making," *Organizational Science* 16 (2005): 409–421; C. Smith and P. Ellsworth, "Patterns of Cognitive Appraisals in Emotions," *Journal of Personality and Social Psychology* 48 (1985): 813–838; K. Sutcliffe and T. Vogus, "Organizing for Resilience," in *Positive Organizational Scholarship: Foundations of a New Discipline*, ed. K. Cameron, J. Dutton, and R. Quinn (San Francisco: Berrett-Koehler, 2003), 94–110; I. Mitroff, "Crisis Management: Cutting Through the Confusion," *Sloan Management Review* 29 (1988): 15–20.

responding to the crisis. The project relied heavily on secondary sources for historical and factual information, but on primary as well as secondary sources to validate facts and uncover leadership challenges not addressed by the available data on the event. Sixteen interviews were conducted with participants using a questionnaire developed by the authors, supplemented by a thirty-four-item questionnaire based on G. Klann's work.[16] Participants in the study were the leaders of the units that acted as first responders and members of the rank and file. The study also included an interview with the governor of Rhode Island, who played a critical leadership role.

This study presents in-depth research on leadership issues that arose during the fire. Note that there are scientific gaps in this qualitative approach. First, data provided are subject to the interpretation of the participants, and the research was guided by the official record of the incident. Second, it is impossible to know how this crisis might have been handled differently since reconstructing it was not an option. While the findings of this qualitative study cannot be generalized to other crises, the Station club fire represents a crisis with significant leadership challenges. Much can be learned from it.

BACKGROUND

Built in 1946 as a restaurant, the small (4,484 square foot) one-story, wood-frame building at 211 Cowesset Avenue in West Warwick, Rhode Island, had undergone an occupancy change in March 2000 to become a rock-themed nightclub. At the time of the change in occupancy, the club owners were required to install a sprinkler system, but they did not.[17] On the evening of the fire, the band had just begun to play when the tour manager set off pyrotechnic displays on both sides of the stage.[18] Within minutes, a night of anticipated entertainment turned to tragedy.

Many musical groups use proximate pyrotechnics to enhance live shows.[19] In the majority of jurisdictions (including Rhode Island), special training and licensing must be obtained from local authorities to prepare and use them. In this case, there was no fire permit for the pyrotechnics. Figure 14.1 shows the Station layout, including the location of exits. Flammable sound insulation in the ceiling and wood paneling on the walls ignited. Within five and a half minutes, the club was engulfed in a flash fire.[20] Table 14.2 provides a summary of incident data. A June 2005 report by the National Institute of Standards and Technology (NIST) asserted that a sprinkler system would have permitted occupants to escape safely.[21] A timeline of key events is presented in Table 14.3.

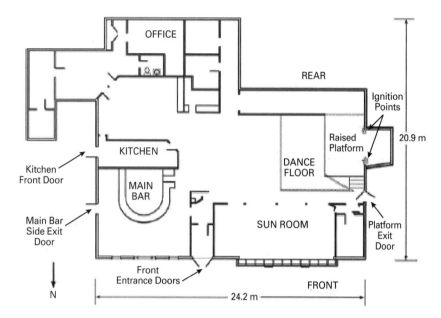

FIGURE 14.1 Floor plan of the Station club showing available exits

Source: National Institute of Standards and Technology, "Report of the Technical Investigation of the Station Nightclub Fire," NIST NCSTAR 2, vol. 1, http://fire.nist.gov/bfrlpubs/fire05/PDF/f05032.pdf.

Table 14.2 Profile of the Station Club Fire

Nightclub capacity	317
Number of people in the club	466
Number killed in the club	96 (92 patrons, 4 employees)
Number who died in hospitals	4
Total deaths	100
Injured (many with serious, life-threatening injuries)	230
Escaped unharmed	132
Survivors and spouses of the dead	23
Children who lost one or both parents	78
Number of emergency personnel responding	583

Source: *Providence Journal*.

Note: The pyrotechnics at the Station were gerbs, cylindrical devices that produce a controlled spray of sparks.

Table 14.3 Station Club Fire: Timeline of Key Events

February 20, 2003	
11:07:00 p.m.	Foam ignites, first flames on upper wall, left of platform
11:07:16	Flames reach ceiling to right of platform
11:07:30	Band stops playing; evacuation begins
11:07:32	Flames extend fully across ceiling above platform
11:08:13	Fire alarm recorded at the West Warwick Fire Department; fire dispatcher initiates a standard structure fire response
11:08:30	Thick, black smoke pours from sun room windows; smoke appears to be at floor level inside; occupants exiting though windows; dance floor and adjacent areas too hot for human survival two feet above the floor; cooler temperatures closer to the floor explain how some people still escaped later
11:09	Engine 4, Engine 2, Engine 3, Ladder 1, Battalion 1 assigned and dispatched
	Battalion 1 activates Warwick Task Force mutual aid (chief officer, 3 engines, 1 truck, 2 rescue) from Warwick Fire Department; triage set up at nearby restaurant by fire department
11:28:20	Three hose streams, three hand lines streaming on front door area; unified command established
11:40	Rescue 2 at Kent County Hospital (first arrival)
11:58	Warwick Ladder platform water on building
1 hour	Fire extinguished
2 hours	All occupants requiring medical treatment evacuated
4:00 a.m.	Command group meets to demobilize incident
February 21, 2003	
Late afternoon	Final body recovery efforts completed

Source: Department of Homeland Security, Office of Domestic Preparedness, "Rhode Island—The Station Club Fire After-Action Report," October 2004.

After the tragedy, the band, the nightclub owners, the manufacturers and distributors of the foam material and the pyrotechnics, and the concert promoters pointed fingers at one another. The band and the club owners disagreed about whether permission had been given for pyrotechnics. Questions were raised about the failure of town building and fire inspectors to enforce sprinkler system laws and to follow up about an inward-opening rear exit door they had cited but which had not been corrected.

ELEMENTS OF CRISIS LEADERSHIP CHALLENGES

This section reports on leadership themes and challenges specific to the fire. Detailed, factual background drawn from official reports and supplemented by interview data is presented here and serves as evidence to support the theoretical model. This section follows the flow of the incident and is divided into the following subsections based upon a compilation of participant interview data and "Rhode Island—The Station Club Fire After-Action Report."[22]

1. Technical assessment
2. Assess situation / manage risks
3. Command and control authority
4. When to stop rescue operations
5. When to transition to recovery
6. Manage subordinates' emotions
7. Media relations / control of airspace
8. Governor's role
9. Interface with other agencies
10. Provide support services after the fire

Technical Assessment

The fire at the Station club—given the information in the resources available—was not a type of fire that is difficult to suppress. There were no exposures (other structures close enough to the building of origin to allow the fire to spread), the water supply was more than sufficient to fight and suppress the fire, and the amount of manpower and apparatuses ultimately available to the West Warwick Fire Department via mutual aid from surrounding towns was sufficient to extinguish the blaze. If the building had been vacant, the incident would have been categorized as a routine fire. The life hazard in the building, however (even at normal occupancy), constituted a tremendous challenge. The combination of an overcapacity crowd and a rapidly spreading fire created a disaster.

Mutual aid was provided to the West Warwick Fire Department, in conjunction with the Southern New England Fire Emergency Assistance Plan (SNEFRAP), to provide surge capabilities and to cover departments already at the Station.[23] The Warwick Fire Department provided two additional apparatuses (one engine and one fire truck), supplemented with an additional engine company, rescue ambulance, and special hazards unit. The Cranston Fire Department and the Coventry Fire Department also provided substantial equipment and staffing, including approximately 100 firefighters and command officers, to support on-scene operations and to cover the West Warwick Fire Department stations and services during the incident. Significant numbers of the officers and staff of the mutual aid units were deployed to provide critical on-site cadre to initiate and maintain casualty collection, triage, pre-hospital victim care, and survivor support operations. West Warwick Fire Station 4 was only a half mile from the nightclub. A restaurant right across the street, the Cowesett Inn, became a triage site.

Assess Situation / Manage Risks

The first responders on the scene of the fire were members of the West Warwick Fire Department. Because West Warwick is a small community with only eighteen firefighters and rescue personnel typically on duty per shift, units from nearby Coventry and Warwick were called. Sixty to seventy on-duty firefighters and rescue personnel from these three communities fought the fire while waiting for backup. It was impossible at that time to determine how many victims remained in the building, alive or dead. Many surviving victims were already outside of the building beginning to receive treatment. Fatalities were assumed early on to be around ten, but another thirty were soon counted.

First responder leaders had to determine how much risk fire personnel should take based on how many people they could potentially rescue. Under normal circumstances, with few or no people in the building, emergency personnel would not have been allowed to enter the building due to the extreme danger. The first leaders on the scene, however, made the decision to risk responders' lives to possibly rescue more victims. Firefighters and rescue personnel were committed to (and vocal about) wanting to enter the building. The fire chiefs empowered them to act because they all believed that the potential to rescue victims outweighed the risk. The leaders listening to involved responders and allowing them to assist in decision making served to motivate them even more. Allowing such input is not a competency previously identified in crisis leadership research.

A ladder truck was positioned so firefighters could enter the building under the protection of a hose stream, an approach referred to as offensive (rescue) and defensive (fire suppression) firefighting. Although exceedingly dangerous and contrary to most standard procedures—firefighters can be crushed under the weight of the water above them—the attempt proved to be extremely successful.[24] Many more people were rescued from the vestibule. This leadership decision was made during the most intense part of the crisis and demonstrates the firefighters' dedication to saving lives.

Table 14.4 Communities Providing Mutual Aid in Fighting the Station Club Fire

Town	Population	Square Miles	Fire Department
Coventry	34,000	62	61 personnel, 6 stations
Cranston	80,000	29	202 personnel, 6 stations
Warwick	86,000	50	220 personnel, 8 stations
West Warwick	30,000	8	66 personnel, 4 stations
North Kingstown	26,000	52	73 personnel, 4 stations (arrived at the end of the fire)

Source: Department of Homeland Security, Office of Domestic Preparedness, "Rhode Island—The Station Club Fire After-Action Report," October 2004.

Command and Control Authority

Fire Chiefs Charles Hall (West Warwick), Robert Warren (Cranston), Wolfgang Baeur (West Warwick), and John Chartier (at the time, fire chief for the City of Warwick) were on the scene. The West Warwick Fire Department had jurisdiction over the incident, with the West Warwick chief in command. He received assistance from other West Warwick officers and those responding from two other communities. Initially, this included a battalion chief from Warwick and a small number of firefighters from Coventry. The crisis management situation became complicated as more communities responded, and communications systems between departments proved incompatible. A more complex organization structure relying on team-based management, rather than the normal chain of command, was required.

Two major operations needed to be managed: the suppression and rescue effort in the Station club and triage, treatment, and transport coordination at a restaurant across the street. Figure 14.2 illustrates a traditional fire response organizational structure while Figure 14.3 shows the greater complexity of the Station fire response. The triage process was a traditional one, but the number of people and the severity of the injuries were extraordinary.

Because of incompatible radio communication systems, the three fire chiefs who managed the fire and rescue operation communicated verbally. Eventually, Hall assumed the role of communicating with the media. He was assisted by the town manager, as many questions were posed and camera crews were on scene. Another chief managed the rescue effort and eventually the recovery component of the incident. The other chief documented events as they occurred and ensured that resources were being allocated appropriately.

The three would meet regularly to update one another on what was happening. With the triage component being managed across the street, face-to-face communication among leaders was difficult. Rescue personnel were sent over periodically to provide information to the chiefs regarding the condition and transport of victims.

The overall operation had a unified command structure consisting of the three fire chiefs, from West Warwick, Warwick, and Cranston (see Figure 14.4). This model is based on a nationally accepted incident command system, referred to as NIMS, the National Incident Management System. The three chiefs had been colleagues for more than twenty years, and their mutual trust and familiarity were key. National standards requiring leaders to wear vests identifying them as incident commanders were unnecessary. The chiefs communicated face-to-face, collaborating and drawing on their combined perspectives and experiences. Acutely aware that their jobs had to be done quickly and in many cases with incomplete information, the chiefs weighed in with ideas before reaching consensus about the best course of action. Each then communicated with his subordinates in-person or by radio. (Radio compatibility existed within departments.)

The emergency rescue captain from Warwick assumed leadership of the triage operation at the restaurant. He knew the capabilities of some of the rescue workers and made quick assessments of others from junior ambulance drivers to more seasoned rescue veterans. Because of the horrific physical condition of some of the victims, rescue workers had to be assigned based upon their perceived ability to handle the situation not only technically but also emotionally.

When to Stop Rescue Operations

The fire chiefs decided to cease rescue operations when the first responders in the building's vestibule indicated that they could no longer see anyone alive. This consensus decision was made based on the chiefs' personal observations about what was transpiring at the scene, input from fire and rescue personnel who had entered the building, and the chiefs' combined experience in fire suppression and rescue situations. Interview data strongly suggest that first responders would not have ceased the rescue operation if there were still victims alive.

The condition of the victims added to the sense of urgency. Firefighters and rescue personnel witnessed countless victims alive and burning, stuck in the front doorway, piled on top of one another trying to get out but unable to move. In the parking lot were people suffering from horrific burns, smoke

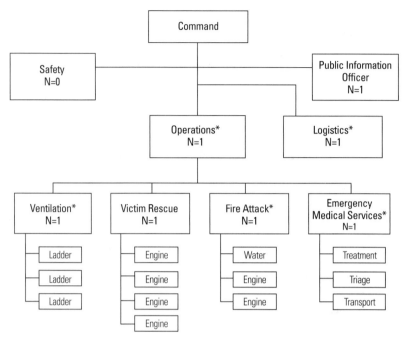

*Span of control 1–5

FIGURE 14.2 A typical building fire management structure. Functions usually performed by individuals were done by teams during the Station fire. This happened across the board.

Source: John Chartier, fire marshal, Rhode Island.

inhalation, and cuts from exiting the building through windows. Across the street at the restaurant, countless more injured were being assisted by companions. Friends and volunteers had taken some victims in private vehicles directly to the closest emergency facility, Kent County Hospital, 2.26 miles from the scene. The responders also arranged for alternate or supplemental transportation. When the evening news began reporting on the fire, friends and family of the club goers and employees began to arrive at the scene, creating crowd-control issues.

When to Transition to Recovery

By morning, news of the fire was being reported not only by the local media, but also by the Associated Press and major news networks. Aircraft attempting to photograph the scene filled the airspace over West Warwick. Hundreds

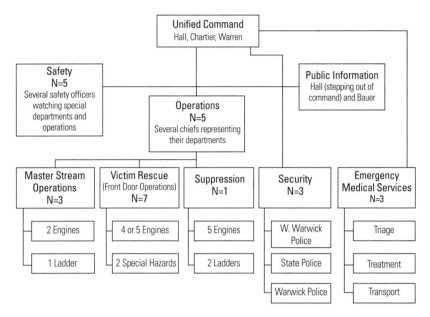

FIGURE 14.3 Station club fire management structure
Source: John Chartier, fire marshal, Rhode Island.

of people arrived looking for missing family members. All this activity posed a dilemma for the leadership team. Because bodies are considered evidence, responsibility for recovering them normally falls to the Coroner's Office, the State Fire Marshal's Office, and local law enforcement, not firefighters. In this case, however, when members of the Coroner's Office arrived, they were not prepared for the magnitude of the situation, having brought only four body bags to the scene in a small truck.

The chiefs determined that they could not leave the bodies in the building. Acting without legal authority, they asked for firefighters to volunteer for body removal. Teams of three were assembled—one officer and two firefighters—who entered what remained of the building with representatives of the Fire Marshal's Office and law enforcement. Victims' bodies were photographed; locations noted. Victims were placed in body bags, and the Warwick Fire Department chaplain led a short prayer for each. The bodies were then delivered to a member of the Coroner's Office.

The West Warwick fire chief, the media spokesperson, acknowledged the multiple fatalities (the exact number was not yet known), indicated the number of transported victims, and promised to identify which trauma center had received which victims as soon as he could. When the decision was made by the Governor's Office to set up a family assistance center, this too was communicated to the media.

Manage Subordinates' Emotions

When the three chiefs made the decision to stop recovery efforts, many of the firefighters were standing outside the building watching what remained of the blaze being completely extinguished by the heavy streams from ladder pipes and deck guns. About thirty Warwick firefighters, the group that had conducted the vestibule rescue for more than three hours, informally assembled around an engine. The Warwick fire chief spoke briefly, offering words of thanks, encouragement, and praise for a job well done, focusing on lives saved rather than those lost. In the days and weeks following the incident, firefighters expressed appreciation for this acknowledgment.

Following the chief's remarks, firefighters were required to report across the street to the restaurant, where an area separate from triage had been set up by critical incident and stress debriefing (CISD) teams called by the leadership team once they realized they would be dealing with multiple fatalities. The CISD teams talked to rescue personnel about what they had seen and done in the hope of minimizing post-traumatic stress disorders. Televisions were on, and responders were watching media coverage of the event. The leader of the CISD team considered turning them off but decided that the news actually helped responders see the bigger picture of what was happening in addition to their own individual roles.

Media Relations / Control of Airspace

Members of the Rhode Island State Police, Federal Bureau of Investigation, and Alcohol, Tobacco and Firearms were also on the scene. Each agency assumed responsibility for issues within its scope. Among the most compelling was protecting the dignity of the dead and their families. Firefighters set up large tarps to prevent media from photographing the scene from across the street. Helicopters also began circling, shooting photographs and live footage. The state police contacted the Federal Aviation Administration to request that the airspace above the scene immediately be closed, which was done.

Governor's Role

Rhode Island governor Donald Carcieri had been in office only six weeks when the Station club fire erupted. He was out of state, but returned as soon as the incident was reported. In his interview for this research, he related a story from his orientation at the National Governors' Conference. His mentor had told him that one of his first decisions as governor should be to appoint a director of emergency services. The rationale: within six months of taking office there would be a crisis, and its handling would define his tenure.

During the crisis, Carcieri played three critical roles. First, he assumed the role of chief communicator. He made himself available to families and the media and went to great lengths to ensure the accuracy of communications. Second, he took charge of the recovery and insisted that each family have certainty about victim identification. This process provided each family with the emotional relief of knowing what had happened. It also created the corollary problem of potentially missing persons reports. The whereabouts of some individuals had to be confirmed so that their loved ones would know that they had not perished in the fire. Third, the governor played the role of consoler, comforting families whose loved ones had perished or been severely burned. His availability and outward and genuine empathy created an impression that lasted throughout his eight years in office. In spite of the difficult economic and political circumstances confronting the state during his tenure, Carcieri's personal image firmly remained that of a leader of empathy and integrity.

Interface with Other Agencies

As the immediate crisis began to dissipate, Governor Carcieri met with the heads of the state police, Fire Marshal's Office, and West Warwick and Warwick police, along with the fire chiefs to discuss opening a family assistance center at a nearby hotel later that day. Rescue personnel along with CISD team members were at the hotel as family members continued to be informed of their relatives' fate. This center was open for the next several days, staffed by the Rhode Island Critical Incident Stress Management Team, the Red Cross, Rhode Island Emergency Management Agency, and staff from the Governor's Office.

Provide Support Services after the Fire

During the early morning hours, after the fire had been completely suppressed and no more victims were found alive, the Cranston and Warwick chiefs, along with a Warwick and Cranston Emergency Medical Service (EMS) and the Coventry fire chief, met with the CISD team to assemble a plan to cover the West Warwick Fire Department (in terms of manpower and equipment) and to provide fire support to the community for the upcoming days. This gave the West Warwick firefighters much needed physical and emotional relief. The firefighters, and fire and rescue personnel from all the responding communities, had experienced the worst disaster of their lives. Many had worked for more than twelve hours with few breaks and little relief. They needed time to recover from the pure exertion, strain, and fatigue caused by the fire.

They had witnessed unimaginable suffering and death. For even the most experienced of them, some of whom were combat veterans, the emotional impact of the experience would be felt for years. They needed to make some sense of what had happened, understand the role they had played and the effect of their efforts, and somehow eventually return to life as usual, knowing that there would be more fires and more casualties in the future. During the four to five days following the fire, the CISD team coordinator opened her home to individuals and small groups for counseling sessions and scheduled meetings. Counseling was done by peer teams, rather than mental health professionals, which in this case was a more effective approach. The responders were already acquainted with the team members, who knew and respected them.

Six massage therapists were sent to the State Medical Examiner's Office to work on staff there who were dealing with the victims' remains. This is an innovative approach—addressing the "body" in addition to the mind and spirit, following standards of care outlined by psychological first aid procedures. There are now seventy-five massage therapists credentialed and trained for critical incidents in Rhode Island.

For two weeks, representatives of CISD arrived from around New England to help provide counseling sessions. Chaplains were also involved. Group and individual sessions were both provided. The sessions were not voluntary; all who were involved in the Station club fire were required to attend. Their family members and others identified some as needing ongoing counseling. Subsequently, family support sessions were held at a local church.

LEADERSHIP COMPETENCIES EXHIBITED DURING THE STATION FIRE

This section examines leadership competencies at each phase of a crisis and relevant leadership actions (see Table 14.1).

Phase 1: Signal Detection

The leadership competencies here are sensemaking and perspective-taking. Sensemaking is *turning circumstances into a situation that is comprehended and that serves as a springboard for action.*[25] Unlike Wooten and James' illustrations involving pre-crisis evidence of impending problems, responders in West Warwick had no information prior to their arrival on the scene of the Station fire.[26] The evidence of their lack of "pre-crisis evidence" from the Station club fire can be seen in five leadership decisions:

- requesting the immediate release of additional resources, thus leaving the city with below-standard protection
- deciding to stop rescue and begin recovery
- assigning triage duty based on responders' experience and hospital capacity
- sending massage therapists to the Medical Examiner's Office
- allowing first responders taking breaks to view television coverage to get information and grasp the scope of the event

Signal-detection is also perspective-taking, that is, *ensuring the well being of those affected by the crisis, to act in the best interests of those involved.* The evidence from the Station club fire is contained in four leadership decisions:

- balancing the risks of potential recovery of victims and firefighter safety
- deciding to use firefighters for the recovery of bodies
- closing airspace and putting up tarps to protect the dignity of victims
- governor assuming roles in communications and identification of victims

Phase 2: Prevention and Preparation

The leadership competencies needed in the second phase of a crisis are issue selling, organizational agility, and creativity. In many instances, these could occur before the crisis. In this case, many of the issues were not planned for due to the severity and low probability of an incident of the Station's magnitude. There had been first responder training on organizational functions and departments, and cross-training was a common occurrence. Responders participated routinely in drills, which required the development of problem-solving skills. Still, this crisis presented unforeseen challenges.

Issue selling is *directing attention to and understanding important issues that would be immediately recognized.* The evidence from the Station club fire is contained in five leadership decisions:

- post-fire grief and trauma care for victims' families and firefighters
- critical incident stress debriefing (CISD) team called almost immediately to begin work with first responders
- family assistance center set up to provide updated information for families of victims

- governor understood importance of clear communications
- recognition of potential lawsuits

Organizational agility involves having *full knowledge of the organization and ability to work cross-functionally (organizational functions, departments, and silos) to fulfill the task.* The evidence from the Station club fire is represented by three decisions:

- traditional fire suppression structure, including chain of command and mutual aid between departments, adapted to meet crisis situation
- body bags—usually supplied by the Medical Examiner's Office—supplemented by a supply from the National Guard
- Federal Aviation Administration contacted to close airspace above the fire scene to protect dignity of victims and their families

Creativity is *identifying problems and solutions that go beyond traditional thinking.* Evidence from the Station club fire include the following:

- leaders adjusting the organizational structure and commingling groups from different communities
- establishment of a three-person leadership team (chiefs from West Warwick, Warwick, Cranston) rather than relying on the traditional mutual aid structure
- creation of a plan to provide staffing for the West Warwick Fire Department for the days following the fire
- sending the injured to surrounding hospitals in non-rescue vehicles and in greater numbers per vehicle than is standard to ensure more immediate care

Phase 3: Containment and Damage Control

Phase 3 of crisis leadership requires three different competencies: decision making under pressure, communicating effectively, and risk-taking. Decision making under pressure is the *capacity to make sound and rapid decisions under pressure, particularly when time pressures and limited information exist.* In situations such as the Station club fire, physiological, emotional, and cognitive constraints can interfere with decision making.[27] Decision making under pressure was evidenced during the Station fire by the following:

- allowing offensive and defensive firefighting simultaneously, contrary to normal procedure

- making hundreds of decisions throughout the crisis up and down organizational structures

Communicating effectively involves *connecting emotionally and psychologically with the audience to create a favorable view of the organization.* The evidence from the Station club fire follows:

- the governor's role in the family support center, including his daily presence
- the governor's demonstration of genuine compassion and empathy toward victims' families
- the Warwick fire chief's speech to subordinates focusing on lives saved
- liaison process between fire suppression, triage, CISD teams
- coordination with local hospitals to determine capability of receiving victims

The remaining competence in Phase Three, risk-taking, is associated with *using creativity and innovation; avoidance of risk narrows the ability to respond.* During the Station club fire, risk-taking was demonstrated in the following ways:

- allowing firefighters to enter the building farther and longer than would ordinarily be safe in order to continue to rescue victims
- stretching firefighter time and exposure without physical or emotional relief
- allowing offensive and defensive firefighting simultaneously, contrary to standard procedure
- releasing Warwick resources to aid in fire suppression and rescue but leaving the city with below-standard protection

Phase 4: Organization Recovery

The resumption of normal operations requires leaders to utilize two competencies: promoting organizational resilience and acting with integrity. A crisis can produce a new view of an organization's potential. Promoting organizational resiliency is the "maintenance of positive adjustment under challenging conditions."[28] The evidence from the Station club fire is as follows:

- the Warwick chief's speech to subordinates
- extensive and mandatory use of CISD team support post-event (Note: some responders are still in counseling as of this printing.)

- enhanced appreciation of mutual aid process and strong trust among leaders

Leaders must also act with integrity: *Ethical decision making and behavior are essential for trust and organization integrity. Trust is important during a crisis to avoid a perception of betrayal by the stakeholders.* At the Station club fire this competency was demonstrated many times:

- rank-and-file firefighters trusted that their leaders would allow them to make critical decisions, for example, when to get out of the burning structure or how to triage a victim
- concern expressed for the dignity of victims as evidenced by the recovery process
- chaplains blessed the victims upon removal from scene
- governor developed trust with victim's families through open communication and genuine empathy
- governor and mayors supported their respective staffs at the scene and after at the family support center
- CISD team used peer counselors who understood and had personal experience in crisis situations rather than only clinical training

Phase 5: Learning and Reflection

The final phase requires learning and reflection and is a learning orientation competency: *exceptional crisis management includes post-crisis assessment based on reflection and learning.*[29] Below are some of the lessons learned and the actions taken post-crisis.[30]

- passage of laws changing fire codes across the country; Rhode Island completely revised its fire code, making it the strictest in the United States
- trust among leaders is critical; the network of fire chiefs and response personnel was strengthened and meets with greater regularity
- grandfathering of buildings, that is, allowing existing structures to operate under old laws and codes, does not work
- empowerment of subordinates is critical to fast and effective response
- recognition of the need to better manage the emotional state of first responders
- recognition of other community hazards
- more proactive fire control established in public assemblies

- massage therapists sent to Medical Examiner's Office to address body concerns (complementing mind and spirit) as outlined in psychological first aid standards)

KEY TAKE-AWAY POINTS

This study of the Station club fire finds significant support for the eleven competencies identified by Wooten and James. In particular, those leading in dangerous contexts may take away the following:

1. Making sense of a situation is essential, in particular, knowing when to transition from one phase to another. This was evidenced by leaders deciding when to stop the rescue process to ensure that no responders would be lost.

2. Organizational agility and creativity in a crisis are important for firefighting organizations, where the standard procedure is based on chain of command. The triage team needed to improvise due to the substantial number of victims, casualties, and transport requirements.

3. Decision making under pressure and risk-taking are to be expected in any crisis situation. These were evidenced by leaders allowing offensive and defensive maneuvers to proceed simultaneously during the rescue and stretching subordinates to their emotional limits. Hundreds of decisions were made in a short period of time.

4. Stress management practice should be mandatory to promote organizational resiliency and individual mental health. The CISD team provided support to the Medical Examiners Office after the incident by providing massage therapists.[31]

5. Leaders must be seen as acting with integrity. This was evidenced when it came to protecting the dignity of the victims.

6. The feedback process is important for learning and for preventing future crises. Across Rhode Island and among the communities affected by the Station fire, numerous changes in fire laws and procedures were implemented. A similar fire in Perm, Russia, in 2009 had equally tragic consequences as an overcapacity crowd was trapped when fireworks designed for outdoor use ignited a low, plastic ceiling. There were no fire extinguishers, and one side of double-exit doors was sealed shut.[32]

We do not find support for the leadership competencies being specific to the phases as suggested by Wooten and James. Rather, leadership competencies tend to occur at multiple phases of a crisis. Restricting competencies to specific phases may be an unnecessary theoretical complexity to be avoided in future studies. At a minimum, efforts should be made to reveal competencies at more than one stage of the crisis. We also found an additional potential leadership competency, which we call improvisational leadership— the ability to adapt quickly and in a novel way to unforeseen circumstances well beyond training and preparation that would be typical for a crisis. This area of research will continue to be a difficult one. Only multiple studies that offer the opportunity for meta-analytic techniques will move the research from incidents to more general models.

NOTES

1. C. Pearson and J. Claire, "Reframing Crisis Management," *Academy of Management Review* 23 (1998): 58–76.

2. National Transportation Safety Board, accident report, www.ntsb.gov/Events/2000/Aka261/default.htm.

3. *Securities and Exchange Commission v. L. Dennis Koslowski, Mark H. Swartz and Mark A. Belnick,* Civil Action no. CV 7312, September 12, 2002, www.sec.gov/litigation/litreleases/lr17722.htm.

4. Firestone Tire Recall Legal Information Center, "Overview of the Recall," 2000, www.firestone-tire-recall.com/pages/overview.html.

5. *Gonzalez v. Abercrombie & Fitch,* 2005. See www.afjustice.com.

6. D. Smith and D. Eliott, "Responding to the Demands of Crisis: Issues around Future Developments in Theory and Practice," in *Key Readings in Crisis Management,* ed. D. Smith and D. Eliott (New York: Routledge, 2006), 415–525.

7. H. Hutchings and J. Wang, "Organizational Crisis Management and Human Resource Development: A Review of the Literature and Implications to HRD Research and Practice," *Advances in Developing Human Resources* 10 (June 2008): 310–330.

8. G. Klann, *Crisis Leadership* (Greensboro, N.C.: Center for Creative Leadership, 2003).

9. L. P. Wooten and E. H. James, "Linking Crisis Management and Leadership Competencies: The Role of Human Resource Development," *Advances in Developing Human Resources* 10 (2008): 353.

10. T. Kolditz, *In Extremis Leadership: Leading As If Your Life Depended On It* (San Francisco: Jossey-Bass, 2007).

11. T. Kolditz and D. Brazil, "Authentic Leadership in *In Extremis* Settings: A Concept for Extraordinary Leaders in Exceptional Situations," in *Authentic Leadership Theory and Practice: Origins, Effects and Development,* ed. W. L. Gardner, B. J. Avolio, and F. O. Walumbwa, Monographs in Leadership and Management, vol. 3 (Oxford: Elsevier, 2005), 346.

12. Ibid., 347.

13. Ibid., 353.

14. Wooten and James, "Linking Crisis Management."

15. W. Coombs, *Ongoing Crisis Communication: Planning, Managing and Responding* (Thousand Oaks, Calif.: Sage, 1999); I. Mitroff and C. Pearson, *Crisis Management: A Diagnostic Guide for Improving Your Organization's Crisis Preparedness* (San Francisco, Jossey-Bass, 1993); L. Pheng, D. Ho, and Y. Ann, "Crisis Management: A Survey of Property Development Firms," *Property Management* 17 (1999): 231–251.

16. Klann, *Crisis Leadership,* 81.

17. The club owners were Jeffrey and Michael Dederian. See the *Providence Journal,* www.projo.com/extra/2003/stationfire, for detailed coverage, including an investigation of the town's fire, police, and building inspection processes; a report of the emergency response to the fire; profiles of the club's owners; and indictment and civil complaint documents. Also see M. Arsenault, "Building Official: R.I. Code Required Sprinklers," *Providence Journal,* December 3, 2007.

18. The pyrotechnics were gerbs, cylindrical devices that produce a controlled spray of sparks.

19. Proximate refers to the pyrotechnic devices' location relative to an audience.

20. Video footage of the fire (recorded by Brian Butler, WPRI-TV) can be viewed at www.youtube.com (search "Station Club Fire").

21. W. Grosshandler et al., *Report of the Technical Investigation of the Station Nightclub Fire* (Washington, D.C.: National Institute of Standards and Technology, 2005), http://www.nist.gov/public_affairs/releases/ri_finalreport_june2905.cfm.

22. Department of Homeland Security, Office of Domestic Preparedness, "Rhode Island—The Station Club Fire After-Action Report," October 2004.

23. Grosshandler et al., *Report of the Technical Investigation.*

24. Each gallon of water weighs eight pounds, and the ladder truck is able to deliver 1,200 gallons per minute.

25. K. Weick, K. Sutcliffe, and D. Obstfeld, "Organizing and the Process of Sense-Making," *Organizational Science* 16 (2005): 409.

26. L. P. Wooten and E. H. James, "Linking Crisis Management and Leadership Competencies: The Role of Human Resource Development," *Advances in Developing Human Resources* 10, no. (2008): 363–364.

27. C. Smith and P. Ellsworth, "Patterns of Cognitive Appraisals in Emotions," *Journal of Personality and Social Psychology* 48 (1985): 813–838.

28. K. Sutcliffe and T. Vogus, "Organizing for Resilience," in *Positive Organizational Scholarship: Foundations of a New Discipline,* ed. K. Cameron, J. Dutton, and R. Quinn (San Francisco: Berrett-Koehler, 2003), 94–110.

29. I. Mitroff, "Crisis Management: Cutting Through the Confusion," *Sloan Management Review* 29 (1988): 15–20.

30. Between June 17 and July 3, 2003, the project team met with leaders and selected staff members of key state and municipal organizations to describe the process and seek their support and cooperation, which was forthcoming almost without reservation. The grand jury investigation of the fire, ongoing at the time, produced hesitancy, as might be expected among some responders, but in most cases did not

prohibit efforts to gather data from alternate sources. Concerns voiced by the Rhode Island Attorney General's Office, however, affected the timely completion of this report by prohibiting discussion with first responders and other critical organizations for a period of approximately eighty days while agreements among the various parties were worked out. In addition, access was denied to a report published by the Rhode Island Association of Fire Chiefs. The report would have added more certainty to some of the facts regarding the numbers and identity of responding organizations. Department of Homeland Security, "Rhode Island—The Station Club Fire After-Action Report."

31. J. Mitchell and G. Everly, *Critical Incident Stress Management: A New Era and Standard of Care in Crisis Intervention* (Ellicott City, Md.: Chevron, 1997).

32. On December 5, 2009, pyrotechnics ignited the ceiling of a club in Perm, Russia, killing 153 and injuring 62. See C. Levy, "Club Fire Recalls Station Blaze," *Providence Journal,* December 6, 2009; and M. Tkachenko and L. Graham-Yooll, "Five Detained as Investigators Probe Deadly Russian Nightclub Fire," CNN, December 5, 2009, http://www.cnn.com/2009/WORLD/europe/12/05/russia.nightclub.fire.

CHAPTER 15

Leading and Managing Those Working and Living in Captive Environments

John T. Eggers, Rebecca I. Porter, and James W. Gray

I magine you are the warden of a prison or the administrator of a jail, you enter the facility, and the heavy metal door clangs shut behind you. A riot breaks out and several members of your staff are taken hostage. Fires are set in various locations. The rioting inmates, members of a gang, attack other inmates who want no part in the rebellion and are only concerned for their safety. The decisions you as a leader make are literally matters of life or death, not only for yourself, but also for your staff and those incarcerated. The dynamics of power and guarding against potential corruption are also a constant concern. The leader of an incarceration facility must account for and respond to public opinion and political demands, as well as the individual needs and group dynamics of corrections officers and inmates.

Some of the desired outcomes for leaders in a confinement setting are a reduction in recidivism, security of the facility, prevention of escape, and efforts at rehabilitation. While some would argue that depending upon the reason for incarceration, the inmates do not deserve much more consideration than would an animal in a zoo, others—leaders—in this situation strive for much more. Accomplished leaders in a confinement setting seek to develop a culture that creates and sustains the psychological health and well-being of the corrections officers and provides inmates opportunities to develop skills and their potential. After all, they are in the "people business." Such an approach would conceivably result in an institution that functions based on the strengths of the corrections officers and inmates, thereby allowing them the greatest opportunity for self-development, physical and psychological security, and indirectly decreased chances of recidivism.

This chapter discusses the contexts of confinement, the psychology of corrections officers and inmates, and the forces at work on a leader and the population being led.

CONTEXT AND ENVIRONMENTAL DIFFERENCES

Leading and managing in captive environments, such as jails, prisons, detention centers, brigs, and disciplinary barracks, differ from leading and managing in private sector or other public sector arenas. Captive environments are for housing individuals—detainees, prisoners, offenders, inmates, and so on—with whom staff interact as part of their jobs. The potential danger leaders working in captive environments confront is rarely experienced by leaders in more traditional workplaces. One's thinking, emotions, and behaviors are put to the test in a variety of ways in the former; one must constantly be "on your toes," so to speak, because the environment can move swiftly from calm to all-out violence. Accordingly, leading and managing in this context adds an element of complexity not experienced by leaders and managers outside such an environment.

Correctional facility staff at executive, senior, manager, supervisor, and line staff levels need to function as role models for each other and for the inmates. Leaders outline the parameters of what is appropriate when it comes to the performance of their followers. Managers operate within these parameters, following the rules and regulations, and pursuing goals and objectives.[1] In essence, leaders create the boundaries within which staff and inmates work and reside. Thus, leaders create opportunities for positive change in the correctional environment, while managers maintain the established status quo.

Secure environments often operate in a routinized manner. Eating meals, exercising in the yard, visiting the canteen, and talking with visitors are a few examples of routines limited by specified periods of time, all in part focusing on the enhancement of physical safety. Both staff and inmates are involved in the routines. Sustaining these functions in accordance with policies and procedures requires sound management skills and behaviors, which also play a role when contemplating and implementing policy and procedural changes.

Correctional leaders must have a vision of the future as it could be. This is different from the managers' perspective, which may only be to operate in the present. Having the ability and willingness to adapt when necessary, rather than being merely consistent, is another trait that differentiates leaders from managers.[2] We suggest that a leader's vision be rolled out throughout the organization, so everyone can imagine it, and that a strategy be created to enhance employee ownership of it. For example, at the beginning of his tenure, the commandant of the U.S. Disciplinary Barracks (USDB) issues his correctional philosophy (in writing), so all staff members know it and work within it. In general, this philosophy is developed within the larger framework of two long-standing principles of the USDB. First, the treatment of inmates by all staff is governed by the notion that they are "in prison as punishment, not for punishment." In other words, staff members are never to exact punishment upon the inmates; the mere fact the inmates are incarcerated is all the punishment the court intended upon sentencing. Second, the USDB's motto—"Our Mission, Your Future"—sums up the institution's goals of rehabilitation and preparation of inmates for eventual release. A large portion of the USDBs staff is dedicated to treating, training, and educating inmates so that upon release they have a chance to be successful citizens, who have paid their debt to society by serving a sentence.

CORRECTIONAL MANAGEMENT MODELS

Three correctional management models—authoritarian, bureaucratic, and participative—influence the choices one has in leading or managing. The authoritarian model suggests that a leader maintain firm control and that any deviation from prescribed, centralized authority be met with a high level of disdain and punishment. All decisions are essentially made by the power holder. The bureaucratic model proposes a chain of command approach, with an emphasis on rules and regulations. In short, it advocates "going by the book," which makes it difficult to be flexible and adaptive when it comes to innovation. This protocol does, however, allow staff to move in, out of, and around the organization, using rules and regulations as guideposts. This model advocates a managerial, rather than a leadership approach. The participative model promotes staff involvement in how the organization should do business. As a result, employees may feel a sense of ownership, moving from a business as usual approach to a business beyond usual approach. This model requires a greater investment in time compared to the authoritarian and bureaucratic models. The latter two are the more common today. According to P. Carlson and J. Garrett, "Many successful agencies have adapted the bureaucratic model to include elements of the participatory style."[3]

An example of a management model is based loosely on the USDB's Inmate Advisory Council. The leadership of the Bagram Theater Internment Facility (BTIF) in Afghanistan—the U.S. military's largest detention facility supporting the Afghan campaign and holding several hundred unlawful enemy combatants—created a representative system whereby the detainees selected leaders from each of their respective communal cells to meet with the BTIF leadership and discuss current issues over a traditional Afghan meal on a monthly basis. The goal was to give the detainees a voice and a forum in which they and the leadership could mutually affect positive change. This forum proved hugely successful, and along with the implementation of a behavior-based "carrot and stick" privileges system, dramatically reduced detainee assaults and disturbances.

It is particularly important that one knows when to manage and when to lead. The full-range leadership model may be helpful in this respect.[4] It proffers that transactional leadership is comprised of two components: contingency reward and management-by-exception (active). Contingency reward can be looked at as a quid pro quo situation, whereby the leader and follower together decide on goals the follower will work on, and if the follower is successful, he or she receives a reward for goal achievement. Management-by-exception (active) leader behaviors focus on coaching and counseling the follower not to continue to make mistakes. Here, the leader does not engage the follower unless a problem presents itself.

Management behaviors exhibited in a leader-follower relationship inside the correctional facility may focus on planning, directing, and organizing, for example, overseeing inmate movement, cell shakedowns, inmate classification, staffing patterns, and so on. Management behavior, for the most part, does not promote the development of followers, nor does it typically create positive change inside the organization. Rather, as noted above, it maintains the status quo. In no way, however, does this suggest that management is not a good thing. It is critical.

Transformational leadership, in line with the full-range leadership model, promotes positive change within the workplace. Transformational leaders focus on assisting their followers in elevating their own self-interest for the interest of the organization. They also help their followers become more self-aware, so they can self-regulate their thinking, feelings, and behavior, and as a result, become more self-developed. These leaders focus on four components (or "4 I's"):

- Idealized influence—works to create trust and respect with the follower; demonstrates a strong sense of purpose, ethics, and values whereby followers can emulate the leader
- Inspirational motivation—talks optimistically about the future, articulates a vision for the future, and displays enthusiasm about what needs to be accomplished

- Intellectual stimulation—prompts followers to look at challenges from a variety of angles and welcomes different perspectives from followers on how to solve problems
- Individual consideration—focuses on the needs, expectations, and wants of the followers; spends time coaching and teaching followers, which promotes follower self-development

Transformational leadership essentially augments or builds upon transactional leadership (management). This type of leadership moves individuals, teams, and the organization in a positive direction. It should be used to create and sustain succession-planning efforts inside the organization. This leadership influences follower awareness of what is important, going beyond what needs to be done to explain the how, the why, and the what is being done. It creates a buy-in from followers whereby they feel a part of, rather than apart from, the organization. As a result, followers are better positioned to carry out the mission, vision, goals, and values of the organization. Transformational leadership comes to life when leaders practice the 4 I's.

A number of characteristics and behaviors, some of them noted above as well as below, differentiate management from leadership.[5]

Table 15.1 Management and Leadership Characteristics and Behaviors

Management	Leadership
▸ Does planning, directing, controlling	▸ Promotes change
▸ Provides predictability and order	▸ Examines and motivates others to new directions
▸ Organizes and structures plans	▸ Focuses on improving group members and the organization; develops a culture that promotes growth and learning

If individuals in supervisory positions do not take the time to establish positive relations with their followers, chances are the status quo will prevail. Promoting change implies possible risk. Asking followers to elevate the interest of their organization above their own and to take risks requires a sound, positive working relationship between leader and follower. Ideally, leaders and followers together make sense out of what's important as they compare their personal values and personal visions with the values and visions of their organization. Values such as competence, care, character, integrity, respect, responsiveness, innovation, and accountability, along with professional development, are key to a sound organization.

When asked what one needs to do to manage and lead effectively in the correctional sector, several leaders stressed the need to establish and maintain trust, be constantly aware of the situation at all times (situational awareness), and to empower their employees to get work done in a manner that increases individual and organizational capacity:

The Importance of trust

"Our business involves direct personal dangers which increase the importance of trust throughout the organization."

—*Trust is important for leading in captive environments.*

"To lead in a correctional environment you must have credibility. Staff places their well-being in your care and must have confidence that you know what you are doing from vast experience. Without that credibility, staff will elect to follow their own course of action."

—*Leaders develop credibility and trust through competence, character, and caring.*

Need for situational awareness

"Decisions made in corrections are often influenced by public policies and external stakeholders versus CEO's in the corporate world [who] lead the organization and are influenced by stakeholders in the form of stakeholders and consumers."

—*Managing the external environment is key.*

"One must balance the requirements of departmental policy, state and federal law, OSHA requirements, public opinion, contractual elements and lead in a manner that fosters growth in your subordinates, promoting change, and provide a secure, structured and safe workplace. Human rights laws and DoD regulations are also key as captivity operations during war time can lead to tribunals and other serious challenges if not done correctly. You must do these things under the scrutiny of the inmates who may not wish for you to succeed, but cannot afford for you to fail."

—*The need for situational awareness is clear.*

"We have to be vigilant about our surroundings and continue to evaluate our methods and tailor our approach to have the greatest impact on our staff without compromising safety and security."

—*Situational awareness must be constant.*

Empower to lead

"You need to know your staff and your inmates, and you need to know the policies and procedures that govern your agency. You have to be able to enable your staff to do their job and make decisions, but be ready to take over at a minute's notice during an emergency."

—*Knowing when and how to empower staff is paramount.*

"A leader in corrections needs to stay calm under pressure and should not make quick decisions unless the situation dictates it. Bounce decisions off of others and make an informed decision. In most cases, unless lives are imminently at risk, time is on the side of the correctional leader and their staff. Leaders should resist the temptation to react and employ use of force too swiftly. Be careful not to rush to a failure that will endure long in the minds of both staff and inmates."

—*Empower others when possible.*

"Our leadership style must have a component of courage as well as an emphasis on control and order—for the sake of safety. It is important to stay safe but it is also important to view inmates in a manner other than that they are dangerous to us. We must also view them as human beings whose lives we are trying to influence in a positive manner."

—*Staff need to be able to balance rehabilitation with appropriate safety protocols.*

As noted above, leading in a prison is in some ways quite different from leading in a traditional business environment due primarily to safety and security factors. The issue of personal safety, due to the threat of physical violence because of the nature and background of offenders, makes it essential for employees to be able to trust each other. A lack of trust is definitely a concern. Public safety is number one, but public opinion is also a serious matter in corrections. Correctional leaders must be aware of how employees carry themselves in the community and must accept as a condition of employment a code of conduct stricter than that of private sector or other public sector positions. They are required to answer to agency leaders, legislators, offenders' families, and the general public, all of whom have concerns and questions. The trust necessary when leading in a captive environment is similar to the trust needed among members of military units, for very much the same reason: members of the organization depend on their leader and one another for their physical safety and security.

In analyzing the above comments from correctional practitioners on how to lead in a correctional environment, it becomes clear that one needs to establish a balance between managing and leading. Leaders, to be effective, must develop high-quality relationships with their followers. These relationships need to involve a high degree of trust, respect, and sense of mutual obligation. Relationships between leaders and followers that are considered high quality tend to promote safety-related behaviors in the organization.[6]

TRUST AND PSYCHOLOGICAL SAFETY

Psychological safety is defined as someone's perception of consequences for taking interpersonal risks at his or her place of work.[7] Leaders need to work to create a culture of trust to promote psychological safety. The construct of team psychological safety suggests that it is "a shared belief held by members of a team that the team is safe for interpersonal risk taking."[8] Leaders need to ensure that all voices are raised and heard. Employees are rewarded for challenging processes if their leaders clear the way for them to do so. A "willingness to think of new ideas, explore novel directions, and behave creatively may require a safety net provided by a climate of psychological safety, since the process of exploration may be risky."[9]

Creating a culture whereby trust exists between leaders and followers, particularly in a correctional environment, is not always easy. "To earn trust, leaders must demonstrate competence, strong character, and caring."[10] They also need to invest time in establishing positive, cooperative relationships that empower group members. The level of trust employees have in leaders determines the amount of influence leaders can exercise."[11] (To learn more about building trust and creating a culture based on trust, please see Chapters 9 and 17, in this volume.)

POWER AND ABUSE OF IT

Individuals in leadership positions are granted power based on their position (positional power), and power based on their personality (personal power). Power is "an individual's relative capacity to modify others' states by providing or withholding resources or administering punishments."[12] Power can be used in both a positive and a negative manner. If used appropriately, power can benefit a relationship, but it can damage a relationship if used inappropriately. In short, it can help, and it can corrupt.

People holding power may value it above everything else and pursue the acquisition of it throughout their lives; those who are motivated by personal gain perhaps pursue it in relation to the office they hold. Power may cause one to believe he or she is above reproach, particularly as one's power increases, perhaps leading to corruption, cognitively, affectively, and behaviorally. D. Kipnis notes, "Corruption can also refer to the way in which the control of power changes the power holder's self-perceptions and his perceptions of others."[13] Concerns arise when those holding power believe they can influence others based on the power they hold. This can promote the belief in the power holder that he is superior in his views over those with less power (typically his subordinates), resulting in leaders behaving counter to their values and beliefs. The power holders may also be led to believe that they are special, particularly if their subordinates flatter them.[14]

Power can be abused when the power holder has a strong need for it and is in control of resources. According to Kipnis, (a) "with the control of resources goes increased temptation to influence others' behavior to satisfy personal wants; (b) if power holders use strong and controlling means of influence to satisfy these personal wants, and compliance follows, (c) there arises the belief that the behavior of the target person is not self-controlled but has been caused by the power holder; as a result (d) there is a devaluation of the target persons' abilities, and (e) the preference to maintain social and psychological distance from target person; (f) simultaneously the power holder's evaluation of himself changes so that he views himself more favorably than the target person."[15]

This has applications for the 1974 Zimbardo Stanford prison experiment, in which student volunteers acted as prisoners and prison guards (Zimbardo's choice of words; we prefer correctional officers) for five days. Those assigned to be correctional officers had the most dislike and lack of respect for those assigned to be compliant prisoners. As the officers' ability to control the prisoners increased due to compliance, rather than the officers liking the prisoners, the opposite occurred.[16] "With regard to prisons, we can state that the mere act of assigning labels to people and putting them into a situation in which those labels acquire validity and meaning is sufficient to elicit pathological behavior."[17] (To learn more about fostering a sense of personal responsibility in group members, please see Chapter 6.)

In the real world, supermax correctional facilities maintain total control over inmate movement. The actions of correctional officers are routinized in accordance with supermax rules:

> Because guards are encouraged to punish, repress, and forcefully oppose—by virtue of the fact that they are provided with no alternative strategies for managing prisoners—they have no choice but to escalate the punishment when their treatment of prisoners fails to produce the desired results (as it frequently does). Of course, over time, the correctional staff becomes accustomed to inflicting a certain level of pain and degradation—it is the

essence of the regime that they control and whose mandates they implement. They naturally become desensitized to these actions and, in the absence of any alternative approaches (both the lack of conceptual alternatives or the means to implement them), they deliver more of the same.[18]

Regarding comments on moral disengagement, "Civilized conduct requires, in addition to humane personal codes, social systems that uphold compassionate behavior and renounce cruelty."[19]

MAINTAINING A POSITIVE AND SAFE ENVIRONMENT

One important responsibility of leadership is to address the potential for desensitization of the correctional staff to degrading and unnecessarily painful treatment. Leaders can do this through the use of training programs that educate staff about the potential for behavioral drift, when staff slide toward inappropriate and counterproductive activities, as well as using objective, trained observers (i.e., psychologists) to monitor correctional staff behavior.[20] In the wake of the abuse of detainees held at the Abu Ghraib prison in Iraq, the U.S. military established behavioral science consultant teams (BSCT, referred to endearingly as "biscuit" teams) at most major detention facilities in Iraq and Afghanistan. Their primary purpose was to objectively observe the leadership and the guard forces to detect and report on any possible evidence of behavioral drift, or shift in climate where abuses could occur or even be condoned by leadership.

Individuals who feel powerful exhibit approach-related moods and emotions, focus on social rewards, and view others through a prism of how others could assist in satisfying their needs and wants. The powerful also often act in a less inhibited fashion. Less-powerful individuals experience more negative moods, attend to punishment rather than rewards, and inhibit their behavior.[21] Leaders should use their personal power as much as they can to gain commitments from staff and inmates. Positional power is used when necessary, typically when personal power does not achieve the desired results. For a leader to successfully use personal power, he or she must understand the psychology of inmates.

Psychology of Inmates

As stated earlier, leading effectively in a confinement setting is complex because of the population of inmates being led. They are varied in their attitudes toward the institution, their experiences, their education levels, and their psychological health. A leader must consider not only how his or her actions will influence the corrections staff, but also how they will, in turn, affect the inmates. A leader must cultivate a style that appropriately develops the leader-follower relationship with staff to produce the most effective interactions between the followers and their charges—the inmates.

Reason for Confinement. Perhaps the most salient difference among people who are confined or detained is the reason for their detention. The reasons can range from having been convicted of a property crime to having committed violent acts against other human beings. In the case of military detention centers in a war zone, detainees may simply have been identified as possibly posing a security risk, but are not necessarily guilty of having committed any crime It seems obvious that reasons for confinement likely result in differences in psychology among those who are to be led and managed by the corrections staff.

The reason an individual is confined is sometimes an indication of the inmate's psychological makeup. There are marked psychological differences between people who are convicted of murder and cannibalism compared to those who are convicted of theft, burglary, or assault. Such differences can be presumed to be tied to behavior, attitudes, and motivational styles.[22] Thus, they will respond differently to the confinement setting and the context set by leaders. A leader should not have high expectations of appealing to the humanity of someone convicted of a crime against human beings. On the other hand, inmates convicted of crimes against property might respond to a leader's personal power.[23]

Education Level. Differences in education level can be seen as reflective of intelligence or sophistication or, perhaps more accurately and relevantly, as an indication of the communication styles and means that will be most effective with the population. Leaders must consider how to publish and implement policy, directives, or other programs.

Length of Confinement. Prisoners who are confined for much of their adult lives do not age like unbound individuals who have been subjected to the typical environmental stressors of life outside a penitentiary.[24] Thus one might surmise that those inmates who have been imprisoned at different stages in their lives and for different lengths of time will have different reactions to various leadership styles or methodologies.

Leaders can anticipate that there will be wide variation in attitudes toward the institution and leadership, as well as varying motives and motivation toward rehabilitation, depending on the length and age of confinement. For example, someone who is confined with a life sentence and no possibility of parole might not be motivated to embrace the policies and restrictions of the system if he or she does not see a reason beyond possible release to conform and comply.

Anecdotal reporting from the USDB suggests that there is often disproportionate representation of life without parole inmates housed in disciplinary segregation because they commit higher instances of serious misconduct. Often, those who agree to carry out sanctioned retribution against others within the inmate's informal justice system are "lifers" because they have nothing to lose. By the same token, other prisoners in a similar situation might be motivated to conform or to take advantage of rehabilitation or other educational opportunities for the sake of self-improvement or some other motivation, even if they believe they can never hope for release. These individuals, and the largely unexplainable differences among them, influence the efficacy of different leadership styles.

Psychopathology. While being an inmate does not unilaterally imply that an individual has a psychological disorder, a significant percentage of the inmate population meets the diagnostic criteria for having one or more psychological disorders. In a review of 2004 data from the Survey of Inmates in State and Federal Correctional Facilities and 2002 data from the Survey of Inmates in Local Jails, a 2006 report from the National Criminal Justice Reference Service notes that 73 percent of females and 55 percent of males have a mental health problem.[25] It is not clear whether these problems were preexistent. Within federal prisons, the incidence breaks down to 61 percent of females and 44 percent of males, and in local jails, 75 percent of females and 63 percent of males. According to the 2006 report, more than 33 percent of state prisoners with a mental health problem and more than 25 percent of federal prisoners with a mental health problem had received treatment since incarceration.[26]

All of these variables come together to produce a complex picture for leaders. In addition to considering the motivations, education, and possible psychopathology of inmates, leaders must respond to public opinion about how they perform their jobs when local and national politics call into question their actions and decisions. In some ways it is helpful to think of leaders in this environment as being at the center of numerous intersecting circles, all of which exert some pressure on them and which leaders need to appropriately and effectively balance, all while maintaining a legal and ethical posture. Positive psychology and its associated concepts are useful constructs for conceptualizing the task of leading in captivity and maintaining the delicate balance it requires.

LEVERAGING POSITIVE PSYCHOLOGY AND
AUTHENTIC LEADERSHIP

Correctional leaders can positively influence their culture when they view stumbling blocks as stepping-stones, when they foster hope, confidence, resilience, and optimism, and when they are true to themselves and to others. In 1998, Martin Seligman, president of the American Psychological Association at the time, coined the term "positive psychology." He offered, "Positive psychology is an umbrella term for the study of positive emotions, positive character traits, and enabling institutions."[27] Positive psychology consists of positive experiences that look at joy and happiness, positive individual traits, such as character, and potentially positive institutions, like the workplace, families, and schools.[28]

Positive psychology also opened the door for the exploration of positive organizational behavior (POB), which "applies positively oriented human resource strengths and psychological capacities that can be measured, developed and managed for performance improvement in today's workplace."[29] Capacities of POB include hope, confidence, resilience, and optimism. These comprise what is termed psychological capital, or PsyCap.

Hope is "a positive motivational state that is based on an interactively derived sense of successful (a) agency (goal-oriented energy) and (b) pathways (planning to meet goals)."[30] Individuals who have an abundance of hope are able to devise healthy ways to get the things they want.[31] In the correctional arena, hope has important implications for the workforce and inmates, both of whom need to set goals and generate pathways for achieving them.

Confidence, or self-efficacy, is the "individual's conviction about his or her abilities to mobilize the motivation, cognitive resources, and courses of action needed to successfully execute a specific task within a given context."[32] When staff and inmates work on building their confidence levels to achieve specific tasks, both the inmate and the organization will benefit. Confidence building can result in enhanced job performance inside the facility for both inmates and staff and perhaps assist the inmate in obtaining a possible early release and help a staff member get a promotion.

Resilience is one's ability to recover, or bounce back, from adverse situations, sometimes with even greater levels of performance. People with high levels of resilience learn along the way. Resiliency has three components: "staunch acceptance of reality; a deep belief, often reinforced by strongly held values, that life is meaningful; and an uncanny ability to improvise and adapt to significant change."[33] In confinement environments, one's ability to bounce back from episodes is critical for staff and inmates. Leaders need to constantly monitor their well-being. Both are subject to a variety of trying circumstances, typically involving high levels of stress.

Optimism is the fourth component of psychological capital. People view both good and bad things that happen to them as either temporary or permanent. An optimist will look at a negative setback as temporary. A pessimist will view the negative occurrence as permanent. If an encounter or experience is good, the optimist will make a permanent attribution, but the pessimist sees the positive experience as only temporary.[34] According to Peterson and colleagues, "PsyCap is a critical component of what inspires and sustains follower motivation."[35] Leaders can help staff and inmates in self-discovery and ascertaining their potential by assisting them in setting stretch goals, talking optimistically about the future, being a role model, and focusing on the positive.

AUTHENTIC LEADERSHIP

Authentic leadership can be referenced to Greek philosophy, particularly, "To thine own self be true." Authentic leaders are true to themselves. Their beliefs, attitudes, values, and behaviors essentially model the way for their followers to become leaders. Authentic leaders are not overly concerned about their own self-interest. This type of leader believes in doing what's right, narrowing the gap between espoused values and values in action. He or she is aware of personal vulnerabilities and is comfortable speaking about them, models psychological capital components, leads from the front, is concerned for the development of followers, and handles moral concerns appropriately.[36]

Authentic leaders are transparent. What you see is what you get. Their leadership incorporates elements of positive psychology (looking at people's strengths rather than weaknesses) and the components of psychological capital (hope, efficacy, resilience, and optimism). Authentic leadership development is a "process that draws upon a leader's life course, psychological capital, moral perspective, and a 'highly developed' supporting organizational climate to produce even greater self-awareness and self-regulated positive behaviors, which in turn foster continuous, positive self-development resulting in veritable, sustained performance."[37]

Key components that comprise authentic leadership development are self-awareness (personal insight), self-regulation (realizing where one is currently in relation to where one wants to go), balanced processing (the unbiased collection and the interpretation of self-related information, positive and negative), and relational transparency (openness and trust in relationships). Accordingly, authentic leaders function as a positive role model in the development of their subordinates.[38]

Self-awareness is realized when people take the time to reflect through introspection and make sense and meaning of what's going on around them. Self-regulation involves internalized regulation (when one's regulatory system is self-driven as opposed to being led by external forces), balanced processing (the collection and sensemaking of information), authentic behavior (exhibited by one's core values and beliefs, not others'), and relational transparency (seeing through a leader because he or she is open and trusting with those in close relationships).[39]

In an unpublished study focusing on a western state's department of corrections, the National Institute of Corrections Academy and the Gallup Leadership Institute found that followers of authentic leaders expressed 16.2 percent greater trust in their leader than followers of leaders deemed less authentic. This was associated with 7.1 percent lower intent to quit, 5.2 percent more citizenship/helping behavior, and 7.7 percent higher performance. These data suggest that perhaps attention be given to the delivery of programs that focus on the enhancement of authentic leadership development and psychological capital.

For correctional leaders to become authentic leaders, they need to act in ways consistent with their inner thoughts as well as feelings. They must also be transparent in their intentions. Furthermore, the values and behaviors they espouse should be the same as their real values and behaviors.[40] Being aware of one's power sources and bases and influence strategies, creating and maintaining psychological safety, looking for the good in the bad, developing psychological capital, and practicing authentic leadership, will take one far while leading in captive environments.

Leaders in confinement environments should heed advice to create a culture that perpetuates solid beliefs, attitudes, and values that encourage frank dialogue; squelch in-fighting and nurture trust among all who lead; behave in a fair, firm, and consistent way to become trustworthy; and identify the strengths of corrections staff and inmates and leverage those strengths. Finally, they should rely on trained, objective professionals to provide them with the feedback on the environment and how they are doing.[41]

KEY TAKE-AWAY POINTS

Good leaders and managers in captive environments should remember and strive to do the following:

1. Be firm, fair, and consistent with staff and inmates.
2. Build a culture that brings alive its mission, vision, core values, and goals.

3. Be true to oneself and to others.

4. Be a "people developer."

5. Realize that inmates are people too and treat them with respect.

6. Create and sustain trust and promote psychological safety.

7. Create positive leader-follower relationships.

8. Become a lifelong learner.

KEY REFERENCES

Edmonson, A. C. "Psychological Safety, Trust, and Learning in Organizations: A Group-Level Lens." In *Trust and Distrust in Organizations: Dilemmas and Approaches*, ed. R. M. Kramer and K.S. Cook, 239–272. New York: Russell Sage Foundation, 2004.

Gardner, W. L., et al. "'Can you see the real me?' A Self-Based Model of Authentic Leader and Follower Development." *Leadership Quarterly* 16 (2005): 343–372.

Hannah, S. T., et al. "Leadership Efficacy: Review and Future Directions." *Leadership Quarterly* 19 (2008): 669–692.

Luthans, F., and B. J. Avolio. "Authentic Leadership Development." In *Positive Organizational Scholarship: Foundations of a New Discipline*, ed. K. S. Cameron, J. E. Dutton, and R. E. Quinn. San Francisco: Berrett-Koehler, 2003.

Seligman, M. E. P., et al. "Positive Psychology Progress: Empirical Validation of Interventions." *American Psychologist* 60, no. 5 (2005): 410–421.

NOTES

The thoughts in this paper are those of the authors and do not necessarily represent those of the U.S. Department of Justice or the U.S. Department of Defense.

1. S. Stojkovic and M. A. Farkas, *Correctional Leadership: A Cultural Perspective* (Belmont, Calif.: Thomson/Wadsworth, 2003).

2. M. Brown and D. R. Beto, "Effective Correctional Leadership for the 21st Century," *Corrections Management Quarterly* 3, no. 1 (1999).

3. P. M. Carlson and J. S. Garrett, *Prison and Jail Administration: Practice and Theory* (Gaithersburg, Md.: Aspen Publishers, 1999), 28.

4. B. J. Avolio, *Full Leadership Development: Building the Vital Forces in Organizations* (Thousand Oaks, Calif.: Sage Publications, 1999).

5. B. M. Bass and B. J. Avolio, *Training Full Range Leadership* (Menlo Park, Calif.: Mind Garden, 1999).

6. D. A. Hofmann, F. P. Morgeson, and S. J. Gerras, "Climate as a Moderator of the Relationship between Leader-Member Exchange and Content Specific Citizenship: Safety Climate as an Exemplar," *Journal of Applied Psychology* 88 (2003): 170–178.

7. A. C. Edmonson, "Psychological Safety, Trust, and Learning in Organizations: A Group-Level Lens," in *Trust and Distrust in Organizations: Dilemmas and Approaches,*

ed. R. M. Kramer and K. S. Cook (New York: Russell Sage Foundation, 2004), 239–272.

8. A. Edmondson, "Psychological Safety and Learning Behavior in Work Teams," *Administrative Science Quarterly* 44 (1999): 350–383.

9. R. Kark and A. Carmeli, "Alive and Creating: The Mediating Role of Vitality and Aliveness in the Relationship between Psychological Safety and Creative Work Involvement," *Journal of Organizational Behavior* 30 (2009): 785–804.

10. Robert Mayer, James Davis, and F. David Schoorman, "An Integrative Model of Organization Trust," *Academy of Management Review* 20, no. 3 (1995): 709–734.

11. P. J. Sweeney, V. Thompson, and H. Blanton, "Trust and Influence in Combat: An Interdependence Model," *Journal of Applied Social Psychology* 39 (2009): 235–264.

12. D. Keltner, C. Anderson, and D. H. Gruenfeld, "Power, Approach, and Inhibition," *Psychological Review* 110, no. 2 (2003): 265–284.

13. D. Kipnis, "Does Power Corrupt?" *Journal of Personality and Social Psychology* 24, no. 1 (1972): 33–41.

14. H. H. Brower et al., "A Closer Look at Trust between Managers and Subordinates: Understanding the Effects of Both Trusting and Being Trusted on Subordinate Outcomes," *Journal of Management* 35 (2009): 327.

15. D. Kipnis, *The Powerholders* (Chicago: University of Chicago Press, 1976).

16. P. Zimbardo, *The Lucifer Effect: Understanding How Good People Turn Evil* (New York: Random House, 2007).

17. P. Zimbardo, "Pathology of Imprisonment," *Society* 9, no. 6 (1972): 4–8.

18. C. Haney, "A Culture of Harm: Taming the Dynamics of Cruelty in Supermax Prisons," *Criminal Justice and Behavior* 35 (2008): 956.

19. A. Bandura, "Mechanisms of Moral Disengagement," in *Origins of Terrorism: Psychologies, Ideologies, Theologies, States of Mind,* ed. W. Reich (Cambridge: Cambridge University Press, 1990).

20. S. Behnke, "Ethics and Interrogations: Comparing and Contrasting the American Psychological, American Medical and American Psychiatric Association Positions," *American Psychologist* 37, no. 7 (2006): 66.

21. J. Brehm, and S. Gates, "Supervisors as Trust Brokers in Social-Work Bureaucracies," in *Trust and Distrust in Organizations: Dilemmas and Approaches,* ed. R. M. Kramer and K. S. Cook (New York: Russell Sage Foundation, 2004).

22. A. Raine, *The Psychopathology of Crime: Criminal Behavior as a Clinical Disorder* (San Diego: Academic Press, 1993).

23. H. J. Eysenck, "Personality and Crime," in *Psychopathy: Antisocial, Criminal, and Violent Behavior,* ed. T. Millon et al. (New York: Guildford Press, 1998), 40–49.

24. M. B. Reed and F. D. Glamser, "Aging in Total Institution: The Case of Older Prisoners," *Gerontologist* 19 (1979): 354–360.

25. D. J. James and L. E. Glaze, "Mental Health Problems of Prison and Jail Inmates," U.S. Department of Justice, Bureau of Justice Statistics, 2006, http://www.ncjrs.gov/App/Publications/abstract.aspx?ID=235099.

26. Eysenck, "Personality and Crime."

27. M. E. P. Seligman et al., "Positive Psychology Progress: Empirical Validation of Interventions," *American Psychologist* 60, no. 5 (2005): 410–421.

28. M. E. P. Seligman, *Authentic Happiness* (New York: Free Press, 2002).

29. F. Luthans and C. M. Youssef, "Human, Social, and Now Positive Psychological Capital Management," *Organizational Dynamics* 33, no. 2 (2004): 143–160.

30. C. Snyder, L. M. Irving, and S. A. Anderson, "Hope and Health: Measuring the Will and the Ways," in *Handbook of Social and Clinical Psychology: The Health Perspective*, ed. C. R. Snyder and D. R. Forsyth (Elmsford, N.Y.: Pergamon, 1991), 285–305.

31. Seligman et al., "Positive Psychology Progress."

32. A. D. Stajkovic and F. Luthans, "Self-Efficacy and Work-Related Performance: A Meta-analysis," *Psychological Bulletin* 124, no. 2 (1998): 240–261.

33. Seligman et al., "Positive Psychology Progress."

34. Eysenck, "Personality and Crime."

35. S. J. Peterson et al., "Neuroscientific Implications of Psychological Capital: Are the Brains of Optimistic, Hopeful, Confident, and Resilient Leaders Different?" *Organizational Dynamics* 37, no. 4 (2008): 342–353.

36. F. Luthans and B. J. Avolio, "Authentic Leadership Development," in *Positive Organizational Scholarship: Foundations of a New Discipline*, ed. K. S. Cameron, J. E. Dutton, and R. E. Quinn (San Francisco: Berrett-Koehler Publishers, 2003). On leadership efficacy, see S. T. Hannah et al., "Leadership Efficacy: Review and Future Directions," *Leadership Quarterly* 19 (2008): 669–692. Leadership efficacy is "a specific form of efficacy associated with the level of confidence in the knowledge, skills, and abilities associated with leading others. It can thus be clearly differentiated from confidence in the knowledge, skills, and abilities one holds associated with other social roles such as a teacher (i.e., teacher efficacy)."

37. B. J. Avolio and F. Luthans, *The High Impact Leader: Moments Matter in Accelerating Authentic Leadership* (New York: McGraw-Hill, 2006).

38. W. L. Gardner, "'Can you see the real me?' A Self-Based Model of Authentic Leader and Follower Development," *Leadership Quarterly* 16 (2005): 343–372.

39. R. Ilies, F. P. Morgeson, and J. D. Nahrgang, "Authentic Leadership and Eudemonic Well-Being: Understanding Leader-Follower Outcomes," *Leadership Quarterly* 16 (2005): 373–394.

40. S. Michie and J. Gooty, "Values, Emotions, and Authenticity: Will the Real Leader Please Stand Up?" *Leadership Quarterly* 16 (2005): 441–457.

41. The authors would like to thank Craig Crossley, a member of the Gallup Leadership Institute team involved in the western state department of corrections study, for providing us data regarding the outcomes of authentic leadership.

CHAPTER 16

Leading across Cultures

Janice H. Laurence

World War IV will cause a shift in classical centers of gravity from the will of governments and armies to the perceptions of populations. Victory will be defined more in terms of capturing the psycho-cultural rather than the geographical high ground. Understanding and empathy will be important weapons of war. Soldier conduct will be as important as skill at arms. Cultural awareness and the ability to build ties of trust will offer protection to [U.S.] troops more effectively than body armor. Leaders will seek wisdom and quick but reflective thought rather than operational planning skills as essential intellectual tools for guaranteeing future victories.[1]

L eadership is an intractable, if not elusive, construct. Even for behavioral and social scientists, who routinely tackle "squishy" topics, leadership can be frustrating. There seem to be countless and conflicting dimensions of leadership, including different traits, styles, and situations.[2] Yet, despite the unwieldy and inexact nature of this construct, leadership research, development, and practice remain important. Leadership is of interest to scientists and practitioners of many disciplines as well as being an everyday phenomenon. Descriptions and discussions of leadership may therefore omit definitions given its "common knowledge" nature or contain nuances unique to the perspective in question. Despite such variety in definitional expression, the notion of influence on others is central to all definitions of leadership.[3]

Influencing individuals and groups to achieve goals highlights the relational aspects of leadership. Indeed, leadership involves relationships and communication with followers or collaborators and therefore demands not only cognitive competencies but social and emotional intelligence as well. Increasingly, these relationships are taking place across cultural divides, imposing an intercultural dimension to the requirements of social and emotional competence. As if the demands of leadership were not already tough enough, oftentimes leaders must exert intercultural leadership under conditions where there is high stress, risk, uncertainty, and danger. Although relationships and communication, and hence social and emotional intelligence, are fundamental for all leaders, conditions of high stress, risk, and danger—typical conditions for military and law enforcement leaders—pose unique demands. In the United States, business leaders may face cultural challenges in light of increasing diversity in the population and multinational operations, military and law enforcement leaders face such challenges while under fire, literally.

Before attempting to shed light on the interactions between leadership and culture, it is important to note that both constructs lack conceptual clarity. As a result, the elusive nature of "leadership" is compounded by the equally, if not more, perplexing concept of "culture." Although hard to define, both are nonetheless critical. Culture includes socially learned and shared knowledge, beliefs, values, customs, symbols, behaviors, and practices. It is the way that a group, community, society, or the like tends commonly to view the world.[4] Overlapping cultural identities exist across national, regional, organizational, and generational lines. Also, subcultures—based on characteristics such as gender, race, ethnicity, religion, and social class—are identifiable within and apart from broader cultures.

Military and law enforcement officers experience leadership and culture on multiple levels and within varying contexts. Given the organized chaos they sometimes encounter, or what Clausewitz calls the "friction" or "fog of war," they rely heavily on top-down command, control, and communication.[5] The gravity of military and police missions requires cohesion, which is enhanced through a strong institutional culture. Within the traditionally male-dominated military and police cultures, formal leadership and authority are ingrained with symbolic reminders of rank, status, and experience readily and publicly displayed. The insignia of rank and unit patches on uniforms, medals, salutes, ribbons, emblems, and other adornments are among the easily recognizable signs of legitimate authority that promote role clarity. Furthermore, shared values and cultural experiences confer trust in and respect for leaders. Trust and value congruence are critical for leadership effectiveness.[6] Respect is crucial as well.[7]

CLOSE CULTURAL CLASHES

Although the military and law enforcement establishments are heralded for their leadership, one does encounter difficulties among the ranks of these controlled and cohesive cultures. Although racial tensions have greatly subsided within them, women have yet to be fully embraced within the profession of arms or across the "thin blue line." Subgroup members who are seen as different from those who dominate the culture may find it difficult to gain full acceptance within the institution let alone attain leadership positions and credibility.[8] While not common, sexual harassment and assault still require ongoing prevention efforts within the military.

Prior to the 1970s, women worked with the police as matrons and juvenile aid officers within the Philadelphia, Pennsylvania, police force. Upon the graduation of the first group of women from the Philadelphia Police Academy in 1976, female officers were not warmly accepted. Women were required to cut their hair to male standards and wear t-shirts to hide the silhouettes of their bras beneath their uniform blouse. They were tested and mocked for their upper body strength and derided for their emotionality. In addition to these assimilation requirements, the women were isolated and excluded from full institutional membership and were assigned to the six worst districts in the city. Further, they were not permitted to ride with men for fear of inspiring a backseat sexual encounter, so they were assigned either to a foot beat or to patrol alone in a car. New, or rookie, male officers, however, were permitted to ride with veteran officers until a court ruled against this discriminatory practice. The leadership "solution" was to put rookie men on their own as well, rather than to further mentor and train women. This failure to lead across subcultures put organizational newcomers, especially women, not just at a learning disadvantage but also in mortal danger.

Just beyond the organizational boundaries of the U.S. military and local law enforcement, a clash of cultures can be detected among "sister" services and police jurisdictions, as well as across government agencies and task forces and coalitions assembled for complex, multidimensional missions. An Army officer who was among those first deployed to Afghanistan in 2001 described Operation Anaconda—a joint operation involving military air and ground units, Special Forces, the CIA, and coalition forces to root out the Taliban—as a disaster. Morale was low and integration was problematic. Each actor wanted to do things its way. The dangerous context went well beyond the old adage that too many cooks spoil the pot. Confusion regarding leader and follower roles is thought to have contributed to such "friendly fire" incidents as the one in which Army ranger and former football star Pat Tillman was killed while on patrol in the mountains of Afghanistan.

These cooperation and coordination—and hence leadership—deficiencies were not malicious or evil in nature. The leaders were not callous or uncaring, refusing to take care of "their own." Rather, they lacked an emotional attachment to the unfamiliar outsiders. Leadership is a social or relational enterprise. According to the relational perspective on leadership, three phases describe the tenor of leader-follower interactions. At first, they are strangers who interact according to formal roles with leader requests and follower compliance based on self-interest. Next, they progress to acquaintanceship, where social and task information is exchanged, thus facilitating more productive working relationships. After that, they form a partnership, the highest level of leader-member exchange, wherein mutual respect, trust, and influence propel productivity.[9] There are different faces of leadership. To insiders, or the in-group, leaders are trusted and influential. To outsiders, or the out-group, there are low levels of support and influence for U.S. leaders. Out-group members have less influence on decision making. This relationship pattern is consistent with the vertical dyad linkage model.[10] In-group membership may be influenced by similarity in values and personality, that is, culture. Going beyond the in-group–out-group distinction, leader-member exchange (LMX) theory highlights the effects of differences in leader-follower relationship quality, with high-quality relationships linked to greater personal and organizational effectiveness.[11]

DISTANT CULTURAL CLASHES

Clashes between subgroups and similar cultures highlight that leadership requires more than technical proficiency. Effective leadership across cultures has emotional and social components and demands attention to the unfamiliar and promotion of change. While these noncognitive exigencies can be formidable across more proximal cultural boundaries, imagine the potential difficulties under conditions where there are even less similarity and more widely divergent perspectives. Police and military officers tend not to live in the places that they work—e.g., in high-crime areas and in Afghanistan and Iraq—so negative perceptions and a lack of cultural understanding can impede necessary interactions. It might be argued that cultural sensitivity is not vital for pursuing criminals and engaging in war with one's enemy, but protecting communities and carrying out counterinsurgency operations and nation building suffer greatly in the absence of cultural competence.

Cross-cultural interactions, even enriching ones, can be challenging under business, professional, and personal circumstances. Adjustment difficulties among government and corporate employees sometimes result in high turnover and low productivity.[12] The psychology and business literatures warn that not all temperaments are suited for transnational assignment. People sent abroad must be open to new experiences among other things. Further, their social or cultural adaptation skills must be cultivated, especially when there are large discrepancies between cultures. That is, tactical skills alone are not enough; the same is true for language skills. Although language is an important cultural component, cultural competence goes beyond words to include understanding gestures, body language, cultural norms, social networks, perspectives, and so on. Interpreting behavior is more complex than interpreting words.[13]

Communication and diplomatic skills or the capacity to perceive, monitor, manage, understand, and employ social, emotional, and cultural information to guide reasoning and action must be cultivated as well. Under conditions of high stress and danger, awareness and management of affect—fear, rage, anger, hatred, grief, joy, and love—can be decisive. Social, emotional, and cultural literacy and intelligence underlie such skills, which are gained not from a technical manual but develop over time through exposure, experience, and discourse.[14]

Within military and law enforcement units, formal and recognized leadership structures with command and control features enhance good order and discipline. Within these organizations, leaders are respected and trusted, so things work relatively smoothly. Within these units, authority has legitimacy; the role of leaders is recognized as appropriate, proper, and just, so followers are personally obligated to defer voluntarily without leaders resorting to coercion.[15] Our senior officers have legitimacy with their subordinates—they have been in their shoes. In such cases, the leader-follower relationship is developmental; members have trained and fought together.

Legitimacy is different from power, which relies on rewards and punishments. Legitimacy is important, especially in times of scarcity, crisis, and conflict. Leadership influence rises above transactional means—that is, pay and promotions, ribbons and honors, as well as court-martials and other punishments—to be transformational in nature. Whereas transactional leadership is highly contractual, with great reliance on individual reward, transformational leadership is communicative and interactional. Transformational leadership involves identifying with followers as well as identifying and articulating a shared vision. Thus, it is likely to engender trust and respect.

When combatants face off or police pursue criminals, culture may not be of critical concern. On the other hand, when relationships and influence are important, as when trying to make friends among foes in a neighborhood in

Iraq or in Philadelphia, culture looms large. Soldiers and cops deal with not just enemies and criminals, but local populations and residents as well. These latter interactions demand the judicious use of force and require sociocultural competence. Unlike in traditional, high-impact war and crime fighting, engaging a local population is essential when conducting counterinsurgency and community policing. One must avoid raising the ire of the public but at the same time address the underlying roots of violence and social problems. First responders and disaster relief workers should be mindful of the perspectives and values of those to whom they offer their professional and technical services. Although trite, there is wisdom in Mary Poppins' advice that "a spoonful of sugar helps the medicine go down."A spoonful of understanding and respect can enhance acceptance and effects.

How does a leader in the U.S military go beyond his or her ethnocentric worldview to influence Sunni, Shiite, and Kurdish Iraqis to advance rather than hinder reconciliation, reconstruction, and development efforts, while not making enemies? How does he identify hostile outsiders while promoting security and foiling attacks by insurgents and militias? How does he negotiate and maintain a cease-fire with Muqtada al-Sadr and his Jaish al-Mahdi (JAM) forces? Precision-guided munitions and other technology are not the solution. While there may not be one specific solution, cross-cultural awareness and nonlethal options should be part of the operational agenda or courses of action to avoid alienating a neutral or friendly populace. Relationships with local tribal leaders must be developed and nurtured and collaboration pursued with such groups as the Sons of Iraq (SoI) in Sadr City and the Sunni Triangle. U.S. military leaders need to engage in dialogue and come to learn the interests and desires of the local people. It is important to show empathy and tact and otherwise understand and act appropriately within their sociocultural contexts.

Engaging in dialogue goes well beyond language proficiency. Certainly, language is part of the cultural conundrum, but English to Arabic and Arabic to English translations alone are deficient for understanding culture. There are numerous stories of interpreters or "terps" fluent in Arabic who contributed to cultural *mis*understanding. Some native Iraqis and Arabic linguists living in the United States have been recruited without regard to culture. Whether the terp is Sunni, Shiite, or Christian may have quite an impact on communication. Aside from words, body language, attitudes, and bias may enter into messages sent and received.

Although the U.S. military employs a transformational approach to leading its own troops, there is evidence of a reliance on a transactional approach in dealings with local populations in Iraq and Afghanistan. Influence techniques are in large part based on money and the simplistic notion that the United States will do something for them to get them to do something for it. In 2003, U.S. troops confronted Iraqi citizens who were angry over the death and destruction left by the "shock and awe" campaign during the U.S.-led invasion. U.S. military leaders instituted a weapons buyback plan, giving people $50 (in Iraqi currency) for an AK-47. Similar to tactics in high-crime neighborhoods in the U.S., the plan was to enhance safety by getting weapons off the street. The plan did not work because average citizens picked up weapons from dead Iraqi soldiers and from depots. The military ran out of interpreters to spread word of the buyback and then ran out of money to continue the program, failing in its goal of providing security for the Iraqi citizens. The plan was naive, and it taught Iraqis to expect money in exchange for helping the U.S. military achieve its goals.. There was a similar type of transaction in the effort to recruit Iraqis for a civil defense corps. U.S. troops lured seventeen-year-old Iraqi youths into a one-week basic training program for a certificate, $50 (U.S.), and an AK-47. Iraqi insurgents later identified these graduates by their certificates and confiscated their weapons.

Transactions without regard to culture also complicated attempts at development in Iraq. Social divisions there are not just geographic and religious, but familial and tribal as well. Within the Shiite and Sunni branches of Islam, there are various schools of thought, movements, divisions, and sects. In Iraq, a complex system of authority existed before and in tandem with the state under Saddam Hussein. Disputes over leadership resurfaced with Hussein's overthrow, and the form of democracy promoted was not consistent with Iraqis' religious or political traditions. Even an engineer tasked with making decisions regarding energy or power distribution had to contend with culture: For example, who got power and for how long could be complicated by whether a Sunni or Shiite owned the power plant and believed that his community should benefit the most. Needless to say, such decisions can have second- and third-order effects.

One must recognize and understand subcultural complexities. In post-Hussein Iraq, leaders needed to facilitate a common identity and cooperation. Because Iraqis lack a collective or shared social identity as Iraqis, the pro-social behaviors that the United States tried to influence failed to gain traction.[16] Given that fairness is important in achieving legitimacy, if leaders are to carry influence in Iraq, they must learn to navigate tribal differences and power relations among the country's various communities. Such negotiations cannot be based on U.S. notions of fairness or ignore power structures already in place. They require time and patience and development of requisite knowledge and relationships.

As the United States tried to restore order, security, infrastructure, and governance to Iraq and transition these functions to Iraqis, leaders had to think outside their own perspectives. For example, seemingly simple development contracting could reduce or increase violence. What happens if a contract goes to the "wrong" tribe? With whom should one form alliances? It is an ethnographic mistake to avoid working with a sheikh because he appears to be corrupt by taking a "cut" of a contract. Seeking an open bid is the American way, but rejecting the Iraqis' way of doing business would challenge their traditional structures and authority.[17] Local leaders want contracts to improve the quality of life for their people, thus securing their power and influence. Thus, if one were to fund local militia leaders directly, rather than through the sheikh, it could trigger an intertribal dispute.

Culturally legitimate leaders will protect their power through force. So although coalition forces may have rid an area of insurgents, such as al-Qaeda in Iraq (AQI), violence may well have continued for other reasons. U.S. military leaders had to learn that negotiating development contracts with opportunistic, "fake" tribal leaders or sheikhs would not advance security. Illegitimate sheikhs, bound by opportunism, would engage in contracts and then sell their services to the highest bidder, be that coalition forces or al-Qaeda. Acknowledged sheikhs are revered by their tribes because of their honor, influence, and power. They consider it humiliating to have fake sheikhs sit beside them at tribal or district council meetings. Americans risked offending these legitimate leaders such that they might use their *wasta,* or influence, to disown the fake sheikhs and forbid their tribal members to enter into business contacts with the Americans. Further, the imposter sheikhs, having shamed themselves and their community, could be killed to restore honor. In short, in such scenarios, outsiders must honor traditional ways, understand locals' sense of nobility and codes of honor, and contract with legitimate sheikhs.

The cost of coercion and reward as a means of influence is high and yields only a short-term "solution" at best. Reliance on transactional leadership had the disadvantage of pitting the U.S. and coalition forces against al-Qaeda or the Taliban; allegiance was up for sale to the highest bidder. According to Tom Tyler, "Those authorities who seek to lead groups through incentives and/or coercion find it difficult to shape behavior effectively through these mechanisms, and they have difficulty maintaining their influence over others. Therefore, those leading groups, organizations, and societies benefit when they have legitimacy among the members of their groups."[18] Legitimacy engenders greater acceptance of decisions. Although decisions should be seen as fair, it is important to grasp that what is considered fair varies by culture.

Only through trust and fairness, and hence legitimacy, is there hope of long-term gain. Without legitimacy, leadership is likely to lose public support.

The transactional approach does not create credibility and is thus recognized as deficient within some organizations.[19] Instead, transformational leadership behavior is recommended. The superiority of identifying and forming an emotional attachment with followers and pursuing a common cause has been well documented. Transformational leadership, with its components of inspiration, consideration, and charisma, is consistent with collectivistic cultures. Although individualized consideration toward followers may seem inconsistent with collectivistic cultures, U.S. leaders are "leading the leader," rather than leading followers; being mindful of such considerations contributes to leader effectiveness. Transformational leadership goes beyond superficial compliance to consider followers' needs. If U.S. leaders do not respect the values of a host society, the cultural differences may thwart the development of partnerships that in turn could stifle security and nation-building efforts.

Legitimacy is a two-way street. If the United States seeks to gain legitimacy in Iraq, the leaders in such an effort must accept tribal leaders as legitimate. Within a leader's own culture or organization, whether engaging in transactional or transformational leadership, he or she must identify common goals and appropriate rewards. When operating cross-culturally, however, a leader has to determine whose goals and whose common vision are to be advanced. In the case of Iraq, developmental relationships were needed to teach governance to the community and to train the Iraqi Army and police. Such development calls for close, rather than distant, relationships and recognition that the relationships may not take hold if basic needs, such as order, survival, and safety, have yet to be met.[20]

Partnerships are key to counterinsurgency and within high-crime and disorderly neighborhoods. Trust in both directions is essential and is earned through contact and the substance of that contact or community context.[21] While U.S. military leaders have expert, reward, and coercive power, they may not have personal or legitimate power with local populations outside of their organization. It was not that long ago in U.S. military history that leader training explicitly heralded the superiority of Anglo-Saxon and Nordic heritage and looked down upon Semites, African Americans, Asians, Italians, Jews, Latinos, and others.[22] Although strict homogeneity of U.S. forces is no longer advocated, elitism survives. For example, U.S. military personnel use epithets such as "Hadji" when referring to Iraqi citizens, and when dealing with local leaders, they expect to get right down to business instead of taking time to have a traditional tea with them. Whereas Americans may believe that "talk is cheap," the value of dialogue, inclusive processes, and ritual cannot be underestimated. Conflict may require a peace ritual or settlement, or *suhl,* to sort things out and allow all to save face. Trust has cognitive and emotional components,[23] so one cannot establish instant rapport based on impressing people outside one's culture with a Combat Infantry Badge or a Purple Heart.

A lack of trust of outsiders creates problems. For example, the U.S. Army's Brigade Combat Team's (BCT) rotation schedule, or relief in place/transfer of authority (RIP/TOA), disrupts the establishment of relationships and development of trust during foreign deployments. Although a BCT may deploy for a year, various activities consume their time besides engaging a local populace and its leaders. Just as the BCT begins to make sociocultural headway, its members redeploy, and a replacement BCT—with its own priorities and ways of doing things—takes over. Of course, just as the foreign community does not trust the U.S. military, the Americans do not trust the foreign community. In Iraq, the U.S. military's missions included training, working with, and empowering Iraqi security forces. Although the U.S. forces had a sense of potency owing to their high levels of social identification with each other,[24] the belief in task accomplishment eroded with the inclusion of outsiders. In short, an Iraqi squad could not be trusted as much as one's own squad buddies. U.S. troops feared that their Iraqi "teammates" would lay down their guns and run. Soldiers also complained that after providing the Iraqis weapons and training, the Iraqis would use these resources against them. Engaging in culturally distant areas requires at a minimum a continuity of approach in lieu of continuity of actual leaders.

Understanding and respect, even under frustrating circumstances, remain necessary. Leadership has a domino effect, with followers modeling the behavior of the leader. Force and distrust beget force and distrust. It is the leader rather than the followers who should set the tone. Bad role models tend to have a stronger effect than do good models.[25] Although maintaining some distance between leaders and followers is necessary for legitimacy, such distance should not prevent identification. A follower does not independently choose to identify with the leader. Rather, the leader's communication and actions enhance the desire to identify. In a counterinsurgency or in community policing, it is important to recognize that communication and cooperation are not abdications of control. Procedural fairness requires more than the ability to deliver rewards or punishments; it demands a focus on and empowerment of those being led.

Leaders' self-presentation is important. They must select the images, messages, and approaches that will get things done. Leaders must practice impression management and adapt their behavior depending on the situation and the audience. Leaders must not only "talk the talk" but "walk the talk"; their actions and words must be consistent and emphasize the collective good of the local or neighborhood people. In another example from Iraq, leaders should have been mindful that under the rule of Saddam Hussein, Iraqis had electricity and water. Members of the U.S. military had these necessities as well at their forward operating bases (FOBs). Therefore, attending to basic human needs was of the highest priority.

Community policing requires a similar establishment of trust and demonstration of respect. Trust increases reports of crime, calls for assistance, and investigative leads. Cooperation, however, can be difficult, especially in minority communities.[26] Subcultures based on age, race, and neighborhood context affect police-citizen relations.[27] Police tend to distrust and have less respect for residents in high-crime neighborhoods. Unwarranted stops, pushing, shoving, handcuffing, and verbal abuse are dehumanizing and can provoke citizens to have a reason to assault their supposed protectors. Leaders must recognize that gangs and other criminal elements exert considerable influence on local residents and remain in neighborhoods long after the police depart. Residents may be reluctant to place their long-term security in the hands of transient police officers. Community policing, as with counterinsurgency, would do well to adopt charismatic, team-oriented, and participative leadership dimensions. Unfortunately, while research on leadership has found these dimensions to be global transformational behaviors that facilitate leadership effectiveness, specific behaviors have not been pinpointed. Further, while common leadership dimensions have been identified within various cultures, leadership styles appropriate for cross-cultural contact have yet to be investigated.[28]

The physical presence of a leader is important, and image-based communications will likely be more effective than concept-based communications in unfamiliar, cross-cultural contexts.[29] To demonstrate respect or consideration in collectivist societies, leaders may need to interact more often with followers than they would in individualistic societies.[30] It is important to establish a collective level of identity and refrain from communicating, "I want you to cooperate" rather than "we need to cooperate." With insurgents, one must project power but also understand that they are exerting power over local people. In protecting local residents, one must not dehumanize or bully them. For instance, having Iraqi workers enter a military base through a narrow path lined with concertina wire as if they were criminals is disrespectful and potentially dangerous for the workers on the base. Combat patrols that "haul ass" in their five-ton trucks through narrow, unpaved Kabul roads to avoid an improvised explosive device (IED) endanger civilians. Similarly, in the streets of north Philadelphia, racial profiling and the use of unnecessary force do not engender perceptions of procedural fairness, but instead may result in the loss

of needed public support in managing community problems. Military leaders must understand the reluctance of local people, even if provided food and
supplies to act as informants against insurgents who have planted a road-
side bomb. Although the United States might give Afghani farmers money to
grow wheat instead of the poppies used in opium production, the Afghans
may renege if the Taliban threatens to slaughter their families. Effective Iraqi
and Afghani helpers have been assassinated. Police officers must appreciate
that snitching is dangerous in neighborhoods where poverty is prevalent. Iraqi
citizens who make IEDs may not be jihadists but might instead be reluctant
accomplices of insurgents who have threatened them and their families.

The military and law enforcement organizations must not only fight
against insurgents and criminals, they must also work with noncombatant and
innocent local populations. Slow response times and poor services in minority neighborhoods and negative interactions between police and community
members affect not only particular situations or individuals, but bystanders
to such encounters as well. Rather than stopping one crime or detaining one
criminal, police must focus on the long term in finding solutions to problems.
Leaders can have far-reaching indirect effects. For example, when a maneu-
ver company was conducting an operation in a small rural village in Iraq in
2007, an elderly Muslim man was wrongly detained under suspicion of having
cooperated with al-Qaeda in Iraq. During the operation, sociocultural advisors
from a new Army program, the Human Terrain System (HTS), facilitated his
release and coached the company commander on how to remedy the insult
by offering a public apology in front of witnesses from his village.[31] On the
day following the release of the elderly man, the tribal sheikh came to the
FOB and said that the "respectful" nature of the operation (and the release of
his uncle) had prompted him to seek coalition assistance in securing his village from AQI. At the conclusion of the meeting as a gesture of goodwill, the
sheikh told the commander the location of an IED buried in front of a mosque.
Indeed, cultural sensitivity has significant indirect effects.

A cultural lens is important at the strategic, operational, and tactical levels. It is at the tactical levels that one experiences close cultural encounters.
Ranking leaders must understand the local culture and the issues and difficulties experienced by the junior ranks.[32] Effective leadership requires experience,
but what experience is needed? Is it experience in combat or in crime fighting?
Is it familiarity with people and cultures? Counterinsurgency and community
building rely on experience and skills that more-senior leaders may lack. The
dual responsibility of leaders toward the local population and their own troops
requires deviation from established, rigid, top-down command and control

channels. Leaders should allow for upward communication, obtaining the real-time input of tactical and patrol officers.[33]

Top leaderships need to be in touch and get accurate pictures of morale and situations on the ground. Low morale and casualties can lead to stress that in turn can result in the desire to kill "Joe Taliban" when your buddy gets "whacked." Higher-ranking unit leaders must understand the environment in which their soldiers operate. The lower ranks conducting foot patrols and interacting with working-class locals see and perceive a much different environment than their superiors, who interact at another level, with local community leaders. Combat deaths have a significantly greater impact at the lower level. The boss enforcing a "shut up and row" mentality is counterproductive and unhelpful to junior leaders.

Listening to the experience of followers does not come easily within military and law enforcement cultures. When a Baghdad sniper was targeting gunners, a corporal (E-4) who was a counter-sniper trainer told battalion leaders that the shooter was not a jihadist but a mercenary with a video camera getting paid to capture successful hits. He surmised this because during a patrol with the platoon, he sensed the sniper's presence but was not "taken out" because there was a platoon behind him. A jihadist would have killed him, but a mercenary who wanted to live to collect his money would not. The more-senior officer, a major, dismissed the corporal's assessment. The value of followers' experiences within the Philadelphia police force is exemplified by the different way that men and women tend to handle domestic disturbances and other calls. With female officers, machismo is not usually in play, so encounters in response to calls are less physical. Drunken men are apt to be more aggressive toward a male cop than toward a female officer, with whom the men feel there is nothing to prove.

Administrative and bureaucratic sources of stress can impact morale and resilience and thus compromise success in life-threatening or grave situations.[34] A lack of respect for or acceptance of women, particularly within dangerous context organizations, not only poses a threat to the women, who are considered as interlopers or outsiders, but can also compromise cross-cultural effectiveness. The evidence for gender differences with regard to traits is beyond the scope of this chapter, but social science findings indicate that women tend to be more expressive, collaborative, and participative than men. Women also tend to be identified with social or collective roles. Given that these traits correspond to transformational leadership and are critical for cultural competence, relegating women to less important status than men could well jeopardize cross-cultural interactions.

SWITCHING CULTURAL GEARS

Building relationships and making fair decisions may sound easy, but being in a foreign land among unfamiliar people is stressful, especially within a dangerous context. Based on Clausewitz' notion of friction, ever present in war, even easy things are difficult under these circumstances. A complex style of leadership is called for when trying to understand culture and deal with danger at the same time.[35] There is not much guidance for leading under unfamiliar contexts, let alone the context of culture and counterinsurgency. How does a leader "switch gears" from a command and control, transactional or autocratic style to a transformational style? How does one switch fluidly from exchanging fire to cordoning and searching to engaging the population and back again? Consistent interactions and clear intentions are difficult to maintain.

Deterrence, combat, and stability operations have overlapping but qualitatively unique demands. Leading in situations that go from nation building to war fighting all in one day (or even less than a day) is complex and complicated. District council meetings in Iraq have been disrupted by suicide bombers. Provincial reconstruction teams on missions to build schools routinely come under attack, and so may need to include machine guns along with their architectural tools. Policing too is unpredictable. Those good at battle may not be the best at statesmanship. Providing clear goals, direction, and guidance is difficult in volatile, uncertain, complex, and ambiguous, or in military parlance, VUCA, situations. Military leaders do not have the luxury of football coaches in fielding a team with different players in offensive and defensive roles. Yet, they do have different sets of followers—their subordinates, coalition members, and local populations—who respond differently to the highly directive command and control approach. Indeed, leadership approaches, styles, and entire theories may not be readily transferable cross-culturally.

It is imperative that leaders consider the operative cultural value system when attempting to influence others and reach goals. The differences between individualistic and collectivist cultures mitigate the effectiveness of certain motivation techniques.[36] This is important for working with coalition and local population partners. The relationship between transformational leadership and organizational culture has been highlighted. Leaders must motivate followers for the good of the organization through consideration and inspiration. Organizational context can facilitate or constrain leadership.[37] Leadership and culture influence each other. Dealing with subpopulations based on gender, race, sexual orientation, and the like is difficult enough. Imagine the impact of decreasing the cultural similarity. Both the military and law enforcement are male-dominated cultures that espouse rational, emotionless, detached leadership styles. To suppress or control one's own emotional reaction is one thing, but leaders must recognize and deal with emotional responses among other people. Indeed there may be value in emotional display rules, such as showing no warmness with perpetrators, but this may work against forging relationships with average citizens. To be sure, there are attachments within military and police units but outside the military and the thin blue line, VUCA constrains the relationships and social bonds necessary for achieving security and stability. While those who lead in dangerous contexts may eschew emotion, they will need to add emotional, social, and cultural competencies to their arsenals. Even Clausewitz seems to agree, hinting that emotion is a prime ingredient of leadership:"In addition to his emotional qualities, the intellectual qualities of the commander are of major importance."[38]

LEARNING TO LEAD ACROSS CULTURES

While leading in situations of ever-present danger is nothing new to people in professions such as the military and law enforcement, the added dimensions posed by cultural demands are beyond their traditional expertise. Leading across a confluence of cultures, both proximal and distant, is complicated and complex. Counterinsurgency requires not just lethal action against al-Qaeda and the Taliban, the enemy, but cooperation with the population. Superior lethal force may backfire and create enemies if collateral damage results in the population perceiving that security rests in the hands of the insurgents rather than coalition forces. Not only is cross-cultural competence required across geographic boundaries, but also to form partnerships with experts in governance, communications, economic development, and security. This requires a cultural shift within the military.[39] Law enforcement must also be prepared to go beyond the use of force and come to understand and interact in positive ways with neighborhood residents. This too is difficult and requires communication and diplomatic skills in addition to tactical skills. Such abilities are promoted through developing social, emotional, and cultural competence. Further, cross-cultural success requires such traits as empathy, respect, open-mindedness, and sociability.[40]

Not only must military and law enforcement leaders rely on engineering, science, math, and other"practical" disciplines, but the social sciences as well. They strive to be decisive and to quantify success, whether in terms of numbers of people and equipment on mission or dollars spent. To become experts in counterinsurgency and community policing requires being comfortable with measuring culture and success qualitatively. Leaders must ensure that cross-cultural interactions go beyond concrete details of customs and language translation. The Human Terrain System has patched the sociocultural knowledge deficit in the military to an extent. This innovative project, with its human terrain teams of civilian social scientists, has supplemented the military's war fighting expertise with cultural expertise and "non-kinetic" alternative courses of action. As when bringing together members of interagency and coalition forces for an operation, however, a cultural schism between the military and the social science community impedes the efficacy of the partnership. Members of the military must recognize that their profession has changed and must value social, emotional, and cultural competencies and advice from outsiders and subordinates. They must incorporate sociocultural knowledge and skills development as a legitimate and critical part of leadership education and training. The Human Terrain System promotes cross-culturally competent transformational leadership, but it remains an appendage. The military and other organizations that confront cultural differences along with dangerous contexts must ensure that sociocultural knowledge and relationship skills become a required and rewarded core competency of soldiers.

The United States' global commitments are extensive and are not likely to dissipate. U.S. leaders and organizations must gain sociocultural competence through education, training, and experience with proximal and distal cultures. The military faces challenges much different than the anticipated Cold War battles that never occurred. The senior military leaders now responsible for establishing training curricula for future leaders continue to pass along their heritage of training for massive tank battles across the Fulda Gap. Modern warfare has changed more quickly than the curriculum. Continued reluctance to embrace the reality of current warfare and acknowledge a transition from Cold War tactics to counterinsurgency delays success on the battlefields of Iraq and Afghanistan. Yet, cultural competency requires going beyond the facts as they concern Iraq and Afghanistan. Just as the United States has certain enemies and challenges today, it may confront cultures in Africa, China, Indonesia, and beyond tomorrow.

Leaders assigned to an area of operations, precinct, or district that encompasses a variety of cultures should be educated in the cultures that they serve. This competence must penetrate numerous layers of leadership, from direct to strategic levels. Cultural ignorance contributed to the success of al-Qaeda's surprise attacks on September 11, 2001. Western notions of government and economics are countercultural and unrealistic in others' contexts, so transformational rather than transactional leadership and concomitant legitimacy requires that one be knowledgeable of different cultures, histories, and cognitive lenses. To get to the *sulh* and be seated to the right of a tribal leader, and hence to gain legitimacy and authority, leaders must be change agents. They must lead within and across cultures.

CULTURAL COMPETENCE: THE WAY AHEAD

In addition to tactical and technical competencies, social, emotional, and cultural competencies must be valued, taught, and rewarded by organizations that confront danger and must deal with cultures that are not their own. Indeed, the military needs war fighters, police forces need crime fighters, and disaster relief organizations need technicians, but they also need skilled communicators and negotiators who understand the perspectives and behaviors of the (sub)cultural groups that they are saving, securing, and serving. Gaps in sociocultural knowledge and deficits in cross-cultural communication and openness to alternate points of view will not, however, be closed overnight. It will require time and a combination of approaches, such as selecting the right young leaders with high social, emotional, and cultural intelligence, appropriate education and training, and exposure to and experience with other cultures. Robert Scales offers, "Experiences in Iraq and Afghanistan have convinced many in the military intellectual community of the value of psychocultural factors in war, but the idea that these factors are now decisive, that indeed they comprise the battle space, may be a tough sell."[41] Leaders of dangerous context organizations do and will continue to face cultural challenges. One can only hope that despite the imprecise nature of leadership and culture, learning to lead across cultures will not be a tough sell.

NOTES

The author is indebted to Maureen Kelly, former Philadelphia police officer who was among the first female graduates of the Philadelphia Police Academy in 1976, for her insights regarding the importance of culture to policing. Also, discussions with leaders in Temple University's Reserve Officers Training Corps (ROTC) unit proved invaluable and enjoyable. The ROTC commander, LTC James Castelli, as well as 2nd Lieutenant Michael Cubbage, Master Sergeant Leonard Wilson, and Sergeant First Class Michael Woody provided insights and reflections from their deployment experiences in Afghanistan and Iraq. I thank all of these fine soldiers for their time, candor, and selfless service.

1. Robert H. Scales, "Clausewitz and World War IV," *Military Psychology* 21, suppl. 1 (2009): S27.

2. Steven J. Zaccaro, "Trait-Based Perspectives of Leadership," *American Psychologist* 62, no. 1 (2007): 6–16.

3. Robert G. Lord and Douglas J. Brown, *Leadership Processes and Follower Self-Identity* (Mahwah, N.J.: Lawrence Erlbaum, 2004).

4. John Monaghan and Peter Just, *Social and Cultural Anthropology: A Very Short Introduction* (New York: Oxford University Press, 2000).

5. Carl von Clausewitz, *On War*, trans. and ed. Michael Howard and Peter Paret (Princeton, N.J.: Princeton University Press, 1976), 140.

6. Dongil Jung, Francis J. Yammarino, and Jin K. Lee, "Moderating Role of Subordinates' Attitudes on Transformational Leadership and Effectiveness: A Multi-Cultural and Multi-Level Perspective," *Leadership Quarterly* 20 (2009): 586–603.

7. Sarah L. Glover and Kelly M. Hannum, "Learning Respect: Showing and Earning Esteem Is Crucial for Leaders," *Leadership in Action* 28, no. 4 (2008): 3–7.

8. Office of the Under Secretary of Defense, Personnel and Readiness, "Career Progression of Minority and Women Officers," Washington, D.C., August 1999.

9. George B. Graen and Mary Uhl-Bien, "Relationship-Based Approach to Leadership: Development of Leader-Member Exchange (LMX) Theory of Leadership over 25 Years: Applying a Multi-Level Multi-Domain Perspective," in *Leadership: The Multiple-Level Approaches*, ed. Fred Dansereau and Francis J. Yammarino (New York: Elsevier, 1998), 24, 103–158.

10. George B. Graen and Terri A. Scandura, "Toward a Psychology of Dyadic Organizing," *Research in Organizational Behavior* 9 (1987): 175–208.

11. Charlotte R. Gerstner and David V. Day, "Meta-Analytic Review of Leader-Member Exchange Theory: Correlates and Construct Issues," *Journal of Applied Psychology* 82 (1997): 827–844.

12. Schahresad Forman and Peter Zachar, "Cross-Cultural Adjustment of International Officers during Professional Military Education in the United States," *Military Psychology* 13, no. 2 (2001): 117–128.

13. P. Christopher Earley and Soon Ang, *Cultural Intelligence: Individual Interactions across Cultures* (Stanford, Calif.: Stanford Business Books, 2003).

14. Scales, "Clausewitz and World War IV"; and John D. Mayer, Peter Salovey, and David R. Caruso, "Emotional Intelligence," *American Psychologist* 63, no. 6 (2008): 503–517.

15. Tom R. Tyler, "Psychological Perspectives on Legitimacy and Legitimation," *Annual Review of Psychology* 57 (2006): 375–400.

16. Boas Shamir et al., "Leadership and Social Identification in Military Units: Direct and Indirect Relationships," *Journal of Applied Social Psychology* 30, no. 3 (2000): 612–640.

17. Robert Gleave, "Conceptions of Authority in Iraqi Shi'ism: Baqui al-Hakim, Ha'iri and Sistani on Ijtihad, Taqlid and Marja'iyya," *Theory, Culture and Society* 24, no. 2 (2007): 59–78.

18. Tyler, "Psychological Perspectives," 393.

19. Paresha N. Sinha and Brad Jackson, "A Burkean Inquiry into Leader-Follower Identification Motives," *Culture and Organization* 12, no. 3 (2006): 233–247.

20. Micha Popper, "Leadership as Relationship," *Journal for the Theory of Social Behavior* 32, no. 2 (2004): 107–125.

21. Patrick J. Carr, Laura Napolitano, and Jessica Keating, "We Never Call the Cops and Here Is Why: A Qualitative Examination of Legal Cynicism in Three Philadelphia Neighborhoods," *Criminology* 45, no. 2 (2007): 445–480.

22. Joseph W. Bendersky, "'Panic': The Impact of LeBon's Crowd Psychology on U.S. Military Thought," *Journal of the History of the Behavioral Sciences* 43, no. 3 (2007): 257–283.

23. Kurt T. Dirks, "Trust in Leadership and Team Performance: Evidence from NCAA Basketball," *Journal of Applied Psychology* 85, no. 6 (2000): 1004–1012.

24. Shamir et al., "Leadership and Social Identification."

25. Gerry Larsson, "Leader Development in Natural Context," in *Handbook of Military Psychology*, ed. Janice H. Laurence and Michael D. Matthews (forthcoming, Oxford University Press).

26. Jamie L. Flexon, Arthur J. Lurigio, and Richard G. Greenleaf, "Exploring the Dimensions of Trust in the Police among Chicago Juveniles," *Journal of Criminal Justice* 37 (2009): 180–189.

27. Rod K. Brunson and Ronald Weitzer, "Police Relations with Black and White Youth in Different Urban Neighborhoods," *Urban Affairs Review* 44, no. 6 (2009): 858–885.

28. Peter W. Dorfman, Paul J. Hanges, and Felix C. Brodbeck, "Leadership and Cultural Variation: The Identification of Culturally Endorsed Leadership Profiles," in *Culture, Leadership, and Organizations: The GLOBE Study of 62 Societies*, ed. Robert J. House et al. (Thousand Oaks, Calif.: Sage, 2004), 669–719; and Mansour Javidan et al., "Conclusions and Future Directions," in *Culture, Leadership, and Organizations*, 723–732.

29. Lord and Brown, *Leadership Processes*, 80–81.

30. Peter B. Smith et al., "On the Generality of Leadership Style Measures across Cultures," *Journal of Occupational Psychology* 62 (1989): 97–109.

31. J. P. Lawrence, "Army Deploys Scientists to Study Iraqi Culture," *Army.mil*, June 4, 2009, http://www.army.mil/news.

32. Michael Rowe, "Following the Leader: Front-Line Narratives on Police Leadership," *Policing: An International Journal of Police Strategies and Management* 29, no. 4 (2006): 757–767.

33. Scales, "Clausewitz and World War IV," S33.

34. Mark Chapin et al., "Training Police Leadership to Recognize and Address Operational Stress," *Police Quarterly* 11, no. 3 (2008): 338–352.

35. Sean T. Hannah et al., "A Framework for Examining Leadership in Extreme Contexts," *Leadership Quarterly* 20 (2009): 897–919.

36. Geert Hofstede, *Culture's Consequences: Comparing Values, Behaviors, Institutions, and Organizations across Nations*, 2nd ed. (Thousand Oaks, Calif.: Sage, 2001); idem, "Cultural Constraints in Management Theories," *Academy of Management Executive* 7 (1993): 81–94; and idem, "Motivation, Leadership and Organization: Do American Theories Apply Abroad?" *Organizational Dynamics* 9 (1980): 42–63.

37. Steven A. Murphy, "The Role of Emotions and Transformational Leadership on Police Culture: An Autoethnographic Account," *International Journal of Police Science and Management* 10, no. 2 (2008): 165–178.

38. Clausewitz, *On War*, 139.

39. David Harper, "Targeting the American Will," *Military Review*, March–April 2007, 94–104.

40. P. Christopher Earley and Soon Ang, *Cultural Intelligence: Individual Interactions across Cultures* (Stanford, Calif.: Stanford Business Books, 2003).

41. Scales, "Clausewitz and World War IV," S26.

Leveraging the Organization

CHAPTER 17

Creating a Culture for Leading and Performing in the Extreme

Donald H. Horner Jr., Luann P. Pannell, and Dennis W. Yates

Inside the Surge: When Judgment Blurs and Cultures Collide

By early 2008 in the Iraq War, the positive effects of the U.S. "surge" had started to become visible in the streets of Baghdad, as shops began to reopen and people again filled the streets.[1] Despite these outwardly positive appearances, a sinister undercurrent flowed through the population. Rumors ran rampant in Iraqi military and government circles that the radical cleric Muqtada al-Sadr's Mahdi Army was about to launch an offensive against the government of Prime Minister Nuri al-Maliki, a fellow Shiite, because of Sadr's unhappiness with his waning political influence.

In the neighborhood of Zafaraniyah, in Baghdad's southeastern quadrant, Sadrist fighters started to make trouble. The unit responsible for Zafaraniyah had been trained by its commander to act with a great deal of restraint in order to avoid unnecessary civilian deaths. This was in keeping with guidance issued by General David Petraeus, commanding general of the Multi-National Forces–Iraq. The success or failure of Petraeus' strategy of limiting civilian deaths depended solely on the support of the Iraqi people and their perceptions of American and Iraqi forces. What Petraeus was attempting to do on a large scale was to change the organizational culture of both forces. The events of February and March 2008 would put Petraeus' vision and strategy to the test and offer evidence of what happens when old ways of doing business compete with the new.

On the second night of what would come to be called "the uprising," a fight erupted between a dozen young Sadrist fighters and a platoon of American and Iraqi soldiers in the most troubled neighborhood in Zafaraniyah. The engaged platoon was well trained, had the situation well in hand, and acted with restraint. What unfolded was a textbook example of the tendency of higher headquarters to use available technological innovations regardless of the logic (or illogic) of doing so and in contravention of a subordinate commander's wishes.

The battalion watch officer, or "battle captain," ran from the tactical operations center (TOC) to the battalion commander's office to notify him of the firefight. The battle captain explained that the brigade headquarters wanted to drop a 500-pound bomb from an F/A-18 Super Hornet onto the house where it was believed that twelve or so fighters had gone to make a last stand. The brigade TOC was watching the house from several miles away via a live camera feed from an aerial drone.

Rushing to the TOC, the battalion commander attempted to call off the strike. "For God's sake—our job here is to protect the Iraqi people! It's the first sentence in our f——g mission statement! And you want to drop a damned bomb on someone's house?!"

Every soldier in the TOC broke eye contact. They knew they were wrong. Their error: they got caught up in viewing the action as nothing more than a video game. They failed to assess whether dropping a bomb on an Iraqi house was consistent with the commander's intent to exercise restraint and minimize civilian casualties.

Within minutes, the battalion commander was on his way to the scene of the fighting to assess the situation. Almost immediately, he heard the boom of a Hellfire missile striking its target to the east of the commander's location, followed by the staccato report of a string of 30mm shells from the helicopter's main gun. Several minutes later, the commander found the platoon. The two small units and the Iraqi soldiers began fighting their way deep into the neighborhood to find the target house. It appeared that the missile strike had taken the spirit out of the enemy fighters, and friendly forces surrounded the house. They found surprisingly little damage. Fortunately, the Apache helicopter had fired a newly developed missile, specifically designed to limit destruction in urban terrain. Nonetheless, there was still collateral damage to other houses and pools of blood on the ground, along with bloody Iraqi National Police uniforms.

This all-too-real story illustrates what happens when judgment blurs and cultures collide. Despite a battalion commander's best efforts to comply with a general order to protect Iraqis, well-intentioned, but detached, soldiers ordered an air strike that effectively bombed an Iraqi home and generated unnecessary collateral damage. The incompatible, video game–like world of a TOC encroached upon the soldier-on-the-ground culture that sought to build positive perceptions and relationships among the local population. The established Army culture—to identify and target an enemy with all available weaponry despite potentially deleterious effects to the local civilian population—trumped the new guidance and intent of General Petraeus and subordinate commanders.

This chapter examines methods of creating a culture for leading and performing in extreme environments. A theoretical framework is provided to help in understanding what culture is and what culture does and to offer insight into why it is so difficult to change a culture. The chapter combines a military view of culture with a police department's perspective to provide a broad sense of what culture means for organizations operating in extreme environments.

CULTURE: LITERATURE REVIEW AND THEORETICAL FRAMEWORK

The structural-functional school of anthropology and sociology is an appropriate point of departure for a discussion about creating an organizational culture expected to perform in *in extremis* contexts. The notion of culture as a structural element of society was introduced by Polish anthropologist Stanislaw Malinowski in his ethnographic research on tribes in the southwest Pacific islands, Africa, and elsewhere. Malinowski views culture as a collective system of shared habits and emphasized the functionality and utility of these habits for society. This functional view of culture "lays down the principle that in every type of civilization, every custom, material object, idea and belief fulfills some vital function."[2]

Though Malinowski's contemporary, Alfred Radcliffe-Brown rejects the structural-functional view as tautological, he highlights that the relational aspects of culture help form bonds of kinship that extend beyond family, marriage, or blood into groups or teams through which blood kinship is metaphorical.[3] Radcliffe-Brown argues that culture can be created, learned, and transmitted in meaningful ways within groups, teams, and organizations. The American sociologist Talcott Parsons acknowledges this distinction and notes that "culture is intrinsically transmissible from one action system to another by learning and diffusion."[4] From a leadership perspective, this would be good news because it suggests that once identified, the proper culture for functioning in dangerous contexts can be replicated, taught, and reinforced. Another implication is that cultures can be adjusted and changed.

Parsons goes on to argue that culture creation and transmission are essential tasks required of all social systems.[5] In Parsonian terms, "[T]he problem of creating, preserving, and transmitting the system's distinctive culture and values" is an issue of survival for the social system.[6] The American industrialist Chester I. Barnard went a step further, arguing that transmission of a company's culture and values is an essential leadership task. Barnard views the creation, maintenance, and transmission of culture as a primary function of the chief executive. "The distinguishing mark of the executive responsibility is that it requires not merely conformance to a complex code of morals but also the creation of a moral code for others. The most generally recognized aspect of this function is called securing, creating, inspiring of 'morale' in an organization. This is the process of inculcating points of view, fundamental attitudes, loyalties, to the organization or cooperative system, and to the system of objective authority."[7]

Barnard asserts that it is a meaningful pattern of relationships within an organization—the culture—that creates "a condition of communion and the opportunity for commandership."[8] Embedded in this framework are the elements of esprit de corps and élan indicative of high-performing teams and organizations operating in extreme environments. Barnard's *Functions of the Executive* is foundational to conceptions linking leadership with organizational culture.

Tom Peters and Robert Waterman's *In Search of Excellence* extend the view of culture from something that an organization *has* to something that an organization *is*. Linda Smircich agrees, noting that initial usages described culture as "an attribute or quality internal to the group . . . and a fairly stable set of taken-for-granted assumptions, shared beliefs, meanings, and values that form the backdrop for action."[9] In this way, organizations actually take on the identity of the cultures they espouse, becoming part myth, part legend, and part reality. Peters and Waterman note that companies become identified with their cultures and contend that "excellent companies are marked by very strong cultures, so strong that you either buy into their norms or get out."[10]

Edgar Schein's *Organizational Culture and Leadership* offers a relevant and useful conception of culture for leaders and teams performing in extreme environments.[11] Schein's views are appealing because they operationalize, or make concrete, many of the variables implicit in earlier theoretical formulations. Schein's conception is a derivation of the structural-functional approaches blended with insights garnered from years as an organizational scholar. Schein defines culture as a "pattern of shared basic assumptions that the group [or team or organization] learned as it solved its problems of external adaptation and internal integration, that has worked well enough to be considered valid and, therefore, to be taught to new members as the correct way to perceive, think, and feel in relation to those problems."[12]

Schein's definition is densely packed. His theory notes that culture is relational, learned, transmitted, patterned, and perception based. It also suggests that most people in an organization presume the culture to sanction certain perceptions, thoughts, feelings, and behaviors based on a past history of problem solving within the organization and with outsiders. At the risk of distorting Schein's views, a simpler definition is offered here to demystify the concept: Culture refers to a basic pattern of assumptions, norms, behaviors, and values learned by members of a group or organization as the proper way to think and behave and includes a general sense of "how things work" in the group or organization. In plain language, culture refers to "how things are done" by an organization and "what matters" to an organization. This definition of culture serves as the basis for the discussion here.

Schein proposes that there are three levels of culture within an organization. "Levels" refers to "the degree to which the cultural phenomenon is visible to the observer."[13] The distinction between levels is significant because it implies that (1) not all elements of culture are readily discernable and (2) there can be matches and mismatches between levels—meaning that one can encounter mixed cultural signals at various levels of the organization. Figure 17.1 depicts the three levels of culture.

The easiest level to observe are artifacts, which are "all the phenomena that one sees, hears, and feels" when encountering a group or organization.[14] Artifacts appeal to the senses and include such elements as the physical plant

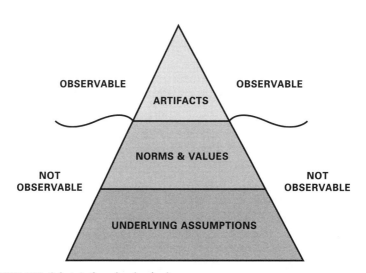

FIGURE 17.1 Schein's three levels of culture

Source: Stephen J. Gerras, Leonard Wong, and Charles D. Allen, "Organizational Culture: Applying a Hybrid Model to the U.S. Army" (unpublished working paper, U.S. Army War College, 2008), based on Edgar H. Schein, *Organizational Culture and Leadership* (San Francisco: Jossey-Bass, 1992).

and environs, language, colors, attire, signage, behavioral interactions, stories, myths, legends, ceremonies, and the like. Artifacts are what visitors and new employees most immediately notice when dealing with the organization. Artifacts are, however, but one aspect of culture, providing only a hint of what the organization may or may not actually value. The degree to which artifacts "reflect deeper values in the minds of organization members" is uncovered only after having spent a good deal of time observing or working in the organization.[15]

At the next level are espoused values or norms and values.[16] They are deeper, less readily observable aspects of culture than artifacts. Norms and values are transmitted to members of the group through learning, practice, and assimilation. Values are judgments about what is important in an organization, while norms represent unwritten rules that allow members of a culture to know what is expected of them in various situations. What one values will affect what one perceives as "normal" behavior in an organization. Values and beliefs define the organization, are a mechanism for social control, and also influence identity development.

Those who best embody, transmit, and propagate norms and values to other members of the group become recognized as leaders. Because of this, Schein argues that "culture and leadership are two sides of the same coin."[17] By this he means that leaders create and reinforce culture, and culture determines the criteria for who advances in an organization. The transformation of members from value and norm conformists to norm and value instructors is cognitively significant because it represents a shift from "must" to "ought." Assessing the degree to which all members of the group or organization buy-in to norms and values provides some sense of the cohesiveness and strength of the culture. For example, the story opening this chapter illustrates how difficult it was for Army leaders to get subordinates to buy in to the new culture that valued restraint and protection of the Iraqi people instead of the heavy-handed application of advanced weaponry.

The most difficult level of culture to discern, and yet the most important, is basic underlying assumptions. Paradoxically, basic underlying assumptions are hard to decipher because they are so fundamental and taken for granted. Schein notes, "When a solution to a problem works repeatedly, it becomes taken for granted. What was once a hypothesis, supported only by a hunch or value, comes gradually to be treated as reality. We come to believe that . . . things work this way."[18]

Basic underlying assumptions are similar to what Chris Argyris calls "theories-in-use." Argyris explains that "human beings have programs in their heads about how to be in control."[19] These organizational rules to live by are so basic, so underlying, that they are unconscious and unspoken. Basic underlying assumptions define "what to pay attention to, what things mean, how to react emotionally to what is going on, and what actions to take in various kinds of situations."[20]

The opening scenario illustrates the three levels of culture. During the surge, an underlying assumption was that technology is good. This assumption leads to the norm of using technology whenever necessary to target combatants. The artifact is the firing of the Hellfire missile into the house containing combatants. Mismatches between levels of culture offer a valuable metric for leaders. Artifacts representative of norms and values, and norms and values consistent with basic underlying assumptions, yield a consistency that reinforces and guides behaviors. For *in extremis* organizations and leaders, mismatches could produce a measure of indecisiveness that might result in unnecessary injuries and casualties. The Iraq story reflects what happens when the culture that a leader is trying to create is out of step with previous norms and values and basic underlying assumptions.

John Kotter's *Leading Change* reinforces just how difficult it is to lead cultural change.[21] He argues that change "sticks" only after it becomes part of how the majority of people in the organization, about 75 percent or more, do business. Kotter suggests that lasting change will not occur "until new behaviors are rooted in social norms and shared values."[22] Three factors weigh heavily in such change: a conscious effort to demonstrate and model the new way of doing things, rewarding behaviors consistent with the new culture, and appointing leaders that embody the new culture.

PRACTICAL APPLICATION OF CULTURAL CONCEPTS: THE LOS ANGELES POLICE DEPARTMENT

For leaders and operators in dangerous contexts, the opening story illustrates how the demands of safety, complex ethical responsibilities, and the consequences of action or inaction must be simultaneously weighed in a short, ultra-high-intensity time frame. To cultivate a culture of sound leadership for such contexts, one must examine the role of training. Training becomes the premium vehicle for not only promoting organizational change, but also for inculcating those changes into values and beliefs that influence the culture. It is the training of an organization's most precious assets—its people—that determines how they think, feel, and act while facing critical situations.

It is within this framework that the Los Angeles Police Department began to examine traditional models of police training. As a practical matter, the

LAPD anticipated that it needed to adjust its policing for its force to adequately address the demands of future generations. Such a mental and cultural shift is easier said than done, however, particularly given the rich, tradition-based entities that police forces tend to be. It is not sufficient to simply add more training; it must be training that will shift thought processes so that a variety of new questions is asked.

Techniques for Assessing Culture and Change

Frequently, the inability of an organization to accept change is connected to a failure to adequately assess the cultures affected by the change. The formidable social forces of formal and informal cultures can often block even the best initiatives. In the case of the LAPD, knowing that a solid understanding of the concerns from the frontline of policing would be critical, the principles of "leadership by walking around" were applied in numerous situations and by several different leaders in collaboration with one another.[23]

Leadership by walking around was employed during the course of everyday tasks. Various leaders in the training office looked for transitional opportunities to develop meaningful conversations, such as while officers were on break from a class, waiting in line for firearms qualification at the shooting range, training to hold a perimeter, or preparing for physical training. Running with classes of recruits allowed trainers to glean elements of accepted culture based on the recruits' chants. They also observed the use of positive and negative reinforcement by staff and noted the response to high and low achievement.

LAPD leaders derived insights from walking around and paying attention to those who were "invisible" in the organization. This technique helped to include the perspective of the parking attendant, the records clerk, and the student workers and trainees. Focus groups alone would not have allowed these perspectives to surface. From the collection of observations through informal interactions, a framework, vocabulary, and subcultures were identified for examination through more formal assessment procedures.

Army leaders likewise employ leadership by walking around as a technique for assessing culture. During such interactions, the leader exerts little direct influence because, for the most part, members of the unit are actually doing things properly. The leader exerts direct influence only on those parts of the organization that are not behaving in a manner consistent with cultural norms and values. Put differently, the leader touches on, or uses "touch points," to correct aberrant behaviors.[24]

Although examining culture may seem unnecessary or labor intensive, to do otherwise is to invite failure. In the case of the LAPD police academy, the following six cultures or subcultures were examined:

- current culture of the department
- culture of the community being served
- culture of the recruit
- culture of the training instructors
- culture of field training officers
- the envisioned future culture

More structured assessments were conducted through focus groups, discussions with key stakeholders, and a review of documentation and procedures. Investigations revealed a myriad of issues that had to be accounted for in order to adequately address a redesigned training model. Generational differences between recruits and senior officers proved significant. In contrast to their trainers, new recruits are "millennials," who tend to have short and selective attention spans and operate with the expectation that information should be readily accessible. Tending toward nonconfrontation, millennials are "joiners" who want to be a part of something with a greater purpose, something larger than themselves. Given that this segment of the population represents the bulk of new trainees entering the LAPD police academy, two questions arose: "How do they learn?" and "How can they be reached?" The academy had been designed originally to meet the needs of a different kind of recruit, community, and environment. The LAPD had to thoroughly evaluate what training (and culture) needed to change in order to ensure success for the next generation of officers in a media-driven world of high expectations, incessant scrutiny, and constant demands.

Similar to the military, traditional police training had typically emphasized pride, discipline, and performance. Police recruits sat at attention with minimal class discussion. Formal and informal instruction, including recruit-to-recruit blogs and internet sites, told recruits to sit still, learn the material, and spout the textbook response. In essence, the mind-set required to succeed in the police academy was antithetical to the previous expectation of engagement held by the community and officers in the field.

The LAPD police academy aspired to do more than simply pass mandated state standards. Though it was determined that continuation of strong tactical training was necessary, improvements had to be made to encourage critical thinking and reward initiative. Training had to evolve so that new officers could be confident in their abilities to think through and master emergent *in extremis* scenarios. The new goal was to complement tactical strengths by developing officers who were self-motivated, community-oriented critical thinkers and problem solvers. This revised goal demanded a new training paradigm and a new culture.

THE LAPD POLICE ACADEMY TRAINING PARADIGM

Part I: Peak Performance by Training the Whole Person

"Training the whole person" requires that all elements of the human condition be considered in the process in order to replicate the real-world policing environment. To reflect the shared importance of all aspects of a human response, the LAPD training triangle was created as a representation of all learning domains to be debriefed in training (see Figure 17.2):

- affective domain, or emotions
- cognitive domain, or thoughts
- psychomotor domain, or behaviors

The concept of developing the "whole person" is endemic to leadership paradigms and is rooted in the Army's "be-know-do" leadership development model.[25]

The challenge of LAPD police academy instructional teams was to ensure that each trainee gets pushed to deeper levels of skill acquisition. Training must mimic real life, which means that often one domain may be more dominant than another. A significant shift in LAPD training culture was changing the definition of success from simply passing a cognitive test to one that involved all elements—emotions, behaviors, and thoughts—of a realistic training scenario.

Though representative of a cultural shift for the law enforcement training community, these concepts are not new to those who study peak performance and sports psychology. Not having the advantage of classes full of highly disciplined, gifted athletes, the LAPD's aspiration was to get exceptional response capability out of normal people. This is where the potential of human motivation needs to be accessed the most, and this represents a significant contrast to the traditional police academy classroom, which involved instructor-to-student lectures with little exchange between the two. The older approach did not reflect the dynamic, interactive nature of community policing, which values critical thinking and problem solving. The latter is the culture the LAPD police academy sought to create.

IN EXTREMIS CONTEXT

FIGURE 17.2 Los Angeles Police Department police academy training model

Older models for police training were focused primarily on training a skill set—typically represented by cognitive or psychomotor learning domains—without much discussion of how an individual's affective state would influence either. The police academy wanted trained officers confident in their ability to assess and understand the role of emotion in human conflict. Consistent with Schein's notion of basic underlying assumptions, the new culture emphasized knowing, instead of ignoring, the affective component of training.

The focal point for teaching affective responses is the LAPD's mission, vision, and values. These concepts represent the meaning of and motivation for why the LAPD does what it does. Acknowledging the numerous emotions experienced with policing, the department's mission, vision, and values help channel police officers' affective responses by causing them to consider what the response ought to be in a given scenario.

Part II: Trained in a Team, by a Team, To Be a Team

The LAPD police academy emphasizes that individuals are embedded in teams. It is not a trivial matter that the police academy's emphasis on team flies in the face of American society, which stresses individualism. Even the notion of the American Dream reinforces individuality by noting that the United States is a "land in which life should be better and richer and fuller for every man, with opportunity for each according to ability or achievement."[26]

The deep roots of individuality point to the potential challenge and struggle of inculcating the value of teams in police academy training. This represents a foundational clash of underlying values and cultures.

Solutions for *in extremis* events are more commonly team-based and involve a coordinated, collective action. Police forces dispatch their most elite teams to intervene in the most dangerous situations. Though respected for their individual skills, these teams are best known for their well-coordinated, synchronized efforts and movements. These teams are cross-trained for full awareness and appreciation of the complexity of each person's role. As Figure 17.2 connotes, extensive team training is conducted in a continuous cycle. Strong teams require strong individuals, so remediation is done at both the micro (individual) and macro (team) levels of analysis.

By deemphasizing individual grades and skills acquisition in the LAPD police academy, the organization leverages the social environment to create a different, more critical and more team-based, officer. The vision is that the organization will succeed or fail based on the aggregate performance of its coordinated teams. The intent is to create the building blocks for team collaboration, roles, and responsibilities early in one's development as a police officer.

Ultimately the LAPD of the future will reflect an interdependent organization that values teams for their specific functions and for their contribution to the force. Having officers train in teams creates ownership, responsibility, and a better awareness of how one team's response fits within the larger operational context. This creates a more resilient workforce. Research suggests that resiliency is increased when those exposed to life-threatening, *in extremis* environments feel an affinity for and social connection to colleagues in meaningful ways.[27]

Part III: The Context—Training through an Event, Not to It

The final portion of the LAPD police academy model requires that the dynamic development of the individual and the team occurs within an experiential learning environment. This necessitates officers training "through" an event and not to it. Training through an event includes training not only for the extreme event, but also for events following or preceding the crisis. The latter tend to encompass the preponderance of daily police work.

Laudably, the law enforcement community spends significant training dollars preparing for *in extremis* events meant to test certain psychomotor (behavioral) capabilities. Often ignored, however, are the cognitive (thoughts) and affective (emotion) domains. After an *in extremis* event, it is incumbent on leaders to ensure that individuals, teams, and organizations return to functioning at a neutral level. Cultivating a healthy police culture requires that officers return to functioning in the relative calm of more "normal" situations.

This LAPD model incorporates many aspects of what is already known to cultivate resilience in those who chose the career path of a first responder. Taken as a whole, the model speaks to the deliberate, practical, and informed manner in which the LAPD has gone about the process of building a culture of policing based on the contribution of every individual as a leader and the value of every team in completing the mission.

LEADER AND LEADERSHIP DEVELOPMENT IMPLICATIONS: AN INTEGRATED ARMY (GREEN) AND LAPD (BLUE) PERSPECTIVE

Envisioning and enacting a positive culture capable of sustaining high-level performance in extreme environments takes an enormous commitment of time and energy. While much has been written about culture or "command climate," the pragmatic view suggests that complex written perspectives generally lose their luster in practice.[28] This bias toward "doing" hints at the need to keep guidance regarding leadership and leadership development simple. Providing subordinates a general framework within which to work and allowing them the freedom to innovate within that framework also fits within the broader American culture. What follows are tips about leading effectively in extreme situations. The intent is to offer a perspective that readers can use to develop their leadership style in the context of creating a sustainable organizational culture capable of winning during extreme circumstances. The insights apply to a leader's attempt to assess, discover, change, or transmit the appropriate culture.

- *Keep your command philosophy simple and provide a framework for winning in extreme environments.* Army commanders have traditionally been encouraged to publish a "command philosophy" upon assumption of their position. Some command philosophies are several pages long, for example, ten single-spaced pages or more. The problem with this approach is that often the leader's words do not match subsequent actions. In Scheinian terms, a mismatch is created between espoused values—what the leader says—and actual behaviors—what the leader does. This disconnect between espoused values and basic underlying assumptions results in cynicism among organization members.

- *Get the big ideas right.* Leadership is about getting the "big ideas" right.[29] A small number of big ideas—modeled by the organizational leader every day and copied by subordinates—are better than tenfold ideas published in an unread philosophical epic. Consider the following command philosophy, a scant two sentences long: "Do the right thing" and "Treat others the way you want to be treated." Consider adding a qualifier at the end of the document and one has the essence of the philosophy: "You will learn more about me and my beliefs as we meet each other during the course of our operations and day-to-day life within the unit."

- *Lead by example in all things—and teach.* Avoid the common misperception that leading by example simply means being the fastest or the strongest. Teaching is an indispensable part of being a leader—and never more so than in extreme environments. As Admiral James Bond Stockdale noted, "Every great leader I've ever known has been a great teacher, able to give those around him a sense of perspective. . . . Teachership is indispensable to leadership and an integral part of duty."[30] This theme, that leadership is teachership, is essential in dangerous environments.

- *Seek personal balance in order to protect your ability to make decisions.* Current literature cites balance as a critical element of holistic leadership.[31] The notion is simple: do not ignore one's very real need to read, reflect, and rest. The organization depends on the individual and the collective abilities of its leaders and members to make sound decisions, and sound decisions are affected by one's emotional, physical, social, and spiritual health. To illustrate, General Douglas MacArthur is rumored to have never made a serious decision after 3 p.m., preferring instead to spend his evenings in quiet reflection and to postpone big decisions until the morning.

- *Periodically review your philosophy for subordinates.* It is easy to get caught up in the gravitational pull of the day-to-day running of an organization. Take the larger organizational view. One should not assume that new members of the group will absorb leaders' beliefs or philosophy through osmosis. Much as big ships do not make sharp turns, it takes time and reinforcement to change organizational culture. Remember the opening story about Iraq?

- *Develop the ability and tacit knowledge to identify where you are needed and at the precise time you are needed.* In Army parlance, the notion of being where needed most is known as the decisive point. The ability to identify the decisive point and to be present as necessary accrues through experience, training, and trial by fire. Leaders must be present and vigilant because even well-intentioned subordinates can get off track. Be mindful of this dynamic.

- *Attend to all elements of extreme events, whether during training or real life.* This chapter's opening story highlights how a given tactical situation can elicit numerous applicable solutions. Some solutions are consistent with and others are in opposition to the desired organizational culture. Although predictable in the Iraq situation as told, the responses of embarrassment and shame are emotions largely excluded from training development or tactical debriefs. If only tactical operations are debriefed, only tactical operations will be improved. *In extremis* events require leaders to attend to all facets of an operation.

- *Train the whole person.* First responders to dangerous events, whether wars abroad or emergencies at home, are challenged in a number of ways. The challenges occur before, during, and after the events. These include battles for scarce resources, lack of support from senior leaders, and bureaucratic red tape to train for all elements of an operation. Organizations that fail to train the whole person and challenge their capabilities across all domains fail to adequately prepare team members for the totality of the experience.

  A best practice focused on training the whole person is a technique used by the German Army Quick Reaction Force (QRF) in Afghanistan.[32] In summer 2008, a German army military psychologist offered psychological education and mental training to the soldiers and leaders of a platoon earmarked for duty with a second contingent of the QRF. Military psychologists in the German army work as consultants in psychological matters, preventive specialists focusing on post-traumatic stress disorder and other psychological outcomes, coordinators for after-care measures following critical incidents, and counselors for soldiers before, during, and after operations.

  This particular psychologist designed two instruments for psychological self-assessments: (1) a self-check for mental readiness to engage in a fight-and-survive scenario and (2) a self-check for leadership and team capability during a fight. Instruction was provided regarding how to adapt to unusual, *in extremis* situations and how to adequately perform self-checks for combat readiness.

  Results showed that 63 percent of participants felt better prepared for combat, and 86 percent acknowledged the utility of a self-check to make them more aware of combat stressors. Similarly, 90 percent of participants fully agreed that mental preparation is necessary as a means of anticipating psychological stressors associated with combat operations. Researchers concluded that interventions by military psychologists paid huge dividends before, during, and after QRF missions.

- *Train all the way through an event, not just to it.* A derivative of the preceding discussion is that events leading to a dangerous context and recovery from the actual event engender significant additional challenges. Leaders cannot stop leading once the tactical operation has concluded. Leaders must anticipate the ongoing needs of their people, consider the political environment and constructs within which operations are conducted, and acquire the resources needed after the extreme event.

- *Demonstrate righteous anger judiciously.* The notion of losing one's temper judiciously appears to be oxymoronic. Yet, this prescription is both interesting and supported by the leadership literature. Research shows that leaders only have so many silver bullets, and if fired all at once, the werewolves become immune. This is often referred to as the "silver bullet theory" of leadership, coined by former Stanford University president Donald Kennedy.[33]

  The argument here is not advocating behaving badly. Rather, the intent is to leverage the affective response of subordinates by judiciously using anger as a motivator. Daniel Goleman, Richard Boyatzis, and Annie McKee suggest this approach in Primal Leadership. They argue that this commanding style should be part of a leader's repertoire and is best used "in a crisis, to kick-start a turnaround, or with problem employees."[34]

  In Sacred Hoops, the basketball coach Phil Jackson speaks about "righteous anger" and how to deliver it. He states, "As a rule I try not to unleash my anger at players.... When it happens, I say what I have to say, then let it pass, so the bad feelings won't linger in the air and poison the team. Sometimes what my father called 'righteous anger' is the most skillful means to shake up a team. But, it has to be dispensed judiciously."[35] Jackson's points are reinforced by research suggesting that "emotional arousal in moderation may also have a positive impact on human learning."[36] Admiral Stockdale supports Jackson's contention: "Every so often, I would play that 'irrational' role and come completely unglued" in order to stimulate the desired arousal in subordinates.[37] His point: being theatrical at the right time really helped him during his *in extremis* imprisonment in the Hanoi Hilton.

- *Link mission, vision, and values, and make them meaningful.* Full commitment is necessary for success in extreme environments, and for human beings, commitment is linked to meaning. Hence, the values and vision of an organization must be devised, communicated, and reinforced in a manner that stimulates full commitment to accomplishing the organizational mission. These are essential tasks for creating the desired culture.

Napoleon warns leaders that this sort of commitment cannot be bought and is not for sale. He cautions, "A man does not have himself killed for a half-pence a day or for a petty distinction. You must speak to the soul in order to electrify him."[38] Stockdale agrees: "More than any other factor . . . success or failure depends on the moral sentiment, the ethos, the spirit of the man."[39]

In extreme environments, the binding force of individual commitment is manifested by unit cohesion. Cohesiveness of the variety required to succeed *in extremis* is derived from membership in a team of professionals fully committed to subjugating one's needs for the good of the team. Membership in such teams must be earned, standards must be high and consistently enforced, and there must exist overarching meaning of the rarest form. In these environs, leadership is as much about communicating meaning as it is anything else.[40]

- *Conduct training in teams by teams early.* A well-established body of sociological literature demonstrates that human beings endure and operate in extreme conditions essentially for each other. S. L. A. Marshall's *Men against Fire* (1947), Morris Janowitz and Edward A. Shils' classic "Cohesion and Disintegration of the German Wehrmacht in World War II" (1948), Samuel Stouffer's *American Soldier* (1949), and Charles Moskos' "Why Men Fight" (1969) equally contend that trust in and overriding commitment to the team serves as the tonic that keeps soldiers fighting in combat.

  The same motivational foundation applies to first responders. Evidence suggests that identification with one's team, the cohesiveness of the team, and the team's commitment to organizational goals are linked with successful functioning in extreme environments. For these reasons, it makes sense to form teams early and to conduct training in teams in order to bind individuals into an identifiable, functional collective.

- *Seek continuous improvement.* The literature on "learning organizations" also applies to organizations operating *in extremis*.[41] Seeking continuous improvement implies double-loop learning, which Argyris describes as learning that changes the system. This involves unlearning old ways of doing business and continually seeking new ways to operate. A culture of continuous improvement is necessitated by the enormity of the dangers and risks associated with operating in extreme environments and by the ingenuity of the opposition.

KEY REFERENCES

In addition to the referenced citations, there are several relevant texts that speak to aspects of producing an organization capable of sustaining high performance in extreme environments. This short list of seminal works is valuable for addressing the topic of culture:

Blaber, Pete. *The Mission, the Men and Me: Lessons from a Former Delta Force Commander.* New York: Penguin, 2008.

Kotter, John P., and James L. Heskett. *Corporate Culture and Performance.* New York: Free Press, 1992.

Loftus, Bethan. *Police Culture in a Changing World.* New York: Oxford University Press, 2010.

Building and sustaining a culture capable of winning in extreme environments ultimately comes down to whether people—soldiers, police officers, fire fighters, and first-responders of other types—are willing to fight for each other. The true test of a winning culture is whether unit members consistently run toward and rather than away from the fight—be it a fight against a raging fire, criminals with bad intentions, or enemy combatants. For an exhaustive look at unit cohesion in extreme environments, see the following:

Henderson, William Darryl. *Cohesion: The Human Element in Combat.* Washington, D.C.: National Defense University Press, 1985.

Wong, Leonard, et al. *Why They Fight: Combat Motivation in the Iraq War.* Carlisle, Pa.: Strategic Studies Institute, 2003.

NOTES

1. The surge refers to the increase in the number of American troops ordered deployed in 2007 by President George W. Bush to provide additional security and combat power. Approximately 20,000 additional soldiers were deployed to Baghdad.
2. Abram Kardiner and Edward Preble, *They Studied Man* (Cleveland, Ohio: World, 1961), 24.
3. A. R. Radcliffe-Brown, *Structure and Function in Primitive Society* (London: Routledge, 1952).
4. Talcott Parsons and Edward Shils, *Toward a Theory of Social Action* (New York: Harper and Row, 1951), 159.
5. W. Richard Scott, *Organizations: Rational, Natural, and Open Systems* (Englewood Cliffs, N.J.: Prentice-Hall, 1987).
6. Ibid., 68.
7. Chester I. Barnard, *The Functions of the Executive* (Cambridge, Mass.: Harvard University Press, 1938), 279.

8. Scott, *Organizations,* 63.

9. Linda Smircich, "Concepts of Culture and Organizational Analysis," *Administrative Science Quarterly* 28, no. 1 (1983): 58.

10. Thomas J. Peters and Robert H. Waterman Jr., *In Search of Excellence* (New York: Harper and Row, 1982), 77.

11. Edgar H. Schein, *Organizational Culture and Leadership* (San Francisco: Jossey-Bass, 1992).

12. Ibid., 12.

13. Ibid., 16.

14. Schein, *Organizational Culture,* 17.

15. Richard L. Daft, *Organization Theory and Design,* 10th ed. (Mason, Ohio: South-Western, 2010), 375.

16. Schein uses the term "espoused values." The authors find "norms and values" to be more descriptive of the processes involved.

17. Schein, *Organizational Culture,* 2.

18. Ibid., 21–22.

19. Chris Argyris, *Overcoming Organizational Defenses* (Boston: Allyn and Bacon, 1990), 13.

20. Schein, *Organizational Culture,* 22.

21. John P. Kotter, *Leading Change* (Boston: Harvard Business School Press, 1996).

22. Ibid., 15.

23. See Peters and Waterman, *In Search of Excellence,* for a comprehensive discussion of this leadership technique. The practice was used by senior executives at Hewlett-Packard and originally called "management by walking around" (MBWA).

24. The term "touch points" is also referred to as "negative control": if while walking around the commander finds things are going well in the unit, there is no need for corrective action. When things are going awry, the leader takes action and exerts control to positively affect the situation.

25. See the whole-person paradigm by Franklin-Covey at www.franklincovey.com; see *Army Field Manual 22–100 Army Leadership: Be, Know, Do,* August 1999, for a thorough discussion of the Army's model; another source is Richard E. Cavanaugh, *Be-Know-Do: Leadership the Army Way* (San Francisco: Jossey-Bass, 2004).

26. James Truslow Adams, *Epic of America* (Boston: Little, Brown, 1931), 15.

27. Merle Friedman and Craig Higson-Smith, "Building Psychological Resilience: Learning from the South African Police Service," in *Promoting Capabilities to Manage Posttraumatic Stress: Perspectives on Resilience,* ed. D. Paton, J. M. Violanti, and L. M. Smith (Springfield, Ill.: Charles C. Thomas, 2003), 103–118. To clarify, positive resilience can be thought of as the capacity to endure and adapt to repeated exposure to potentially traumatic events while retaining the ability to live a well-rounded, healthy life with positive relationships.

28. The authors concur with Edgar Schein conceptually: Climate is an element of culture, not vice versa. The comment as written reflects the Army's perspective, which tends to broadly view culture and climate as interchangeable concepts.

29. For a more thorough discussion, see Robert J. Allio, "Leadership: The Five Big Ideas," *Strategy and Leadership* 37, no. 2 (2009): 4–12.

30. James Bond Stockdale, *Ten Years of Reflection: A Vietnam Experience* (Palo Alto, Calif.: Stanford University Press, 1984), 73–74.

31. The term "holistic leadership" is not new. See Gordon L. Lippitt, *Organizational Renewal: A Holistic Approach to Leadership Development* (New York: Prentice Hall, 1981). The *Journal of Leadership Studies* devotes its spring 2012 edition to the topic of holistic leadership and sustaining high performance.

32. The authors wish to thank Jochen Grigutsch for his contribution to this paper. This section is largely written by him or adapted from his work.

33. For a discussion of this and other nontraditional leadership theories, see Donald H. Horner Jr., "A Different Twist: Non-Rational Views of Leadership," *Military Review*, November–December 1996, 45–50.

34. Daniel Goleman, Richard Boyatzis, and Annie McKee, *Primal Leadership: Realizing the Power of Emotional Intelligence* (Boston: Harvard Business School, 2002), 55.

35. Phil Jackson, *Sacred Hoops* (New York: Hyperion, 1995), 141–142.

36. Russell Shilling, Michael Zyda, and E. Casey Wardynski, "Introducing Emotion into Military Simulation and Videogame Design: America's Army: Operations and VIRTE," *Proceedings of the GameOn Conference* (London, 2002), 3.

37. Stockdale, *Ten Years of Reflection*, 37.

38. Kevin Kiley, "Thumbing through the Napoleonic Wars: The Words of Napoleon and Others Who May Have Influenced His Methods," The Napoleon Series, 2010, http://www.napoleon-series.org/research/napoleon/c_quotes.html.

39. Stockdale, *Ten Years of Reflection*, 95.

40. Louis R. Pondy, "Leadership Is a Language Game," in *Leadership: Where Else Can We Go?* ed. Morgan W. McCall Jr. and Michael M. Lombards (Durham, N.C.: Duke University Press, 1978), 87–99.

41. For a thorough discussion of double-loop learning, see Chris Argyris, *Overcoming Organizational Defenses* (Boston: Allyn and Bacon, 1990).

CHAPTER 18

Choosing the Elite
Recruitment, Assessment, and Selection in Law Enforcement Tactical Teams and Military Special Forces

Ole Boe, Kristin K. Woolley, and John Durkin

NYPD Emergency Service Unit

In the early morning hours of July 31, 2007, Gazi Abu Mezer and Lafi Khalil, two Palestinians who had entered the United States after exploiting loopholes in the immigration system, were in the operational phase of a planned suicide bombing of the New York City Transit system. Their weapons: simple pipe bombs with electrical detonating switches packed into knapsacks. Two things would stand in the way of their attempt at martyrdom—their Egyptian roommate and the New York City Police Department's Emergency Service Unit (ESU).

Mossabah, the roommate, had been taken to the New York Police Department's 88th Precinct. When the ESU tour commander, a veteran lieutenant, arrived at the precinct, he interviewed Mossabah, having him start at the beginning of his recollections, interrupting him for clarifications and details. After digesting what he had heard, the commander began apprising his leadership of the situation and stressing that he believed Mossabah. He then looked at the roster of ESU officers working his shift, from midnight to 8 a.m. The urgency of the situation prohibited him from calling in people from home and handpicking a team to enter the apartment Mossabah shared with the two suspects; he would have to go with those already available. The commander called a sergeant and four police officers and told them to meet him at the precinct.

After the five arrived, Mossabah was again asked to tell his story from the beginning. They interrupted him with even more questions and requests for clarification and had him draw an extensive diagram of his apartment building's exterior and his apartment's interior, highlighting the locations of the backpacks as well as the spaces Mezer and Khalil normally occupied. The commander took his team into another room and devised his tactical plan, giving out assignments as they progressed. The team would execute a standard dynamic search warrant entry. Mossabah would lead them to the building, and they would enter using his key. The building the team saw upon exiting their vehicle looked nothing like the one Mossabah had sketched at the precinct. Thoughts of an ambush ran through the officers' minds. Mossabah then led the team through a narrow alley, at the end of which the team saw a building resembling the one he had drawn.

The lead officer, protected by a hand-held body bunker, put the key in the lock, turned it, and opened the door. The team flooded the apartment, yelling, "Police! Get down on the floor!" The first officer through the door was met by a man who attempted to physically disarm him. The officer fired one shot from his 9-mm pistol, hitting his target. The wounded man stumbled backwards, toward a black canvas bag in the corner of the room. As he flipped one of four toggles on the front of the bag, another officer fired two 5.56-mm rounds into him, and he crumpled into a corner of the room. As the team pressed on, a second man in another room lunged toward a backpack in a corner. Two shots from an officer's pistol dropped him before he could reach it. The entry was over in less than ninety seconds. Both men were taken into custody.

The FBI reconstructed both backpack improvised explosive devises, determining them to be functional with a blast radius of more than 100 yards. Their analysis also revealed that the toggle thrown on the first backpack should have detonated the device. It is not known why it failed.

JOINING THE ELITE

This incident highlights the challenges faced by leaders of law enforcement tactical teams: A crisis situation arises suddenly. Urgency calls for action. There is no time to handpick a response team. The leader must work with whoever is on duty. What can a law enforcement leader do to ensure that whoever is working counts among the best the agency has? Perhaps through a framework for a selection process of tactical teams that ensures transparency, provides a multilayered approach for weeding out the unqualified, and has a multitiered means of selecting from the strongest of the remaining candidates those capable of performing in dangerous, high-stress operations.

The Emergency Service Unit, Special Weapons and Tactics (SWAT), Emergency Response Team, and Emergency Incident Team are a few of the types of outfits called upon to handle and diffuse the most complex and dangerous situations law enforcement officers encounter. They deal with armed, barricaded suspects, hostage situations, shooters, and high-risk search warrants. It is sometimes said that when the public needs help, they call the police; when the police need help, they call Emergency Service. How does one become a member of these elite units? More important, how do leaders select applicants for assignment to the agency's special response teams? The process is similar to that of any other job: recruitment, an interview (selection), and training followed by a probationary period (assessment). The recruitment, selection, and assessment "training" procedures of three high-performing and high-stakes organizations will be examined here.

Recruitment

Although some officers will "walk in" to apply to join a unit, implementing a formal recruitment program lends legitimacy as well as transparency to the process. It also helps debunk the myth of an "old boy" network, possibly preventing future allegations of exclusion, and improve diversity. Two recommended courses of action are publication of a formal bulletin along with briefings or presentations to roll calls department wide.

Publication and dissemination of a bulletin serves several purposes. It reaches the largest pool of potential applicants because it is distributed throughout the department. The bulletin should clearly state the minimum requirements for assignment as time in service, education, special skills, evaluations, and physical requirements if any. Department-wide roll call presentations, given by members of the unit, validate the inclusiveness of the recruitment process and allow prospective applicants the ability to pose questions to unit members. The application form itself should allow the applicant to provide a detailed assignment history covering their entire career. Additional information might include education, prior military service, and special skills. It should also include a section in which the applicant can explain why he or she should be selected and what they would bring to the unit. No application should be considered without a signed recommendation and comments from the applicant's commanding officer.

Selection

The next step in the process is an oral interview. Any commander of a law enforcement tactical unit who does not conduct oral interviews for applicants to their team is committing a grave error. There is simply no other way to fully appraise an applicant than through a face-to-face meeting. Prior to conducting interviews, complete packages for all of the applicants must be assembled that include at a minimum the completed application, the applicant's previous evaluations and personnel file (or a synopsis of the latter), disciplinary records, and details of any previous firearms discharges, force complaints, and open internal investigations. Applicants with multiple firearms discharges or force complaints and open internal investigations must be rigorously evaluated.

The interview panel should include frontline and ranking or executive-level supervisors. The ranking officers should not only chair the interview, but ask the majority of the questions. This tactic allows the panel to gauge the applicant's ability to interact with ranking officers, that is, to operate in a somewhat stressful situation. Being able to function and communicate well under stress is a requirement of any member of a law enforcement tactical team. At the scene of a major event, the incident commander will usually want to confer and coordinate directly with the members of the tactical team. Team members must be able to calmly and coherently respond and not be intimidated by rank. Asking applicants about their hobbies, off-duty activities, and volunteer or community service offers insight into the person rather than the officer. There are two main methods of conducting an interview: asking direct questions or asking situational questions. In the direct method, questions will elicit either a negative or an affirmative answer. Usually these questions focus on integrity and procedure. The situational method, in which the applicant is presented with a situation and asked to indicate how he or she would respond, requires more detailed answers. Some situational questions should not and do not have a right or wrong answer. The objective is to evaluate the applicant's analytical skills and gain insight into their decision-making process. For instance, a sample situation might probe their response to an active shooter on a crowded playground. Another method to evaluate a candidate's analytical ability is to provide them with a written, mechanical-reasoning test whose goal is not to evaluate their mechanical abilities but rather their analytical ability.

There are many reasons why a police officer wants to become a member of their department's tactical team. Some relish the challenge and want to belong to an elite unit. Others have prior military service and enjoy the camaraderie of a small unit with a specific mission. One type looking to join the team that must be identified during the oral interview is the one enthralled by the "glamour factor," whose sole desire is to be near the action and to look good in the tactical uniform. These people tend not to be team oriented. Posing situational questions where the desired answers are team focused will help identify them. Fortunately, glory seekers rarely pass the team-related parts of the physical tests.

The use of heavy body armor, additional weapons, and equipment combined, with the often drawn-out time frames of tactical situations require team members to be in excellent physical condition. A physical fitness exam can help determine a candidate's overall level of fitness and endurance and commitment to a personal fitness program. Some departments use a military-style physical fitness test to evaluate applicants' levels of fitness, but collective bargaining agreements may preclude an agency from using this method. An alternative is a test comprised of job-specific tasks, such as but not limited to a timed stair climb while wearing tactical equipment and carrying tools, moving and carrying heavy equipment, and simulated door ramming. The list is limited only by the imagination. As long as the task is job specific, it should survive a union grievance. During the test, instructors and evaluators should ratchet up the mental stress but refrain from hazing candidates.

A tactical law enforcement officer must be able to function in a high-stress environment, often for an extended period. The applicant must be able to deal with the physical and mental stress while preventing his personal feelings and emotions from interfering with a safe resolution of the incident. Also, some incidents will be ended by the application of deadly physical force. The interview process and the physical should weed out the majority of unacceptable candidates, but no system is perfect; one or two undesirables may give all the right answers in an interview and max the physical. Interviewing well and being in good shape does not automatically translate into being qualified for selection. Instinct, or gut feeling, is one of a police officer's greatest tools. If during the selection process a member of the selection committee thinks that something just doesn't feel right about an applicant, his or her instinct is probably right. The applicant should not be selected for assignment.

Training

After the interviews and physicals and selection process, the next step is training. Most large departments have a formal training school, but smaller ones may only have a field training, or an on-the-job program, where the newly assigned are mentored by a senior team member. Regardless of the size or the location, the training program must be structured and formalized with clearly measurable objectives for each part of the curriculum. The training curriculum should be focused on the unit's mission. Some units may encompass all aspects of a tactical situation, ranging from breaching, to hostage negotiation, to rendering explosives safe. Others may focus on breaching and subject apprehension. Regardless of the team's mission, the student's initial training curriculum must cover each aspect of its core function.

Selection for training does not guarantee selection for the unit. Regardless of a trainee's rank, the cadre must be in charge. The training program should be mentally and physically taxing while devoid of hazing. The tactical team and the department's leadership must give the cadre the authority to remove any trainee for unsatisfactory performance. Prior to the start of training, students should be provided with a list of the required standards for performance in training. Flagrant safety violations, such as accidental discharges and unsafe weapons handling, should be automatic cause for dismissal. Upon completion of the training program, the new team member should be assigned to a senior team member for assessment. This officer acts as a field training officer and mentor for at least six months. A newly assigned team member should not be considered fully qualified for at least twelve to eighteen months after completion of his or her training.

U.S. ARMY SPECIAL FORCES

The Taliban move freely throughout Helmand province in Afghanistan. They run a well-established web of safe houses that crisscross the desert, shuttling resources throughout the area. These "rat lines" are numerous, flexible, and almost invisible, but are the key leads to finding and capturing Taliban leaders and their large caches of equipment and supplies. In fall 2009 Captain M and his Special Forces Operational Detachment Alpha (SFODA) team of twelve men sought to disrupt one of these networks and question the men involved. They planned and executed a five-day operation equivalent in size and scope to managing a large multinational corporation. It involved more than 200 soldiers, civilians, and support personnel. Captain M had to request, and coordinate more than ten separate supporting elements, including two dedicated Blackhawk helicopters, logistical support from a U.S. Marine Corps unit, translators, interrogators, demolitions, and a force of twelve Afghan soldiers to spearhead the mission. Captain M was twenty-seven years old.

What made this operation different from the myriad of conventional operations soldiers and marines conduct every day in Afghanistan is that Captain M and his team conceived and carried out the entire mission on their own. This is typical of a SFODA that is expected to function independently, think creatively, and use the "by, with, and through" method of engagement common to Special Operations forces (SOF) missions. Such missions include short, violent, and direct engagements using host nation troops to augment the SFODA or the SFODA will train and prepare host nation armies to defend their country against an insurgency. Captain M. had to rehearse the entire plan, de-conflict his operation with Marine and Spanish general officers, and be prepared to take responsibility for billions of dollars worth of assets not to mention the lives of the personnel working under him.

How did Captain M come to join this elite organization? How was he able to stand out among his peers to excel during the assessment and selection phase? A brief historical review reveals that elite groups are usually created because of a demonstrated need. The Green Berets, a Special Forces unit, were born out of necessity, tracing their roots to the demands of the Office of Strategic Services (OSS) in the early 1940s. Colonel "Wild Bill" Donovan, the founder of OSS, conceived of a force of individuals whose mission would be to go behind enemy lines and train indigenous forces to disrupt and ultimately defeat enemy capabilities, all undetected.[1] Performance of these tasks required exceptional individual intelligence, physical agility, special language and technical skills, and nerves of steel. Operators were initially selected based on their personal connections, leading to the joke that OSS stood for "Oh so social."

As is often the case in the military, mistakes in the field drive innovation. Operators were often unprepared and overwhelmed by the psychological demands of the job, which included maintaining a cover, working in isolation, and being under the constant threat of captivity.[2] It became necessary to develop better methods of selecting operators for these unconventional missions. Colonel Donovan eventually elicited the support of prominent psychologists to help form a nucleus of professionals to advise commanders about the best practices for the recruitment, assessment, and selection of men and women for the OSS. A thorough account of this program was recorded in *The Assessment of Men*.[3] Aspects of it are still used today at the U.S. Army John F. Kennedy Special Warfare Center and School (USAJFKSWCS).

Recruitment

How do the Special Forces find what they are looking for? The Army has a standardized process involving a permanent group of SF soldiers trained in marketing and "selling" SF to find and prepare quality soldiers for SF duty. The Special Operations Recruiting Battalion's (SORB) sole purpose is to educate, promote, and advise soldiers and their families about Special Operations (SO) jobs in the Army. There are several benefits to this dedicated asset. First, the recruiters know and have lived as SF operators. They are the best possible representatives of the organization. Second, the SORB recruiters are constantly communicating with USAJFKSWCS, maintaining an awareness of changing requirements and the needs of the force. Third, marketing efforts, such as the Special Operations Parachute Demonstration Team, internet outreach campaigns, promotional videos and documentaries, and a chance to experience SF training through virtual reality technology can make being an SF operator the job of choice.

Once an applicant is interested, he is required to sit down with a recruiter to discuss basic requirements. If all basic requirements are met, soldiers are invited to attend the Special Forces Assessment and Selection (SFAS), located at Ft. Bragg, North Carolina. SFAS is a rigorous three-week test of physical and mental stamina. The program assesses and selects the best soldiers for the organization by measuring individual and group performance in a series of stressful events, such as land navigation, extended road marches, and team problem-solving tasks. If a candidate's performance is acceptable, he will be given the opportunity to enroll in the Special Forces Qualification Course (SFQC) where he will learn a specialized skill and a language and complete a culmination training exercise called Robin Sage, where all his skills are tested. Once a graduate and awarded the coveted Green Beret, he is assigned to a Special Forces group and begins to perform his duties and responsibilities on an Operational Detachment Alpha (ODA). The entire process can take up to twenty-four months, so the recruiter must critically evaluate the commitment of the applicant.

Recruiting for elite organizations like SF can benefit from the support of former SF operators and their families. These include retirees and families of wounded and fallen comrades. Probably the most effective recruiting tool is the loyalty and constancy found among the SF community. It is unmatched in the conventional Army.

Assessment

What kind of person emerges when he or she is faced with great adversity? Teddy Roosevelt said, "The boy who is going to make a great man must not make up his mind merely to overcome a thousand obstacles, but to win in spite of a thousand defeats."[4] SFAS gives each candidate an opportunity to demonstrate an ability to learn, work as part of a team, and maintain motivation through intense physical and psychological challenges. Each candidate is made equal during the assessment phase; rank, experience, and connections are all disregarded. Many of those who complete the assessment phase report that the program was the most difficult test of their lives. This is because the psychological stressors of unpredictability, physical discomfort, fatigue, and constant evaluation over several weeks are fairly effective at exposing the fortitude of each candidate. It is in this environment that people like Captain M slowly rise to the top and stand out among their peers. Research has shown that Special Forces soldiers produce more of a protein-like molecule in the blood known as neuropeptide Y. This molecule helps calm the brain in stressful situations.[5]

Intelligence, character, and commitment are the three most important traits looked for during the assessment phase. Each candidate is evaluated using the Whole Man model, which is a Gestalt approach following the OSS model.[6] This means that the assessment phase combines a myriad of tasks over time to reduce error and provide the selection committee with the best "snapshot" of the candidate. There are many opportunities for the candidate to fail and to succeed, and many opportunities for the candidate's traits to be observed.

The tasks used to test candidates are designed to be stressful, but each task can be accomplished with some basic physical preparation and grit. For example, one well-known candidate exercise is the "Nasty Nick" obstacle course, aptly named after Colonel Nick Rowe. Rowe, best known for his book *Five Years to Freedom,* was an SF officer, POW, and strong advocate for physically and mentally preparing SF soldiers for captivity and to return home with honor.[7] His story is a reminder to SF candidates to show courage and strength in the face of adversity. The course is grueling, with more than twenty obstacle features. The assessors are particularly interested in how the candidates react to "perceived failure." Does a candidate bounce back and demonstrate a commitment to improve his performance? In addition, a candidate's character may be tested for "cheating" during certain tasks. Will the candidate cheat again if given another opportunity? These assessments are designed to relate directly to real-world issues commonly confronted by SF soldiers in combat. These kinds of situations require an uncommon resilience or ability to bounce back and continue with the mission. SF operators need to be exceptionally stress tolerant, as their numbers are few, their missions more dangerous than those conventional forces may conduct, and their impact on the battlefield greater because of their special type of missions.

Candidates are constantly reminded that they are "always being assessed," but how and when will usually be unknown to them. Events and tests are not always what they seem. This fact is even more pronounced during team assessment events, which are designed to evaluate how well candidates work together to accomplish a task: how well do they plan, communicate their plan, adjust to changing conditions, accomplish the task, and lead by example? Candidates are not necessarily judged on whether they finish a task; what matters is their approach and how they organize the effort. In addition, candidates are judged on how well they follow the leader. In some cases, a leader is not identified. This practice was a common assessment technique used during British officer selection after World War I.[8] Leaderless tasks help evaluators determine who in a group has natural leadership skills. Team assessment events also give evaluators insight into peer-to-peer relationships.

Peer evaluations are another tool used to gauge a candidate's performance within a group. Fellow candidates often are more candid and direct when it comes to the men they feel they can serve and live with on an ODA. Peer evaluations are criticized by some who claim that they are useful only for measuring the "popularity" of an individual. Research suggests, however, that peer evaluations are helpful in providing feedback to individuals about their performance. Such evaluations also give individuals specific, concrete information on what they can improve about their behavior.[9] Peer evaluations reflect a unique dynamic on an SFODA: the ability to accept and give blunt and practical feedback.

The assessment phase ends with the requisite data collected for each candidate, and the process of reviewing each candidate begins. The assessors utilize a large database to collect and store data for every class that attends SFAS. The database includes more than 27,000 individual records. This way, data can be reviewed across, between, and within groups. Trends are monitored and changes to the program can be made based on the available data.

Selection

Selection decisions are made based on the needs of the SF community as well as the data collected on each candidate. SF leaders involved in selecting the newest member of the regiment are guided by what are called Special Operations Forces Truths.[10] These are inscribed in the halls of the Special Warfare Center and School and are helpful reminders of the boundaries that limit decisions about hiring the right kind of person for the job.

Humans are more important than hardware. No matter what technology offers, the individual operator and his ability to master and use that technology are critical. This means that the ability to solve problems, learn and use a language in a foreign country, and build relationships with the indigenous population is more important than the newest weapons system, the fastest computer program, or the best long-range surveillance optics. With these basic mental skills, SF operators can and will excel in any kind of environment. The organization seeks individuals like Captain M who can perform when help does not arrive on time and can carry on in spite of failure.

Quality is better than quantity. This statement is under constant scrutiny as SF grows exponentially to meet the needs of the force. Soldiers that show character and integrity and an ability to resist temptation and to cope with perceived negative life events are highly regarded. At the same time, high energy, adventurousness, and risk-taking behaviors are equally regarded. Individuals who push limits are acceptable as long as they demonstrate an awareness of boundaries and self-regulation. Captain M learned during the assessment phase to seek and accept constant scrutiny by his subordinates, peers, and superiors. This habit forces them to always perform their best regardless of the circumstances and is a hallmark trait of an elite operator.

Special Operations forces cannot be mass produced. This statement reminds the leaders selecting soldiers for this elite organization that individual attention, coaching, mentoring, and learning takes time. Training cannot be rushed.

Competent Special Operations forces cannot be created after emergencies occur. It is crucial that SF operators be ready to perform their job at any time. It is equally crucial that the SF "pipeline" continue to feed SFODAs with competent men. Fortunately, SF has a unique system that ensures that recruiters, assessors, and commanders are up to date on force needs. SF operators are routinely rotated back to the SORB and the Special Warfare Center and School as instructors or training company commanders.

The Special Operations Forces Truths guide selection decisions but there are also some checks and balances. The commander balances his judgment of candidate performance with the input of other senior SF leaders and support personnel on a selection board consisting of current and former commanders, command sergeants major, staff officers, psychologists, and civilians with expertise in the SF community. Although the psychologist or other board member may have the power to influence, the commander retains the authority to make the final decision regarding the selection of a candidate. Another practice is to identify candidates who may not be a good fit for the job of SF operator. As stated in one assessment text, "Results of wise decisions can range from the mere absence of problems to genuinely excellent outcomes promoting organizational purposes[.] . . . [C]onsequences of unwise decisions can range from inconvenience to disaster."[11]

Selection errors exist even when rigorous recruitment and assessment tools are in place. Individuals who pass the selection gates are usually persons with exceptional qualities. Those who enter the Special Forces regiment without these qualities will typically be exposed and removed from further training.

THE NORWEGIAN ARMY SPECIAL FORCES

The special forces team in the MH-47D Chinook helicopter had prepared themselves well for the upcoming mission—tracking down members of the Taliban in a remote area of Afghanistan. The low-level flight toward their drop-off point was not an easy ride for the team and their leader. The loadmaster gave the first signal, indicating ten minutes to drop-off. The team leader turned on his GPS and reviewed the infiltration route one more time. The team then made the necessary last-minute checks.

As the loadmaster gave the signal for one minute to drop-off, the pilots decreased the speed of the helicopter. The team grabbed their backpacks by their handles, preparing to start dragging them toward the ramp of the helicopter. When the Chinook hovered over the drop-off point, the load-master got down on his knee, turned around, and commanded, "Go! Go! Go!" The team dragged their heavy backpacks toward the ramp and down it. They then threw themselves to the ground amid an inferno of dust and small rocks whipped up by the rotor blades. The Chinook lifted off and disappeared quickly in the darkness. The team got their weapons up and secured the 360 degrees around them. The silence they experienced was incredible. The team leader knew that they were on their own now, surrounded by enemies that wanted nothing more than to capture, torture, and kill them. The team leader focused on the job they had to do, and the team soon started moving. The hunt had begun.

The Norwegian army special forces, Forsvarets Spesialkommando / Hærens Jegerkommando (FSK/HJK), took part during Operation Enduring Freedom, Task Force K-Bar, and Operation Anaconda in Afghanistan. The size of the unit is classified. Operators from FSK/HJK were decorated with the U.S. Navy Presidential Unit Citation for their contributions in Afghanistan from December 2001 to April 2002.[12] These operations, as well as the one described above, can place a heavy mental and physical burden on the personnel involved, especially those responsible for leading in such situations. Men and women who lead units in the world's harshest environments are referred to as *in extremis* leaders.[13]

Recruitment

Imagine being the team leader in the chopper before being dropped on the ground in Afghanistan. Where would you find people like yourself to follow you on such a mission? What kind of person can cope with the type of training required? Training soldiers to handle the extra load and weight has been shown to be a decisive factor for success in operations in Afghanistan.[14]

Table 18.1 Physical Requirements for Norwegian Special Forces Candidates

Test	Minimum Required	Performance/Time Limits
Push-ups	45	Feet together, hands shoulder-width apart
Sit-ups	45	For 2 minutes
Pull-ups	8	Chin over the bar for each pull-up
Back raise	20	Repeated at 5-second intervals
Step test	140	Take 70 steps with each foot carrying a 25 kilogram backpack
Running	32	Complete 32 laps on a 15-by-7-meter short track dropping and touching chest to ground on one 15-meter side, and on the other 15-meter side dropping to the ground and rolling onto the back
Swimming		Swim 400 meters freestyle under 11 minutes; swim 25 meters underwater; dive to a depth of 4 meters
Speed march		Complete 30 kilometers, with a 25-kilogram backpack and weapon, in under 4 hours and 45 minutes
Orienteering		Navigate various lengths of terrain while carrying different loads in a backpack

FSK/HJK operators come from all classes of society.[15] At the age of seventeen, they receive a letter from the Norwegian National Service Administration requiring them to appear at a nearby National Service Centre to be tested on their suitability for military service. Those who are determined to be qualified for military service are called to a military service center close to where they live. There they undergo a series of physical and mental tests. Applying for the special forces is popular. The minimum requirements for are listed in Table 18.1.

These requirements should be within reach of most potential candidates, but the drop-out rate can be as high as 90 percent once the selection period begins. Not many become an SF operator. After basic education as an SF operator, some members receive further education, up to a master's level.[16]

Many candidates applying to FSK/HJK have already served as airborne rangers for one year during their compulsory military service. Only 4 to 5 percent of new soldiers make it through the selection period to become rangers in the first place.[17] The airborne rangers who serve the year usually are good candidates for SF education. Table 18.2 provides a brief overview of the traits and characteristics that FSK/HJK finds desirable in candidates.

Table 18.2 Desired Traits and Characteristics of Norwegian Special Forces Candidates

▸ Likes to push their own limits

▸ Knows how to follow rules and regulations

▸ Able to think and operate independently

▸ Willing to obey an order and to commit to the team

▸ Possesses above average control over emotions and a high tolerance for stress

▸ Manages stress and ambiguity well

▸ Has stamina

▸ Able to cope well with people

▸ Has a goal-driven behavior that allows for making detached and realistic judgments and exhibits coherent cognition

FSK/HJK searches for fast learners who can apply knowledge quickly. It also emphasizes general intelligence, and good psychomotor skills in candidates.[18] One might easily imagine that while riding in a chopper before being dropped in Afghanistan is a demanding exercise. Being able to handle the unknown, the unknowable, and the subsequent stress over time is a crucial component of the physical and psychological makeup of an SF operator or team leader.

Assessment

After completing basic education, an operator only needs to make small adjustments to shift focus from winter warfare in Norway to operations in Afghanistan or other places in the world. However, common knowledge, an understanding of other people's culture, occupational proficiency, language skills, and the ability to improvise are some of the most important factors that contributed to the success of FSK/HJK operators in Afghanistan. These skills have to be developed over years.

Trust, integrity, and flexibility are also important for an SF operator. FSK/HJK operators are taught from the start to work in pairs. They are allowed to go to the commander and say that they cannot work with so and so, a type of peer evaluation similar to that in the U.S. Special Forces. Trust is also manifest in the high degree of openness among team members. After conducting missions, operators must attend a debriefing and talk to the unit's psychologist.[19]

Selection

Selection is an extensive process, based upon the experiences, practices, and knowledge of FSK/HJK operators, officers, and psychologists over the years. The first selection phase lasts three weeks and has many of the same elements as in SFAS to test potential candidates' physical and mental stamina. This includes, for instance, long marches with heavy backpacks. Research on paratrooper aspirants has revealed these individuals to be gifted with above average intelligence.[20] An SF operator needs to be an individualist and a good team player at the same time. Believing that one will succeed can be decisive in accomplishing a mission.[21] Therefore, belief in one's ability to solve whatever problems arise provides an advantage when applying to an SF unit.

The soldiers in Afghanistan have experienced a significant number of knee and back injuries, so testing future FSK/HJK candidates' capacity for marching while carrying heavy loads for long stretches would be a good idea.[22] The history of FSK/HJK reveals that the best predictor of which candidates will make it through the selection process is the ability to manage physical loads over time. In the opening scenario here, all the team members, including the leader, had heavy packs that they knew they would have to carry for long distances over unforgiving terrain.

As in the British Special Air Service, most of FSK/HJK's selection process is done by experienced SF officers.[23] Many of them have gut feelings about who will make it through the experience. They most likely have been subjected to similar situations as the team and team leader in Afghanistan and know what traits and characteristics to look for in a potential candidate.

CONCLUSION

Members in military special forces and law enforcement emergency service units have a lot in common, including working in dangerous and unknowable situations, coping with uncertainty, and making quick decisions. Members of such units are normally of above average intelligent and have the willpower to go the extra mile. Establishing a formal recruitment system is critical, otherwise these units might confront a shortage of candidates applying to them. Using experienced officers during selection or mentors during the assessment periods is recommended.

Putting candidates through one or several well-organized interviews will reveal important information about a potential candidate. Identifying a candidate's motivation for wanting to join a unit is crucial. A strong inner drive is necessary, but must be combined with the right attitude. Successful candidates will show that they have the ability to learn fast and to put acquired knowledge into action when needed.

Several tests should be conducted to determine whether a candidate can withstand the physical and mental stresses of the job. The traits to look for are intelligence, commitment, and good character along with a high tolerance for stress. Testing how candidates function under physical stress also reveals personality traits, willpower, and ability to work with others. An ability to bounce back from bad or difficult situations and the level of comfort with ambiguity must be determined. Honest feedback through peer evaluation, and candidates' response to it, is critical. They must function well on an individual and team level, displaying cooperation, trust, and integrity. It takes time to find individuals through the recruitment, assessment, and selection process with the physical and mental stamina needed to perform in the type of units under discussion.

KEY TAKE-AWAY POINTS

1. Elite organizations use dedicated assets to recruit, assess, and select members. These duties are separate from training.

2. Assessment for elite organizations is multidimensional and longitudinal. No one task or test is the sole basis for selection or rejection.

3. Operators in elite organizations accept, seek, and provide constant performance feedback.

4. Psychologists in elite organizations serve primarily as consultants in the assessment and selection processes. Commanders have sole decision-making authority.

KEY REFERENCES

Couch, Dick. *Chosen Soldier: The Making of a Special Forces Warrior*. New York: Crown, 2007.

OSS Assessment Staff. *Assessment of Men: Selection of Personnel for the Office of Strategic Services*. New York: Rinehart and Co., 1948.

Robinson, Linda. *Masters of Chaos: The Secret History of the Special Forces*. Cambridge, Mass.: Perseus Books, 2004.

NOTES

1. A. T. Bank, *From OSS to Green Beret: The Birth of Special Forces* (Novato: Presidio Press, 1986).

2. L. M. Banks, "Selection and Assessment of the OSS" (master's thesis, 1989).

3. OSS Assessment Staff, *Assessment of Men: Selection of Personnel for the Office of Strategic Services* (New York: Rinehart & Co., 1948).

4. H. P. Jeffers, *The Bully Pulpit: A Teddy Roosevelt Book of Quotations* (Lanham, Md.: Taylor Trade Publishing, 2002).

5. S. P. Rosen, *War and Human Nature* (Princeton, N.J.: Princeton University Press, 2010).

6. H. L. Ansbacher, "Murray's and Simoneit's (German Military) Methods of Personality Study," *Journal of Abnormal and Social Psychology* 36, no. 4 (1941): 589–592.

7. J. N. Rowe, *Five Years to Freedom* (New York: Ballantine, 1971).

8. H. L. Ansbacher, "The History of the Leaderless Group Discussion Technique," *Psychological Bulletin* 48, no. 5 (1951): 383–391.

9. M. Cracraft et al., "Self-Awareness: Getting the Ground Truth from Peer Evaluations," *Special Warfare*, November 1, 2006.

10. U.S. Army Special Operations Command, 2009, www.soc.mil.

11. R. M. Guion and S. Highhouse, *Essentials of Personnel Assessment and Selection* (Mahwah, N.J.: Lawrence Erlbaum Associates, 2006), 5.

12. Norwegian Armed Forces, Norwegian Armed Forces, 2009, www.mil.no.

13. T. A. Kolditz, *In Extremis Leadership: Leading As If Your Life Depended On It* (New York: Wiley, 2007).

14. J. J. Knapik, "Soldier Load Carriage: Historical, Physiological, Biomechanical and Medical Aspects," *Military Medicine* 169 (2004): 45–56.

15. T. Bakkeli, *Norges hemmelige krigere* (Norway's secret warriors) (Oslo: Kagge Forlag AS, 2007).

16. Norwegian Armed Forces, Norwegian Armed Forces, 2009, www.mil.no.

17. A. Nilsen and A. Løset, *Fallskjermjeger* (Airborne ranger) (Oslo: Kagge Forlag AS, 2008).

18. W. Kristensen and T. Sunde, *Uttak av soldater til en Norsk militær spesialstyrke: Personlighet, evner og egnethet* (Selection of military personnel to the Naval Special Forces of Norway: Personality, ability, and fitness) (unpublished manuscript, University of Tromsø, Norway, 1998).

19. A. Lysgård, *Kampstress* (Combat stress) (term paper, Norwegian Military Academy, 2005).

20. E. Baade et al., "Physiology, Psychology and Performance," in *Psychology of Stress: A Study of Coping Men*, ed. H. Ursin, E. Baade, and S. Levine (New York: Academic, 1978), 125–160.

21. B. K. Siddle, *Sharpening the Warrior's Edge: The Psychology and Science of Training* (PPCT Research Publications, 1995).

22. K. G. Sørensen, "Physical Health Conditions during Deployment in Afghanistan" (paper presented at the Nordic Military Sports Leaders Conference, Oslo, Norway, 2009).

23. Personal e-mail communication to Boe from Jon Reichelt, chief psychiatrist for the Norwegian Armed Forces, September 2009.

CHAPTER 19

Leader Development for Dangerous Contexts

Noel F. Palmer, Sean T. Hannah, and Daniel E. Sosnowik

Looking back, it was almost funny how we were all detached emotionally from the emergency we were responding to. Our marked police van, with its lights and sirens blaring, was racing down the center lane of the FDR Drive. We, the officers inside, were trying to consider what type of stupendous pilot error landed an aircraft into the WTC tower. As the van screeched to a halt near the site, our "therapy"—or was it avoidance—of nervously joking about the incident ended quickly as the severity of the event became apparent. Now, it wasn't just one tower burning, it was two. People were running scared; the NYPD radio was filled with a mixture of orders, screams, and confusion; and the towers in the distance had small items dripping off their sides, like drops of glue out of a bottle. One officer cleared his throat and said what we already knew: "Holy shit, those are people jumping out of the windows!"

I quickly lost all sense of time and purpose; I think we all did. Our sergeant offered the one and only instruction of that day: "Everyone stay together." What else could she say? Each of us was trying to remember the ride in the van. . . . Did we talk tactics? Did we have an emergency response plan for this, an obvious terrorist attack? Or should we just go on a quick search and rescue mission, a mission for which we really didn't have enough training either? It didn't matter in the end; just a few minutes after our arrival, the majestic south tower collapsed. The memory of civilians scampering for their lives, humans seeking cover in any nook and cranny available, dust and debris filling the air and our lungs, was a sure indication that if there was a hell on earth, we were in it at that moment.

—Officer Walsh, New York City Police Department,
assigned to respond to the World Trade Center, September 11, 2001

R esearch of human behavior in organizations has for the most part been decontextualized.[1] As a result, behavior is generally understood, but without an adequate grasp of the various social and situational contingencies that affect it. Further, scholars point to a similar, limited understanding of the contextualization of leadership in organizations, both generally and more specifically in military and other extreme contexts.[2] Yet, as made clear in the opening epigraph, extreme contexts may include extensive contingencies that influence leadership processes, such as the presence of fear, complexity, moral challenges, and mental and physical fatigue.

Understanding effective leadership for dangerous contexts requires a focus on context-specific factors and the integration of context into models of leader and leadership development.[3] Creating an integrated leader development framework for dangerous contexts should accomplish three goals: clarify the demands placed upon leaders; explain the capacities that need to be developed so that leaders can adapt well to demands and changes in situations and circumstances; and recognize that the demands on leaders differ across the phases of dangerous contexts.[4] Thus, a framework is suggested here that recognizes the importance of development through three phases of dangerous contexts: (1) anticipation of involvement in a dangerous context; (2) effective functioning in situ (e.g., during dangerous contexts); and (3) post hoc functioning, which addresses outcomes of involvement in dangerous contexts (see Figure 19.1). This framework was chosen in part because it aligns with theories of stress and coping, where stressful encounters are recognized as a "dynamic, unfolding process, not as a static, unitary event."[5] This taxonomy allows leader developers to recognize that the requirements on leaders may differ substantively across the phases of dangerous contexts.

DEFINING DANGEROUS CONTEXTS

An underlying assumption in this chapter is that when confronting danger such as that experienced by the New York City police and fire departments on September 11, 2001, leadership is uniquely contextualized or distinct from that in non-dangerous contexts. Hannah and colleagues, in their typology of leadership in extreme contexts, suggest that "unique factors influence leadership in important ways depending on where and when it is occurring relevant to the extreme event and context, and across periods before, during, or after an extreme event."[6]

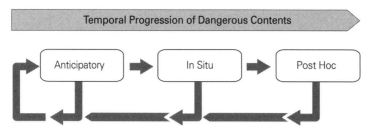

FIGURE 19.1 Cyclical phases of leadership in dangerous contexts

Hannah and colleagues also delineated five dimensions across which dangerous contexts vary: location in time (pre, in situ, post hoc), potential magnitude of consequences, probability event may occur, proximity or closeness, and the form of threat (e.g., physical or property loss).[7] These factors combine in a myriad of ways to create variable inputs into the overall level of danger experienced and the responses of leaders and followers.

DEFINING LEADER AND LEADERSHIP DEVELOPMENT FOR DANGEROUS CONTEXTS

Learning is defined as "an increase or change in knowledge or skill that occurs as a result of some experience," whereas "development is an ongoing, longer-term change or evolution that occurs through many learning experiences."[8] An important discussion for leadership researchers has been one of distinguishing between leader and leadership development. Leader development is a process that builds competencies to make individual leaders more effective, while leadership development is a process that expands "collective capacity of organizational members to engage effectively in leadership roles and processes."[9]

In dangerous contexts, leaders require the capacity to meet certain objectives under conditions of danger. The discussion here takes a more cognitive and affective, process-oriented approach and outlines the individual capacities that need to be developed in leaders for successful functioning in dangerous contexts. Further, it is suggested that leadership is an influence process that draws from a highly developed organizational context to foster positive interactions within and across individuals and groups and within a dynamic external environment.[10] Extending this to dangerous contexts, the following definition of leadership in extreme contexts is used: "Adaptive and administrative processes of influencing others to understand and agree about what needs to be done and how to do it, and the process of facilitating individual and collective efforts to accomplish shared objectives and purpose under conditions where an extensive and intolerable magnitude of physical, psychological, or material consequences may. . . occur."[11]

Combining the definition of development presented above with this definition of leadership in extreme contexts, it is suggested that leadership development for dangerous contexts be defined as a process that builds individual and collective capacities and the organizational systems and context to foster adaptive response across phases of preparation for, function during, and post hoc recovery from dangerous contexts. This definition accentuates that the demands of leadership vary across cycles of dangerous events, requiring different developed capacities. Targets of development must provide social, psychological, and organizational resources for managing coping under stress and enabling successful adaptation to extreme and volatile conditions that then foster mitigation of harm, successful post hoc restorative processes, and the development and maintenance of organizational systems that support these objectives and related socialization processes.

TARGETS OF DEVELOPMENT FOR DANGEROUS CONTEXTS

A number of recent reviews of leadership development have endeavored to create integrative models of the development process. These reviews in aggregate provide a sense of the developmental targets most commonly cited as important for leader development (see Table 19.1). In reviewing these theories, we sought to evaluate and highlight those developmental targets from among them that best facilitate success for leaders who operate in dangerous contexts. We identified several commonly cited capacities and used these as a starting point for identifying targets for the development of dangerous context leaders.

Eight major concepts were common among theories of leader development: identity, moral/ethical capacity, cognitive capacity, experiences and expertise, self-regulatory capacities, efficacy beliefs, goals and goal orientation, and organizational context. Many of these are individual capacities that were defined in a context-free sense, so here we suggest how these and related constructs are relevant to dangerous contexts.

Identity

Identity—a compilation of individual experiences, values, and knowledge—serves as a structure around which development is motivated and organized. One's identity, or self-concept, is a multifaceted, organized structure of

Table 19.1 Summary of Integrative Leadership Development Theories

Development Theory	Identity	Moral/Ethical Capacity	Cognitive Capacity	Experiences and Expertise	Self-Regulatory Capacities	Efficacy Beliefs	Goals and Goal Orientation	Organizational Context
Avolio (1999)	Self-awareness and identification		Perspective-taking and intellectual stimulation	Life stream events	Adopt new ways of leading			Context and supporting mechanisms
Day et al. (2009)*	Identity, self-awareness	Moral development	Cognitive: ability, frames, and processes; sensemaking	Expertise	Regulatory strength, goal orientation	Self-efficacy	Implementation intentions; goal orientation	Social capital
Gardner et al. (2005)	Self-awareness	Moral integrity; moral development		Trigger events	Self-regulation		Goals and motives	Organizational climate and positive modeling
Maurer (2002)*	Self-schemas		Attitudes toward learning and development			Developmental efficacy	Learning goals	Work content and work context
Olivares (2008)*	Shared intentions		Sensemaking	Learning through beneficial experiences	Agency	Efficacy beliefs	Goals	
Russell and Kuhnert (1992)*			Information-processing and perspective-taking capacity	Task-related experience and skill acquisition	Self-regulatory abilities			Social context

Sources: B. J. Avolio, *Full Leadership Development: Building the Vital Forces in Organizations* (Thousand Oaks, Calif.: Sage Publications, 1999); D. V. Day, M. M. Harrison, and S. M. Halpin, *An Integrative Theory of Leadership Development: Connecting Adult Development, Identity, and Expertise* (New York: Psychology Press, 2009); W. L. Gardner et al., "Can You See the Real Me? A Self-Based Model of Authentic Leader and Follower Development," *Leadership Quarterly* 16 (2005): 343–372; T. J. Maurer, "Employee Learning and Developmental Orientation: Toward an Integrative Model of Involvement in Continuous Learning," *Human Resource Development Journal* 1 (2002): 9–44; O. J. Olivares, "The Formulation of a Leadership Development Praxis: Linking Intentions to Outcomes," *Leadership and Organization Development Journal* 29 (2008): 530–543; C. J. Russell and K. W. Kuhnert, "Integrating Skill Acquisitions and Perspective Taking Capacity in the Development of Leaders," *Leadership Quarterly* 3 (1992): 335–353.

*Individual-level focus

knowledge that contains traits, values, and memories and controls the processing of self-relevant information.[12] As such, identity is an important construct in a number of leadership theories. For example, authentic leaders are described as having the following attributes: "(a) the role of the leader is a central component of their self-concept, (b) they have achieved a high level of self-resolution or self-concept clarity, (c) their goals are self-concordant, and (d) their behavior is self-expressive."[13] Significant experiences can assist in changing an individual's identity to incorporate possible selves—for example, who the individual wants to be and believes they can become as a leader.[14] In general, leaders choose to relate events and experiences based upon what they perceive to be reflective of their current or possible self-views as a leader.[15] Thus, a focus on identity is important because it emphasizes one's interpretation of events in a self-relevant manner, rather than the events themselves.

The intense experiences faced by leaders in dangerous contexts place unique demands on their identity. First, these challenges, often coupled with physical, mental and emotional fatigue may push leaders and their units to the breaking point. Such situations require high levels of self-awareness for leaders to maintain a sense of self and to understand their strengths and weaknesses when challenged. Further, they need to understand how the extreme context is influencing their emotions and cognition as well as how their subsequent behaviors are affecting those around them.

Second, dangerous contexts normally lack control and structure, and as a result, leaders may be thrust into a myriad of demands in close succession. This requires leaders to have a multifaceted identity.[16] For example, a recent study of combat-experienced leaders found that the current operational environment requires tactical-level leaders to have complex identities that allow them to adapt to fill multiple roles: intelligence manager, tactical war fighter and commander, diplomat and negotiator, nation builder, and troop and unit leader.[17] Successful leadership in this context is in part contingent upon a leader's ability to strategically think and consider the impact of chosen tactics, maintain shared and coordinated situational awareness among his or her soldiers and coordinating units, assess insurgence threats, and remain prepared to react to threat while concurrently working with local security and civilian organizations. Tactical leaders must therefore have high levels of self-complexity in these domains. For example, bringing a "war fighter" identity to a negotiation exchange may elicit an undesired response from another leader (e.g., aggression) that would hamper success in that context.

Merely being self-complex is insufficient for achieving the adaptability leaders need to successfully meet their role demands. Self-complexity is context-specific in that leaders need to be multifaceted in those particular identity aspects relevant to dangerous contexts.[18] While the complexities of modern tactical warfare are not characteristic of all dangerous contexts, this example highlights the need for leaders to develop capacities linked to identity structures that extend beyond surface traits and behaviors.

Moral / Ethical Capacity

> We took fire from insurgents hiding in the middle of a crowd. We could have fired into the crowd and been within the ROE [rules of engagement], but it just wouldn't have been right.

> —An infantry captain in Iraq

Beyond the complexities and threat of dangerous contexts, the potential ethical implications of one's actions (or inaction) also make the context inherently morality laden. Leaders thus require highly developed moral character. Moral character involves those values and beliefs that are central to one's self-conception and that guide one's behavior. It includes the internalization of one's moral identity as demonstrated in the alignment of behavior with espoused values (i.e., integrity).[19] Moral identity is the view of the self "as one who acts on the basis of respect and/or concern for the rights and/or welfare of others."[20]

Leaders act as important role models and demonstrate through their decisions and behavior what the acceptable standards of behavior are.[21] Through observation, followers learn from and emulate their leader's behavior. In dangerous contexts, the development of moral identity is important for guiding leader behavior, in accordance with his or her values and beliefs. It is also important in that the moral behavior that flows from moral identity also influences the behavior of others in that context.

Ethos. The concept of ethos is a construct related to moral character and professional ethics that is of central importance to organizations operating in dangerous contexts. Many such organizations have codified ethos. Examples include the U.S. Marine Corps Rifleman's Creed and the U.S. Army's Warrior's Ethos. The latter states, "I will always place the mission first; I will never accept defeat; I will never quit; and I will never leave a fallen comrade."[22]

Ethos is characterized by levels of character, values, and beliefs sufficient to motivate a willingness to endure the cognitive, emotional, and physical hardships associated with dangerous contexts and, if needed, risk physical injury or death. Ethos, as an aspect of moral character, goes beyond ordinary commitment to an organization or cause. With serious injury or death as real possibilities, one's identity as a dangerous context leader goes beyond superficial externalities and may demand commitment at a level that would be considered extreme in most other contexts.

People tend to seek opportunities for development in those areas consistent with their self-identity. Hence, a person who sees himself as a moral leader would be prompted to further engage in and learn from moral experiences,[23] reinforcing self-complexity, leading "functional flexibility . . . adaptive psychological functioning and a heightened sense of personal agency."[24] Identity development can thus promote the development of expertise and equip leaders with cognitive and self-regulatory abilities that foster adaptability. Through the alignment of behavior with self-relevant standards, leaders model appropriate behavior for their followers.

Cognitive Capacity

Officer Valerio and the other police officers in the van were intently listening to radio transmissions as they raced to Lower Manhattan from their home precinct in the Bronx. They didn't need to say what they were all thinking: This is bad, really bad. None of the officers knew what they would find when they got there, and they certainly hoped that there would be some ample direction and recognizable "cues" when they did.

What Officer Valerio remembers most, however, is the captain she found at the mobilization point for her group; she didn't even get his name. She approached him, expecting to be quickly put into action. Instead, she noticed that the captain's eyes were fixated on the flames billowing out of the upper half of Two World Trade Center. She watched those same eyes following each body as it came hurtling down from the upper floors of the building. With each thunderous crash signifying the end of another human life, the captain—giving no direction and in fact, saying nothing—returned his eyes to the upper half of the building, wordlessly awaiting the next victim.

Dangerous contexts often involve quick and violent episodes where the demands for planning, coordination, and employment of resources may challenge or overwhelm leaders' and their followers' cognitive abilities.[25] Indeed, an area of consensus in leadership research is that in highly complex situations timely adaptation to change is needed.[26] For example, individuals can become so overly emotional when exposed to catastrophic events that the way they process information and make decisions becomes distorted.[27]

Expansion of leader adaptive capacity requires development of more than just the surface skills identified in most competency models (i.e., the immediately observable traits and behaviors leaders exhibit). It also necessitates development of the deeper knowledge structures and metacognitive skills that allow leaders to construct sophisticated understandings of situations and guide their thoughts and behaviors.[28] These deep knowledge structures refer to the individual's mental organization of information related to a particular domain, such as leading firefighting units. Leaders also require metacognitive skills that facilitate awareness and understanding of the relationship between task requirements and individual capabilities.[29] Metacognitive capacity acts as an "executive control" function for planning, monitoring, and regulating mental strategies, and thus for accessing deep knowledge structures and applying knowledge to specific situations.[30] Together the development of deep knowledge structures and metacognitive skills enhance leader adaptive capacity. Adaptive experts have developed detailed knowledge about relevant task domains and effectively organized that knowledge into memory.[31]

As these knowledge structures develop, it is important that leadership roles, traits, skills, and behaviors become increasingly central to and ultimately inextricably integrated with development of the leader's self-concept, enabling him or her to take on multiple leadership roles and to be adaptive to the demands of complex situations.[32] The linkage between knowledge structures and identity may be cultivated through a clear understanding of one's identity and interest in the development of roles, skills, and behaviors related to dangerous contexts.[33]

Experiences and Expertise

"As leaders progress from novice to expert, they become increasingly capable of flexibly drawing on internal resources such as identities, values, and mental representations of subordinates and situations."[34] Expertise is knowledge of tasks and social issues related to leadership, recognizing that the knowledge available to a leader may depend on the current context. Expert leaders possess a richer set of skills and behaviors than that of a novice or less-skilled leader.[35] Also, expert leaders have richer conceptualizations of leadership than lesser-skilled leaders.[36] Thus, those with a greater knowledge base specific to their organizational context may be better equipped to succeed as leaders.

Self-knowledge, self-concept clarity, and the merging of personal and role identities are derived from individuals' experiences, which implies that experiences are an important part of leader development.[37] Indeed, individual experiences are antecedents for many of the developmental targets highlighted here. Without experiences, there is little basis for self-knowledge or developing clarity around one's self-concept. It is through individual experience that people make sense of their environment and their position in it.

Unique experiences across all phases of dangerous contexts are essential for leaders to situate their identity as a leader within the context of danger.

Self-Regulatory Capacities

> Pondering the importance of military leader development, I can't help but think of a recent report discussing how the people in Helmand province are taking on the insurgents. A key mission for our forces has been attacking Taliban strongholds in Helmand. As the Marines continue operations there, the people in this region have also begun to take action against the insurgents. Some would argue that the locals were finally fed up and mad enough to respond to the harshness of the Taliban, but the threats and intimidation they've experienced over the last decade have been constant. Why have they now decided to fight back?
>
> Conditions changed this year with the presence of U.S. and coalition forces conducting deliberate operations to root out and destroy the Taliban. The success of our forces in fighting the Taliban has given the people the confidence to fight and defeat their oppressors, and when one Afghani fights back, this confidence spreads to others. In their day-to-day lives, local Afghanis face death threats and murder for providing support to the Afghan government and coalition forces. Yet these civilians have developed the confidence to fight this ruthless enemy, marking a positive development for the people and villages who've felt helpless in the face of intimidation. They serve as a model for our military leaders; through their example we understand the importance of building confidence to fight and defeat the enemy.
>
> —A U.S. officer in Afghanistan

Efficacy Beliefs. To face the intense demands of dangerous contexts, leaders require high levels of leader efficacy. Self-efficacy is individual confidence in one's ability "to organize and execute courses of action required to attain designated types of performances."[38] One's efficacy beliefs enable self-regulation of behavior. This is because self-efficacy beliefs help determine what individuals do with the knowledge and skills they have. Therefore, how people behave can often be better predicted by their beliefs about their capabilities than by their actual capabilities. Self-efficacy beliefs are contextually specific and developable, being influenced most through mastery experiences and vicarious experiences provided by role models.[39]

To say that efficacy beliefs are contextually specific means that they apply to specific tasks or domains of behavior but not to others. In the case of leader self-efficacy, these beliefs concern a person's confidence in his or her ability to successfully enact the set of behaviors associated with leading. Leader self-efficacy beliefs have been demonstrated to contribute to leader effectiveness.[40] Efficacy beliefs are important for leadership in that they motivate efforts at effective leadership and overcoming challenges faced in the leadership process.[41]

Efficacy is required to motivate one to attempt a task and to persist when beset by challenges. As the epigraph above notes, the people in Helmand province did not fight back until they gained sufficient efficacy due to the context created by the military forces. Efficacy beliefs inform leaders that despite failures or setbacks, they have the ability to accomplish the task at hand. Further, research in stress and coping highlights the relevance of self-efficacy as a context-specific variable beneficial for managing stressors.[42] For leader development, it is important to understand that these beliefs develop through experience, both personal and through observation of others.

Sensemaking. Sensemaking is a process by which individuals "construct meaningful explanations for situations and their experiences within those situations."[43] Sensemaking theory is built on the idea that individuals are "continuously bombarded by ambiguous environmental and organizational information that must be somehow noticed, interpreted, and acted upon."[44] It is distinctly applicable to dangerous contexts, where leaders play an important role in giving meaning or interpreting what is happening within organizations.[45]

Sensemaking in situ (e.g., during extreme events) may be the most critical when individuals face novel and ill-defined events. Effective leaders provide followers with a sense of meaning to "get their bearings and then create fuller, more accurate views of what is happening and what their options are."[46] In dynamic, novel situations people think by acting and interpreting the response to those actions. Therefore they must not only be guided by current knowledge, but must also filter and process new knowledge from the unfolding situation.[47]

Goals and Goal Orientation. Another important leader capacity— particularly for the in situ dangerous context—is one's learning goal orientation. Individuals generally fall into one of two major classes of goal orientation: learning-goal oriented and performance-goal oriented. Learning-goal oriented individuals develop competence and expand abilities by seeking to master challenging situations, and performance-goal oriented individuals attempt to validate their competence by seeking favorable judgments and avoiding negative judgments.[48] It has been demonstrated that a learning-goal orientation is important for shifting focus during complex tasks from the end result to the process.[49] In a dangerous context, a process focus may be important because learning-goal-oriented individuals deal well with negative feedback and handling distress;[50] performance-goal-oriented individuals tend to be apprehensive of failure and are concerned with consequences of poor performance. Thus, a learning-based approach serves in a functional capacity for complex, challenging circumstances.

Developmental Readiness. The concept of leader developmental readiness integrates many of the capacities outlined thus far.[51] Developmental readiness is defined as "the ability and motivation to attend to, make meaning of, and appropriate new leader KSAAs (knowledge, skills, abilities, and attributes) into knowledge structures along with concomitant changes in identity to employ those KSAAs."[52] Further, "motivation to develop is promoted through interest and goals, learning goal orientation, and developmental efficacy, while ability to develop is promoted through leaders' self-awareness, self-complexity, and meta-cognitive ability."[53] In accordance, developmental readiness is a capacity supported by other key developmental targets highlighted above and may be most relevant for leaders in the anticipatory and post hoc phases of dangerous contexts. For the anticipatory phase, leaders must be motivated to establish goals and learn the complexities of the presented context. For the post hoc phase, learning experienced in dangerous contexts must be synthesized for future use into the leader's knowledge structures.

Optimism, Resiliency, and Courage. The intense challenges posed by dangerous contexts require leaders and their followers to possess ample psychological resources with which to face traumatic experiences. Fear and negative emotions tend to narrow the scope of cognition and attention, limiting potential thought-action repertoires (e.g., creating a fight or flight response). It is argued, however, that positive psychological capacities, such as optimism or resiliency, offer personal resources to overcome such narrowing effects and that these resources offset negative emotions during stress, thus creating an "undoing effect," which "loosen[s] the hold that a negative emotion has gained on that person's mind and body by dismantling or undoing preparation for specific action."[54]

Leader Optimism. Optimism primarily focuses on explanatory style[55] and to a lesser degree, future expectancies.[56] Drawing from classic attribution theory,[57] positive leaders have an optimistic explanatory style, in which they tend to attribute positive events or outcomes to intrapersonal, permanent, and persistent causes; they attribute negative events or outcomes to external, transitory, and situation-specific causes.[58] This helps them maintain the view that they can personally bring about positive change in their context. Setbacks are seen as externally imposed events that they can react to and overcome.

Leader Resiliency. Resiliency is the "positive psychological capacity to rebound, to 'bounce back' from adversity, uncertainty, conflict, failure or even positive change, progress and increased responsibility."[59] Unlike optimism, which focuses on future expectations, resiliency is reactive and focuses on reactions to previous or expected setbacks. Resiliency is "a class of phenomena characterized by patterns of positive adaptation in the context of significant adversity or risk."[60] It is critical for leaders and followers operating in dangerous contexts, where volatility may create cycles of successes and failures, thus requiring them to pick themselves up after failures, make sense of and learn from their failures, and avoid ruminating on the failures and instead focus (with optimism) on the next challenge.

FUTURE DIRECTIONS

In preparing this chapter we sought to integrate current work on leadership development and lay a basic foundation for future work on leadership development for dangerous contexts. To a degree, there is an assumption in our focus on key developmental targets that they are collectively important across all the phases of dangerous contexts. Though we make suggestions as to when capacities may be most beneficial, clearly the profile of important developmental targets changes as an organization moves through the phases of the context. Such changes then lead us to question whether it is possible to have a leader capable of effectively meeting the demands of all three phases of dangerous contexts.

If different roles require different leadership capabilities, individual leaders need to be adaptive and self-complex experts, or they will be rigid or ineffective in certain phases of extreme contexts. As organizations in these contexts are rarely afforded the luxury of swapping out leaders who best fill each role or situation, it raises the question of what collective leadership mechanisms, such as social systems and organizational strategies, may provide the collective capacity (i.e., leadership) to meet the demands across all phases when such expectations are impractical for individual leaders. This requires integrating theories of shared leadership, team leadership, and social network leadership.[61]

We have discussed the difference between leader and leadership development, with the primary focus being on development of individual leader capacities. That is, we detailed what it is that develops within leaders (i.e., self-regulation, identity, ethos, and so on); however, for future discussions of leadership development for dangerous contexts, it will be important to consider the collective or organizational processes that influence or even foster individual development. It has been demonstrated that there are three major components of jobs: physical demands, complexity, and the social environment.[62] Whereas dangerous contexts are in and of themselves complex and physically and psychologically demanding, it is leadership that shapes the social context of the organization (see Table 19.1). In accordance, group processes, such as collective identification, adaptive systems, socialization, and collective expertise may be important as developmental targets for collective leadership. For example, Zaccaro and colleagues highlight the importance of organizational culture, group cohesion, and a number of other collective factors that are important in shaping the organizational context (see Chapter 10 in this volume).

Further, some individual-level constructs can be elevated to the collective level where "through social interaction, exchange, and amplification— [constructs] have emergent properties that manifest at higher levels."[63] Here collective-level phenomena emerge from the discontinuous interactions of agents, which creates distinct team-level phenomena, such as positive team cognitive, motivational, and affective states (e.g., cohesion). These states then over time facilitate future team performance.[64] One example is self-efficacy: over time, when highly efficacious team members interact, they create a form of collective efficacy where they come to jointly believe that the team can operate effectively.[65]

Collectives reinforce certain values and identities among their members through normative pressures and informational means whereby members seek to teach new members the "correct" way to act.[66] Collectives are thus powerful instruments of social influence and create substantial effects on the behavior of team members.[67] Constructs at the individual level can be similarly raised to the collective level. For example, positive emotions are contagious and can serve to make others in a group more positive.[68]

Space did not allow for an in-depth discussion of the specific processes through which to develop the capacities in our model in dangerous context leaders. Yet, we believe the specific processes of leader development likely do not fundamentally differ between developing leaders for non-dangerous contexts versus dangerous contexts. The process of providing challenge, feedback, reflection, and support, for example, is highly relevant across contexts.[69] We suggest that interested readers review the frameworks in Table 1 for further guidance on these processes. We should be clear, however, that while the process may be the same, the content of the training, education, and development must be directly relevant to dangerous contexts and target capacities such as those we have laid out here. The context in which training, education, and development occurs must be ecologically valid, replicating or simulating the factors present in dangerous contexts as best able within safety considerations.

In conclusion, we have outlined various facets of dangerous contexts and provided a set of developable capacities that we believe are critical for preparing leaders to operate in such contexts. This list is by no means comprehensive, but may serve as a starting point to inform future leader development efforts for leadership in dangerous contexts.

KEY TAKE-AWAY POINTS

1. In order to effectively develop leaders, it is necessary to understand the context for which they are being developed and the developmental targets that foster success within that context.

2. Leadership development for dangerous contexts is defined as a process that builds individual and collective capacities and the organizational systems and contexts to foster adaptive response across phases of preparation for, function during, and post hoc recovery from dangerous contexts.

3. Important developmental targets for dangerous context leaders include identity, moral/ethical capacity, cognitive capacity, adaptive expertise, self-regulatory abilities, and psychological capacities.

4. Leaders should operate successfully across all phases of dangerous contexts (i.e., pre, in situ, and post hoc), therefore, it is important to communicate clear expectations for development of individual leaders as adaptive and self-complex experts, or they will be rigid or ineffective in certain phases of extreme contexts.

KEY REFERENCES

Day, D. V., M. M. Harrison, and S. M. Halpin. *An Integrative Theory of Leadership Development: Connecting Adult Development, Identity, and Expertise.* New York: Psychology Press, 2009.

Hannah, S. T., et al. "A Framework for Examining Leadership in Extreme Contexts." *Leadership Quarterly* 20 (2009): 897–919.

NOTES

Noel F. Palmer is the corresponding author.

1. M. J. Gelfand, L. M. Leslie, and R. Fehar, "To Prosper, Organizational Psychology Should . . . Adopt a Global Perspective," *Journal of Organizational Behavior* 29 (2008): 493–517; L. W. Porter, "Organizational Psychology: A Look Backward, Outward, and Forward," *Journal of Organizational Behavior* 29 (2008): 519–526.

2. B. J. Avolio, "Promoting More Integrative Strategies for Leadership Theory-Building," *American Psychologist* 62 (2007): 25–33; S. T. Hannah, D. J., Campbell, and M. D. Matthews, "Advancing a Research Agenda for Leadership in Dangerous Contexts," *Military Psychology* 22 (2010): S157–S189.

3. S. T. Hannah et al., "A Framework for Examining Leadership in Extreme Contexts," *Leadership Quarterly* 20 (2009): 897–919; J. D. Blair and J. G. Hunt, "Getting Inside the Head of the Management Researcher One More Time: Context-Free and Context-Specific Orientations in Research," *Journal of Management* 12 (1986): 147–166; Y. Berson et al., "Leadership and Organizational Learning: A Multiple Levels Perspective," *Leadership Quarterly* 17 (2006): 577–594.

4. O. J. Olivares, "The Formulation of a Leadership Development Praxis: Linking Intentions to Outcomes," *Leadership and Organization Development Journal* 29 (2008): 530–543.

5. S. Folkman and R. S. Lazarus, "If It Changes It Must Be a Process: Study of Emotion and Coping during Three Stages of a College Examination," *Journal of Personality and Social Psychology* 48 (1987): 150.

6. Hannah et al., "A Framework for Examining Leadership in Dangerous Contexts," 897–919, 898.

7. Hannah et al., "A Framework for Examining Leadership in Dangerous Contexts."

8. T. J. Maurer, "Employee Learning and Developmental Orientation: Toward an Integrative Model of Involvement in Continuous Learning," *Human Resource Development Journal* 1 (2002): 14.

9. D. V. Day, "Leadership Development: A Review in Context," *Leadership Quarterly* 11 (2000): 582.

10. J. Antonakis, A. T. Cianciolo, and R. J. Sternberg, introduction in *The Nature of Leadership*, ed. J. Antonakis, A. T. Cianciolo, and R. J. Sternberg (Thousand Oaks, Calif.: Sage, 2004), 3–15.

11. Hannah et al., "A Framework for Examining Leadership in Dangerous Contexts," 913.

12. H. Markus and E. Wurf, "The Dynamic Self-Concept: A Social Psychological Perspective," *Annual Review of Psychology* 38 (1987): 299–337.

13. B. Shamir and G. Eilam, "'What's your story?' A Life-Stories Approach to Authentic Leadership Development," *Leadership Quarterly* 16 (2005): 399.

14. B. J. Avolio et al., "Unlocking the Mask: A Look at the Process by Which Authentic Leaders Impact Follower Attitudes and Behaviors," *Leadership Quarterly* 15 (2004): 801–823.

15. Shamir and Eilam, "Life-Stories Approach," 395–417.

16. S. T. Hannah, L. Woolfolk, and R. G. Lord, "Leader Self-Structure: A Framework for Positive Leadership," *Journal of Organizational Behavior* 30 (2009): 269–290.

17. S. T. Hannah, P. Jennings, and O. Ben-Yoav Nobel, "Tactical Military Leader Requisite Complexity: Toward a Referent Structure," *Military Psychology* 22 (2010): 1–38.

18. R. G. Lord, S. T. Hannah, and P. L. Jennings, "A Framework for Understanding Leadership and Individual Requisite Complexity," *Organizational Psychology Review* 2 (2011): 104–127.

19. T. Simons, "Behavioral Integrity: The Perceived Alignment between Managers' Words and Deeds as a Research Focus," *Organization Science* 13 (2002): 18–35.

20. D. Moshman, *Adolescent Psychological Development: Rationality, Morality, and Identity*, 2nd ed. (Mahwah, N.J.: Erlbaum, 2005), 121.

21. M. E. Brown, L. K. Treviño, and D. A. Harrison, "Ethical Leadership: A Social Learning Perspective for Construct Development and Testing," *Organizational Behavior and Human Decision Processes* 97 (2005): 117–134.

22. Department of the Army, *Army Leadership: Competent, Confident, and Agile* (Washington, D.C., 2001).

23. R. G. Lord and R. J. Hall, "Identity, Deep Structure and the Development of Leadership Skills," *Leadership Quarterly* 16 (2005): 591–615.

24. Hannah, Woolfolk, and Lord, "Leader Self-Structure," 277.

25. P. Shrivastava et al., "Understanding Industrial Crisis," *Journal of Management Studies* 25 (1988): 285–303; K. E. Weick, "The Collapse of Sensemaking in Organizations: The Mann Gulch Disaster," *Administrative Science Quarterly* 38 (1993): 628–652.

26. S. T. Hunter, K. E. Bedell-Avers, and M. D. Mumford, "The Typical Leadership Study: Assumptions, Implications, and Potential Remedies," *Leadership Quarterly* 18 (2007): 435–446; R. Marion and M. Uhl-Bien, "Leadership in Complex Organizations," *Leadership Quarterly* 12 (2001): 389–418.

27. P. A. Sorokin, *Man and Society in Calamity* (New York: Dutton, 1943).

28. Lord and Hall, "Identity, Deep Structure and the Development of Leadership Skills," 591–615.

29. M. Pressley et al., "Perceived Readiness for Examination Performance (PREP) Produced by Initial Reading of Text and Text Containing Adjunct Questions," *Reading Research Quarterly* 22 (1987): 219–236.

30. J. Metcalf and A. P. Shimamura (eds.), *Metacognition: Knowing about Knowing* (Cambridge, Mass.: MIT Press, 1994).

31. M. L. Gick and K. J. Holyoak, "The Cognitive Basis of Knowledge Transfer," in *Transfer of Learning: Contemporary Research and Applications*, ed. S. M. Cormier and J. D. Hagman (Orlando: Academic Press, 1987), 9–46.

32. Lord and Hall, "Identity, Deep Structure and the Development of Leadership Skills," 591–615.

33. S. T. Hannah and B. J. Avolio, "Ready or Not: How Do We Accelerate the Developmental Readiness of Leaders?" *Journal of Organizational Behavior* 30 (2010): 1–7.

34. Lord and Hall, "Identity, Deep Structure and the Development of Leadership Skills," 592.

35. Ibid.

36. Hannah, Woolfolk, and Lord, "Leader Self-Structure," 269–290.

37. Shamir and Eilam, "Life-Stories Approach," 395–417.

38. A. Bandura, *Social Foundations of Thought and Action: A Social Cognitive Theory* (Englewood Cliffs, N.J.: Prentice Hall, 1986), 391.

39. Ibid., 2.

40. M. M. Chemers, C. B. Watson, and S. T. May, "Dispositional Affect and Leadership Effectiveness: A Comparison of Self-Esteem, Optimism, and Efficacy," *Personality and Social Psychology Bulletin* 26 (2000): 267–277.

41. K. Y. Chan and F. Drasgow, "Toward a Theory of Differences and Leadership: Understanding the Motivation to Lead," *Journal of Applied Psychology* 86 (2001): 481–498; S. T. Hannah et al., "Leadership Efficacy: Review and Future Directions," *Leadership Quarterly* 19 (2008): 669–692; L. L. Paglis and S. G. Green, "Leadership Self-Efficacy and Managers' Motivation for Leading Change," *Journal of Organizational Behavior* 23 (2002): 215–235.

42. S. Folkman, "Commentary on the Special Section 'Theory-Based Approaches to Stress and Coping' Questions, Answers, Issues, and Next Steps in Stress and Coping Research," *European Psychologist* 14 (2009): 72–77.

43. D. A. Gioia, "Symbols, Scripts, and Sensemaking: Creating Meaning in the Organizational Experience," in *The Thinking Organization*, ed. H. P. Sims Jr., D.A. Gioia, and Associates (San Francisco: Jossey-Bass, 1986), 61.

44. M. J. O'Fallon and K. D. Butterfield, "A Review of the Empirical Ethical Decision-Making Literature: 1996–2003," *Journal of Business Ethics* 59 (2005): 375–413.

45. D. V. Day, "Leadership Development: A Review in Context," *Leadership Quarterly* 11 (2000): 581–614.

46. K. E. Weick, "Drop Your Tools: An Allegory for Organizational Studies," *Administrative Science Quarterly* 41 (1996): 310.

47. Ibid.

48. D. VandeWalle, W. L. Cron, and J. W. Slocum, "The Role of Goal Orientation Following Performance Feedback," *Journal of Applied Psychology* 86 (2001): 629–640.

49. G. H. Seijts et al., "Goal Setting and Goal Orientation: An Integration of Two Different Yet Related Literatures," *Academy of Management Journal* 47 (2004): 227–239.

50. D. VandeWalle et al., "An Integrated Model of Feedback-Seeking Behavior: Disposition, Context, and Cognition," *Journal of Applied Psychology* 85 (2000): 996–1003.

51. S. T. Hannah and B. J. Avolio, "Leader Character, Ethos, and Virtue: Individual and Collective Considerations," *Leadership Quarterly* (in press).

52. Ibid.

53. Ibid.; B. J. Avolio and S. T. Hannah, "Developmental Readiness: Accelerating Leader Development," *Consulting Psychology Journal* 60 (2008): 331–347.

54. B. L. Fredrickson, "The Role of Positive Emotions in Positive Psychology: The Broaden-and-Build Theory of Positive Emotions," *American Psychologist* 56 (2001): 218–226; B. L. Fredrickson et al., "What Good Are Positive Emotions in Crisis? A

Prospective Study of Resilience and Emotions Following the Leader Self-Structure Terrorist Attacks on the US on Sept 11th, 2001," *Journal of Personality and Social Psychology* 84 (2003): 365–376.

55. F. Luthans, C. M.Youssef, and B. J. Avolio, *Psychological Capital: Developing the Human Competitive Edge* (Oxford: Oxford University Press, 2007); M. E. P. Seligman, *Learned Optimism* (NewYork: Knopf, 1991).

56. C. S. Carver and M. F. Scheier, "Optimism," in *Handbook of Positive Psychology*, ed. C. R. Snyder and S. Lopez (Oxford: Oxford University Press, 2002), 231–243; M. F. Scheier and C. S. Carver, "Optimism, Coping, and Health: Assessment and Implications of Generalized Outcome Expectancies," *Health Psychology* 4 (1985): 219–247.

57. H. H. Kelley, *Attribution in Social Interaction* (Morristown, N.J.: General Learning Press, 1971); B. Weiner, *Achievement Motivation and Attribution Theory* (Morristown, N.J.: General Learning Press, 1974).

58. Seligman, *Learned Optimism*.

59. F. Luthans,"The Need for and Meaning of Positive Organizational Behavior,"*Journal of Organizational Behavior* 23 (2002): 702.

60. A. S. Masten and M. G. J. Reed,"Resilience in Development,"in *Handbook of Positive Psychology*, ed. C. R. E. L. Snyder and J. Shane (London: Oxford University Press, 2002), 75.

61. J. B. Carson, P. E. Tesluk, and J. A. Marrone, "Shared Leadership in Teams: An Investigation of Antecedent Conditions and Performance,"*Academy of Management Journal* 50 (2007): 1217–1234; S. T. Hannah, J. T. Eggers, and P. L. Jennings,"Complex Adaptive Leadership," in *Knowledge Driven Corporation: A Discontinuous Model,* ed. G. B. Graen and J. A. Graen, LMX Leadership: The Series, vol. 6 (Charlotte, N.C.: Information Age Publishing, 2008); S. W. J. Kozlowski and B. S. Bell,"Work Groups and Teams in Organizations,"in *Comprehensive Handbook of Psychology: Industrial and Organizational Psychology*, ed. W. C. Borman and D. R. Ilgen, vol. 12 (NewYork: Wiley, 2003), 333–375; C. L. Pearce and J. A. Conger, *Shared Leadership: Reframing the Hows and Whys of Leadership* (Thousand Oaks, Calif.: Sage, 2003).

62. F. P. Morgeson and M. A. Campion,"Avoiding Tradeoffs When Redesigning Work: Evidence from a Longitudinal Quasi-experiment," *Personnel Psychology* 55 (2002): 589–612.

63. S. W. J. Kozlowski and K. J. Klein,"A Multilevel Approach to Theory and Research in Organizations: Contextual, Temporal, and Emerging Processes,"in *Multilevel Theory, Research and Methods in Organizations: Foundations, Extensions, and New Directions*, ed. K. J. Klein and S. W. J. Kozlowski (San Francisco: Jossey-Bass, 2000), 15.

64. J. R. Hackman, *Groups That Work (and Those That Don't)* (San Francisco: Jossey-Bass, 1990); M. A. Marks, J. E. Mathieu, and S. J. Zaccaro,"A Temporally Based Framework and Taxonomy of Team Processes," *Academy of Management Review* 26 (2001): 356–376.

65. Hannah et al.,"Leadership Efficacy,"669–692.

66. P. J. Hinds and M. Mortensen, "Understanding Conflict in Geographically Distributed Teams: The Moderating Effects of Shared Identity, Shared Context, and Spontaneous Communication," *Organization Science* 16 (2005): 290–307; P. Selznick, *The Moral Commonwealth* (Berkeley: University of California Press, 1992).

67. G. R. Salancik and J. Pfeffer, "A Social Information Processing Approach to Job Attitudes and Task Design," *Administrative Science Quarterly* 23 (1978): 224–253.

68. P. D. Cherulnik et al., "Charisma Is Contagious: The Effects of Leaders' Charisma on Follower Affect," *Journal of Applied Social Psychology* 31 (2001): 2149–2159; E. Hatfield, J. T. Cacioppo, and R. L. Rapson, *Emotional Contagion* (Cambridge: Cambridge University Press, 1994).

69. Day, Harrison, and Halpin, *An Integrative Theory of Leadership Development.*

Conclusion

CHAPTER 20

A Holistic Approach to Leading in Dangerous Situations

Patrick J. Sweeney and Michael D. Matthews

D
angerous contexts place unique psychological, physical, and social demands on leaders and organizations. To prepare for these unique demands, leaders, group members, and organizations need to develop greater levels of trustworthiness, psychological hardiness, and cohesion and stronger leader–follower partnership relationships compared to leaders and organizations that operate in non-dangerous contexts. Given that the demands of dangerous contexts affect all individuals and their relationships with the group and the organization's systems, a systems-based perspective seems to be a logical foundation for fostering holistic development to prepare for the unique challenges of leading and operating in dangerous situations.

A systems approach to understanding the impact of context provides leaders with an appreciation of how the unique challenges of leading in dangerous contexts influence the interdependencies between leaders, followers, their relationships, and organizations. Also, a holistic developmental model with a systems view presents leaders with a common framework for understanding context impact, a shared language for discussing development, and common targets for assessing and engaging in purposeful development. Figure 20.1 introduces such a model to help leaders build their own and their organizations' capacity to lead in dangerous contexts.

A HOLISTIC DEVELOPMENTAL MODEL FOR INDIVIDUALS OPERATING IN DANGEROUS CONTEXTS

This model focuses on interrelated psychological structures, capacities, traits, and skills—that is, worldview (perspective), self-awareness, sense of agency, self-regulation, self-motivation, and social awareness and connection to others—that facilitate the development of leaders' and followers' capacities to operate in dangerous contexts. The model acknowledges the influence that

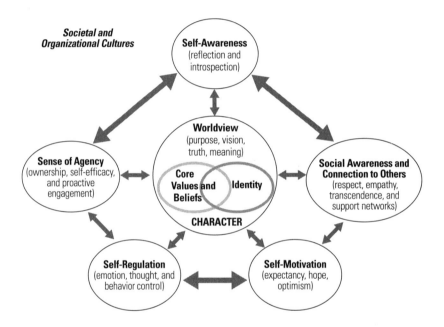

FIGURE 20.1 A holistic development model for dangerous contexts leaders and organizations

Source: Adapted from Patrick J. Sweeney, Sean T. Hannah, and Don M. Snider, "Domain of the Human Spirit," in *Forging the Warrior's Character: Moral Precepts from the Cadet Prayer,* ed. D. Snider and L. Matthews (Sisters, Ore.: Jerico, 2007; repr. Boston: McGraw Hill, 2008), 64.

membership in various social groups—such as a unit, a profession, a society, and so on—have on the development of leaders and followers. This is a versatile model in that the focal point for development can be the individual leader or a follower or even a group. Themes from the various chapters in this volume relate to the model. The process of examining themes through the model provides leaders greater insight into leader and leadership development.

Worldview

The foundation of who leaders and followers are, how they view and interpret events, and most important, how they act and make meaning from their experiences depends on their worldview, which is comprised of an individual's most central core values and beliefs concerning purposes and meaning in life, identity, truths about the world, and visions for realizing one's full potential.[1] Leaders' worldviews are the lens they use to observe, interpret, and make sense of life, events, and their actions.[2] It influences attention, perceptions, thoughts, motivation, behavior, and meaning-making and embodies the foundation of leaders' and followers' character. A person's worldview regulates inputs and outputs from the external environment, allocates attention and memory resources, facilitates the processing of information, and influences the execution of behavior. Thus, worldview needs to be the central target of development in any program preparing leaders and followers to meet the psychological and social demands of operating in dangerous contexts.

To develop one's worldview, a person first needs to gain awareness of his or her components (e.g., core values and beliefs, assumptions about the world, identity, and so on) and internal workings (e.g., how assumptions influence perceptions and behavior) through a process of reflective thought. This may be done in a variety of ways, ranging from formal education to life experiences that expose one to different ways of viewing and conceiving of the world. Exposure to different perspectives may alter one's worldview or alternatively reinforce it. An array of lenses through which to view the world tends to facilitate reflection and introspection about one's own perspectives, create openness to learning from diverse views and ideas, and possibly allow for a less judgmental approach to differences among people.

Challenging and adverse experiences (e.g., having a demanding job, being passed over for promotion, experiencing a death in the family, being injured on the job, confronting ethical issues, and the like) also facilitate the development of one's worldview by pushing to the limit one's established system of understanding the world. When individuals cannot make sense of their experiences, feelings of disequilibrium or uneasiness may ensue. The need to restore balance or equilibrium might drive one to build additional complexity into existing meaning-making systems until an event is understood and unease reduced.[3] Thus, experiences that take people out of their comfort zones or usual ways of viewing life promote the development of worldview.

Core Values, Identity, and Character. One of the major themes of *Leadership in Dangerous Situations* is the importance of leaders' and followers' character for operating in dangerous environments. Character can be viewed as the extent to which one's core values are integrated into one's self-identity. The more leaders and followers define themselves by their core values, the more consistent they will behave in accordance with those values in all situations.[4] Such people use their values to define themselves; that is, they become their values. One reasonable assumption is that the core values of an individual who chooses to work in dangerous contexts would tend to have values in line with an organization operating in such an environment and that espouses values of duty, service, integrity, loyalty, courage, and respect. Being a person of character is an integral part of the identity of dangerous context leaders and "warriors," defined here as leaders who take on tough challenges, place duty first, never accept defeat, never quit, and never leave a fallen comrade on the battlefield (commitment to teammates). Once leaders integrate the warrior ethos into their identities, they approach leading and living with a proactive, resilient, and winning spirit.[5]

A leader's character provides the moral compass that guides decisions and behavior, especially when using lethal force. Some people draw courage and strength from leaders who model courage in threatening conditions. Character is a motivational source for perseverance. When group members are physically, emotionally, and mentally fatigued, they look to their leader, who models perseverance, to summon the strength to continue the mission and to accomplish it. Leaders modeling good coping skills, based on being true to their own and their organization's values, positively influence followers' coping skills, which promotes resilience to adversity. Character also forms the foundation for leaders and followers to understand and make meaning out of their experiences. Furthermore, leaders and followers who model their organization's values are likely to earn a reputation of trustworthiness, which facilitates the development of trust in others and enhances the ability to influence (lead).[6]

Purpose. Finding purpose in serving is important in preparing leaders and followers to meet the psychological challenges of leading and operating in dangerous contexts. Purpose is a powerful motivational force for transcending self-interest and facing the risks of injury or death to serve others. Core values linked with a sense of purpose promote the strength of will to endure, bounce back from (resilience), and make meaning out of adverse or traumatic experiences. For instance, Admiral James Stockdale endured eight years of torture and indignities in a North Vietnamese POW camp by sustaining the belief (faith) that he would get out and turn the experience into a defining event in his life (purpose).[7] Furthermore, getting members to rally around a common, worthy purpose influences the development of trust and task cohesion within teams and also facilitates the use of transformational leadership behaviors.

Another important theme is that leaders be in the business of shaping meaning within their organizations. Shared meaning-making within a group influences leaders' and followers' worldviews. Exchanging perspectives provides members a wealth of information with which to test assumptions about the world, to redefine truths, to understand larger purposes, gain insight into how values influence decisions and behavior, and find the limits of their current way of thinking. Leaders can proactively engage in shared meaning-making by identifying the purpose of missions for followers, sharing rationales for decisions (and how they align with the organization's core values), being transparent with information, and providing their team an opportunity to conduct an after-action review upon completion of each mission. Every opportunity leaders have to engage group members is an opportunity to shape and strengthen their worldviews.

Self-Awareness

Families, schools, teams, and other social groups have a tremendous impact on shaping general worldviews. Leaders and followers transform these general views into personalized perspectives through the process of reflection and introspection. Through reflection on core values and beliefs, identity, purpose and meaning in life, and truths, an individual can begin to "customize" his or her worldview. Reflection also plays an important role in the development of identity and the integration of core values into it or the formation of one's character. The ability to start to identify and assess identity, values, truths, purpose, and vision provides individuals with the autonomy to take charge of their development and to regulate their thoughts, emotions, and behavior.

Awareness of one's capabilities, core values, identity, purpose, mental models, and perception of truths plays a key role in managing stress, promoting courageous actions, building hardiness, enhancing perseverance, and mitigating post-traumatic stress symptoms. Self-awareness allows leaders to frame experiences so they are viewed as challenges that have the purpose of increasing growth. Awareness of contextual variables and how they influence internal states lets individuals engage in proactive strategies to manage stress or harness additional motivational forces to effectively adapt. Also, a good sense of oneself influences ethical decisions and behavior and provides an individual with a firm foundation through which to interpret and make meaning out of experiences. Knowing oneself and being authentic is important to the development of relationships based on trust and engaging in higher order leadership behaviors, such as transformational and authentic leadership.

Sense of Agency

Agency entails leaders assuming control and responsibility for their actions and effective functioning. Leaders make a commitment to intentionally seek out opportunities for growth and ways to improve their effectiveness. They accept their shortfalls and realize they are the primary authors of their actions and developmental journeys toward being leaders of character. Agency is largely determined by leaders' self-efficacy or personal beliefs. If leaders believe that they can positively influence their destiny, they will engage in proactive, purposeful actions to take advantage of opportunities to do so. Thus, leaders' behavior is controlled internally, not dictated by environmental forces. Efficacy beliefs influence leaders' decisions (e.g., take the challenge or play it safe), how much effort they expend toward a goal, the strength of will to persevere when confronted with obstacles and danger, self-enabling or self-hindering thought patterns, ability to adapt and cope with changing circumstances, and levels of stress they experience. These beliefs also influence one's regulation of thought processes, emotions, and motivation.[8]

Leaders can enhance their sense of agency through building self-efficacy beliefs, which are bolstered through the development of competence. Throughout *Leadership in Dangerous Situations*, competence emerges as a primary factor in determining leader effectiveness. Realistic training that replicates the conditions of dangerous contexts develops the skill sets—that is, decision making, technical and tactical knowledge, stress management, and social skills—and the mental models that raise members' self-efficacy beliefs. These beliefs have a synergistic effect by allowing leaders to apply various skill sets in adapting to situations. The more competence leaders possess, the more diverse and broad their plans of action (scripts), the greater the options to adapt to uncertainty, all of which bolsters self-efficacy and agency. Skilled leaders who doubt themselves can undermine their own performance. Thus, effective performance depends on competence as well as efficacy beliefs.[9]

Physical courage is developed by placing leaders in training situations (e.g., live-fire training exercises) with increasing threat. Similarly, training exercises designed to place leaders in morally ambiguous situations like those they might experience in the real world or requiring them to incur risk to stand-up for their group members or beliefs assists in developing personal responsibility and moral courage. Each time leaders successfully demonstrate courageous behavior in a training setting, efficacy beliefs deepen, as does agency.

Tough, realistic training can be used to develop stress management skills and resilience. Self-efficacy beliefs play a key role in leaders accurately assessing their ability to meet the demands of dangerous situations and assist in managing stress. Training that introduces adversity helps develop leaders' coping and resilience strategies as well as their meaning-making abilities. Each time they successfully handle a tough challenge or setback, their efficacy beliefs should increase, along with agency.

From a collective perspective, realistic training facilitates the development of trust between group members, enhances team cohesion, increases group viability, builds team resilience, and most important, enhances the team's perception of its efficacy. Collective efficacy lifts morale, assists in the management of stress, and facilitates the mitigation of post-traumatic stress symptoms.[10] Shared perceptions of efficacy beliefs are instrumental in a team's performance and resilience to adversity.

Self-Regulation

Self-regulation is the ability to monitor, understand, assess, and control one's thoughts, goals, emotions, and behavior—or the ability to lead the self.[11] Self-awareness and agency play significant roles in the development of an individual's ability to self-regulate.[12] Leaders who can assess their mental models for accuracy and bias, and understand the source of their emotions and how their patterns of thought influence motivation and behavior, are empowered to implement measures to control them and start to master self-influence.[13] This ability to reflect on the causes and consequences of past patterns of thoughts, emotions, and behaviors allows leaders to choose future patterns of thought and behavior that align with values, beliefs, and goals. Thus, self-regulation is a prerequisite for integrity, authentic leadership, and development as a leader and a person.[14]

Self-regulation also influences leaders' and followers' abilities to maintain attention focus, perseverance to accomplish a task, and strength of will to behave in accordance with their own and their organization's values. One's ability to monitor and regulate thoughts, emotions, and behavior is a resource that can be developed through self-awareness and practice. An individual's self-regulation resource can also be depleted through overuse and fatigue.[15] Superb physical fitness and disciplined sleep plans serve to mitigate the rate of depletion of this scarce resource. Leaders and group members need to be aware when their self-regulation strength is depleted to the level where it is about to adversely influence judgment and behavior.

Self-regulation plays a pivotal role in developing leaders' psychological body armor to meet the unique challenges of operating in dangerous contexts. From an individual perspective, self-regulation influences leaders' ability to act courageously, moral and ethical behaviors, resilience, stress management, and meaning-making. Regarding courage, leaders and followers use self-regulation to acknowledge the threats in a situation, control their emotions, and motivate themselves to take action to accomplish their duties. In terms of stress and resilience, leaders use regulation processes to frame perceptions of the situational demands (challenge versus threat), assess capabilities, and execute adaptive strategies for coping with stress and accomplishing the mission.

When confronted with adversity, self-regulation provides leaders a sense of control over their thoughts, emotional reactions, and behavioral responses to the event. The regulation process assists them in evaluating the cause of the event, developing plans to prevent similar events in the future, and most important, how to adaptively respond to the event. Leaders use their self-regulation abilities to frame the event in a way that assists the meaning-making process. The ability to understand and control one's thoughts, emotions, and behavior promotes within leaders a sense of agency, optimism, and resilience to handle the challenges of dangerous contexts.

Self-regulation is critical to effective decision making in high stress and dynamic situations. Leaders must be able to control their own emotions, balance competing goals (e.g., accomplish the mission but also minimize danger to the team members), and manage their thoughts to make adaptive decisions. Self-regulation provides leaders with the ability to remain calm and composed in dangerous and crisis environments. This skill is honed by decision making during realistic training and reflective thought.

In terms of the social perspective, lessons from the various chapters here indicate that leaders' self-regulation is instrumental in the development of trust, cohesion, team resilience, morale, and influence. In the area of trust, leaders' ability to influence their attitudes and direct their behavior toward developing competence, demonstrating good values, and genuine caring for members helps them to earn a reputation of credibility and gives them the opportunity to establish positive relationships that foster trust. Trust bonds in leader-follower relationships assist in the development of cohesion within the team. Furthermore, we propose that leaders with good self-regulation abilities are more likely to set high standards, focus on building team competence through tough training, communicate in a clear and open manner, and work cooperatively, which bolsters team resilience compared to low self-regulating leaders. Team resilience coupled with trusted, self-regulating leaders serves to bolster morale or the general well-being of organizations.[16] Finally, leaders' ability to control their thoughts, emotions, and behavior facilitates the development of their power bases—expert and referent—related to the person. High levels of expert and referent power allows leaders to exercise a higher level of influence through the use of transformational and authentic leadership actions.

Self-Motivation

Self-motivation refers to leaders' and followers' ability to marshal various internal sources to drive action, in this case, in the face of risk or to persist toward a goal when faced with challenges. The ability to motivate oneself is closely linked to an individual's efficacy beliefs. Leaders and followers who expect or believe they can perform a required behavior to achieve a goal are more likely to engage and persist in that specific, goal-directed behavior.[17] Similarly, leaders' and followers' beliefs about their ability to control their thoughts, feelings, and behavior influence their intentional attempts to regulate or lead the self. Thus, self-efficacy is an important internal source of motivation that is developed through realistic training, education, and reflective thought.

Behaving consistently true to one's identity and core values is another important internal source of self-motivation. The more centrally integrated a person's core values are with his or her self-identity, the stronger the internal force to act congruently with those values and identity, thus preserving the concept of self.[18] As the integration of core values into identity develops, the sources influencing behavior shift from external to internal. Therefore, leaders' and followers' actions become consistently more values based and authentic in response to internal motivational forces. They behave in a consistently moral and ethical manner because that is who they are. One's desire to stay true to core values and identity provides the wellspring of motivation to strengthen an individual's will to persevere and prevail.

Striving to achieve a worthy purpose is another powerful internal motivating force that influences behavior in dangerous contexts. A higher purpose inspires people to step beyond self-interest, to the point of risking their safety or lives, to serve or achieve something greater than themselves. Purpose provides people with the ability to frame their actions in a larger perspective and provides meaning. Admiral Stockdale was able to endure the horrifying experience of being a prisoner of war for eight years because he found purpose in surviving with honor and made it the defining point of his life. As Victor Frankl gleaned from his experience in the concentration camps, if people can find meaning and purpose in their suffering, there is almost nothing they cannot endure.[19]

One's desire to survive and also to uphold a commitment to shared trust between team members is a powerful internal motivating force that influences behavior in dangerous contexts. An individual's will to survive can motivate one to engage in behaviors up to the point of taking another human's life in service to one's country or society. A person's commitment to fulfilling the trust that teammates have placed in him or her acts as a powerful motivational force. Studies conducted in combat zones found survival and upholding trust to be two primary sources of motivation that get soldiers to fight.[20]

Various chapters in this book proffer that self-motivation impacts strength of will, physical and moral courage, resilience to stress and adversity, meaning-making, and trust development. The strength of leaders' and followers' will or spirit rests in their motivation to act in a manner consistent with their core values and beliefs, identity, and achievement of their purpose.[21] Self-motivation influences one's ability to act courageously and in a moral and ethical manner. When confronted with situations that are dangerous or contain a moral or ethical challenge, one must balance the need for survival and social approval against the internal need to act consistently with core values and beliefs, identity, and purpose. Likewise, self-motivation plays a significant role in bolstering resilience to stress and adversity and making meaning out of one's experiences. Again, a worthy purpose that provides meaning or the desire to maintain consistency with oneself tends to fuel coping strategies that promote resilience as well as efforts to understand experiences.

Social Awareness and Connection to Others

Social awareness refers to an individual's realization that relationships with others play an important role in one's development and that one needs certain attributes to build positive connections with others. Uplifting relationships with important persons (i.e., family, mentors, teachers, coaches, and so on) assist in developing core values and beliefs, discovering and creating identity, finding truth in the world, learning moral and ethical decision making, understanding and making meaning from experiences, and determining one's purpose and direction in life in order to realize one's potential.[22]

To harness the developmental potential of positive relationships with others, one must be able to demonstrate respect, empathy, compassion, transcendence of self-interest, and trust in others.[23] Regarding respect, it is important that an individual recognize that other people have the right to hold different values, beliefs, and cultural practices and that one must, without giving up one's beliefs, show others due consideration and openness to these alternative perspectives. Showing respect to others' worldviews validates them as humans on equal footing and opens the door to the development of relationships based on trust. Moreover, empathy—the ability to see the world through another person's lens to understand their situation in life, needs, goals, motivations, culture, and potential feelings—affects one's ability to demonstrate respect and also facilitates the establishment of cooperative relationships. Compassion, being moved to assist others in reducing suffering or improving themselves by providing support, communicates care that facilitates the establishment of positive relationships.

An individual's ability to transcend or step beyond self-interest to work cooperatively for the good of all in the relationship facilitates the development of trust. Transcendence of self-interest is important because it empowers leaders and followers to serve or strive to achieve something greater than themselves and engage in selfless behavior. Exhibiting selfless behavior in relationships reassures all parties involved that the common good will be served, which promotes trust. Furthermore, one's willingness to trust others or willingness to be vulnerable to others' actions communicates intent to deepen a relationship and initiates the trust building cycle. Being vulnerable to another person's actions provides the individual with information about their character, motives, and competence to determine if one wants to pursue the relationship at a deeper level. After an individual extends trust, others will feel a psychological pressure to reciprocate in kind.[24]

Positive connections with others are critical for one's development and social resilience.[25] An individual may possess the requisite attributes to form positive relationships with others, but still not perceive that he or she is connected with others. Developing robust and diverse social networks to assist one in solving work and personal problems, obtaining feedback, providing a safe forum in which to share thoughts and feelings, and benefiting from career coaching are continuous processes. Here we introduce the concept of network efficacy, which entail's a person's beliefs about the ability to leverage networks to provide or obtain needed support. Thus, feeling connected with others entails the skills and abilities to build robust and diverse networks of trusting relationships and also involves one's efficacy beliefs about the ability to connect to and leverage existing networks to provide the needed social support.

Relationship networks are critical in assisting leaders and followers in meeting the unique psychological and social challenges of leading and operating in dangerous contexts. Support networks are important in managing stress and promoting resilience. Feeling connected and supported by others tends to boost people's perceptions of their capabilities by giving them access to various adaptive problem-solving or coping strategies, a forum to express feelings and thoughts, and exposure to diverse perspectives to assist in making meaning and finding purpose in the stress or adversity they face. Such connections and support help reduce stress, promote resilience, and mitigate symptoms of post-traumatic stress.

Social support networks can also serve as powerful motivational forces to encourage leaders and followers to behave in a courageous and honorable manner. Significant others modeling behavior consistent with the organizations' values creates a social reality that communicates that the individual is expected to behave in an honorable fashion. In these situations, support from others provides external pressure that is congruent with and amplifies a person's internal motivation to behave consistently with one's value and identity.

The bonds that unite people in social networks are based on trust. Leaders' and followers' credibility (competence, character, and care), the quality of the cooperative relationships they build, and the supportiveness of an organization's culture and systems influence the development of trust. Competence encompasses the basic social abilities and skills needed to develop quality relationships. An individual's ability to develop positive relationships contributes to the development of trust.[26] Trust enhances the forging of social bonds, team viability, perceptions of collective efficacy, and organizational resilience needed to meet the psychological and social challenges associated with dangerous situations.

Relationships based on trust provide leaders with the opportunity to exercise the high level of influence associated with transformational and authentic leadership that induces followers to change the way they think about themselves, their responsibilities, and the values and purpose of their organization. Trust relationships are also critical for influencing people and actions across cultures and in prison settings. Strong bonds of trust in leader–follower relationships promote morale (group well-being) and mitigate post-traumatic stress symptoms. Therefore, leaders' and followers' ability to build relationships based on trust determines the level of perceived support, the level of influence they can exercise, and the viability of the group.

Societal and Organizational Cultures

Leaders' and followers' developmental journeys are influenced on multiple levels: individual self-development, relationship networks, and organization cultures. As previously discussed, an individual's development efforts are influenced by the various social networks to which he or she has connections. An individual's group memberships have a significant affect on development by influencing one's worldview and relationships. Most people's worldviews are shaped by their families, philosophical or faith groups, schools, teams, communities, and society. Groups possess, communicate, and hold members accountable to a set of common values, norms, assumptions about how to operate and function, collective identity, and purpose—that is, culture.[27]

Living and working in various organizational cultures creates for people social realities that influence their perceptions of right and wrong, values to lead and live by, how to treat each other, what provides work and life meaning, and noble purposes to pursue. Organizational cultures can reinforce a person's values, identity, truths about the world, meaning, and purpose as well as broaden their perspective. On the other hand, organizational cultures can also have a detrimental impact on one's core values, identity, and perspective. This is why most parents are concerned about who their children's close friends are during their formative, adolescent years; friends networks have the potential to significantly influence the development of worldview.

Leaders can leverage an organization's culture to assist in shaping and reinforcing each member's development of worldview and the various psychological attributes that support it (see Figure 20.1). The organization's core values and purpose must be clearly articulated and communicated to all the members of the organization. The purpose should be of a high-enough order to motivate members to transcend their self-interest. People seek groups whose values and purpose are congruent with their own.

Another important part of clarifying the organization's culture is the vision statement. The vision communicates to group members the compelling future state the organization is moving toward if it accomplishes its purpose; it communicates hope and stirs passion. Regardless of the diversity of the organization, the culture is the cornerstone that unites members in a common purpose and a shared belief system to which they commit to hold themselves and others accountable. Thus, culture is a powerful mechanism for exercising influence and also a force that can bring people together in a worthy quest.

One of the most powerful ways to communicate an organization's culture is through role models. Select formal leaders based on the embodiment of an organization's core values and their belief in the core purpose and vision. Formal leaders who are role models help ensure that the organization's espoused values are the values actually being practiced. Also, these role models play a significant part in assisting group members in making meaning regarding core values, purpose, vision, and their duties.

Reviews of organizational policies, procedures, practices, and systems are necessary to ensure that espoused values, norms, purpose, and vision are being communicated accurately and reinforced. A review of the organization's espoused values and perceived values in practice is a good place for leaders to start to identify gaps because policies, procedures, practices, and systems tend to take on a life of their own. Review each one and ask whether it is needed and whether it supports the espoused culture. For instance, if teamwork is one of the organization's core values and it is common practice to evaluate and reward members only on individual performance, then the organization's systems are hindering the practice of this value.

Impact on Individual Development. An organization's culture has a tremendous impact on individuals' preparation and development to meet the unique challenges of operating in a dangerous environment. Organizations that value learning and development allocate necessary resources, such as time, money, quality people, facilities, and equipment, to conduct realistic training and education to ensure that every member is prepared to perform their duties in the face of danger. After each training or educational event, the organization conducts formal after-action reviews (AARs) to facilitate learning and also to decide how to improve in the future. Such investment in development and learning bolsters members' self-efficacy, which contributes to effective performance, helps manage stress, and promotes resilience.

An organization's values can provide members with a reinforced moral compass to raise awareness of individual responsibility, determine what is right, and act in a moral and ethical manner. These values, along with the organization's purpose, influence the development of member's identities and provide a source from which to draw strength during adversity. The organization's values and purpose also shape members' meaning-making and attitudes about seeking help. Organizations that view seeking behavioral health as an adaptive means for maintaining the human system (center of gravity of the organization), not as a weakness, promote resiliency and mitigate the symptoms of post-traumatic stress.

Organizations that value open communication and empower members promote individual agency and efficacy. Open communication allows for mutual influence, leverages the collective wisdom of the team, facilitates learning, allows for the expression of concern (especially on moral and ethical issues), promotes shared meaning-making, and provides members with a sense of control. Empowerment gives members the agency to make or influence decisions to adapt to dynamic situations, use their full array of talents, and have some degree of control. Both open communication and empowerment influence the development of trust at the individual and collective levels.

Impact on Relationships. An organization's culture, policies, procedures, practices, and systems affect the development of relationships within and outside the organization. If the organization's culture entails values such as loyalty, teamwork, integrity, selfless service, and duty, people within the organization are likely to behave in a cooperative manner to achieve a common purpose that enhances the development of positive relationships. Likewise, organizational practices, policies, and systems that encourage fairness and open and honest communication promote the development of relationships. Rewards and performance evaluation systems can have a pervasive influence on the development of relationships in organizations. If both of the systems recognize, assess, and reward cooperative behavior and collective achievement, relationships based on trust will flourish. Organizations that recognize, assess, and reward individual achievement only, hinder the development of cooperative relationships.[28]

HOLISTIC DEVELOPMENT FOR
DANGEROUS CONTEXT ORGANIZATIONS

The holistic development model presented here can also be used for developing organizations to operate in dangerous contexts. The focal point for development simply changes from the individual to the organization. Again, the power of the model lies in its providing leaders with a common framework for thinking about organizational development, a common language for discussing development, and most important, offering specific targets for purposeful development. Below is a brief discussion on how to apply the model to an organization.

Worldview

The organization's culture entails its core values and beliefs, assumptions about the world, norms governing how to interact, truths, and purpose. An organization's culture is the lens through which it perceives itself and the world. Culture is the organization's worldview. Leaders who invest time and effort in shaping and developing their organizations' culture are leveraging a very powerful source of influence.

Self-Awareness

Organizations need to be aware of their internal operating principles and systems. It is through purposeful reflection and introspection that leaders will see the true culture in practice. Taking the organization through a vision development process is a superb mechanism for getting members to reflect on core values and purpose and to construct a shared meaning of them. Using participative vision development processes gets group members involved and promotes reflection on the organization's strengths and weaknesses and what it needs to do to adapt to a constantly changing world. Conducting formal AARs after major events provides members the time to reflect on their performance and make recommendations to improve in the future. Also, periodic review of policies, procedures, practices, and systems through an organization inspection program allows leaders to ensure these structures are synchronized with espoused values, purpose, and vision.

Sense of Agency

As with an individual, organizational agency involves the belief that the group can control its destiny and a commitment to proactively engage in activities to do so. At the heart of agency are collective efficacy beliefs. Members of the group must believe they have the skills, means, and leadership necessary to adapt to a changing world. Organizations that invest in the development, education, and training of its members are bolstering collective efficacy. Also, participative, transparent strategic-planning practices assist the organization in identifying its strengths, weaknesses, opportunities, and threats. An awareness of the changing environment allows leaders to develop and execute plans to ensure the organization remains viable in the future and boosts agency and collective efficacy.

Self-Regulation

At the collective level, self-regulation involves culture, policies, practices, procedures, and systems to shape and control how the organization views and executes its role and purpose. The art is to develop organizational structures that empower individuals but at the same time shape common thought patterns and behaviors. Leaders engaging in open communications and shared meaning-making assist in shaping how the organization reacts emotionally to its performance and adversity. Leaders can draw on the organization's values and purpose to assist members in understanding and making meaning out of experiences. Communicating the hard facts and how the organization will adapt and be successful in the future assists in developing resilience and optimism.

Self-Motivation

An organization's core values and purpose serve as important motivational sources that govern collective behavior. The desire to maintain consistency with their collective and individual identities drives members to behave consistently with values and purpose. Collective efficacy beliefs are also a powerful motivating force that governs members' pursuit of organizational goals.

Social Awareness and Connection to Others

Organizations need to develop within their culture the attributes of respect, empathy, compassion, transcendence of self-interest, and trust of others to form positive relationships within the parent organization, the community they serve, or the countries in which they operate in order to increase effectiveness. Feedback from outside constituents provides organizations with information they can use to further their development to enhance effectiveness. Also, an individual organization can leverage outside organizational networks to provide necessary support to accomplish a mission. Thus, an organization's ability to connect positively with outside organizations promotes development and enhances effectiveness.

Societal and Organizational Cultures

The culture of the parent organization and to some extent the cultures of constituent organizations have the ability to influence the culture of a subordinate organization. The parent organization has a significant influence on a sub-organization's core values and beliefs, collective identity, purpose, norms governing behavior, and assumptions. Furthermore, the parent organization usually has policies, procedures, practices, and systems to ensure that subordinate organizations share similar espoused cultures. Leaders have the responsibility and opportunity to ensure that the espoused culture is the culture in practice and to extend the culture. Constituent organizations that one serves or supports can also impact an organization's culture. For instance, if an organization is conducting major operations overseas and forecasts it will continue to do so in the future, it might want to change its selection, training, rewards, and evaluation systems to reflect the importance of cultural competence.

The holistic development model provides leaders a common framework and language through which to assist in preparing individuals and organizations to meet the unique challenges of operating in dangerous contexts. This approach centers development on individuals' and organizations' worldviews. The model illustrates as developmental targets the supporting psychological attributes, states, and capabilities, and the primary targets of social influence.

It is important to note that societal and organizational cultures can have a powerful influence on the shaping of individuals' worldviews and also on the importance individuals place on the supporting psychological components of the model. For instance, a person from a collective society is likely to have core values and assumptions about the world that subordinate the individual's interest in order to support cooperative interaction with others. Also, this person is likely to place a greater emphasis on the social awareness and connection with others component of the model to gain information for forming one's identity. The power of this model is that it is holistic and universal.

The team of authors for this volume hopes it has furthered your understanding of the unique challenges associated with leading in dangerous contexts and will contribute to making you a more effective leader or operator. We are honored by the opportunity to contribute to your development. Thank you for your service, and continue to lead the way.

NOTES

1. Abraham H. Maslow, *Motivation and Personality,* 2nd ed. (New York: Harper and Row, 1970), 80–97; and Kenneth I. Pargament and Patrick J. Sweeney, "Building Spiritual Fitness in the Army: An Innovative Approach to a Vital Aspect of Human Development," *American Psychologist* 66 (2011): 58–64.

2. Patrick J. Sweeney, Sean T. Hannah, and Don M. Snider, "Domain of the Human Spirit," in *Forging the Warrior's Character: Moral Precepts from the Cadet Prayer,* ed. D. Snider and L. Matthews (Sisters, Ore.: Jerico, 2007), 63–72; Patrick J. Sweeney, Sean T. Hannah, and Don M. Snider, "Domain of the Human Spirit," in *Forging the Warrior's Character: Moral Precepts from the Cadet Prayer,* ed. D. Snider and L. Matthews (Boston: McGraw Hill, 2008), 28–34.

3. Ellen Van Velsor and Wilfred H. Drath, "A Lifelong Developmental Perspective on Leader Development," in *The Center for Creative Leadership Handbook of Leader Development,* ed. Cynthia D. McCauley and Ellen Van Velsor, 2nd ed. (San Francisco: Jossey-Bass, 2003), 388–393.

4. Augusto Blasi, "The Development of Identity: Some Implications for Moral Functioning," in *The Moral Self,* ed. G. Noam and T. Wren (Cambridge, Mass.: MIT Press, 1993), 99–122.

5. U.S. Department of the Army, *Army Leadership: Competent, Confident, and Agile, FM 6-22* (Washington, D.C.: Headquarters, Department of the Army, 2006), 4–10.

6. Patrick Sweeney, Vaida Thompson, and Hart Blanton, "Trust and Influence in Combat: An Interdependence Model," *Journal of Applied Social Psychology* 39 (2009): 235–264.

7. Jim Collins, *Good to Great* (New York: Harper Collins, 2001), 83–85.

8. Albert Bandura, *Self-Efficacy: The Exercise of Control* (New York: W. H. Freeman, 1997), 3.

9. Ibid., 36–37.

10. Gregory L. Belenky, Shabtai Noy, and Zahava Solomon, "Battle Stress: The Israeli Experience," *Military Review,* July 1985, 11–20.

11. Roy F. Baumeister, *The Cultural Animal: Human Nature, Meaning, and Social Life* (New York: Oxford University Press, 2005), 310–315; and Daniel Goleman, *Emotional Intelligence* (New York: Bantam Books, 1995), xi–xii.

12. Bandura, *Self-Efficacy,* 1.

13. David V. Day, Michelle M. Harrison, and Stanley M. Halpin, *An Integrative Approach to Leader Development: Connecting Adult Development, Identity, and Expertise* (New York: Routledge, 2009): 191–194; and Sara B. Algoe and Barbara L. Fredrickson, "Emotional Fitness and the Movement of Affective Science from Lab to Field," *American Psychologist* 66 (2011): 35–42.

14. Day, Harrison, and Halpin, *An Integrative Approach,* 191–194.

15. Ibid.

16. Christopher Peterson, Nansook Park, and Patrick J. Sweeney, "Group Well-Being: Morale from a Positive Psychology Perspective," *Applied Psychology: An International Review* 57 (2008): 19–36.

17. Bandura, *Self-Efficacy,* 3.

18. Blasi, "The Development of Identity," 99–122.

19. Victor Frankl, *Man's Search for Meaning* (New York: Washington Square Press, 1994), 86–88.

20. S. Stouffer et al., *The American Soldier: Combat and Its Aftermath,* vol. 2 (Princeton, N.J.: Princeton University Press, 1965), 136–149.

21. Sweeney, Hannah, and Snider, "Domain of the Human Spirit," 55–99.

22. Pargament and Sweeney, "Building Spiritual Fitness in the Army," 58–64.

23. Daniel Goleman, "What Makes a Leader?" *Harvard Business Review* 76, no. 6 (1998): 93–102.

24. Harold Kelley and John Thibaut, *Interpersonal Relationships: A Theory of Interdependence* (New York: Wiley, 1978), 231–237.

25. John T. Cacioppo, Harry T. Reis, and Alex J. Zautra, "Social Resilience: The Value of Social Fitness with an Application to the Military," *American Psychologist* 66 (2011): 43–51.

26. Kelley and Thibaut, *Interpersonal Relationships,* 231–237.

27. Edgar H. Schein, *Organizational Culture and Leadership,* 3rd ed. (San Francisco: Jossey-Bass, 2004), 3–23.

28. See Chapter 9, in this volume: Patrick J. Sweeney, Kurt T. Dirks, David C. Sundberg, and Paul B. Lester, "Trust: The Key to Leading When Lives Are on the Line."

ABOUT THE EDITORS

Patrick J. Sweeney, Ph.D., Colonel, U.S. Army, is currently serving as an associate professor and director of the Eisenhower Leader Development Program in the Department of Behavioral Sciences and Leadership, United States Military Academy, West Point. He commanded the 3rd Battalion, 320 Field Artillery, 101st Airborne Division, and served with the 101st during Operation Iraqi Freedom I.

Michael D. Matthews, Ph.D., is currently professor of engineering psychology at the United States Military Academy, West Point. He served as president of the American Psychological Association's Division of Military Psychology from 2007 to 2008 and is a Templeton Foundation Senior Positive Psychology Fellow. His research focuses on soldier performance in combat and other dangerous contexts.

Paul B. Lester, Ph.D., Captain, U.S. Army, is currently serving as a research psychologist for the Comprehensive Soldier Fitness Directorate at Headquarters, Department of the Army. His previous military assignments include Ft. Benning, Ft. Campbell, Republic of Korea, the United States Military Academy, Iraq, and Afghanistan.

ABOUT THE CONTRIBUTORS

Michael Albanese, Captain, Commanding Officer, Uniformed Operations, Burbank Police Department, Los Angeles Police Department, Special Weapons and Tactics (Retired)

Mike Baker, Team Leader, Special Weapons and Tactics, Los Angeles Police Department

C. Kevin Banks, Captain (Chaplain), U.S. Army, Former Task Force Chaplain

David M. Barnes, Ph.D., Lieutenant Colonel, Armor, Assistant Professor of Philosophy, United States Military Academy

Ole Boe, Ph.D., Associate Professor, Department of Leadership, Norwegian Military Academy, Oslo

George Bonanno, Ph.D., Professor of Education and Psychology, Teachers College, Columbia University

John E. Chartier, Fire Marshal, State of Rhode Island

Lee M. Chartier, Ph.D., Assistant Professor of Business Administration, Community College of Rhode Island

Michael J. Craw, Los Angeles Police Department

Kurt T. Dirks, Ph.D., Bank of America Professor of Managerial Leadership, Washington University in St. Louis

Joe Doty, Ph.D., Lieutenant Colonel, U.S. Army, Deputy Director, Center for the Army Profession and Ethic, United States Military Academy

John Durkin, Deputy Inspector, Commanding Officer, Aviation Unit, New York City Police Department

John T. Eggers, Ph.D., Correctional Program Specialist,
National Institute of Corrections Academy

Michael S. Erwin, Captain, U.S. Army, Military Intelligence,
United States Military Academy

Joseph Geraci, Major, Infantry, U.S. Army, Assistant Professor,
United States Military Academy

James W. Gray, Director, Management Specialty and Training Center,
Colonel (Retired), U.S. Army

Sean T. Hannah, Ph.D., Colonel, U.S. Army, Director,
Center for the Army Profession and Ethic

Rita M. Hilton, Ph.D., Leadership & OD Consultant, Arlington, Virginia

Donald H. Horner Jr., Ph.D., Director, Davis Leadership Center,
Davis College of Business, Jacksonville University,
Lieutenant Colonel (Retired), U.S. Army

Michael Hurley, Inspector, Commanding Officer,
Fire Arms and Tactics Section, New York City Police Department

Denise Jablonski-Kaye, Ph.D., Assistant Chief of Clinical Services,
Los Angeles Police Department

Jack Jefferies, Guttman Development Strategies, Boulder, Colorado

Angela Karrasch, Ph.D., Army Research Institute, Fort Leavenworth, Kansas

Susann Kimmelman, Queens Internal Affairs Bureau,
New York City Police Department

Thomas Kolditz, Ph.D., Colonel, U.S. Army, Head, Department of
Behavioral Sciences and Leadership, United States Military Academy

David M. Lam, M.D., M.P.H., U.S. Army Telemedicine and Advanced
Technology Research Center and University of Maryland School of Medicine
National Study Center for Trauma and Emergency Medical Systems,
Brussels, Belgium

Janice H. Laurence, Ph.D., Associate Professor, Adult and Organizational
Development, College of Education, Temple University

Alison Levine, Founder of Daredevil Strategies, Adjunct Professor,
United States Military Academy

George R. Mastroianni, Ph.D., Professor of Psychology,
United States Air Force Academy

James L. Merlo, Ph.D., Lieutenant Colonel, Infantry, U.S. Army, United States Military Academy

Chris Midberry, Major, U.S. Army, Infantry, United States Military Academy

James Ness, Ph.D., Colonel, U.S. Army, United States Military Academy

Isabell Obigt, Ph.D., Gruppe Wehrpsychologie, Streitkäfteamt, Bonn, Germany

Raymond Ortiz, Sergeant, New York City Police Department

Noel F. Palmer, Ph.D., Major, U.S. Army, Assistant Professor, Department of Management, University of Nebraska at Kearney

Luann P. Pannell, Ph.D., Director, Police Training and Education, Los Angeles Police Department

Nansook Park, Ph.D., Associate Professor, Department of Psychology, University of Michigan

Christopher Peterson, Ph.D., Professor of Psychology, Department of Psychology, University of Michigan

C. Anthony Pfaff, Colonel, U.S. Army, Foreign Area Officer for the Middle East, Former Assistant Professor of Philosophy, United States Military Academy

Joseph W. Pfeifer, Assistant Chief, New York City Fire Department

Rebecca I. Porter, Ph.D., Colonel, U.S. Army, Office of the Surgeon General

Cynthia Pury, Ph.D., Professor of Psychology, Department of Psychology, Clemson University

James Redding, Major, U.S. Marine Corps, United States Military Academy

Walter Redman, Senior Police Advisor, Office of Civilian Police and Rule of Law, Department of State

Brian Reed, Ph.D., Colonel, Infantry, U.S. Army, Assistant Professor, United States Military Academy

Ted Reich, Lieutenant Colonel, U.S. Army, Assistant Professor, Department of English, United States Military Academy

Michael H. Schuster, J.D., Ph.D., Professor of Management, United States Coast Guard Academy

Daniel E. Sosnowik, Captain, New York City Police Department, Commanding Officer, Executive Development Section, New York City Police Academy

Michael F. Steger, Ph.D., Assistant Professor, Counseling Psychology and Applied Social Psychology Director, Laboratory for the Study of Meaning and Quality of Life, Colorado State University

David C. Sundberg, Federal Bureau of Investigation

Loree Sutton, Psychiatrist, Brigadier General (Retired), U.S. Army

Joseph J. Thomas, Ph.D., Colonel (Retired), U.S. Marine Corps, United States Naval Academy

Jason Toole, Major, Engineer, U.S. Army, United States Military Academy

Barend Tussenbroek, Ph.D., Lieutenant Colonel, Clinical Psychologist, Royal Netherlands Army

Eric J. Weis, Lieutenant Colonel, Infantry, U.S. Army, George Mason University

Kristin K. Woolley, Ph.D., Lieutenant Colonel, U.S. Army, Command Psychologist, 7th Special Forces Group (Airborne)

Dennis W. Yates, Lieutenant Colonel, Field Artillery, U.S. Army, Senior Fire Support Trainer / Mentor, Joint Readiness Training Center, Fort Polk, Louisiana

Stephen J. Zaccaro, Ph.D., Professor of Industrial and Organizational Psychology, Department of Psychology, George Mason University

INDEX

A

Abu Ghraib prison, 15, 98–99, 103, 105, 108–9, 110, 112, 282

accidents, 50, 249, 251

after-action reviews, 184, 191, 194, 197–98, 327, 386, 388

agency, 354; key to sense of, 7; requirement for, 7; sense of, 374, 378–79, 388

aggression: absences of social experiences and, 45; aggressively motivated humans, 124, 136n9

Ambuhl, Megan, 99

ambushing, 125

Anaconda, Operation, 293

analytical thinking, 233, 234–39, 243

Andreotta, Glenn, 21

anger, righteous, 328

Antonovsky, Aaron, 145–46

approach/avoidance motivation, 227–28

Argyris, Chris, 318–19

Army, U.S.: Be-Know-Do model, 150, 322; Comprehensive Soldier Fitness, 157, 196; core values, 28–29, 195; ethical behavior, 156; Five Core Competencies of Combat Leadership, 153, 154–55; motto of, 142; organizational culture, 325–29; security force advisors, 221, 224–25, 227; Special Forces, 32, 186, 338–43; stress reaction, culturally modified, 41, 45; walking around, leadership by, 320, 331n24; Warrior's Ethos, 356

Army Air Corps, U.S.: 332nd Fighter Group, 64; morale during World War II, 203–4

artifacts, 208, 210–11, 216–17n16, 317–18, 319

Auschwitz, 144–45, 381–82

authentic leaders: characteristics and concept of, 172, 250, 286, 290n36, 355; detention and captive environments, 15, 285–88; development of, 286–87; influence and power of, 226; relationships and, 175, 286; success of leaders and, 250; trust and, 286, 287

authoritarian correctional management models, 275

authorization, 105, 109

autobiographical memories, 47–48

B

Bagram Theater Internment Facility (BTIF), 275–76

balanced processing, 286, 287

banality of evil, 104

Barnard, Chester I., 315–16

beer and Jack example, 51–52, 55

meaning-making and, 143, 145, 146; morale and, 206, 213–14; organizational culture and, 386–87, 389; PTE preparation and, 89–90; relational perspective on leadership, 294; requirement for cohesive, 7–9, 10; social awareness, 374, 382–84, 389; transparency in, 287; trust and, 117, 167, 172–74, 383, 384

religion, 46–47, 55

repressive coping, 107

resilience: challenge and, 70; characteristics and concept of, 61–64, 73, 285, 331n27, 362; cognitive resilience, 183, 191–94; commitment and, 69, 70; control and, 69, 70; core value integration and, 9; development of, 14, 67–69, 70–73, 314, 325, 331n27, 376; emotional resilience, 183, 192, 195–98; examples of, 60, 64; hardiness and, 69–73, 196; meaning-making and, 5, 13, 376–77; optimism and, 66, 73; organizational resilience, 252, 267–68, 269; promotion of, 11–12; psychological capital, 285–86; PTE exposure and, 84, 87–93; requirement for capabilities, 5–6, 361, 362; self-regulation and, 380–81; social resilience, 183, 192, 194–95, 383; team resilience, 182, 183, 191–98, 380–81; team resilience, example of, 183–85; unit/group resilience, 64, 73

respect: common respect and combat leadership, 154; cultural and social diversity and, 292, 300–302, 303, 382–83; dehumanization and, 106–7; ethics and respect for human rights and humanity, 12, 123, 125–26, 134; morale and, 205, 206, 210–11; trustworthiness and credibility and, 172–73

reward and evaluation systems: courage, recognition of, 32–33, 35; peer evaluations, 342, 348; to support of core purpose, 10; transparency of, 176; trust development and, 176

risk: courage and, 23, 24–26, 27, 31–32, 35; ethics and balancing risks, 122–23; ethics of, 130–33; expectations of acceptance of, 27; fear and, 25–26; personal risk, 23, 24–25, 122, 132–33, 135, 138n30; stress risk factors, 52; subjectivity of, 27; taking risks, 252, 267, 269

Rivers, Mendal, 22

role models. *See* modeling and role models

routinization, 105–6, 109

Rowe, Nick, 341

S

scandals, 249

Schein, Edgar, 207, 316–19, 331n28

self-actualization, 144–45

self-awareness, 16, 92, 119, 276, 286, 287, 354, 355, 374, 377–78, 387–88

self-complexity, 355–56

self-efficacy, 285, 354, 359–60, 363, 378–79

self-knowledge, 358–59

self-motivation, 374, 381–82, 388

self-regulation, 119, 276, 286, 287, 354, 359–62, 374, 379–81, 388

self-worth, 152

sense of coherence, 146

sensemaking, 252, 264–65, 269, 354, 360. *See also* meaning-making

service, 9

sexual harassment and assault, 293

signal detection, 251, 252, 264–65

silver bullet theory, 328

Simpson, Varnado, 100